GOVERNMENT HANDOUT

A Da Capo Press Reprint Series

THE AMERICAN SCENE
Comments and Commentators

GENERAL EDITOR: WALLACE D. FARNHAM
University of Illinois

GOVERNMENT HANDOUT

A Study in the Administration
of the Public Lands
1875-1891

BY HAROLD H. DUNHAM

DA CAPO PRESS • NEW YORK • 1970

A Da Capo Press Reprint Edition

333.1
D917

This Da Capo Press edition of
Government Handout is an unabridged
republication of the first edition
published in New York in 1941.

Library of Congress Catalog Card Number 79-87564

SBN 306-71433-7

Copyright 1941 by Harold H. Dunham

Published by Da Capo Press
A Division of Plenum Publishing Corporation
227 West 17th Street, New York, N.Y. 10011

All Rights Reserved

Manufactured in the United States of America

GOVERNMENT HANDOUT

A Study in the Administration
of the Public Lands
1875-1891

HAROLD HATHAWAY DUNHAM

SUBMITTED IN PARTIAL FULFILLMENT OF THE REQUIREMENTS
FOR THE DEGREE OF DOCTOR OF PHILOSOPHY, IN THE
FACULTY OF POLITICAL SCIENCE
COLUMBIA UNIVERSITY

NEW YORK
1941

To

Constance Holmes Dunham

Alonzo Hathaway Dunham

PREFACE

The questions which arose after reading the reports of William A. J. Sparks, Land Office Commissioner
under President Grover Cleveland, are largely responsible for this monograph. How was it possible for so
many abuses to exist in the public land system and what
was accomplished by Mr. Sparks' vigorous attacks on
those abuses? It soon became evident that the questions
could be answered only by a rather full study of the
land policies in the post-Civil War era. Many works on
the public lands were already in print. The writings of
B. J. Hibbard, John Ise, E. S. Osgood, L. H. Haney,
M. J. Conover, Thomas Donaldson and numerous others,
some of whom are continuing to publish the results of
their researches, seemed to preclude the need for additional accounts. None of these writings, however, dealt
extensively with the many phases of the public land system for the limited period under review, 1875-1891.
Consequently I have endeavored to bring together the
timber land, mineral land, desert land, swamp land,
farming land, railroad land grant and private land
claims policies that were such an important factor in
the development of the great region west of the Missouri
River. I have also attempted to set these policies
against the background of the times and to examine them
particularly from the administrative angle. How far
these efforts have been successful the reader may judge
for himself.

Emphasis on the administration of the public
lands did not call for an exhaustive analysis of the
literature of the West. I have made an effort, however,
to examine relevant Government publications - Congressional debates; Congressional Committee reports; legislative enactments; judicial reports, and the testimony
on which the decisions for some of the cases were made;
Presidential messages; and reports from administrative
officials that were connected with public lands - newspaper files, magazine articles and books that treat of
leading men and events. Reminiscences of men living and
dead were also used. The General Land Office files

contain a great mass of material, portions of which were
sifted for special topics. The use of the foregoing
sources entailed considerable imposition on the time
and efforts of numerous individuals; and handling the
problem of organizing the results of such use has
brought welcomed assistance from still other persons.
My obligations, therefore, are great to officials in
the Columbia University Library, the New York Public
Library, and the Library of Congress. I also owe a
debt of gratitude to staff members of the Land Office
and the Interior Department. For specific help I wish
to thank S. V. Proudfit, Dayton Phillips and Henry
Steele Commager. My greatest thanks are due Allan
Nevins for guiding the work through many vicissitudes.
If I have struck pay dirt or if there is a satisfactory
round-up of information much of the credit is due him.
Finally, I wish to offer tribute to the person who,
while the work was in progress, might have worn, but
did not, a martyr's cloak - my wife, Lydia Roberts
Dunham. Needless to say none of the above is responsible for any errors of omission or commission which may
have occurred.

                                        H. H. D.

Wagner College.

CONTENTS

Chapter I

NEW PROBLEMS IN PUBLIC LAND ADMINISTRATION

The twenty-five years following the American Civil War brought a tremendous influx of settlers in the region west of the Missouri River. While a considerable number of individuals and frontier families had migrated there before the War the great push came afterwards and in a short time the West was alive with important and colorful activities. Farmers appropriated for cultivation the fertile soil of the plains and mountain valleys. Government troops participated in a ruthless warfare to clear the land of Indians who resented the approach of the white man. Prospectors and miners discovered and exploited silver, gold, copper and coal lands in the mountain areas. Ranchers fattened herds of cattle on the extensive prairies. Promoters and builders spanned half a continent with railroads and telegraph lines. And lumber corporations acquired or despoiled some of the most magnificent timber stands in the world.

Each of these activities has been the subject of extended study but the important fact that they took place on what had recently been, or still was, Government property has received too little attention. This property, the American public lands, had been acquired by the United States through cession and purchase. Consequently the Federal Government was responsible for supervising the lands and distributing them to its citizens. And the manner in which it discharged these functions basically influenced western growth. In fact its policies influenced the growth of the entire country and many of the economic, political and social issues of recent times find their origin in the methods adopted for supervising the public lands. The property which it controlled made the American Government probably the wealthiest land owner that had ever existed. By 1865 it still possessed nearly 1,000,000,000 acres, an amount

equal in area to one-half the United States. Five years
later the Census valued this undeveloped region at approximately $5,000,000,000. In the light, therefore, of
its far-reaching influence and of the value of the property handled there is ample warrant for examining in
some detail the Government's land policies after 1865.[1]

Settlement in the trans-Missouri country was facilitated by the fact that during the Civil War the Government was more than open-handed with its resources.
Almost any individual, after 1862, was permitted to obtain a portion of the public domain free, merely by settling on it. In addition large grants were made to
States for use in promoting education. And corporations
received huge land subsidies to encourage the construction of transcontinental railroads. This generosity was
soon followed by other and less fortunate developments
that fall under two broad classifications: the enactment of ill-advised measures to meet special western
conditions and the failure to provide appropriate administrative machinery for enforcing any of the nation's
land laws.

One of the most important administrative obligations which the Government failed to fulfill, in the
post-Civil War era especially, was connected with the
method of surveying the public domain. Surveying should
have included a scientific investigation of the character of the public lands, their classification under appropriate types, such as mineral, timber, pastoral, arable and desert lands, and the establishment of subdivi-
sions which could be secured readily by those desiring
to use them. Nevertheless the Government adopted and retained a method of surveying that was primarily suited
to farming land alone.

Moreover the Government's methods for supervising the distribution of the semi-arid grasslands of the
trans-Missouri country were woefully deficient from the

---

1. The public lands of the United States have included 1,442,200,320
   acres out of a total area of 1,937,144,960. Land Office Report,
   1931, p. 57. (Hereafter cited as L.O.R.) The 1,000,000,000
   acres noted above was calculated from Thomas Donaldson's "Public
   Domain" and the L.O.R's. for 1879 and 1880.

standpoint of both the farmer and the rancher.   During
the period of the growth of the cattle business, as
well as long afterwards, there was no law designed specifically to meet the needs of the cattlemen.   And such
laws as were adopted in behalf of settlers were almost
entirely of a mistaken if not a vicious character.   In
addition laws which provided for the acquisition of
timber and timber lands can be described as stop-gap
measures which, despite their obvious failure to meet
the needs of either the country or the timber companies,
remained on the statute books unchanged for decades. The
mineral land laws growing out of the customs of Far
Western miners and the desires of greedy mining interests served as the basis for wasteful, speculative or
litigious activities; frequently, also, such activities
were founded upon a clever evasion of the mining laws
themselves.   The Government's extensive land grants to
railroads were accompanied by no adequate provision for
supervising the use of the gifts.   In the subsequent
period there was practically no correction for this
omission: no provision for making the roads live up to
a strict construction of their granting acts; or for ensuring that the grant would not be exploited before it
was earned; or for seeing that settlers were protected
in their rights on the granted land; or finally, for
preventing the railroads from appropriating more land
than they were entitled to receive.   In short, one of
the most shameful chapters in American History is to be
found in the records of the Government's land policies
during the post-Civil War era.   It contrasts strangely
with the story of the West's heroic and constructive
enterprises.

        The questions readily arise, how did these la-
mentable features occur: what, more exactly, was the
nature of western development, and why did the Government fail so fundamentally in its obligations?   The answers can be found by examining the methods of disposal
and administration which existed prior to 1865; the actions of individuals and groups which exploited western
resources; the policies of the executive, legislative
and judicial branches of the Government; and finally,
the status of public opinion.

At the risk of some repetition it is necessary
first to review the public land policies which developed
with the growth of the country.   In the early days of
the Republic, lands were used to help solve fiscal problems.   For instance, Revolutionary War soldiers received
a portion of their pay in military bounty warrants.
These warrants were, in effect, checks to be cashed for
land and their number increased as the result of subsequent wars until the amount of land called for totaled
61,000,000 acres, representing an area equal to the
State of Oregon.[2]   In 1852 warrants were made transferrable so that soldiers did not have to take advantage of
their privileges personally.   Consequently large quantities were bought by speculators and land brokers at a
rate of from fifty cents to $1.00 an acre.   The warrants
were then used to acquire land worth from $5.00   to
$50.00 an acre, unless it was timberland which might be
worth vastly more, and they frequently contributed to
the formation of large holdings.[3]

Congress also used public lands for relieving
the burdens of the Treasury.   Under a law of 1796 land
was sold in 640-acre lots for $2.00 an acre, and the
proceeds were pledged to the discharge of Secretary
Hamilton's funded debt.[4]   But within a few decades the
methods of distribution became dominated by two facts:
the interests of the poor settler and the need to encourage internal improvements.   Land laws were modified
in 1800 and again in 1820 so that by the latter date
anyone could purchase as little as 80 acres at a $1.25
an acre minimum.   But because the "squatter" who had already taken up land must purchase it at public auction
after the official surveys had been made, he ran the
risk of being outbid for his land by a wealthy person
with ready cash.[5]   Consequently western Representatives
demanded that Congress protect a squatter's preëmptive
rights and finally in 1830 Congress enacted a Preëmption

---

2. John Ise, "American Forest Policy," p. 49. Quoted from the Bureau
   of Corporation, "Report on the Lumber Industry," vol. I, p. 258.
3. A. E. Sheldon, "Land Systems and Land Politics in Nebraska," p. 87.
4. P. J. Treat, "National Land System, 1785-1820."
5. B. J. Hibbard, "A History of Public Land Policies," p. 144ff.

law to be valid for only a year. Later, however, the
law was repassed several times until it was ultimately
put into permanent form as the Preëmption Act of 1841.
Under it a squatter who had resided on and improved his
lands for one year after making entry with the Government, could purchase prior to public sale, 160 acre at
the minimum price.

Incidentally, about 1830, western squatters developed another method of protecting their interests
through the institution of the Claim Association.[6]
Groups of settlers, particularly in Nebraska, Iowa and
Kansas, banded themselves together into Associations for
the purpose of securing their lands at auction time. The
Association adopted rules and regulations and chose officers who were to bid in their lands, sometimes twice
the 160 acre limit, at the minimum price. The members
of these Associations attended the auctions in a body
and threatened any outsider who might attempt to defeat
their carefully laid plans. State but not Federal laws
recognized these groups and their widespread occurrence
was justified on the ground of protecting the bona fide
settler against the speculator.

Western demands had also modified the land laws
in behalf of the poor settler in another direction. During the 1840's agitation developed for a homestead law
which would permit any settler who had fulfilled the
residence requirements of the Preëmption law, to receive
his land free of charge.[7] The demand for such a law
continued with increasing vigor but it was blocked chiefly by Southern opposition. There is considerable interest in speculating on the development of the United
States if the Southern slave owners had maintained their
political alliance with the Northwestern farmers by favoring the homestead movement. But it was left to the
Republican Party to reward one wing of its adherents by
enacting the Homestead law of 1862 after the Southern
States had seceded.[8]

---

6. Ibid., p. 198ff; and Sheldon, op. cit., pp. 30-5.
7. G. W. Stephenson, "The Political History of the Public Lands,
   1840-1862"; Hibbard, op. cit., chaps. XVII-XVIII.
8. But it was also delayed so long that its effective use was restricted by the conditions in the plains country where water
   rights were important. Cf. Hibbard, op. cit., p. 454; and post,
   p. 28.

The adoption of this act completed the change in policy inaugurated by the preëmption laws. The public lands were to be used thereafter, as Milton Conover phrased it, "for national development rather than national revenue."[9] The Homestead law allowed any settler a quarter section, 160 acres, without price if he resided on it, cultivated it and improved it for five years. An applicant was required to swear that he took the land in good faith for the purpose of making a home. If for any reason he wanted to reduce his period of residence or secure his patent sooner than the five years the law allowed him to "commute" his entry and purchase the land at $1.25 an acre. This provision became subject to extensive abuse later, largely because the law did not specify any time after entry when commutation could take place.

If the encouragement of small farming homesteads was one basic element of the Government's public land policy, the use of land as a subsidy to stimulate various State and Federal improvements was another. For instance from the time of the Northwest Ordinance of 1787, Congress adopted a practice which had its roots in Colonial practices of reserving one or more sections in each township for promoting schools.[10] It would make an interesting story to relate the manner in which the States discharged their guardianship of these school lands but it cannot be dealt with here. In 1862, however, at the time of the adoption of the Homestead settlement law, Congress passed the Morrill Act for the purpose of further assisting education. This latter act provided that for every Congressman and Senator in the National Legislature each State was to receive 30,000 acres of public land, the proceeds of the sale of which were to be used for establishing agricultural and industrial colleges. States which had no public land were given scrip which could be sold and returned to the Government by the purchaser in exchange for public land in the regions where it did exist. One of the principle results of the Morrill Act was the creation of or

9. Milton Conover, "The General Land Office," p. 26.
10. N. M. Orfield, "Federal Land Grants to the States"; Hibbard, op. cit., p. 305ff.

assistance given to sixty-eight land grant colleges by
1916, and another was the facility offered for the establishment of large scale holdings through the purchase
of scrip.[11]

      Generous grants of public land were also used to
stimulate the building of roads, canals and railroads.
The most important of these three were the railroad
grants.[12] One of the first was made in 1833 when the
Government transferred an unused donation intended to
encourage the construction of an Illinois canal, to the
proposed construction of a railroad. Extensive grants
began in 1850 with the 2,500,000 acre subsidy to the
Illinois Central Railroad. Then in the prolific land
law year, 1862, Congress passed the first of the vast
concessions for transcontinental roads. In addition to
these grants to major lines, like the Union Pacific, the
Central Pacific, the Northern Pacific and the Atlantic
and Pacific, Congress also gave land subsidies to many
lesser western roads. Before it ceased making grants
the Government had turned over to the railroads more
than 132,000,000 acres.[13] Such an extensive amount of
land not only represented an exceedingly valuable investment but it also proved to be a source of complicated problems. For example indemnity claims developed
from the granting act provisions which permitted the
railroads to secure indemnity for lands which had been
entered by settlers or reserved for Indians within the
granted limits of the roads. At least until 1939 the
Government was still endeavoring to adjust some of the
indemnity claims that arose from grants made in the
1860's.[14]

      Another type of grant to stimulate internal im-
provements developed from the desire to reclaim swamp

---

11. Hibbard, op. cit., chap. XVI.
12. Ibid., p. 228ff; Donaldson, op. cit., p. 261; Orfield, op. cit.,
    Introduction; and J. B. Sanford, "Congressional Grants of Land
    in Aid of Railroads."
13. 132,425,574 acres were patented to railroads by 1934 when se-
    lections and adjustments were still in progress. Sec. of Int.
    Report, 1934, p. 73.
14. Cf. N.Y. Times, June 29, 1939. For a discussion of indemnity
    claims see post, chap. V.

lands. In 1849 Congress made the first of the swamp
land grants when it sought to encourage Louisiana "in
constructing the necessary levees and drains to reclaim
the swamp and overflow lands which may be unfit for cultivation."[15] The next year the granting act was extended to include Arkansas and other States with similar un-
usable lands. The granting acts stipulated that the
proceeds derived from the sale or use of the lands
should be applied to their reclamation. Although it was
thought at the time that there were only about five or
six million acres that would be affected by the acts,
the estimate proved to be too modest because it ignored
what a later Secretary of Interior called "the ingenuity
of the seekers of the landed wealth of the Government."
For instance the States soon requested additional land
as indemnity for the swampy lands that had been taken up
by settlers. Ignoring the obvious fact that if the land
had been satisfactory for private ownership without
State reclamation it did not come within the meaning of
the acts, the States nevertheless sought and obtained
indemnity either in lands or money.[16] Since there was
no time limit for selecting lands or indemnity the Land
Office was annually plagued with applications. But when
in 1860 Minnesota and Oregon received their donations
Congress profited by its experience and established both
a time limit for selection and a provision that there
could be no indemnity. Unfortunately, however, the early grants dragged along for decades and yet their purposes were achieved only to a limited degree.

One form of land disposal which had arisen early in the country's history, but which does not lend itself readily to classification, resulted from the approval of titles in regions formerly owned by Great
Britain, France, Spain and Mexico.[17] The American Government ultimately ratified private land claims totaling

---

15. Donaldson, op..cit., p. 220; and Hibbard, op. cit., p. 296ff.
16. In 1857 the Commissioner of the Land Office estimated that
    840,000 acres were all that would be involved in indemnity
    claims. He was greatly mistaken. L.O.R., 1891, p. 60.
17. Report of the Public Land Commission, 1880. H. Ex. Doc. #46.
    46 Cong. 2 Sess., Serial #1923, pp. 41-3.

33,000,000 acres but there was a costly delay in adjusting many of them.[18] This delay resulted from two facts: first, the manner in which some of the grants were originally made and, second, the method which the American Government adopted for adjusting those in various Southern States, particularly those of the Southwest. In the days when Spain and Mexico held seemingly limitless areas on the west of the North American continent, their Governments made extensive grants with vague boundary lines. Ascertaining boundaries with accuracy at a later date required a nice skill. In 1850 the American Congress created a fairly satisfactory Land Court for California where claims were adjusted promptly even though fraud and mistakes crept in. But for the remainder of the Southwest the Government provided that ratification of titles should be secured from both the Surveyor General of each Territory and Congress. This method proved so unsatisfactory that for over thirty-five years practically no titles were ratified and fraud became rampant. As a subsequent chapter will show Congress finally established another Land Court which had to spend more than a dozen years in disentangling hundreds of claims, principally for land in New Mexico, Arizona and Colorado. It is interesting to note that until recently lawyers could collect fees to contest the alleged fraudulent adjustment of private land claims in the hope that the patent to the land would be set aside and the donor of the fee would have a chance to acquire the land so released.[19]

Although there were other laws for the disposition of the public domain and numerous amendments to some of those already mentioned, the principle measures that influenced developments after 1865 have been noted.[20] But the significance of this heritage cannot be fully understood without noting important gaps in the system of distribution. As indicated above, one of the

18. Hibbard, op. cit., Table, p. 29.
19. L.O.R., 1891, pp. 30-1.
20. Certain details such as the fact that Homestead entires required small fees have been omitted. Incidentally the right of private entry and purchase at $1.25 an acre still existed.

most important omissions is found in the failure to provide any adequate means for classifying the lands of the
public domain. Laws had been framed chiefly from the
standpoint of their application to agricultural regions
and not only were such classifications as swamp lands
improperly provided for but exceedingly valuable natural
resources such as timber and minerals were virtually
ignored. This failure to recognize the need for taking
an inventory of its wealth meant that the Government had
made practically no provision for distributing timber
and mineral lands.

But since the Old Northwest and the South were
rich in timber, citizens who desired to acquire it
either trespassed under a lax enforcement of the penal
laws or obtained timberland in the same manner as they
secured agricultural land, at regular public auctions.
It frequently happened that bidders agreed among themselves before auction time, not to compete so that the
Government did not receive more than the $1.25 an acre
minimum for land worth perhaps fifty times as much. And
occasionally the laws were abused because the officials
of the Local Land Offices sold timberlands to favored
buyers before public sale. The important point to note,
however, is that because timber could be obtained the
need for a distinctive timber law was not evident until
the middle of the 1870's, after lumbermen had begun tap-
ping the valuable forest lands of the Far West and after
Government officials endeavored to enforce more string-
ently the laws against trespass.

The development of mining in the United States
had also failed to draw adequate federal attention because until the 1840's mining needs were met chiefly by
the English common law which held that an owner of a
surface claim was also the owner of all subsurface
rights. But gold discoveries in California had produced
a new doctrine that permitted a miner to follow a vein
of ore underground to its end, even though it led outside the perpendicular boundaries of his surface claim.
This western custom not only departed from English
precedent but from Spanish and Mexican as well. But
prior to the close of the Civil War it received recognition only in State and Territorial laws.

There was, however, a Federal statute passed in 1864 for the purpose of disposing of coal lands.[21]   By its provisions the President could offer coal land to the person who made the highest bid above the minimum price of $20.00 an acre. In the following year the law was amended in order to protect those who were already working mines without proprietory rights. Clever operators found, nevertheless, that they could evade the new measure by using the agricultural land laws. If they did not resort to outright fraud operators could take advantage of the Preëmption Act which contained a provision permitting entry on all lands where there were no "known mines." This meant that lands whose geological structure or outcroppings promised rich mineral wealth could be obtained as agricultural land, although their official character was changed as soon as a mine was opened.[22] In any case since there was no Federal law to provide for the distribution of metal bearing lands and since the coal land law could be easily evaded, it is evident that the Government needed to adopt appropriate measures for the distribution of mineral lands.

Besides the several serious gaps in the system of disposing of public lands the Government had neglected to provide adequately for administering them. Administration of the land laws and supervision of the public domain were the responsibility of a few closely related agencies which comprised what has been called the land department. The department was composed of the President, the Secretary of Interior, and a few subordinates in his office, the staff of the General Land Office and the officials in the Local Land Offices and the Surveyor Generals' offices. A brief analysis of the duties and responsibilities of each agency will illustrate the fact that the entire group was handicapped in its efforts to furnish efficient land administration.

21. From the wording of the law it seems to offer protection to those who were, apparently without warrant, already engaged in mining operations. 13 Stat., 343.
22. In 1864 the Land Office had suggested that the Government keep possession of its mineral lands and then license or tax those who mined gold. L.O.R., 1864, p. 25ff.

There can be little question of the fact that
the President was unable to devote much attention to
land affairs. He could indeed, emphasize policies, make
recommendations to Congress and decide questions of particular importance, but he was forced to rely heavily on
his Cabinet officer, the Secretary of Interior, for the
work of general administration. The Interior Department
had been established as the Home Department in 1849, although objections were then raised on the score that
there was little for its chief officer to do.[23] Yet
gradually the number of his tasks had been increased until by the time of the post-Civil War era he held wide
and varied responsibilities. With many major bureaus
and sundry local bureaus, public works and institutions
in Washington, as well as Cabinet and political responsibilities, the Secretary was too occupied to devote much
time to any one bureau. Questions of policy and the appeal of individual cases from the Land Office, for instance, did receive his decision--with the help of his
law officers; and frequently a Secretary with a personal
interest in some case ordered it brought before him for
review. But in the last analysis responsibility for administering the laws relating to the public domain rested in the Land Office Commissioner.

By 1865 the Commissioner was becoming one of the
most important and burdened officials in Washington. He
was later accurately described as "an executive officer,
a collector of revenue, an auditor, a legislator, a
prosecutor and a judge."[24] It was in the discharge of
these manifold duties that he presided over one of the
principal bureaus of the Government. A survey of Land
Office history reveals that it was established in 1812
under the supervision of the Treasury Department, a connection due to the fact previously noted that at that
time the public lands were looked upon as a source of
revenue. The Office was required only to distribute and
sell lands. But in 1836 it was reorganized and enlarged; the Survey, Public Lands and Private Lands Claims
Divisions were officially established and the Office was

23. 30 Cong. 2 Sess., Cong. Globe, vol. 18, pp. 669-79.
24. Conover, op. cit., p. 32.

required to supervise the work of the Surveying Offices. Unfortunately there was no provision for a subsequent increase of duties and as Milton Conover has pointed out, the Bureau grew by "administration rather than by legislation."[25]

In 1849 the Land Office was transferred to the Interior Department and it has remained there since. Six years after the transfer the Office was required to take over control of public timberland and protect it from depredation. This alone was a heavy responsibility but then with the passage of the Homestead law the Office was also obliged to supervise the making of improvements on every entry. This new obligation increased clerical work eightfold, but the personnel of the Bureau was not correspondingly increased. Consequently, as one writer has stated, the proper discharge of its duties was "not very successful."[26] New Divisions were created by the Commissioner, but without legal authority, as obligations continued to mount. These improvised divisions, some of outstanding importance, were placed at a disadvantage in several respects. Not the least of the disadvantages was to be found in the fact that their chiefs rated as only clerks. It was obviously unbusinesslike as well as unfair to have the chief of the long established but practically inactive Private Land Claims Division outrank and usually receive higher pay than the clerk who headed the new and important Railroad Division.[27] Moreover, when compared with other bureaus, the Land Office as a whole was discriminated against in regard to the number of its employees and the salaries paid them.[28] And finally, the Office was handicapped by the lack of efficiency in the Surveying and the Local Land Offices because, among other things, each set of offices was unwarrantly kept separate from the other.

The various defects and handicaps in the land department prior to 1865 did not hold much promise for

---

25. Ibid., p. 26.
27. F. H. White declared, "The Government obtained unfairly, it must be said, the responsible work of a chief while it was paying only the salary of a clerk." Quoted in Conover, op. cit., p. 22.
28. L.O.R., 1876, p. 14.

successful administration in the following period. Yet
it would be difficult to overemphasize the importance of
adequate facilities for handling the problems that were
to arise from settlement in the trans-Missouri region.
Immigration in the United States was to grow until it
brought in about three-quarters of a million people annually. Moreover as settlers laid claim to land along
their lines there was to be an increasing necessity for
carefully supervising the huge tracts which the railroads had received. The private land claims that had
remained in an inchoate state for nearly a score of
years would also need to be definitely established in
order to avoid various abuses and conflicts with settlers. Swamp land claims were to require greater attention as they increasingly burdened the Land Office by
their growth in number and questionable character. And
official surveys of valuable regions were to demand ever
closer scrutiny as the eagerness to obtain a share of
the nation's wealth promoted efforts to corrupt surveyors.

　　　　If, in the period after 1865, there were to be
unusually important administrative problems the Government was also faced by fundamental legislative issues.
These latter grew out of the need for measures that
would foster the proper disposal of the lands in mountain and plain. Primarily the country's land laws were
framed in terms of fertile farm land in a humid climate
and were intended to build up a nation of small-scale,
independent homesteaders. This intention is evident not
only in the settlement laws but in grants for many internal improvements as well. For instance railroad
grants reserved every other section of land for settlers
who could enter them in eighty-acre lots. But as the
frontier was pushed west of the Missouri River it became
evident that because of the resources, topography and
climatic conditions which existed there, the Government
would have to revise and augment its methods of disposal.[29]

---

29. There is, obviously, some difficulty in selecting the year
　　1865 as the time for the beginning of settlement west of the
　　Missouri River, but the period of extensive settlement begins
　　then.

In the first place the Jeffersonian system of
surveys that extended existing lines and then formed
square townships and sections was not adopted to surveying high mountains, deep gorges and useless alkali des-
erts.[30] Then there was the necessity for improving, as
noted above, federal laws for distributing mineral and
timberlands. Moreover as W. P. Webb has shown in his
study, The Great Plains, the settlement laws were inapplicable to arid and semi-arid regions because access to
water or water rights was essential for purposes of
homesteading.[31] Control of the extensive grasslands of
the plains presented a problem as these lands were increasingly absorbed by cattlemen. There was no federal
regulation for pasture rights and it was quite evident
that ranching required larger units of land than the
laws would permit a rancher to acquire. And finally,
the grasslands were to present a problem which only the
Federal Government could solve, the problem created by
the dispute which arose when, in the post-War era, favorable rains brought farmers into the cattle country to
contest the rights which the cattlemen had assumed for
themselves.

There is no doubt that the public domain east of
the Missouri River was subject to abuse, fraud and speculation, factors which were always a part of American
growth. On the other hand, to a large extent, there was
a close approximation between the needs of that area and
the legislation which Congress adopted. The foregoing
review has emphasized the enactment of a group of laws
molded in response to both frontier and national demands.
It has also pointed out the new problems, both legislative and administrative, which arose with the occupation
of western regions. It therefore becomes necessary to
study in more detail how these problems were met during
the years immediately after the Civil War.

---

30. Improvements in the technique of surveying also suggested revi-
    sion of the Government's surveying methods. See post, chap.
    IV.
31. Webb, op. cit., p. 353ff; passim.

II

The moral standards of business and Government, during the Reconstruction period, sank incredibly low. Reckless speculators, designing business men, corruptionists and irresponsible and dishonest officials became all too prominent in American life. The public lands presented great opportunities for the exploiter and though, in comparison with later periods, the amount of land absorbed was not large, some of the Government's policies encouraged questionable methods for the acquisition of choice areas. Instead of dwelling upon those policies, however, it is sufficient to relate what may be considered the constructive achievements of President Grant's administration. These achievements may be summarized as: a growing official and public consciousness of the necessity for revised land policies; cessation of further railroad land grants; reform of careless and reckless administrative methods; scientific explorations of parts of the West; and tentative steps for providing legislation appropriate to western needs.

The abandonment of further railroad grants in 1871 resulted especially from western indignation at corruption and jobbery in railroad building.[32] The demand for general reforms was more widespread. Labor groups as well as western farmers aimed at revising the methods of distribution and management of the public domain so that it could be protected from monopolies and preserved for the poor settler. The National Labor Congress supported this drive and it was soon backed by the Knights of Labor and the Greenback Labor Party.[33] The split in the Republican party in Missouri brought a similar stand from the Carl Schurz faction.[34] That renowned "fighter for social justice," Peter Cooper, agitated in behalf of the interests of western settlers and against wasteful gifts and careless control of the national heritage.[35]

32. L. H. Haney, "A Congressional History of Railways," p. 20ff.
33. F. E. Haynes, "Third Party Movements Since the Civil War," pp. 93-4; 96-7.
34. N. Fine, "Labor and Farm Parties in the U.S.: 1828-1928," pp. 119-20; 122-3.
35. A. Nevins, "Abram Hewitt," p. 288.

In 1871 Henry George began his campaign to arouse the
country to the realization of the fact that: "We are
monopolizing our lands deliberately." He also declared
that: "If we continue this policy a few years the public domain will be all gone" and the evils of a European manorial system would surely develop.[36] In addition to such individual and group programs there was
some sentiment for timber conservation and for legislation that would assist irrigation projects and cattle
raising on western lands.

        This awakened public sentiment was accompanied
by suggestions for exploring and mapping the West in order to aid science and the development of navigation. By
the time of President Grant's inauguration there were
four independent survey groups carrying on surveys with
Congressional backing.[37] Nevertheless these surveys
were unconnected with the needs of the Land Office. Consequently the land department was denied the advantages
which accrued to the private citizen. On the other hand
Congress did begin to enact measures which implied a
feeling of responsibility for the administration of
western lands. In 1866 it passed a law which reserved
from regular sale "all lands valuable for minerals," unless otherwise provided for.[38] The law did not explain
the meaning of mineral land but it placed the responsibility primarily on the Secretary of Interior for segre-
gating mineral and agricultural lands. It also provided
federal recognition for State and Territorial laws such
as those which granted full rights to follow a lode
wherever it led. W. P. Webb has praised the federal
recognition of western custom and it is true that the
law does exemplify again legislation molded in response

---

36. Henry George, Complete Works, 1901, vol. 9, pp. 97-9.
37. See post, chap. IV.
38. 14 Stat. 86, pp. 252-3. In 1865 Congress had given its recog-
    nition to "the law of possession," 13 Stat. 44. Webb states
    that westerners secured the 1866 law because they feared that
    the Government would try to sell its mineral lands in order to
    pay the public debt arising from the Civil War. Webb, op. cit.,
    p. 446. The law also protected water rights and the right of
    way for the construction of ditches and canals. Though prob-
    ably intended for the protection of mining enterprises this
    provision might have proved useful to cattlemen.

to western demands. But in this case it might have been
better to resist the demands because sanction for the
right to follow a lode aided the instigation of costly
lawsuits like those which plagued the Comstock Lode.[39]
Despite the absence of a definition for mineral land and
the potentialities for litigation the 1866 law was amended six years later chiefly by writing in western provisions.[40] Thereafter miners in "each mining district"
could, under certain restrictions, establish their own
regulations "governing the location, manner of recording
(and) amount of work necessary to hold possession of a
mining claim." This certainly was a flexible provision.
Nevertheless the law was specific in the requirement
that a patent could be issued only after a plat of the
claim and field notes had been officially made.   Moreover the size of all claims was limited. But because
the law still permitted a miner to follow his lode beyond the bounds of his own claim, conflicts between
claimants were certain to continue.

Another law applicable to the trans-Missouri region resulted from an attempt to conquer "The Great
American Desert." The suggestion that homestead applicants should plant a few hundred trees on their claim in
order to supply timber and to induce rainfall, coupled
with the practical experiments of several western States,
inspired a federal statute called the Timber Culture
Act.[41] One eminent writer on prairie land declares that
"Rain making by legislative fiat was something new, even
in the varied history of our public land legislation."[42]
In 1873, however, Senator Phineas Hitchcock of Nebraska
introduced the bill which was intended "To encourage the
growth of timber on the western prairie." The bill made
a fundamental break with the past when it did not require an entryman to settle on his entry. Nevertheless
it did provide for the usual 160-acre entry and it permitted any person who planted and maintained in healthy

39. C. H. Shinn, "The Story of the Mine," especially chap. XIII; and
    C. H. Shinn, "Land Laws and Mining Districts." For additional
    comment on federal response to western suggestions and customs
    see post, p. 35, note.
40. 17 Stat. 91. There were minor changes in the law in 1870.   16
    Stat. 52.
41. Ise, op. cit., p. 35 and pp. 43-5. Sheldon, op. cit., pp. 94-7.
42. E. S. Osgood, "The Day of the Cattlemen," p. 195.

condition 40 acres of timber to secure a patent for the entire quarter section. But since this forest had to be planted within a year of entry the law had to be modified and by 1878 it allowed any citizen to enter 160 acres devoid of timber and, if 675 trees were living on ten acres after eight years, to receive a patent for the entire entry. Unfortunately for the hopes of its backers the act not only did not stimulate rainfall, but according to John Ise it "never had any appreciable effect in stimulating forest growth."[43] It did, however, stimulate cupidity and speculation to an extraordinary degree.[44]

Despite the recognition of western needs which special surveys and mineral and timber culture laws reveal, in 1875 President Grant called Congress' attention to the complete inadequacy of federal land statutes. He had made a tour of the West in the summer of that year and had visited particularly the Territories of Wyoming, Utah and Colorado. He reported that his observations had convinced him "that existing laws regulating the disposition of public lands, timber....and probably the mining laws themselves are very defective and should be carefully amended and at an early date." Since there was "no adequate law" for the disposal of timber the President especially urged that Congress enact some provision which would meet the needs of settlers and so prevent them from becoming trespassers on public property. He also suggested that a joint committee of the two Houses visit the Territories and recommend such specific laws or amendments as seemed appropriate.[45] Since each of the President's suggestions, except that for a change in the mining laws, was adopted within the succeeding five years, chiefly after he had left office, they will be noticed again in more detail.

But during the final years of his second term President Grant also secured improved administration for

43. Ise, op. cit., p. 45.
44. In March, 1872, Congress also established a reservation that became Yellowstone Park. Donaldson, op. cit., pp. 1294-5.
45. J. D. Richardson, "A Compilation of the Messages and Papers of the Presidents," vol. VI, p. 355.

the land department. Under Secretary Columbus Delano of
Ohio the Department of Interior had acquired an evil reputation for abuses in the Indian, Patent and Land Offices. Suspicion was attached to the activities of the
Secretary's son particularly in connection with the latter bureau. In October, 1875, however, President Grant
turned to ex-Senator Zachariah Chandler of Michigan and
asked him to head the Department. After some hesitation
Mr. Chandler accepted.[46] Newspaper comments were caustic as to the new Secretary's capabilities but whatever
may be said of the various political and private activities which reflect unfavorably on his character, it
does appear that he established a more wholesome atmos-
phere in the Department.[47] With the full support of the
President he immediately provided a shake-up for several
bureaus and thereby served notice on others. Beside certain drastic changes in the Indian and Patent Bureaus
the Secretary stopped one glaring fraud in the Land Office. He conspicuously refused a bribe in deciding a
land case appealed to his office and at another time reversed a predecessor's decision, ostensibly to rectify a
fraud. The first case was given much publicity when
charges of fraud and bribery lay over the Republicans in
the election of 1876.[48] It aided the party to portray
its National Chairman, Secretary Chandler, as a model of
official rectitude.

During his short term the Secretary had two able
Land Office Commissioners. Samuel Burdett of Missouri
served from 1874 to 1876 when ill-health forced his
resignation. His report in 1875 showed a broad grasp of
western requirements and promised vigorous administration. On June 24, 1876, however, he was succeeded by
James A. Williamson of Iowa, one of the prominent Commissioners of the post-War period. Commissioner Williamson held office for five years and by continuing policies marked out by his predecessor, established a notable record. He became a leader for land law reform and
ably assisted the Public Land Commission of 1879.   The

---

46. Detroit Post and Tribune, article "Zachariah Chandler"; Dict.
    Am. Biog.
47. N.Y. Tribune, Nov. 25, 1875; N.Y. Times, Jan. 8, 1876.
48. N.Y. Times, Jan. 25, 1876; ibid., Feb. 13, 1877.

Commissioner was born in Columbus, Kentucky, in 1830, but received his college education in Illinois. In the latter State he also studied law and was admitted to the bar.[49] He refused to enter politics and soon moved to Iowa where, during the Civil War, he joined the Iowa volunteers. Leaving the army with the rank of Major-General the young officer acquired an active interest in western lands. He not only preëmpted a quarter section in Utah but obtained extensive investments in coal and iron lands there, while he was acting as an advisor for railroad, mining and land companies. In the meantime the General also spent a considerable period in Europe, studying land problems so that by 1876 he was well qualified for the position of Commissioner. At the time of his appointment, Copp's Land Owner, the leading paper on land affairs, remarked: "He fully appreciates the wants of the settlers and the changed conditions of our public lands, especially in the Territories and the public land States which call so loudly for a new system of sale and disposal."[50]

Before discussing Commissioner Williamson's proposals it is interesting to note that paradoxically enough his reputation for uprightness in office is questionable for he used his position to acquire some of his property. In 1869 he had staked out the settlement claim referred to above but when he applied for his patent in the following year the Land Office found that he had not fulfilled the necessary requirements.[51] General Williamson explained that he had been kept from carrying the entry to completion because of threats which he had received, but he nevertheless felt entitled to a patent. Commissioner Drummond wrote the General that he had no discretion in the matter, for proof of residence and cultivation must be forwarded to the Land Office. The General failed to provide the proof but when he became Commissioner, several years later, "Acting Commissioner" Baxter reopened the case. He went over the record,

49. Appleton's Encyclopedia of American Biography, vol. VI; and National Cyclopedia of American Biography, vol. XII.
50. Copp's Land Owner, Nov. 1876.
51. 46 Cong. 2 Sess., Sen. Ex. Doc. #181, Serial #1886, pp. 129-35.

decided that there was sufficient evidence of settlement
and then passed the entry to patent. In effect, therefore, Commissioner Williamson reversed a predecessor's
decision for his own personal benefit and with little
legal warrant.[52]

On the other hand the Commissioner tackled the
problem of Land Office needs and in his first report
stressed particularly the questions of staff and salaries. The inadequate facilities which had been provided in an earlier time had not been improved to meet a
subsequent increase of business. On the contrary they
had become worse. By 1876 there were 145 employees in
the Office and that number represented a reduction by
one-fourth from that of the preceding year. The Commissioner asserted that it was less than that for the previous twenty years.[53] He also called attention to the
salary discrimination for his Office as compared with
other Bureaus and declared that such discrimination
caused his abler men to seek transfers whenever possible.
Many other men stayed in the Office only long enough to
become acquainted with the land laws and Office procedure and then they were snapped up by "railroads, land
companies and legal firms," which offered salaries far
above those paid by the Government.[54] With pardonable
exasperation Commissioner Williamson declared: "I must
confess that unless Congress provides by law for the re-
organization of the clerical force under my control and
payment of salaries adequate to the ability required, I
feel myself unable to properly administer the laws relating to the public lands and do justice to the thousands of cases now pending, awaiting action for want of
clerks possessing the ability to adjudicate them."[55]

Moreover, although a great many land claims involved a contest between two parties or between the Government and an interested party, the Commissioner revealed that there was no provision for a formal review.
He very rightly felt that: "The establishment of a

52. See also post, chap. XI.
53. L.O.R. 1876, p. 14.
54. Ibid., p. 14.
55. Ibid., p. 14.

proper judicial tribunal for the determination of questions arising before this office is one of such preëmi-
nent importance that it seems a little remarkable that
it has not been made the subject of legislation."[56] Yet
Congress failed to respond to the suggestion for a court
or to reorganize the Office.

The administration of the Local Land Offices also
needed to be revised. In 1877 there were more than ninety such offices and each was presided over by a Register
and a Receiver. These positions had been created many
decades before when the monetary return from lands was
important. The officials were paid a small salary which
was supplemented by commissions for handling contested
cases. Such a method of pay proved injurious to settlers, however, for officials frequently fostered contests in order to secure an adequate income. In fact
Commissioner Williamson charged that the low salary attracted mercenary adventurers who saw the possibilities
that the chance for commissions offered.[57] He then suggested reform by the consolidation of the two positions
and payment of a suitable salary to a single new official; but Congress took no action on this suggestion
either.

In 1877 the Commissioner made an urgent appeal
for a law library because the Office lacked many common
books and State law reports and it possessed only "brok-
en sets of Supreme Court decisions."[58] He declared that
there were only single copies of many volumes, which too
frequently several clerks needed to use at the same time.
Furthermore he showed that no one was authorized to
print official decisions, orders or circulars, nor was
there any codification of laws and decisions. Congress
soon met these deficiencies by supplying a library,
authorizing the printing of official decisions and, in
1879, providing for the codification of land laws and
decisions by the Public Land Commission.

---

56. L.O.R. 1877, p. 4. Conover speaks of the especially complicat-
    ed judicial cases which the Office decided from 1837 to 1891.
    Conover, op. cit., p. 23.
57. Ibid., pp. 30-1.
58. Ibid., pp. 3-4.

Meanwhile the Commissioner continued his efforts for improving administrative equipment and for securing laws appropriate to the western needs of land distribution. Throughout the administration of President Rutherford B. Hayes the Commissioner repeatedly emphasized the importance of meeting the problems which the last frontier raised. The official recognition of these problems at least led to the hope for their practical solution while the Government still held title to the lands. It is therefore necessary to turn to public land issues under President Hayes and see the nature of the solution which developed.

Chapter II

PROVIDING FOR PASTORAL LANDS

An authority on the history of the public domain, Benjamin J. Hibbard, has remarked that Government
lands played a far less significant political role in
the post-Civil War era than in the preceding period.[1]
This was especially true in facing the issues which
arose in the trans-Missouri region for neither of the
major parties took sides on such questions as those
that involved pastoral or timber lands. Democratic and
Republican platforms in 1876 differed somewhat in their
public land planks but these differences were revealed
chiefly in Democratic recrimination on Republican
largess.[2] Having been out of office for fifteen years
the Democrats could accuse their opponents of "profli-
gate waste of public lands" whereby 200,000,000 acres
had been squandered on railroads alone and where out of
more than 600,000,000 acres less than a sixth had been
distributed directly to "tillers of the soil." The
Democrats called for reform and in recognition of popular hostility to their erstwhile liberality the Republicans declared that they too were now opposed to further
grants to corporations and monopolies and in favor of
preserving the public domain as "free homes for the
people."[3] But the presidential candidates who stood on
these platforms, Samuel J. Tilden, Democrat, and Rutherford B. Hayes, Republican, failed to mention the land
question in the letters accepting their respective
party's nominations.

---

1. Op. cit., p. 560.
2. R. P. Ellis, "Platforms of the Two Great Political Parties,"
   p. 40. In 1868 the Democrats had suggested that the proceeds
   of the sale of lands be given the railroads instead of giving
   the lands themselves, p. 27.
3. Ibid., p. 45.

The election was followed by the bitter dispute over the electoral votes so that when Mr. Hayes received the majority he had to begin his term under the shadow of a partisan count and a rumored agreement with politicians over the "Southern question."[4] Nevertheless as a Cincinnati lawyer, a Major General in the Civil War, a Congressman and three times Governor of Ohio, President Hayes had acquired a reputation for deliberation of judgment and scrupulousness of conduct and he continued to display these qualities in the White House.[5] He endeavored not only to overcome the initial handicap of the electoral count but also to replace "Grantism" as a factor in official life. He continued to be handicapped, however, for during the first two years of his term the House of Representatives contained a Democratic majority and the last two years brought a Democratic Senate as well. His own party did not give him strong support partly because he alienated the Stalwart Republicans when he failed to give them any prominent Cabinet positions. Nevertheless his term marks a distinctive period in public land affairs. Its tone was distinctly that of reform for the treatment of major issues and its accomplishments include the passage of two timber laws, the consolidation of western surveys and the creation of the Public Land Commission.

The President showed a special interest in providing for the proper disposal of timber, for offering Federal protection to the cattle industry and for ensuring a well-managed Interior Department.[6] He brought the well-known reformer Carl Schurz to the Department and supported his efforts for an improved administration. The new Secretary had come to America as an immigrant from the 1848 Revolutions in the Germanies and had risen rapidly in public life. Like the President he had rendered distinguished service in the Civil War and had become widely known for his abilities as an author, orator, Senator and diplomat.[7] He also became

---

4. A. Nevins, "Hewitt," op. cit., passim.
5. D. S. Muzzey, "The United States of America," II, pp. 75ff. and 101ff.
6. Richardson, op. cit., Vol. VII, p. 476.
7. Claude M. Fuess, "Carl Schurz," passim.

one of the leaders of the Liberal Republican Movement
in President Grant's first term. His devotion to Civil
Service reform was demonstrated when he became Secretary by the comparatively few staff changes which he
made.[8] His progressive spirit guided administrative
policies though it was somewhat tempered in handling
railroad and timber questions. The Secretary inaugurated what he believed was the first real move for timber
conservation in America[9] and he also initiated the practice of securing annual reports from the Governors of
western Territories in order that the Government could
keep in touch with their problems and development. It
is these reports, along with those which the Surveyors
General sent to the Land Office, that provide valuable
information for the student of public land affairs.

        The reports reveal that one of the major prob-
lems of the West during the Hayes-Schurz administration
was connected with protecting and distributing arid
lands. The term arid or desert land was applied to several types which included barren and worthless land,
land that was suitable for pasturing or for crop raising if irrigated, and finally land which could be cultivated despite an occasional scarcity of water. This
latter class, represented by considerable areas in
Kansas and Nebraska, could be farmed profitably when
rains were favorable, but it was also subject to periods
of drought or insufficient rains so that irrigation
seemed advisable. Irrigation required either windmills,
artesian wells or dams and canals which could utilize
the waters of rivers and streams. Since the use of
streams proved to be the most feasible of these methods,
farming arid lands required access to rivers and a greater capital outlay than lands in humid regions. Moreover semi-arid lands presented another complication in
that a great many of them were covered with sturdy
prairie grasses which invited pasturing. Since they
thus offered opportunities to both farmer and cattle
raiser they fostered many clashes between the two

8. Carl Schurz, "Reminiscences of Carl Schurz," Vol. III, pp. 380-1.
9. Carl Schurz, "Speeches, Correspondence and Political Papers,"
     ed. Bancroft, Vol. V, p. 27.

groups. Western arid lands, therefore, produced the difficult problems of how to classify them and how to provide methods of distribution which would ensure water rights to both farmer and rancher and ample areas for private ranching.

It has already been noted that the settlement laws passed prior to 1877 could not be satisfactorily applied to most of the West and this fact became glaringly apparent as abuses grew to wholesale proportions. Land Office Commissioners explained that many communities were opposed to convicting violators because nearly everyone realized that there was no law which permitted them to acquire adequate amounts of land. Since President Grant had learned of these conditions during his western trip in 1875 he had recommended modifying the land laws. At the same time Commissioner Burdett presented several concrete suggestions. For instance he proposed that Congress provide for selling desert land in sufficient quantities to reimburse those who supplied the capital which would be invested in their purchase and in the construction of dams, canals and ditches.[10] In addition he suggested a law permitting unlimited sale of pastoral land at $1.25 an acre or a law which would follow the Australian method of leasing large areas. During the following year his successor, Commissioner Williamson, urged that Congress adopt some plan for large scale irrigation.[11] He pointed to the reports from Idaho, Wyoming, Utah and Nevada which demonstrated that both settlers and capitalists were eager to appropriate and improve arid lands. He opposed the sale of such lands and advocated instead that the Government donate large tracts in the same way that it had made railroad grants. It should provide, however, a suitable method for supervising the construction of irrigation facilities. As an alternative plan the Commissioner suggested that the Government itself could construct dams and ditches and then distribute the land to be irrigated.

---

10. L.O.R., 1875, pp. 7-9.
11. L.O.R., 1876, p. 3ff. Reports of Surveyors General. *Ibid.*, pp. 220, 271, 278 and 294.

Meanwhile Congress had been considering several bills which were intended to foster irrigation but it had been unable to agree on any of them. In 1877, however, while the country was agitated over the disputed presidential election Congress adopted a Desert Land Act with some surprising features. Ostensibly the Act was framed for settlers yet its requirements were so inappropriate that they could scarcely be met. On the other hand by a process of simple evasion the law served the needs of business enterprise, particularly the cattle business.[12] In fact the Desert Land Act's widespread abuse leads to the belief that it was passed at the behest of large scale operators. Support for this belief can be found first in Commissioner Williamson's statement that the act was pushed through by its "promoters" because there was no way in which to purchase land.[13] It is evident that settlers did not need a new law for buying homesteads since they could secure railroad, school or swamp lands if they did not care to take advantage of the settlement laws. Only ranchers, mining companies and capitalists who wished to build dams for extensive irrigation needed to purchase land, particularly in the larger units which the Desert law permitted. Perhaps there is some significance in its last minute passage prior to President Hayes' reform administration. But the most convincing evidence which supports the belief concerning landed interests can be found by reviewing the act's progress through Congress, the provisions of the law itself, the suggestions which immediately arose for its amendment and finally the forms of abuse to which it was subjected.

On January 6, 1877 the House received a bill which permitted any citizen to enter 640 acres of desert land if he intended to "reclaim" it "by conducting water on the same" within three years.[14] At the end of that time if he showed proof of reclamation and

---

12. Perhaps an answer to W. P. Webb's query regarding the Government's failure to pass a bona fide pastoral land law, op. cit., p. 428.
13. L.O.R., 1877, p. 34.
14. 44 Cong. 2 Sess. Cong. Rec., pp. 331, 464.

paid $1.25 an acre he could receive a patent. Entries were confined to eleven western States and Territories and desert land was defined as all that which, exclusive of timber and mineral land, would not produce "some agricultural crop" without irrigation. The bill had not been accompanied by a report and no one asked how much of the 640 acres must be reclaimed, what reclamation meant, why settlement was not required or why there was no provision for survey; in short, there was no explanation or discussion before the bill passed the House.

The bill received more appropriate attention from the Senate, through the Committee report seemed unnecessarily vague and even misleading. The report gave many indications that the bill was intended for settlers.[15] For instance it noted that settlers had already taken up land along streams where "sufficient moisture exists for cultivation and where irrigation is cheap and easy." This fact pointed to the necessity for a new settlement law which would meet more stringent conditions. The Committee opposed, however, the suggestion for Government construction of dams because it believed that private enterprise was more practical and that in general Government interference in reclamation should be reduced to a minimum. It also opposed the sale of large tracts because it feared speculation. Consequently it rejected the two most feasible plans for assisting the impecunious frontiersman. Furthermore the Committee recognized that the construction of irrigation works was expensive and that this construction must precede settlement. Both of these factors would have handicapped many settlers yet the Committee added another drawback when it rejected donating the land free. It explained its position by stating that irrigation would so increase the value of an entry that the entryman could pay $1.25 an acre. But there is some doubt of the Committee's good faith on this point since Homestead entrymen also increased the value of their lands at comparatively little expense and they were not penalized but rather rewarded for it. The

15. Ibid., pp. 1965-5.

Committee did declare that by granting 640 acres instead of the usual 160, there would be an "additional inducement to settlers to undertake the work of irrigation." Yet one commentator had justly observed that by requiring any settler to irrigate 640 acres of desert land the Committee was expecting a miracle.[16]

The Committee also asserted that the new bill would enable "settlers by combined efforts to construct more extensive works" than was possible under other laws. It is true that cooperative efforts were necessary for reclaiming arid lands but there was no indication in the Desert Land bill that it was intended to foster those methods. The Committee declared that it recommended the bill with greater confidence than was possible if its provisions were entirely new. Perhaps it would have been more realistic to omit such a statement because western lands required a law which would embody a new provision intended to ensure water rights. On the other hand the bill did possess enough unusual features that it seemed practically new. For instance although there had been a special law omitting the requirement for survey in one California County, there never had been a general law which permitted patents in the absence of a survey. Furthermore it was rather novel to require a settler to have considerable capital for improvements and for purchasing his land, or to expect him to improve his land by cooperative labor, or to ignore any requirement for settlement under what was considered a settlement law.

The Senate debate brought out several efforts to tighten up loop-holes in the bill.[17] Senator Chaffee of Colorado was the first to point out that it did contain innovations such as the failure to require surveys.

_____

16. Osgood, op. cit., p. 195. The Committee pointed to a special act which had passed for facilitating irrigation in Lassen County, California after an investigation in 1873. The latter law had hardly been in existence long enough to prove a great deal and it was more carefully drawn than the Desert Land bill of 1877. 18 Stat. 497, and Donaldson, op. cit., p. 363.
17. Cong. Rec., pp. 1964-74.

Senator A. A. Sargent of California was in charge of
the bill and despite his explanation that it was impossible to get Congress to appropriate sufficiently
for surveying needs Senator Boutwell of Massachusetts
secured an amendment requiring survey before patent.
He also secured an amendment which required each entryman to pay twenty-five cents an acre when filing his
claim. The Massachusetts Senator explained that since
the bill contemplated settlers "who already have some
property," he felt that they could give the Government
some security that "the undertaking on which they have
entered would be performed." Unfortunately this provision resulted in a security for the entryman and not
the Government. Senator Ingalls of Kansas obtained an
amendment that excluded the bill's application from
pastoral land. Senator Allison of Iowa raised a pertinent question when he sought an explanation of the meaning of the phrase, "conducting water on" the land. But
he obtained only laughter when he suggested that a mere
spring might suffice for reclamation. A provision
which required that entries be made in a "compact form"
was rejected in view of the survey requirement. There
is some significance however, in the fact that Senator
Sargent laughed down a definition which stated that compact form meant "not more than twice as wide as long"
for he was thereby defending the right to enter as much
land as possible along a stream in order to monopolize
it.[18]

      After the bill passed the Senate on February 27,
1877,[19] it went to conference and did not emerge until
March 3, the last day of the Session.[20] The conference
committee report was then accepted by both Houses without discussion and the bill was immediately signed by
President Grant as one of the last acts of his administration.[21] But a comparison of the new law with the
bill which passed the Senate reveals that the conference committee, composed of four men from California

---

18. Senator Ogelsby of Illinois desired to test the law in Cali-
    fornia and Oregon alone but his amendment to that effect was
    rejected.
19. Cong. Rec., p. 2156.
20. Ibid., p. 2225.
21. 19 Stat., 377.

and Oregon, and one each from Nebraska and Illinois,
had made three important changes. They had made surveys optional and, without defining the term, had added
a provision requiring "compactly" formed entries. They
had also dropped Senator Ingalls' amendment in order to
permit entries on grazing land. In short they had replaced those loop-holes which had existed in the House
bill and which made the measure so suitable for abuse
by corporate interests.[22]

The most charitable interpretation of the law
would class it with other careless measures of the post-
war period.[23] A very critical interpretation would
call it a vicious law. Since it contained practically
the same provisions as the bill which the Senate committee supported, the criticisms of that report and the accompanying bill also largely apply to the law. For the
sake of emphasis, however, it is necessary to repeat
two points which are of special significance. By permitting entrymen to omit surveys there was no certain
method by which the Government could know whether it
was issuing a patent for 500 or 800 acres, or know accurately the character of the land or where it was located. Of course the law required an entryman to describe his boundaries, but western oaths regarding land
were notoriously unreliable. Even if they were honest
the question of reasonably accurate location and amount
still remain. Moreover the failure to require any definite shape for an entry or to stipulate the character
and extent of reclamation, played directly into the
hands of the cattlemen and other large scale operators.
The conference committee must have been aware of the
many defects in the law but it seemingly ignored them
without even the possibility of the excuse that it was
meeting settlers' needs. Incidentally it is interesting to observe that the Desert Land law was almost entirely a western law; that is, it was formulated and
presented by a Committee which was composed almost

22. The conference committee was composed of Representatives J. K.
    Luttrell of California, La F. Lane of Oregon and L. Crouse of
    Nebraska and Senators Sargent, J. K. Kelley of Oregon and R. J.
    Oglesby of Illinois.
23. Cf. Webb, op. cit., p. 414.

wholly of men from the Mississippi Valley or farther
west. Furthermore the law was not materially changed
on the floor of Congress and most of its changes had
been suggested by western men.[24] Tradition may have
caused the bill to be framed with an approximation to
earlier settlement laws in order to have it the more
readily accepted. If that is so it is possible to explain the law's peculiar features as the result of a
compromise between a heritage of providing small land
units for settlers and the reality of western conditions, but it was a compromise that was only an indirect and unrealistic approach to the arid land problem.

                            II

        The unsatisfactory character of the Desert Land
Act, especially its provisions which favored large-
scale operators, were emphasized by the law's abuse and
the recommendations for its amendment during President
Hayes' administration. Soon after its passage land officials criticized the law severely and western reports
stressed the need for laws which would be more appropriate to both ranching and irrigation farming. Taking
up first the question of farming it is necessary to note
that Secretary Schurz believed that the law was intended
for settlers. But in order to protect the Government he
proposed an amendment that would assure officials of
the desert character of the land to be entered.[25] He
also requested a provision that would specify the
amount of land which each entryman must irrigate and
that would prohibit the latter from alienating any right

----

24. W. P. Webb's claim that "The Easterner was reluctant to approve
    any proposal made by the Westerner for new institutions for the
    West" is not entirely accurate. Webb, op. cit., p. 397. Be-
    sides the Desert Land Act, the Timber Culture Law, the Mining
    laws and the two Timber laws of 1878 were western products
    which received little eastern opposition. Moreover westerners
    could be somewhat unrealistic in their proposals. Senator
    Ingalls of Kansas wished to reserve all land for 250 miles east
    of the Rockies and from Canada to the Gulf as pastoral land.
    Cong. Rec., loc. cit., p. 1967.
25. Sec. of Int. Report, 1877, p. xxi.

to the land before title had passed from the Government.
The request for a prohibition on alienating rights
pointed to a fundamental difficulty in managing western
lands: though it was necessary to protect the Government's interest until its requirements had been fulfilled, many settlement law entrymen needed the financial aid of a mortgage, or aid with some other form of
guarantee for the person providing the aid, in meeting
the Government's requirements.

Instead of recommending amendments Commissioner
Williamson's greater knowledge of the West caused him
to declare that the law could not be carried into effect and that it should, therefore, be repealed. In
its place he again proposed that the Government donate
to individuals or corporations large tracts of all land
which was "truly and unmistakably desert in character,"
if it could be reclaimed.[26] He believed that the Government should be as liberal with desert land as it was
with fertile farm land farther east. But Congress was
not prepared to adopt any changes great or small, at
that time.

In the following year, 1878, Major James W.
Powell presented another plan in his "Report on the
Rocky Mountain Region," more commonly called, "The Report on the Arid Regions of the United States."[27] Major
Powell had studied the West at first hand for more than
a decade and his report grew out of a special survey in
the Mountain area. He had left the Army after the Civil
War and had become a professor at an Illinois College.[28]
During the summer of 1867 he took a class of students to
study geology in the West and became interested in exploring the Colorado River. Consequently in 1868 he organized another party and by enduring intensive hardships, succeeded in descending the River by boat. This
feat led to the establishment of a survey for the region. The Smithsonian Institute sponsored the survey
and in 1874 it received Congressional backing and became the Geographical and Geological Survey of the
Rocky Mountain Region.

---

26. L.O.R., 1877, pp. 34-5.
27. 45 Cong. 2 Sess. H. Ex. Doc., #80. Serial #1805.
28. Appleton's Encyclopedia of American Biography. Vol. VI.

Major Powell's report pointed out that since most of the country's arid lands were unused the Government had the opportunity to adopt a comprehensive plan and satisfy the expectations of many settlers. He brought up the all-important question of surveys and foreshadowed his later report on that subject by suggesting the necessity for classifying lands. Next he pointed to the necessity for a system of land parcelling which would provide access to water for the greatest number of settlers.[29] In order to make his suggestions concrete he drew up a bill which provided for nine or more cooperative homesteads that would be built around a common irrigation project.[30] Major Powell believed that if a group of entrymen pooled their resources and labor they could construct irrigation facilities and then obtain at least an 80-acre homestead from the Government. His plan seemed to establish the principles expressed by the Senate Public Land Committee on a practical basis but since the United States had not yet come to believe in community planning the proposal did not find support and so was never adopted.

It was not only eastern land officials and survey specialists that recommended a change in the Desert law but western officials and residents poured suggestions into Washington. Many officials became caustic over Congress' failure to "legislate anew and aright." They could not avoid pointing out the great discrepancy in charging the same price for "worthless lands" as the Government had charged for "well-watered lands a 1,000 miles nearer the markets of the world." Their suggestions centered around plans already presented, namely, large-scale sale or donation that would encourage investment of capital in irrigation works, or Government construction of such works.

A comprehensive treatment of the problem of irrigation is found in the 1879 report of Governor M. Brayman of Idaho. Starting with ancient times he presented an historical survey of Government control of irrigation and he then went on to consider the inadequacy

---

29. Report, p. 41.
30. Report, p. 13; Webb, op. cit., p. 354.

of the Desert act.[31] But he did not believe exclusively in Government construction for he was willing to accept Commissioner Williamson's plan of large-scale donations to corporations. He felt that if the Government
did undertake to build irrigation works there could be
no question of receiving back the cost because both
land and water rights could be sold. If, on the other
hand, private interests were allowed to undertake the
work, the Government should carefully supervise both
the construction and the distribution of land within a
specified time limit. Of course Government supervision
of any large enterprise, if the railroads are taken as
an example, was not certain to be successful but the
alternative of a poor law and practically no supervision was scarcely a triumph in any sense. Nevertheless
the Governor's suggestions were closely followed in the
Public Land Commission's report of the following year,
though they were never enacted into law.[32]

Governor Brayman had brought out another important point when he claimed that, contrary to the as-
sertions in the Committee report on the Desert land bill,
western water rights were not protected. He claimed
that any person who entered land along a stream was apt
to find that his rights to its water were illusory because whole streams were "appropriated by capitalists
and corporations, turned from their channel for mining
or other purposes and in effect treated as private property, to the exclusion of those entitled to common use."
The Governor reported that according to instances in
California, local laws or litigation offered only
hazardous protection against such abuses and he felt
that only the Federal Government could enforce the

---

31. Sec. of Int. Report, 1879, pp. 425-6. Though in 1878 the land
department ruled that entries were not transferrable Commissioner Williamson recognized western needs and agreeing with
one of Governor Brayman's suggestions asked Congress to reverse the rule. L.O.R., 1880, p. 491.
32. The Commission declared the cost would reach into the hundreds
of millions of dollars and that Government expenditures for
such purposes were not in "consonance with the traditions of
the American people and hence not as preferable as private
construction work," op. cit., pp. xxvi-xxix.

rights which had been uniformly recognized in the East.
A recent student, W. P. Webb, has defended the western
custom of prior appropriation rights as not only unique
but particularly suited to western needs. Nevertheless
since the practice involved the antagonism of settlers
and corporate interests and even the good relations between States and Territories it warranted Federal interference.[33] But Congress did not interfere, unless
the complicated phraseology of the Desert land law had
already recognized the western practice.

One mitigating factor in the neglect of arid
regions was introduced in 1878 when Congress enacted
the first measure which permitted official withdrawal
of lands around the headwaters of the Mississippi River.
On the other hand Congress refused to link this effort
at river control with the problem of irrigation.[34] In
1879 Representative Atkins of Tennessee brought up the
question in Congress because it was receiving considerable public attention. He argued in behalf of the construction of "reservoirs, ponds and canals....in the
upper channels of the Missouri and the Arkansas and
other rivers along whose courses the boundless tracts
of arid lands lie." He felt that such construction
would not only provide the water for irrigation of the
dry country but it would also lessen "the flow of those
rivers into the Mississippi River." Moreover he claimed
that it would end the Mississippi's "annual freaks" in
addition to making it a great commercial thoroughfare.[35]
Unfortunately his proposal found little response for it
came nearly thirty years too early.[36]

While Congress was not ready to adopt so bold a
plan nor to modify the Desert act, the West was proving

---

33. See the dispute over use of the Bear River flowing through
    Utah and Idaho. Sec. of Int. Report, 1889, p. xxv.
34. Withdrawals of 168,000 acres in Wisconsin and Minnesota brought
    only minor results. Army engineers considered it impossible to
    work out a plan that would aid navigation though Congress ap-
    propriated $300,000 in 1882. L.O.R., 1882, pp. 28-9.
35. 45 Cong. 3 Sess. Cong. Rec., p. 1175.
36. In 1888, however, Congress took the first step toward with-
    drawing irrigation reservoir sites. See post, chap. XIV.

the validity of large-scale irrigation. Numerous States
and Territories reported construction work or the incorporation of ditch companies, despite the difficulty
of obtaining the necessary amount of land. As long as
Desert act requirements and administrative rules made
the law's use of doubtful worth for extensive projects,
a capitalist or a company needed considerable courage
to proceed with any plans. Of course it is proper to
be suspicious that some of the "Ditch" and "Irrigation"
companies were associated with the cattle business but
if they irrigated the land they were making as proper
use of it as a group of farmers might. One enterprise
which was undertaken primarily for irrigation farming
had been started in the San Joacquin Valley of California in 1871 and it was intended to develop 190,000
acres.[37] Another prominent enterprise was located near
Boise City, Idaho. In 1879 the Governor reported that
a capitalist had secured sufficient persons to make
desert land entries for 17,000 acres.[38] He had also
constructed a canal eight miles long and had made numerous branches from it. Trees had been planted and crops
raised on the irrigated portions of the land; one tract
of 600 acres had produced 16,000 bushels of wheat in a
year. The Governor declared that although the construction work had cost $17,000 it was jeopardized by the
strict interpretation of the Desert act. This handicap
did not, however, deter further undertakings in Idaho
for in 1884 the Governor reported over half a dozen
similar projects.

        A report from Arizona revealed that one region
was profiting by the use of an old Aztek irrigation
ditch which had been reopened in 1878.[39] It served an
extensive area for it was several miles long and its
thirty-foot width enabled it to carry considerable
water. In 1883 the Governor of Wyoming submitted a
list of seventeen irrigation companies which had filed

37. H. K. Norton, "Story of California," p. 334.
38. Sec. of Int. Report, 1879, pp. 417-8. See also J. T. Ganoe,
    "The Desert Land Act in Operation, 1877-1891." Agricultural
    History, April, 1937.
39. Sec. of Int. Report, 1886, p. 919.

petitions for incorporation with the Secretary of the
Territory during the two preceding years. He showed
that the largest company was planning to irrigate
50,000 acres and the smallest, 2,500.[40]

While western developments and recommendations
proved the inadequacy of the Desert land law for farming arid lands they also demonstrated its appropriate-
ness for meeting in a legitimate way the needs of cattle raising. At the same time that he had requested
amendments to protect the settler's use of the law
Secretary Schurz had taken up "the stock raising interests on the plains." He noted that they were reaching
great proportions without authority or the protection
of law and without benefit to the Government.[41] In order to correct these faults he proposed a plan for
leasing large areas of railroad and Government lands.
The proposal had originally come from cattlemen through
the Director of the Union Pacific Railroad and had suggested joint leasing "to responsible stock-growers all
lands lying west of the 100th meridian in blocks of say
fifty to five hundred square miles at such annual rental and for such term of years as will protect all concerned, and warrant the cattleman in fencing his land
and improving it." The Secretary, however, offered an
amendment which would enable the Government to exchange
its alternate sections with the railroad so that each
would own all the land on one side of the road.

H. L. Osgood has stated that during the Eighteen
Seventies and early Eighties, leasing was an "academic"
subject to cattlemen for they preferred to take their
chances on the open range where "priority rights" protected them.[42] Although the author qualifies his statement it is necessary to emphasize the fact that ranchers
differed in their opinions. The suggestion for leasing
originated with cattlemen and western reports indicated
that many others were looking to the Government because

---

40. Sec. of Int. Report, 1883, p. 604. In 1879 a system of irri-
    gation was begun at Garden City, Kansas. Subsequently
    $500,000 was spent in canals 80 miles long. The Nation,
    August 6, 1885.
41. Sec. of Int. Report, 1877, pp. xx-xxi.
42. Osgood, op. cit., pp. 209 and 182-3.

the range was filling up. While the boom period of the
cattle business did not arrive until the middle Eighties
an examination of the official reports from Arizona,
Wyoming, Utah, Dakota, Montana and New Mexico will reveal increasing business, crowded areas and demands for
Federal assistance.[43]

In 1879 the Governor of Utah remarked that
seven-eights of his Territory was "fit only for grazing
purposes" and that it was becoming more and more necessary for stock growers to acquire definite land rights.[44]
He declared that although priority rights used to be re-
spected they no longer were. Not only were cattle becoming numerous but sheep herders were beginning to
move their flocks in from California. In the year before the Surveyor General of Dakota had reported that
"The valleys are all claimed and settled....and the
amounts of money spent by 'ranchmen' in improvements of
all kinds prove them to be what they claim they are,
permanent and actual settlers."[45] Probably the Survey-
or General exaggerated when he claimed that all the valleys were settled. Nevertheless the same official from
Montana presented an appropriate suggestion in 1879
when he proposed survey and classification of lands as
agricultural, irrigable, pastoral and worthless. Then
he advised that the Government sell the pastoral lands
at from twenty-five to fifty cents an acre and he maintained that stock raisers would purchase for self-protection, if for no other reason, because their numbers
were increasing. In answering the argument that large-
scale purchases would create a landed aristocracy which
would not improve the land, the Surveyor General asserted that pastoral land could not be improved beyond
their use for grazing.[46]

---

43. In 1881, L. P. Brockett claimed that cattle land could still be
    obtained in the unsurveyed regions of Colorado and Kansas but
    that "ere long the stock raiser will find himself pushed by the
    tide of farming immigrants." "Our Western Empire," p. 171.
44. Sec. of Int. Report, 1879, p. 455.
45. L.O.R., 1878, p. 246.
46. L.O.R., 1879, p. 793. In 1877 the Governor of Wyoming claimed
    a special law of sale or lease would be an advantage and that
    shortly it would become a necessity. Sec. of Int. Rep. 1878,
    p. 1179. The Surveyor of Arizona repeatedly urged a law.
    L.O.R.,1877, p. 331. Sec. of Int. Report, 1878, p. 1159 and
    1879, p. 404.

Another plan which drew considerable attention
was presented in Major Powell's Report on the Arid
Lands.   Just as he had applied the homestead principle
to irrigation, the Major applied it to ranching and
suggested that nine or more individuals be permitted to
secure pastoral homesteads of at least 2,560 acres each.
He planned to provide water frontage for each entryman
and a grouping of residences which would encourage local
social organization and cooperation in improvements.[47]
His suggestions were endorsed by the Public Land Commission in 1880[48] but they were opposed by such groups
as the Wyoming Stock Growers Association, an organization composed largely of "cattle kings."   The opposition
fostered antagonisms to the proposals by catering to the
American hostility to land monopoly.   It therefore produced a paradoxical situation: cattlemen who were
creating monopolies through illegality, fraud and violence, whipped up sentiment for "beating the land grab"
so successfully that they defeated a legal method for
aiding cattlemen.[49]   Perhaps there is some significance
in the fact that stock growers were beginning to think
of control in terms, not of a few thousand acres but,
of hundreds of thousands of acres.

One of the principle methods used to acquire
control of very large areas sprang from the abuse of
the settlement laws, particularly the Desert Land Act.
It is in this connection that reference has previously
been made to the Desert law as one intended for corporate use.   Within a few months of its enactment the
Land Office was forced to suspend all entries at the
Local Offices because of the many "allegations of fraud"
which were reported to Washington.[50]   The Office then

---

47. The Major felt that his plan would make fencing unnecessary.
48. Report, 1880, p. xxiff.   H. H. Bancroft supported the principle
    of the proposal.   "Hist. of Arizona and New Mexico," 1889,
    p. 769.
49. Osgood, op. cit., p. 198-9.   Webb claims that the bill fitted
    too well the needs of the West to get eastern consideration.
    It is true that the National Cattlemen's Convention at St. Louis
    in November, 1884, adopted a resolution for a similar system.
    "Report in Regard to the Range and Ranch Cattle Business in the
    U.S." Joseph Nimmo, Jr., 1885, p. 46 quoted in the Nation,
    July 2, 1885.
50. Copp's Land Owner, Nov. 1877.

attempted to investigate the charges but in the absence
of surveys or a sufficient number of inspectors it was
almost impossible to prove fraud, so the suspension was
removed and the abuse continued. A complete explanation of the nature and purports of the abuse are found
in the report of Governor Hale of Wyoming. Without intending to expose or indict cattlemen the Governor
showed that any one could obtain 1,120 acres by making
simultaneous entry under the Homestead, Preëmption,
Timber Culture and Desert Land laws.[51] If, therefore,
a rancher secured several of his cowhands to make similar entries along a stream, the combined efforts would
secure enough land for 1,000 head of cattle. Of course
there was no intention of fulfilling the requirements
of the laws and patents could be secured only through
an indulgent Local Land Office and a generous or overburdened General Land Office.[52]

The particular advantage of joint entries lay
in the opportunity which they gave for using the extensive regions behind them. Governor Hale explained that
ranchers supposed that none would want the waterless
backlands so they proceeded to enclose a great deal for
a private range. Furthermore he declared that they
hoped "that in time the government might afford them
some lawful means of acquiring possession of it." Since
the Governor was speaking from one of the great cattle
raising Territories he demonstrates the fact that cattlemen were willing to pay for grazing lands; that some
of them looked to the Government for protection in
their rights; and that in the absence of appropriate
legislation they were willing to pervert the settlement
laws. It is also interesting to observe that the use
of four laws proves that the Desert Land Act did not

51. Sec. of Int. Report, 1883, pp. 583-4. See also Copp's Set-
    tlers Guide, quoted in Donaldson, op. cit., p. 534.
52. The Governor of New Mexico, however, protested against this
    practice and urged the Government to sell large tracts so that
    they could be taxed to support local governments and schools
    and so that boundary disputes could be minimized. Sec. of
    Int. Report, 1881, p. 997; and ibid, 1883, p. 557.

supplant but rather complemented earlier laws for the
purpose of greater frauds.

Another form of abuse provided cattlemen with a
virtual lease on pastoral lands. Since an entryman's
initial payment of twenty-five cents an acre was intended to give evidence of his good faith he was able
to hold the land for three years without reporting to
the Government. But if he did not want to prove up and
pay the remaining $1.00 an acre which the law required,
he could release his entry just before the time limit
expired and immediately regain possession by having one
of his cowhands ready to make a new entry on the same
tract.[53] In this manner cattlemen paid what amounted
to a modest rental; they were not subject to taxation;
and they could use the backlands along a stream just as
completely as though they owned their land. There was
also another abuse when many entrymen endeavored to secure the largest possible water frontage. Whether they
were moved by an effort to comply with the requirement
for irrigating their entire tract or merely by the desire to monopolize a stream they made the backlands
valueless for others.[54] The unadopted Senate amendment
which restricted entries to a length twice their width
could have checked such a violation of the spirit of
the law.

There were two other ways in which the Desert
Land Act was misused, though in these instances not by
cattlemen. Because Congress had not provided any check
for determining the character of an entry, any person
could easily enter on timberland for purposes of depredation. The practice became widespread and in 1881 the
Land Office explained that timbermen made entry "with
no intention of acquiring title, stripped the land of
its timber and moved on to other fields."[55] Speculators also learned that the law could serve their purpose. The Land Office found that after it had been in

---

53. Webb, op. cit., p. 415.
54. The Surveyor General of Arizona reported one entry that covered
    44 corners of surveyed land. It must have been unusual. L.O.R.,
    1877, p. 321.
55. L.O.R., 1881, p. 377.

use for three years entrymen were not endeavoring to
complete their titles. It therefore gave notice to
such entrymen to show cause why they were not proving
up and it sent a second warning later, with little response. The Office concluded that the entries were
speculative and the cases which it was able to examine
proved that the suspicion was true. In other words
entrymen were using the law to hold fertile land until
they could sell it or relinquish it to a bona fide settler.

Since the need for a pastoral land law was
shown by western suggestions and by abuse of the Desert
Land Act the question readily arises as to why there
was no specific provision for cattlemen until well into
the Twentieth century. The answer can be found partly
in the fraudulent use of the settlement laws as a means
to enclosing large tracts. This usurpation of the public domain was frequently protected by friendly Territorial laws and lax administration. Moreover there was
no great demand for a change in the status quo until
the range became crowded and settlers demanded the removal of fences, and until, under President Cleveland,
the Government supervised more carefully the use of the
settlement laws. By that time, however, conditions
were unfavorable to a new law, as later discussion will
show. Meanwhile ranchers' needs were met in a variety
of other ways, without recourse to the Government. For
instance until the range was filled many of them preferred to take their chances on the continuance of large
quantities of free land. Those who wished greater security could purchase or lease from railroads; similar
opportunities were offered in Texas where the Federal
Government had no control of the land; scrip could be
purchased at a low figure and used for acquiring a
ranch; or it was possible to take advantage of private
land claims derived from Spanish and Mexican grants in
California, New Mexico, Arizona and Colorado. And finally, since the Indians possessed extensive reservations, cattlemen were able to lease large blocks, often
with questionable support from Federal administrators.
The development of this latter practice and its over-
throw will be considered in a later chapter along with
further attention to the Desert Land Act.

Chapter III

TIMBER LAWS AND THEIR VIOLATION

The Government's timber policy has usually been characterized either by failure to provide adequately for the disposal of timber lands or failure to protect them from depredation. In the decades 1870-1890 it was characterized by both. During earlier times the Government sold land irrespective of its timber value and so lumbermen had little difficulty in obtaining fresh supplies. After 1862, when the passage of the Homestead Act caused a great reduction in public sale, timber could still be easily secured under an amazing departmental rule which permitted open depredations upon payment of a small fee. This widespread practice was in turn overthrown in 1877 because when Commissioner Williamson discovered that the rule had no basis in law he revoked it and began enforcing the statute for punishment of depredators. As a consequence timbermen were made acutely aware that in order to meet the demands of a rapidly developing country there ought to be some straightforward way to obtain access to the untouched forests. Congress, therefore, became faced with an emphatic demand for a distinctive timber law but instead of accepting the challenge by adopting a well-devised program it enacted two measures which applied solely to western regions. Not only were the needs of the Southern and Northwestern sections of the country ignored but the new laws proved grievously unsuited to the West.[1] Moreover because Congress refused to modify them or appropriate sufficient funds to protect public timber, evasions and depredations became flagrant.

---

1. In 1876 Southern Lands were again sold for cash so the original method of obtaining timber returned there.

Timber stealing became so common that John Ise has remarked: "It would be very easy to exaggerate the moral turpitude involved in stealing timber and timberland in the Seventies and Eighties....and that practice has been too common to be viewed seriously."[2] But there are several objections to this indulgent attitude. Considerable evidence indicates that many observers of the time thought timber thefts just as wrong as any other kind of theft. To take one example, the Land Office asserted, "the timber on the (public) land remaining unsold is as much the property of the Government as money in the Treasury and far more important to its future welfare."[3] Similar comments poured into Washington from the West. Furthermore the Government's failure to check stealing produced gross injustice. The funds which Congress did appropriate enabled the Department of Justice to prosecute annually, hundreds of violators, many of whom served criminal sentences. Yet at the same time a lack of sufficient appropriations meant that other hundreds or even thousands of cases were never brought to court or were thrown out before they could be brought to trial because there was no way to collect sufficient evidence.[4] Congressional parsimony and neglect favored the corporate interests particularly, and as a result railroads, mining concerns and timber companies were able to strip public timber with impunity. And finally the failure to enforce the provisions of the timber laws fostered the growth of large-scale holdings. It will be suggestive to examine more fully the policies which produced injustice, defiance of the Government and monopolies.

Congress had provided protection for timberlands in 1831 by an act "to punish offences committed in cutting, destroying or removing live-oak and other timber trees reserved for naval purposes."[5] The Navy Department had been required to enforce the act.

---

2. Ise, op. cit., p. 79.
3. L.O.R., 1876, p. 8.
4. R. S. Yard, "Our Federal Lands," p. 100.
5. Sec. of Int. Report, 1880, pp. 34-5. (There seems, however, to be a reservation law of 1817. 3 Stat. at Large 347.)

Depredators were fined three times the value of the
timber taken and any ship captain hauling such timber
subjected his ship to forfeiture. There seems to have
been little reason for applying the law to lands other
than Naval Reserves but a Supreme Court decision of
1851 held that it did so apply.[6]

When in 1855 the General Land Office was required to supervise and protect public timber, a circular was sent to the Registers and Receivers of the
various District Land Offices requiring them to investigate depredations and prosecute trespassers. They were
also instructed to make no compromise with violators.
But in 1860 the Secretary of Interior allowed compromises for fifty cents per 1,000 feet of timber cut,
and entry on the land. Four years later the Land Office again modified the original instructions. Registers and Receivers, acting with District Attorneys,
were thereafter to collect quarterly for timber used at
lumber mills.[7] If these Federal officers were unable
to collect a sufficient sum they were to prosecute the
mill owners for using public timber illegally.[8] An accepted rate of $2.50 came to be collected uniformly
throughout the States and Territories. The compromise
scheme would seem to be an amazing bit of usurpation of
legislative authority and perilously close to Government racketeering.

Thefts of timber were far more numerous than
"compromises." In 1870 there were 25,832 lumber manufacturing companies in the United States and lumber interests ranked second in bulk and value in the products
of the country. So many companies were paying nothing
for their supplies that in 1872 Congress made its first
appropriation, $10,000, for special timber agents who
were to assist Registers and Receivers in preventing
depredations.[9] During the ensuing five years Congress
voted approximately $35,600 for these agents. From the
time of Land Office control until 1877 about $200,000

6. H. C. Cummings and C. McFarland, "Federal Justice," p. 261.
7. L.O.R., 1877, pp. 16-19.
8. L.O.R., 1864, pp. 21-2.
9. Sec. of Int. Report, 1880, p. 36.

was collected from depredators.[10] After deducting the expenses of special agents there was a balance of only $150,000 in the Government's favor for the twenty-two years. This equalled the purchase price of about 5,000 acres of good pine land.

In order to provide more effective protection the Land Office reports in the early Seventies had requested amendments exempting pine and fir lands from entry under the Homestead and Preëmption laws. They also recommended surveys to determine the extent and value of Government timberlands, and enactments permitting them to be sold after proclamation, for cash and at not less than appraised value. The explanation for these requests is found in the 1875 Report[11] where it stated, "depredations to an enormous extent are constantly occurring which existing laws are powerless to punish..... It is among the traditions of this office, certified indeed by its records, that from a very early day eagerness to acquire title from the Government to these exceptionally valuable lands has lead to the perpetration of innumerable frauds." The Report also explained that entries were made under the settlement laws with no intention of actually acquiring title, but solely for the purpose of stripping the land of its timber. In the Far West where vast areas of land were not subject to settlement entry until surveyed, timber was freely taken for use if not for the market. Of course there was an undeniable need for construction materials. But there was a tendency toward carelessness which resulted in considerable waste; only the best trees were removed and the smaller ones were slashed or crushed so that a re-growth was retarded. Western reports showed that for miles around mining camps the timber had disappeared. Barren land meant that there was a danger of unregulated water supply, floods and snow-slides with a consequent loss of life.

Commissioner Burdett admitted that the problem presented by these facts was not easy of solution. He believed that perhaps the best method would be for the

10. L.O.R., 1877, p. 20.
11. L.O.R., 1875, p. 10.

United States to retain title to the lands while selling off the timber, judiciously, by sections.[12] As an
alternative he suggested the sale of reasonable amounts
of timberland so that purchasers would feel responsible
for protecting them. The Commissioner declared that
under this plan "the law against depredations which in
the absence of surveys is practically inoperative,
could and ought to be enforced." In either case he
felt that the practical ends to be accomplished were to
stay waste and "to provide for the due return to the
public treasury."

     While Congress was debating methods of timber-
land disposal in June, 1876, Commissioner Williamson
took office. Within a month he discovered the compromise scheme for timber depredators and decided to
abolish it.[13] First he secured a ruling from the Interior Department that no more compromise settlements
were to be made without the approval of the Secretary.
After further consideration it was decided to make the
special agents directly responsible to the General Land
Office rather than to the Registers and Receivers.
These reforms were submitted to Carl Schurz just after
he became Secretary. Being heartily in sympathy with
conservation, he approved them April 5.[14]

     Thereafter timber agents were employed by the
Commissioner. Under his instructions they were detailed for the special duty of determining when, where
and by whom depredations were made. If the Commissioner
felt that their reports warranted proceedings for punishment or collection of damages, he could make recommendations to the Department. No agent was permitted
to compromise for depredations and if offers were made
to him he was to report the full circumstances to the
Land Office for recommendation to the Department. When
an occasion arose requiring prompt action and the evidence was clear and indisputable agents were to secure
the aid of the United States District Attorney where
the depredations were committed. These new regulations

12. Ibid., pp. 11-12.
13. L.O.R., 1877, pp. 19-20.
14. Sec. of Int. Report, 1880, pp. 35-6.

were accompanied by increased appropriations for agents in 1877 and in the following year they were doubled to reach what was still a small amount, $24,000.

Secretary Schurz later declared that when he took office the timber "export trade had grown to enormous proportions on those coasts, (the Atlantic, Pacific and Gulf coasts). Whole fleets of vessels entered the harbors of Puget Sound, the Columbia River, Pensicola, Sabine Pass, Atchafalaya and places along the shore whose cargo consisted mainly of timber taken from public lands for which no compensation was paid the Government and which was not used for the domestic or mining purposes of our own people but for export to foreign countries."[15] In 1877 the Secretary explained that depredations were "a question of law and a question of public economy. As to the first point little need be said..... There may be circumstances under which the rigorous execution of a law may be difficult or inconvenient, or obnoxious to public sentiment or working particular hardship; in such case it is the business of the legislative power to adopt the law to such circumstances. It is the business of the Executive to enforce the law as it stands."[16] He was convinced that within twenty years the existing rate of forest destruction would leave insufficient timber for home consumption. In addition to establishing the principle of conservation the Secretary wanted "to make those who hitherto have carried on these depredations with profit understand that in attempting to steal timber from the public lands they will in any event lose the value of their labors and the expense, and expose themselves to criminal prosecution."[17]

---

15. Sec. of Int. Report, 1880, p. 36. Copp's Land Owner estimated that $60,000,000 worth of timber was shipped from California between 1855 and 1877, Nov., 1877.
16. Sec. of Int. Report, 1877, p. xvi.
17. Copp's Land Owner believed that much of the talk of the disappearance of forests arose from the bull and bear movements of those who wanted to buy and sell timberland. Nevertheless it noted that Maine imported pine from the South and that Michigan and Canada supplied New York whose timber had failed. The propaganda may or may not have influenced Secretary Schurz, op. cit., March, 1878.

But Secretary Schurz soon found that it was both "difficult and inconvenient" to enforce the laws.[18] Mining regions complained that timber was necessary for smelting so the Secretary made an exception in their case because they were "entitled to consideration." He requested the Attorney General to proceed against only the large depredators, those who took large quantities for sale to railroad companies or smelting works or for the supply of the market. Secretary Schurz also made another exception. Railroads complained that they had to have ties, building timber and firewood. Apparently they did not consider their right-of-way privileges sufficient. In any case the Department decided that if they would "pay a fair price" for the property taken "without authority of law," they might do so until "by proper legislation they are enabled to obtain the necessary supply in the legal way."

These two exceptions show that Secretary Schurz tempered his strict reform principles with a sense of expediency. They also show the complexities of handling the timber problem. Since the Secretary was particularly interested in conservation and adequate laws his recommendations may be briefly summarized.[19] He advocated Government control of timber land so as to regulate timber cutting. Moreover he recommended the adoption of an amendment which would make the settlement laws or scrip inapplicable to timberlands. He also suggested that the funds accruing to the Government from suits for depredations should be placed at the disposal of the Secretary of Interior. Since, in 1877 the Government expected to recover $100,000[20] from depredators it was evident that under proper supervision such a sum would aid the Department in materially reducing trespassing.

Two other significant suggestions called for a law to penalize willful or negligent setting of fires on the public lands, and a commission appointed by the

18. Sec. of Int. Report, 1880, p. viii.
19. Ibid., p. xix.
20. L.O.R., 1877, p. 23.

President to study the laws and practices of other
countries for the preservation and cultivation of forests. Commissioner Williamson, however, differed from
his superior by recommending the sale of timberland at
graded prices, without retaining title to the land.[21]
But he was particularly outspoken in calling for control of timber violations. He declared that Congress
ought to "deal with the facts of the wicked and wanton
waste of the timber of the public lands. A national
calamity is being rapidly and surely brought upon the
country by the useless destruction of forests."

Commissioner Williamson could not fail to contrast this widespread destruction with the feeble activities under the Timber Culture law. He declared:
"It is an anomalous fact that the Government is giving
away the rich alluvial soil in Iowa, Nebraska, Kansas
and Minnesota to any citizen who will plant a few acres
of cottonwood or other inferior timber while under the
provisions of the Homestead and Preëmption laws it is
granting a license to destroy millions of acres of pine
forests of almost incalculable value."[22] A bill covering many of Secretary Schurz's suggestions was submitted
to the Senate but did not pass. Congress was developing
its own plans for timberland disposal under the leadership of western Representatives.

II

As stated previously Congress had debated timber legislation for several years. Delay in enacting
any law had been caused by the failure of the two
Houses to agree on the same plan. In March, 1878, however, the Senate received a bill which was destined for
passage; the bill permitted the free cutting of timber
in certain Western States and Territories.[23] The

---

21. L.O.R., 1876, p. 7.
22. He received reports like that from the Surveyor General of
    Washington urging the Government to obtain "something like
    their just value" for timberlands. Ibid., p. 314.
23. 45 Cong. 2 Sess. Cong. Rec., p. 1507. It had originally been
    reported during the first Session.

accompanying Committee report,[24] like that for the
Desert Land Act, was vague and illogical where it
should have been explicit. It stated that after "careful" consideration and "mature deliberation (on) the
best method of preserving, cultivating and disposing
"of timber, the Committee had made a distinction between trees in mountain mineral districts and forests
of pine, oak and other timber in more level parts of
the country. It recognized that the "lumber of the
latter is a regular and important article of commerce
and constantly cut....in large quantities." But the
Committee declared that it was concerned only to provide for cutting trees in the mineral districts because
such timber was unfit for commercial purposes.

        The report did not, however, define mineral dis-
tricts nor tell how they were to be determined. It
neglected to explain why the law did not apply to all
States with mineral resources. It failed to note that
important mining regions like that around the famous
Comstock Lode in Nevada contained no trees. And there
was no explanation for the failure to meet the needs
for timber as an article of commerce. Nevertheless
with practically no discussion and with two slight
amendments the bill passed the Senate, April 18.[25]

        Representative Page of California then intro-
duced it into the House with the assurance that it had
been recommended by the Land Office Commissioner and
the Secretary of Interior.[26] There is considerable
doubt as to the accuracy of that assertion in view of
the objections which the Secretary made immediately
after the bill's passage. Representative Fort of Illinois interrupted the well-oiled procedure when he declared that the bill would "allow unlimited license to
cut timber on the public lands to an unlimited number
of persons." Yet he felt it necessary to offer only
two protective amendments: first, that the act should
not apply to railroads; and second, that the Secretary
of Interior should draw up regulations for the

24. Ibid., pp. 3327-8.
25. Ibid., pp. 2638-40.
26. Ibid., pp. 3327-8.

protection of timber and undergrowth. Then the bill
was approved; the Senate agreed to the amendments and
it was signed by the President, June 1.[27]

In his definitive study of American timber John
Ise has pointed to the looseness with which the bill
was drawn.[28] It referred to "citizens....and other
persons," and the "residents of the State of Colorado
or Nevada, or either of the Territories of New Mexico,
Arizona, Utah, Wyoming, Dakota, Idaho or Montana and
all other mineral districts of the United States." Consequently it required careful judicial interpretation
to determine the true extent of its application as
Secretary of Interior Teller later discovered.

Both Commissioner Williamson and Secretary
Schurz agreed that the machinery for carrying the provisions of the act into effect were entirely inadequate.
They believed that those who saw the "chance to make
money quickly" would take advantage of it. Furthermore
they regretted that it would cut off revenue which the
lands should have provided. The Secretary maintained
that it was "Equivalent to a donation of all the timberlands to the inhabitants of those States and Territories
which will be found to be the largest donation of the
public domain hitherto made by Congress.[29] He also believed that it would foster waste and destruction.

In the absence of adequate surveys there was no
way to determine what was "mineral land" in the regions
where the act applied. Nevertheless Secretary Schurz
ruled that the penal provisions should be "enforced
against persons trespassing upon any other than lands
which are in fact mineral or have been withdrawn as
such."[30] He therefore placed a narrow interpretation
on the law yet there was small danger that it could be
enforced in view of the large distances to be covered
and the paucity of agents. It would also have proved
difficult to enforce the ruling which limited the size
of trees cut to those over eight inches in diameter.

---

27. 20 Stat. 88.
28. Ise, op. cit., p. 62-3.
29. Sec. of Int. Report, 1878, pp. xiii-xiv.
30. L.O.R., 1878, p. 119.

As a supplement to the Timber Cutting Act Congress passed the Timber and Stone Act which provided for the sale of timberland in 160 acre lots. The law applied only to California, Oregon, Washington and Nevada. It was introduced by Senator A. A. Sargent, March 14, 1878 and passed the Senate a month later.[31] There was no discussion on the bill though Senator Sargent himself offered several amendments. One of these gave evidence of a certain haphazard quality to the bill for it struck out a provision that had come from an old bill applying to "all other Territories of the United States not exceeding 40 acres to any one person."[32]

Senator Sargent also offered the infamous section five as another amendment and explained his move with what amounted to a half truth. The section provided that any person guilty of timber trespass, who was apprehended for penalties, would be relieved from prosecution and liability if the timber was not cut for export and if the offender paid $2.50 per acre to the court where the action was pending. Title to this same land could be secured by paying an additional $2.50 an acre. All the money was to be paid into the treasury however and would not therefore accrue to the needs of law enforcement in the Interior Department.

The Senator explained that it was not proposed to excuse past offenders for depredations which had been necessary in the absence of law, but to require them to pay $2.50 an acre whether they had cut "one or twelve trees." He felt that though the land had been stripped the Government received a "fair large price" for it, a price which "seemed to be an equitable settlement." But what Senator Sargent failed to point out was that the amendment not only applied to past offenders but to all future ones as well. In effect the law would permit free timber cutting, or stealing, for those whom the Government did not catch as it; and for those who were caught, a nominal fee would secure release from prosecution. When the bill came before the

---

31. Ibid., p. 1753. It had been passed in the previous Session.
32. Ibid., p. 2842.

House it passed with no discussion.[33]   On June 1, President Hayes gave it his approval.[34]

The law provided for the sale of lands "unfit for cultivation," in quarter sections if they were valuable for timber or stone. They must have been surveyed and must not contain minerals such as gold, silver, copper or coal. The entryman would take an oath that he "verily believes" the land was not mineral. There was a minimum price of $2.50 an acre which curiously enough became the only price because officials did not realize the value of the word "minimum." Every applicant filed a written statement "that he does not apply to purchase the same on speculation, but in good faith to appropriate for his own use and benefit"; and that he had not made any agreement or contract by which the land should inure to the benefit of any person but himself. The pledge was made under oath with the supporting testimony of two witnesses. If the applicant perjured himself he was liable for the forfeiture of land and money. It is perhaps significant that not only citizens but persons who had declared their intention of becoming citizens could make entry under the act. And it will prove interesting to notice later the way in which the Supreme Court interpreted "speculation."

John Ise has stated that the act was dictated mainly by the lumber interests.[35]   Certain of its provisions seem to indicate that origin. Yet it is difficult to reconcile other provisions with the needs of lumbermen. It was obvious to any experienced person that an individual could not finance timber removal from a 160-acre plot.[36]   Lumber could be profitably produced only at a mill which must draw on large districts.

---

33. Ibid., pp. 3387-8.
34. 20 Stat. 89. Ise declares that this attempt of Congress to legalize timber stealing was partly thwarted by the courts for they held that a party which was prosecuted was not discharged from liability by the payment of $2.50 but was still liable to the United States for the value of the timber cut. Op. cit., p. 71, note.
35. Op. cit., p. 77.
36. Nevertheless the law permitted sale to "any person or association of persons."

Perhaps the timber interests felt it was necessary to
cling to the quarter section limit in order to ensure
the bill's passage but they might have tried to obtain
a larger unit. They placed a heavy premium on fraud
and perjury by their inadequate law.

A few months after the bill passed the Secretary of Interior and the Commissioner indicted it on
seven counts.[37] 1. The price was too low, much of the
land subject to entry being worth $5 to $50 per acre.
2. Land would speedily pass into the hands of speculators. 3. Land should not be sold with the timber when
it was unfit for cultivation. 4. The law should be restricted to persons whose home was in the State.
5. Upon receiving his certificate an entryman could
transfer it to another immediately. 6. The penal section calling for $2.50 an acre was not adequate and
would not pay the cost of prosecution. 7. Those who
wanted to make money quickly would take advantage of
the act.

The subsequent complaints of land officials in
the west and in Washington soon showed the unsatisfactory character of the timber laws in actual practice.
Depredations continued, the land department could not
prosecute violators with any great success and the
legitimate needs of the residents of the west went unrequited. In 1878 Congress had appropriated $25,000
for timber protection; that sum enabled the Land Office
to employ eleven special agents. The following year
the amount was raised to $40,000 but both the Secretary
and the Commissioner declared it inadequate.[38] Commissioner Williamson reported: "The powers of the department are so enfeebled by limited appropriations for de-
tecting and punishing timber trespassers that but a
little of the plunder and destruction can be arrested."[39]
Congress did not increase the figure till 1882 when it
voted $75,000. This remained the annual appropriation
for the succeeding eight years in spite of an increasing need. Though the sum was three times that provided

---

37. Sec. of Int. Report, 1878, p. xv.
38. Sec. of Int. Report, 1879, p. 27.
39. L.O.R., 1879, p. 561.

in 1878, only twice the number of agents were employed
by 1885 due to the increased cost of investigation and
prosecution.

The requests of Territorial authorities to modify the Timber Cutting Act so that trespassing would be
unnecessary are illustrated by the report of the Governor of Idaho.[40] In 1879 he asserted that in the Territory the Government was looked upon as a "huge, help-
less impersonality which any may plunder at will. Notwithstanding the vigorous efforts recently employed by
the department to enforce the laws and limit the waste,
the evil goes on,....the people must consume the timber
growing on the public lands or abandon the country." He
believed that even an army could not protect the timber
from depredation. His solution was to sell the land to
individuals at auction, or above a carefully set minimum for cash, and to depend on the purchasers to care
for the timber. The Governor wanted to avoid monopoly
but he may have been oversanguine of the possibility of
preventing it.

In 1880 the Public Lands Commission presented a
comprehensive analysis of timber conditions and several
suggestions for improvement.[41] Its report called attention first to the value of classifying timberland. Then
it pointed to the necessity for capital in manufacturing and transporting lumber. This need made the sale
of small units impractical, when restricted to use by
the purchaser. The Commission therefore recommended
that the Government sell alternate sections in large
quantities, and attach a proviso that all trees less
than eight inches in diameter should be reserved for
the "maintainance and reproduction of the forests." It
believed the "experiment was well worth the trying."
There was need for greater care of forests because "the
rate of consumption and the destruction of timber by

---

40. Sec. of Int. Report, 1879, p. 419.
41. Report, 1880, p. xxxiff.

fires[42] in the United States have been so great during the past twenty-five years as to cause alarm."[43]

The Commission found the difficulties of suppressing depredators were increased by "the impossibility of purchasing in a straightforward, honest way from the Government, either timber or timber bearing lands."[44] In Arkansas, Louisiana, Mississippi, Alabama and Florida the only way to secure timberlands until 1876 had been through the homestead law. Consequently there had been "thousands of fraudulent Homestead entires" until Congress had allowed private entry at $1.25 an acre. Then the fraud and depredation greatly decreased.

The settlement laws had also been greatly abused in the West, prior to 1878. The Commission found "little huts or kennels....that were totally unfit for human habitation" in the redwood sections of California. The huts had enabled some entryman to "prove" he had had a house on his farm. In certain sections of the timber country "where there should be; according to the 'proofs' made, large settlements of industrious agriculturists engaged in tilling the soil, a primeval stillness reigns supreme, the solitude heightened and intensified by the grandeur of high mountain peaks where farms should be." The only traces of human occupation were stumps left by the woodsman's ax.

---

42. The surveyor general of Wyoming had claimed that larger bodies of timber were destroyed annually by "mischievous Indians, careless hunters, and lightning than in any other way." The Governor of Idaho reported a fire which an Indian set to drive a beaver from his nest had finally burned 27,000 acres. Some westerners argued it was better to use timber than to let it be burned. Others suggested rapid sale which would throw the burden of protection on the purchaser. L.O.R., 1879, p. 477; see also Sec. of Int. Report, 1879, p. 419.

43. L. P. Brockett estimated that in 1871 in twenty western States and Territories woodland covered 198,124,802 acres. He also declared that by 1880, that area had diminished by 25% because of the amount used. Op. cit., p. 147.

44. Report, 1880, p. xxxii.

The Timber and Stone Act of 1878 had "ameliorat-
ed previous conditions only slightly." In its revised
report the Commission declared, "Evidence is cumula-
tive" that the act was used by "corporations and wealthy
individual operators....fraudulently to get timber or
to hold it for speculation." Gangs of ten to fifty men
were hired at so much a head to make entries, and they
readily perjured themselves "in many localities." Secretary Schurz' predictions were thus abundantly verified.

The Commission also found that the provisions
of the Timber Cutting Act meant "very little." It declared that not one acre in five thousand was mineral
and not one acre in five thousand of what might be
mineral was known to be such. The Commission was therefore emphatic that "The population of two States and
seven Territories should no longer be compelled by the
laws of the country to be trespassers and criminals on
account of taking timber necessary to enable them to
exist, as is the condition today and as it has been according to law ever since settlements were commenced,
or since the policy of selling lands for cash has been
abandoned by the Government.[45]

Surely this indictment would seem strong enough
to have provoked a remedy. Yet Congress accepted the
timber recommendations - for printing only. In order to
obtain a clearer picture of timber conditions at that
time it is sufficient to read the routine reports of
timber agents to the Land Office in 1880. Similar accounts could be found for other years. Their amazing
disclosures are interesting in view of the comparatively few agents, fifteen, which the Government employed.
The Land Office reported that many investigations in
the South, in Michigan and in Washington Territory had
to be abandoned because funds became exhausted. It
will be noted that the story of depredations was not
confined to the "frontier," for like the sale of bogus
stocks, timber stealing was carried on wherever it was
profitable.

---

45. Ibid., p. xxxiii.

Copp's <u>Land Owner</u> testified in 1879 that Commissioner Williamson's reforms had already lessened depredations.[46] But the land department continued to request Congressional coöperation in order to limit the need for violations. It asked for the repeal of the two timber laws and passage of "more adequate legislation." Secretary Schurz favored a plan for Government timber reservations from which timber could be sold to settlers, miners and commercial groups. President Hayes urged Congress to permit selling "timber without conveying the fee..... The enactment of such a law appears to become a more pressing necessity every day."[47]

Instead of adopting more intelligent measures or endeavoring to check depredation Congress extended protection for timberland violators. It is significant that a Southerner, Representative Herbert of Alabama introduced a bill in May, 1879, to extend the immunities of the Timber and Stone Act to the entire country. His bill has been termed the "License to Timber Thieves Act."[48] It did not apply to future cases, however, but only to offences committed prior to March 1, 1879. It released offenders from prosecution in civil suit through payment of $1.25 an acre instead of $2.50 an acre as provided in the Timber and Stone Act.

In defending the bill Representative Herbert had recalled that no efforts had been made to stop timber stealing prior to Secretary Schurz' time and so "to commence suddenly a system of persecutions, to enforce them rigorously, exacting the supreme penalty of the law was cruel and harsh." Other defenders spoke of the Secretary's "paralyzing the great lumber industries" or "affecting the poor settler." Those who opposed the bill waxed caustic over granting immunity to depredators. Nevertheless the bill passed June 15, 1880.

Such a bill was bound to bring discouragement to the conservation movement. Secretary Schurz claimed

---

46. <u>Op. cit.</u>, May, 1879.
47. Sec. of Int. Report, 1878, p. xii; Richardson, <u>op. cit.</u>, vol. VII, p. 578.
48. Ise, <u>op. cit.</u>, p. 89; L.O.R., 1880, pp. 480-1.

in 1880 that a wholesome sentiment favoring timber
preservation had lately grown up for he had received
many latters from western States and Territories urging
increased protection.[49] Furthermore scarcely a responsible journal had refused to publish something on conservation during the past two years; yet he observed,
"almost all the legislation that has been had on the
subject consists in acts relieving those who have committed depredations in the past of their responsibility
and protecting them against the legal consequences of
their trespasses..... (Such measures) constitute an
encouragement to (other) trespassers" who expect that
"at a future date similar acts condoning their offences
would be passed."

A more progressive public opinion was also revealed by the Land Office claim that hostility to special agents was dying down and that a general feeling
for suppressing depredations was supplanting it. The
Office declared, "It is now much easier to obtain information regarding trespassers and their unlawful acts
than formerly when the community seemed leagued together
for mutual protection against the officers of the Government."[50] Such testimony indicated that the ground
work for a change in the timber laws was inviting Congressional coöperation.

Secretary Schurz' last report summarized his
efforts to prevent depredations and then added the
warning: "Whatever our success in this respect may
have been so far, it is certain that the evil will
spring up again if the efforts of the Government to arrest it be the least bit relaxed in the future, or if
Congress should fail" to pass appropriate legislation.[51]
Subsequent chapters will show how far the Secretary's
prophecy was accurate.

---

49. Sec. of Int. Report, 1880, p. 34.
50. L.O.R., 1881, p. 376.
51. Sec. of Int. Report, 1880, p. 37.

Chapter IV

THE NEGLECT OF WESTERN SURVEYS

As the tide of settlers moved into the trans-
Missouri region the Government faced a great variety of
surveying problems which could have been solved by forthright action. Many of the problems grew out of the fact
that there was no system of land classification to serve
as a basis for disposal under timber, swamp, coal, mineral, arid and arable land laws. Moreover official surveys performed under the direction of the Surveyors General were hurried, unscientific and incomplete and
though there were special surveying projects established
for purposes of scientific exploration, as noted above,
their work was kept entirely separate from that of the
Land Office. Another problem arose from the failure
either to provide for the survey of railroad grants or
secure payment from the roads for the official surveys
which had been made. Defraying the cost of surveys was
a prerequisite for patents and by neglecting to make payments railroads did not receive full title to their
grants and so controlled them tax free. And finally
there were problems which resulted from the difficulties
of surveying arid and mountainous regions and from the
necessity for keeping surveys abreast of the constantly
increasing number of settlers.

One of the most astonishing facts in public land
history arises from the fact that instead of endeavoring
to meet these problems the Government persistently neglected them. It would be difficult to overemphasize the
significance of the Government's ignorance of its treas-
ures even while it was disposing of them. An excellent
opportunity for survey reforms occurred during President
Hayes' administration when the National Academy of Sciences presented Congress with a comprehensive surveying
program. But Congress adopted only portions of the

program and those did not benefit the land department.
Similarly a great many other suggestions from western
sources found little response. Even the most elementary
needs of the service went unrequited while measures
which contributed to defrauding the Government were added to or left on the statute books. Some of the factors
which contributed to this neglect can be noted in a more
detailed account of the surveying system.

Regular Government survey work was performed
under what was known as the contract system.   Under
this system there was a Surveyor General for each of the
sixteen (in 1877), Surveying Offices located in western
States and Territories. These officials, responsible to
the Land Office Commissioner, let surveying contracts to
deputy surveyors. In return for the payment of a Con-
gressionally established rate per mile, these contracts
required the deputies to mark out a stipulated portion
of the public domain.[1] They set stakes along the regulation standard and township lines to form the square
land units which had been established by Thomas Jefferson. The deputies also took notes of the character of
the land traversed and when these notes were returned to
the Surveying Offices they were platted, or put into a
readily usuable form. A copy of the notes and the platting was forwarded to the General Land Office at Washington and another copy was placed in the Local Land Office, nearest the district surveyed. This latter practice enabled prospective settlers and land officials who
received entries, to refer to them when necessary. By
1878 the Government had secured the survey of 728,320,000
acres but the character of the work performed was not
always satisfactory.[2] Moreover, as previously indicated, the topography west of the 100th meridian offered
many problems for the continuance of traditional survey
methods.

In 1875, for instance, Commissioner Burdett
called attention to the difficulties of extending

1. C. S. Woodward,"The Public Domain--Its Surveys and Surveyors";
   and L. O. Stewart, "Public Land Surveys, History, Instructions,
   Methods."
2. J. W. Powell, "Report on Surveying the Public Domain," (printed
   separately, 1878).

mid-western survey lines across dry wastes and mountain
gorges.[3] Two years later, because western surveyors
complained of the contract system, Commissioner Williamson recommended concentrating control of all survey
work in Washington under a Chief Surveyor General who
would employ full-time surveyors at regular salaries;
this method was calculated to save the Government
$90,000 annually.[4] The Commissioner's suggestions were
soon followed by the efforts of the National Academy of
Sciences to consolidate all survey work, not only that
carried on under the Interior Department, which controlled Land Office and certain special surveys, but
that progressing under other Departments as well.

In the decade prior to 1878 there were various
surveys supervised either by the Treasury, War or Interior Departments.[5] The area which they covered frequently overlapped with a consequent waste of money. But
though the field work was duplicated there was no co-
ördination of results. The Coast and Geodetic Survey
efforts under the Treasury Department bore no relation
to those of the Surveyors General and neither of these
systems had any connection with the Army surveys or
those of special groups fostered by Congress.   There
had been four of these latter surveys, three of which
were in progress in 1878, and they had cost $1,685,000.[6]

The efforts for consolidation advanced a step in
1878 when Representative Abram S. Hewitt of New York secured a provision in an appropriation bill, which required the National Academy to prepare a comprehensive
plan for surveying and mapping the Territories.[7] As a
result the Academy secured documentary material and expert testimony from Army Engineers, the Land Office Commissioner and special survey leaders, including James W.
Powell. The value of the recommendations which the
Academy then submitted in its report,[8] November 26, 1878,

3. L.O.R., 1875, p. 16.
4. L.O.R., 1877, pp. 9, 333 and 354. Secretary Schurz backed the
   Commissioner. Sec. of Int. Report, 1877, p. xxiv.
5. 45 Cong. 3 Sess., Cong. Rec., p. 1174.
6. Ibid., p. 1174.
7. Ibid., p. 1170.
8. House Misc. Doc. #5, 45 Cong. 3 Sess., Serial #1861.

can be understood best in the light of Major Powell's
testimony. He presented a full summary of the many
criticisms of the contract system. His report declared
that the system was "in many respects wise" but it had
"never had proper scientific supervision."[9] He therefore considered it wasteful and inaccurate because deputies were anxious chiefly to perform the greatest amount
of work in the shortest possible time. This haste led
to unsatisfactory observation of geographic and geological formations and Major Powell claimed that the
23,000 manuscript maps and reports which had been secured at a cost of $23,000,000 were "incoherent and
worthless" even for maps of general value.[9]

Major Powell also indicted the methods used for
running and marking survey lines and he showed that lat-
itudes and longitudes had never been determined as a
check on survey accuracy.[10] This latter neglect brought
poor results which were evident when survey lines met
State boundaries for frequently it was necessary to
create fractional townships. Furthermore Major Powell
declared that the use of wooden sticks and earthen
mounds to mark surveying lines was wasteful for they
easily perished; and he had found that nitches in trees
were also destroyed easily either intentionally or by
fire.[11] According to the Major these impermanent markings had bequeathed a "heritage of litigation."[12] He
suggested that the remedy lay in the use of triangulation for checking the accuracy of lines and the setting
of iron and stone markers for preserving the lines. The
basis for the change was already provided by the transcontinental triangulation which the Coast Survey was
conducting.[12]

Major Powell favored consolidating the various
survey bodies and he particularly urged that the

---

9. Ibid., p. 17. He also called attention to the surveying suggestions in the Land Office Reports for 1875 and 1877, ibid.,
   p. 6.
10. Ibid., p. 17.
11. Ibid., p. 16.
12. Ibid., p. 23. This was particularly true for mining surveys
    which he considered "barbaric."

scientific study of geological formations should be made available for the work of the Land Office. He explained that the lack of "accurate classification permitted the fraudulent use of the settlement laws to acquire mineral lands.[13] This fraud occurred particularly in areas where the regular surveys had not been made. One of the first steps in this process was to apply for the survey of a likely district under the deposit system, a method which had been established in 1862 to benefit settlers who entered land ahead of the regular surveys.[14] The system enabled a settler to deposit with the Government the cost of surveying his land and to receive a receipt or certificate which was accepted at face value in payment for his purchase of the land. But in addition to benefiting settlers the system also enabled unscrupulous entrymen to bribe a deputy surveyor to return their land as agricultural when it was actually valuable for minerals or timber. After the survey the entrymen would complete the requirements for possession under a settlement law. Major Powell charged that to a large extent both individuals and States had secured land titles under "fraudulent presentations" whether by the deposit system or otherwise.[15] It seemed to himself evident that the Government should protect itself through scientific classification of the lands of the public domain. In concluding his testimony he called attention to his report on arid lands. He noted that since four-tenths of the Rocky Mountain region required irrigation, a proposed Geological Survey Bureau could assist the Government in selecting proper sites for reservoirs while enough land still remained in its possession.[16]

It was partly on the basis of Major Powell's testimony, then, that the National Academy presented its concrete and comprehensive solution to surveying problems.[17] Its report recommended transferring the Coast and Geodetic survey from the Treasury to the Interior Department where it would be given the additional work

13. Ibid., p. 19.
14. L.O.R., 1880, p. 418.
15. H. Misc. Doc. #5, op. cit., p. 20.
16. Ibid., p. 24.
17. Summarized in 45 Cong. 3 Sess., Cong. Rec., pp. 1170-1.

of internal surveying. The enlarged Bureau, to be
called the United States Coast and Interior Survey,
would undertake to mark out in a scientific manner the
remaining 1,101,107,183 unsurveyed acres in the United
States and Alaska. For topographical work, however, the
Academy recommended the creation of a United States Geological Survey Bureau which would also be placed under
the jurisdiction of the Interior Department. It would
take over the work of the various special surveys and
systematically map out the geological structure of the
country for Governmental use but not for private parties or individuals. These two surveying bureaus would
permit the Land Office to concentrate on the disposition
and sale of public land and to supervise all questions
of title and record. Nevertheless each of the three
bureaus would coöperate wherever possible. The Academy
also recommended the appointment of a commission to codify public land laws and to report standards for classifying, evaluating and surveying the public domain.

   The Academy's report was turned over to the
House Committee on Appropriations and early in 1879 its
recommendations were incorporated into sections of the
regular Legislative Appropriations bill.[18] In introduc-
ing the bill Committee Chairman Atkins of Tennessee remarked that "The most important feature in this bill, as
many regard it," was the change in the surveying system.
He commended the Academy "for looking to the solution of
the idea and leaving the scientific feature as a secon-
dary one," and he welcomed the economy that would be
made possible by abolishing the Surveyor Generals' offices.[19]

   But discussion over the proposed changes brought
the fact that western Congressmen seemed determined to
defeat any plan which would permit a stronger administration for surveying, or restrictions on monopolizing
water frontage or a scientific system of classification
which might thwart attempts to appropriate mineral or
timberland fraudulently. All but two of the western
Representatives opposed the Academy's plan and Congress

18. Ibid., (Jan. 28, 1879), p. 791.
19. Ibid., p. 1171.

received petitions against but none in favor of it.[20]
Representative Patterson of Colorado submitted a memorial from the Legislature of his State, protesting against
any survey changes.[21] The memorial contained some of
the principle objections later urged against the bill in
debate, objections which were not wholly plausible or
valid or weighty enough to overbalance the benefits
which it was sure to bring. The memorial stated that
"any changes would create confusion"; the transfer of
all survey business to Washington "would involve expense and loss of time to mine owners"; the modification
of the rectangular surveys "would end in confusion and
disputes regarding boundary lines and cost more than the
present system"; and centralization at Washington would
"cause useless expense to the citizens."...and preclude
the possibility of procuring a patent in a reasonable
time." It hardly seems possible that anyone could believe that definite and accurate markings would confuse
any normal person or that disputes would arise concerning them. Moreover any westerner who cared to inquire
would have learned that expense and trouble to miners
was already a standing grievance because the Land Office
was some 3,600 cases in arrears on mining patents. And
if the settlers were concerned over delay in receiving
patents for bona fide agricultural entries it was not
apparent in the Land Office where there were tens of
thousands of uncalled for patents. There was no great
need to obtain a patent if all the requirements had been
met and final papers had been filed and accepted at the
Local Office. For those who were in a hurry to receive
their patents there was bound to be delay even without
survey changes because the Office work was in arrears
in issuing other than mining patents. The arguments
against the survey changes were not, therefore, very
cogent.

During the ensuing debate Representative Page of
California objected to the adoption of provisions which
would apply to the entire West because they had already
been enacted as a test in California, Nevada and Oregon

20. Ibid., p. 1211.
21. Ibid., p. 1168.

in 1852.[22] These provisions had permitted the geodetic method of survey and a "departure from the rectangular mode of surveying" whenever the Secretary of Interior considered either of them necessary. Representative Page claimed that they had not been used because they were "impractical."[23] He probably meant that mining and cattle raising interests opposed their use for reasons mentioned above. He also objected to the proposed changes because they would upset existing laws like the swamp acts in which the approval of the surveyor General was required. A fellow Californian pointed out that the Commission which the bill would create could suggest remedies for all such conflicts.

Two other western Representatives, Maginnis of Montana and Haskell of Kansas, displayed a curious prejudice when they declaimed against the changes because they had originated among "scientific lobbyists" and "in the interest of a hundred or two purely scientific gentlemen who are now pretty nearly out of a job." The legislators charged that these men proposed "To ingraft themselves on the public land survey."[24] The unfairness of the charge is apparent on its face. Representative Maginnis declared that practical men should be permitted to demonstrate western possibilities without any changes in the existing system. He showed where his real sympathies lay when he objected to the provision which would permit new divisions of land for stockmen.

---

22. Ibid., p. 1197; and Rev. Stat. 2408-10. A preceding section allowed the President to direct the survey of lands "in tracts of two acres width fronting on any river, bayou, lake or water course and running back the depth of 40 acres; which tracts so surveyed shall be offered for sale entire, instead of in half quarter sections." This is somewhat in accord with Major Powell's suggestion but no instance of its use has appeared. Sec. 2407.

23. In the debate on the Desert Land bill the year before Senator Sargent of California explained that the usual method of survey did not apply in the West because of mining claims, private land claims and the conditions of the country. But he was trying to forestall a survey requirement for the Desert bill. 44 Cong. 2 Sess. Cong. Rec., p. 1966.

24. 45 Cong. 3 Sess., op. cit., pp. 1202 and 1210-11.

Representative Hewitt of New York presented one
of the strongest arguments in favor of the proposals and
delivered probably the only prepared speech in the House.
His own treatment of the subject, he declared, sprang
from the "peculiar experience" which he happened "to
have had with reference to the growth of industry in the
country" and from an interest in the economic side of
the propositions.[25] He asserted that his experience
pointed to "The need of a thorough survey, for the wise
organization and distribution of American industry is in
the future as imperative as a constitution on which to
found our laws." He seemed to foreshadow the economic
planners of a later day for he felt that American industry had all the necessary requisites for great development except information on natural resources. Mr. Hewitt
believed that the information could be readily supplied
through scientific surveys.

After this extended debate the Appropriations
bill passed the House and came before the Senate March 1,
just three days before the Session ended.[26] The Senate
rushed the bill through but took time to strike out the
survey proposals. A few other changes were made and a
conference committee became necessary. This committee
failed, however, to reach a compromise before the session ended largely through a conflict over a phase of
the "Southern question," namely, the use of United
States Marshalls at the polls.[27] The Academy's survey
provisions seemed lost until some of them were rescued
by a daring coup which illustrates how both beneficial
and harmful legislation developed.

The Sundry Civil Expenses bill had been passed
by the House, February 24,[28] and it was a clause appropriating $100,000 for the Geological Survey. This sum
was obviously predicated on the passage of the Legislative appropriations bill with the survey changes intact.
When the Senate[29] considered the Civil bill Senator

---

25. Ibid., pp. 1203-6. In part he merely emphasized Major Powell's
    recommendations.
26. Ibid., p. 1909 and pp. 2173-87.
27. Ibid., pp. 2317-39.
28. Ibid., pp. 1864-71.
29. Ibid., pp. 2058-75.

Sargent, feeling certain that the survey provisions
would not pass, amended it by allotting the $100,000 to
the special surveys. Because of other changes also a
conference committee again became necessary.   Senators
Windon of Minnesota, Dorsey of Arkansas and Davis of
West Virginia were therefore appointed to meet with Representatives Atkins, Hewitt and Hale of Maine. The Committee proceeded to take two of the survey sections out
of the stranded Legislative appropriations bill and
placed them in the Civil bill which they were considering. According to Congressional rules no new material
could be inserted by a conference committee, but in this
case the rule was ignored. The committee agreed that it
was expedient to include the provisions establishing a
Geological Survey and a Public Land Commission.

The House immediately accepted the committee report with little discussion but due to a crowded docket
the Senate did not reach it until the evening of March 3,
1879.[30] Senators Edmunds of Vermont and Beck of Kentucky protested that the survey insertions made for "bad
legislation" but the bill passed and the President signed
it that evening. Since it provided for the new Bureau
which would consolidate the work of the various scientific surveys and the Commission, the new law marks a
noteworthy achievement in public land history. Representative Hewitt considered that the one permanent result of his legislative career lay in the unification of
the scientific surveys.[31] Without in any way intending
to detract from his contribution it should be observed
that the benefits of consolidation did not accrue to the
work of land distribution. The Geological Survey was
not permitted to coöperate with the Land Office and occasionally friction developed between them over work
which each had done in the same field.[32]

---

30. Ibid., pp. 2298-2303 and pp. 2355-61.
31. Quoted in Nevins', "Hewitt," op. cit., from "The Education of
    Henry Adams," p. 400.
32. U.S. Geological Survey Report, 1880, and Conover, op. cit.,
    p. 37. They were consolidated, however, in 1910 with obvious
    benefit. Ibid., p. 52.

II

The Public Land Commission had been required to establish certain basic classes of land and a system of surveys adopted to the economic use of each class. Its report of 1880 therefore presented a system of classification and a suggestion that the contract system be abolished so that accurate work could be assured.[33] There was no mention of the Academy's unused proposals though Major Powell's suggestion for regularly employed deputy surveyors was repeated. The Commission also recommended a full salary of $3,000 annually for Surveyors General and significantly added that each of these officials should have scientific and practical knowledge of surveying; it wanted no more political appointees. The Commission reported that it had received many complaints on the financial waste caused by surveying swamp and arid lands into small divisions so it suggested that in the future only major lines should be run over such regions. It also emphasized Major Powell's suggestion for more permanent survey markings and concluded by noting the practicality of inspection for survey work.

If many of the National Academy's suggestions had failed to find adequate support, the Commission's more modest proposals were practically ignored. The Land Office did investigate the feasibility of more permanent monuments but in the last analysis this was a question of larger survey appropriations, a matter over which the Office had little control. The problem of survey inspection was taken up at a Convention of Surveyors General which Commissioner Williamson called at Salt Lake City for the week of October 6, 1880.[34] The Convention adopted three resolutions, one of which urged that ten per cent of the amount annually appropriated for regular surveys should be allotted for inspection.[35] Congress responded by appropriating $8,000 in 1881 for the use of Surveyors General in "occasional examination," but the Land Office became dissatisfied with the results

---

33. Report, 1880, pp. xv-xvii.
34. The Convention Report is in the General Land Office. See also
   L.O.R., 1881, p. 683.
35. L.O.R., 1880, p. 984 and 1881, p. 151.

and requested that inspection be placed under its supervision.[36] Congress approved this request and then from 1882 to 1886 appropriated $30,000 annually for inspection work. Unfortunately even this system did not prove entirely satisfactory because of the unreliability of inspectors, the amount of territory to be inspected and the failure to include inspection of deposit survey work.

Another resolution which the Convention adopted requested that Surveyor Generals be allowed a supplementary fee for inspecting the too frequently complicated mining claim survey plats.[37] This would not add any expense to the Government appropriations for miners were required already to meet the cost of their surveys. But it does not appear that Congress approved the extra charge. A third and final resolution maintained that better work could be secured by increasing maximum rates for difficult regions. Surveying rates had fluctuated from year to year and had brought protests for the low maximums permitted. In 1876, for instance, Congress had reduced standard rates as part of an economy move.[38] Then in 1878, at the time of the passage of the Timber and Stone Act which required surveyed land for its use, Congress allotted a special amount of $30,000 for timber survey. Since no rate was stipulated Secretary Schurz allowed more than the standard rate and received reports that he had stimulated the better class of deputies to bid for work.[39] But such a windfall was not permanent and rates remained unsatisfactorily low, especially for rough and broken regions.[40]

Since Congress had not deemed it feasible to adopt a comprehensive surveying program and had rejected many of the suggestions for improved technique which experts offered, it might have tried to assist the imperfect system which remained. But instead of assistance

---

36. L.O.R., 1881, p. 8.
37. L.O.R. 1880, pp. 984 and 1085.
38. L.O.R., 1880, p. 955.
39. Ibid., p. 446 and p. 984.
40. For continued complaints see Sec. of Int. Report, 1883, p. 542; L.O.R., 1883, p. 246.

it almost constantly crippled the service through inadequate fiscal appropriations. For instance, according
to reports from Colorado, Idaho, Montana, Wyoming and
Dakota, there was an increasing demand for funds to
keep surveys ahead of settlement or to provide for protection and legitimate exploitation. In 1879 Dakota officials had complained that for three years surveys had
lagged behind absorption.[41] The Surveyor General had
been allotted $30,500 which would pay for surveying
1,042,116 acres. But in 1878 Homestead entries alone
had covered 867,775 acres, in addition to large areas
claimed under the Preëmption and Timber Culture laws.
The Surveyor General requested $139,920 for the follow-
ing year but he did not receive it; only the regular
amount was appropriated. Similar conditions and like
results existed in other States and Territories.[42]

        The inconvenience to settlers and the loss to
local and national Governments caused by retarded surveys are revealed in many western reports. The Governor
of Idaho maintained that they held back settlements in
his Territory.[43] He felt that the deposit system which
required settlers to advance the money for surveying
their claims, was "small business for a great nation
like ours to engage in" and that restricted appropriations were "not economy." Other officials pointed out
that the actual settler was often too poor to make a
deposit or that some were too far from standard survey
lines to take advantage of it.[44] In order to aid this
latter class as much as possible, in 1880 the Land Office ordered that where practical, standard and meridian
lines only should be run in the course of regular surveys. This order made for the greatest possible use of
survey funds but it could not satisfy all needs.   The
Governor of Wyoming asserted that settlers had repeatedly appealed to him "for intervention in their behalf."[45]

---

41. L.O.R., 1879, pp. 390 and 607. Donaldson declared that there
    was more land surveyed than necessary. This may have been true
    of amount but not of location; and it was obviously wise to
    keep ahead of possible mining claims.
42. Cf. L.O.R., 1879, pp. 754-5.
43. Sec. of Int. Report, 1880, p. 544.
44. L.O.R., 1879, p. 833; 1880, p. 925.
45. Ibid., pp. 529-30.

The absence of surveys meant that the Territory could not benefit from the use of its school lands because of uncertainty regarding their location. The Governor of Montana asked that surveys be "greatly expedited" and the Surveyor General revealed that settlers had paid deputies something additional in order to secure their services.[46] The Governor also urged survey of railroad lands so that the Territory could tax settlers that had acquired them.[47]

Several western reports indicated that more rapid survey and classification of timber regions would have reduced depredations. The decline in the number of trespasses in the South after surveys and public sale were permitted in 1876 has already been noted.[48] The Surveyor General of Montana has suggested that his territory would be similarly affected if surveys were pushed there.[49] In 1880 officials in Minnesota and Montana felt that surveys would aid private entry and in addition reduce the hazards of fire. The Surveyor General of Oregon maintained that he was able to survey twenty townships a year on his appropriations, "while in the same time five times as many townships" were sought by entrymen.[50] The Timber and Stone Act applied in his State but individuals were not able to find enough surveyed lands to enter and the Surveyor General stated that "the consequence is depredations upon timberland continue and the trespassers trust to their fellows for the protection of the courts."

Congress' failure to appropriate for the lawful salaries of Surveyors General presented another problem for it had its effect on their morale and undoubtedly on their work as well. The biting comment of the official

---

46. L.O.R., 1883, p. 246. The year before Secretary Teller urged "speedy surveys." Report, 1882, pp. xx-xxi.
47. He objected to the use of rectangular surveys in Montana because of the control of water rights which it permitted.
48. L.O.R., 1879, p. 392, and request for increased surveys in Louisiana. L.O.R., 1882, p. 413.
49. L.O.R., 1876, p. 256, and Surveyor General of California, L.O.R., 1879, p. 694.
50. L.O.R., 1881, p. 862.

in Montana will illustrate something of a general reaction. He wrote, "After nearly three years of faithful
service, during which time I have performed not only the
duties required of me by law and instruction but also
much additional clerical labor in order to expedite the
transaction of public business, my salary has been reduced (below the statutory amount), presumably as a reward for merit. While I have very little hope or expec-
tation that anything which I may say will have the
slightest effect....such actions do not tend to increase
the efficiency of the public service or promote the
feelings of enthusiastic devotion to same in the minds
of public servants."[51] The same niggardliness was apparent in appropriations for survey office work. Sometimes
the platting of field work fell behind from one to five
years, defeating one of the major purposes for which
surveys were designed. Small wonder that the Land Office did not always know when an agricultural entry covered timber or mineral land.

        Yet the Federal Government was not in straight-
ened circumstances. On the contrary, during the Seventies and Eighties it had a large Treasury surplus for
every year but 1876. Evidence that it could supply
funds for surveys is shown not only in large appropriations for special scientific undertakings but also in
repayments for deposit surveys which began to increase
surprisingly in 1880. The unusual increase had been
made possible because Congress modified the restriction
on the use of deposit certificates by permitting their
endorsement and acceptance at any land office in payment
for settlement entries. It is interesting to observe
that this seemingly innocent change took place while the
National Academy's proposals were pending before Congress. In 1878 deposits had totaled about $32,000 and
in 1879 when the law had been modified they rose to
$100,000. In the following year nearly $1,000,000 was
deposited, almost three times the annual appropriations
for regular surveying.[52]

---

51. L.O.R., 1880, pp. 984-5.
52. L.O.R., 1885, p. 232.

The Land Office found that the increase was explained by the fact that the amendment permitted extensive fraud.[53] It fostered friendly agreements between
individuals and deputy surveyors whereby the latter secured work on lands easily surveyed and the former sold
their certificates. The office described the process
succinctly by stating that the deposit law caused "the
survey of land of no present and perhaps no prospective
value and the surrender of title to valuable lands in
payment for such surveys."[54] It also claimed that settlers were not availing themselves of the modified law
because in the majority of instances it had found that
the location of settlers placing the deposit was entirely omitted from survey plats, while improvements, if
there were any, were never noted.[55] If contracts were
thus fraudulently secured the Land Office felt that it
was probable that deputies would "fraudulent survey" the
land. It sent out circulars urging Surveyors General to
devote "searching scrutiny" to all contracts submitted
for their approval,[56] but circulars did not remedy nor
prevent further abuses. The Office therefore requested
Congress to repeal the amendment which permitted endorsement. With a show of unusual concern for land frauds,
for in the previous year deposits had totaled over
$2,000,000,[57] Congress finally repealed the amendment,
August 7, 1882. As a consequence the use or abuse of
the law immediately dropped to one-fifth of what it had
been.

It is a curious fact that there was no provision
for punishing individuals who made false application for
surveys. Moreover the provisions for punishment on
false return of surveys by deputies was ineffective.
Every deputy posted a bond for the fulfillment of his
contract but when the Government secured the forfeiture

53. L.O.R., 1881, p. 6.
54. L.O.R., 1881, pp. 7-8.
55. For comments on the use of the law and suggestions for amending
     it see L.O.R., 1879, p. 895; 1881, p. 492; and 1882, p. 522.
     Suggestions for a topographical observer are in ibid., 1881,
     p. 781; 1879, p. 899.
56. Copp's "Public Land Laws, 1875-1882," p. 1428.
57. L.O.R., 1885, p. 232.

of bonds because of fraudulent work they were usually
found to be worthless.[58]   Juries would not convict deputies for perjury so they escaped punishment and the Government received only an inferior or worthless survey
for its expense. Congress failed to safeguard the Government against these abuses and it also ignored requests for penalties in cases of willful destruction of
survey markings.[59] If such penalties had been provided
it would have been necessary to define destruction carefully for perhaps a traveler could not be blamed if he
collected and made a fire for his evening meal from survey stakes which some irresponsible deputy had tossed
out of a wagon or thrown from horseback. There should
have been some check on such useless marking.[60]

Since Congress failed to provide appropriations
for legitimate surveys and proved generous in supplying
means and funds for fraudulent work it severely handicapped the business of land disposal. There was some
benefit to the land department in the fact that the Legislature did provide for resurveys and remarkings but
this was a mistaken generosity; the work should have
been properly attended to in the first place.[61] Even resurveys were not necessarily well performed, and because
of Congress' seemingly purposeful neglect of the system
a powerful survey ring grew up in the West during the
late Seventies and early Eighties. It is difficult to
say, however, which was cause and which effect for the
ring was known to have exerted powerful influence in
Washington. Some record of its work and its exposure
will be noted while considering President Cleveland's
administration.

One of the most important results of the efforts
to improve the surveying service was the creation of the
Public Land Commission. Credit for its existence should

---

58. L.O.R., 1883, p. 25.
59. L.O.R., 1880, p. 692; 1883, p. 25.
60. Stewart, op. cit., p. 125.
61. The first appropriation for resurveys of a general character
    was in August, 1882. Regular appropriations began in 1884.
    Conover, op. cit., pp. 42-3.

be given to such men as Abram S. Hewitt, James A. Williamson, Carl Schurz, James W. Powell and various leaders of the National Academy of Sciences.[62] But viewed
in a broader perspective the Commission grew out of the
movement to deal with the trans-Missouri regions and
though timber, desert and mineral laws had been enacted
by 1878 there was no question but that they were adopted
in a piecemeal manner and that the whole system of land
disposal needed comprehensive treatment. During the
same period Canada had faced many of the same problems
and in 1879 its land laws were completely revised.[63] The
measures which it adopted for timber and grazing lands,
for use of the homestead law and for law enforcement represented realistic solutions which the United States
might well copy.

    The first definite step for revising the United
States system came with the provision for a Commission
in the Sundry Civil Service bill of March 3, 1879. Created from the National Academy's suggestion and by the
conference committee's adroit manoeuver, the Commission
was required to codify the laws for the survey and disposition of the public domain, classify the several
types of land and make recommendations for such measures
as it deemed wise for disposing of the remaining lands
to actual settlers. The law also stated that the Commission should consist of Commissioner Williamson, Clar-
ence King,[64] Director of the newly established Geological Survey, and three civilians appointed by the President. President Hayes promptly selected men well versed
in land matters: Thomas Donaldson[65] of Philadelphia,
soldier, lawyer, author and former land register in Idaho; Alexander T. Britton[66] of Washington, D.C., an experienced land lawyer and former employee of the Land

---

62. In his Congressional speech favoring the survey proposals Rep-
    resentative Hewitt gave the Commissioner credit for originating
    the idea of a Commission. He had mentioned it in his Land Of-
    fice Report for 1877.
63. Donaldson, op. cit., p. 477ff.
64. Cf. Dict. Am. Biog., vol. X, p. 384
65. Lamb's Biographical Dict. of the U.S., vol. II, p. 487.
66. Nat. Cyclop. of Am. Biog., vol. I, p. 267.

Office; and James W. Powell, the author of the reports
previously noted.

The Commission organized its work in Washington
during July, 1879, and then journeyed to Denver, Colorado, as a base for visiting every western State and Territory, except Washington Territory. George L. Converse,
Chairman of the House Committee on Public Lands, accompanied the Commission at his own expense in order to be
prepared to support the Commission's recommendations
when placed before Congress. In addition to the personal inspection which the group made it also secured replies to lengthy questionnaires which were distributed
to well-informed western residents. It included these
replies in 600-page Preliminary Report that contained
its recommendations, February 25, 1880.[67]

The Commission had not then completed its work
of codifying the land laws but with the report it presented a bill embodying certain changes. The Report explained that the Commission approved of the practice of
distributing public lands for settlement rather than for
revenue but that it also believed that the laws and machinery for their execution had not been constructed
"in all respects so as to secure the objects which they
have contemplated."[68] Since many laws were new and "ex-
perimental" the Commission proposed the "means by which
their defects may be remedied." It believed that if the
system had proved too unsatisfactory westerners would
have made "loud and general complaint." And it significantly added: "The ease and rapidity with which any
qualified person may make entry of such public land as
yet remains is apparent to all."[68]

The Commission noted that the purpose of the
settlement laws suffered defeat when one person used
them all to acquire 1,120 acres, for this entailed only
perfunctory or nominal compliance with the laws or complete evasion of them. It also declared that although
some of the defects of the land system, or evils which

67. Preliminary Report of the Public Land Commission, 1880. 46
      Cong. 2 Sess. H. Ex. Doc. #46, Serial #1923.
68. Ibid., p. viii.

stemmed from them, had recently produced new laws, these
in themselves had given rise to other defects. Through
great trouble and expense disputed cases which had been
brought to the courts had brought decisions that filled
in some gaps but they were quite inadequate. The Commission presented, therefore, what it termed "conservative" changes in order to establish a coördinated system.[69]

The scope of these changes affected nearly every
branch of the land service from the Interior Department
to the District Offices and from the Homestead to the
mining laws.[70] Many of its suggestions are taken up in
other chapters of this monograph; they include not only
recommendations for surveys but for the Land Office,
arid and pastoral lands, timber and mineral laws and
private land claims. In addition there were several
minor suggestions such as that to limit the time for ap-
pealing land cases and centralize them either in the
Land Office or the Interior Department. The Commission
also believed that all outstanding land scrip should be
used within two years or forfeited and that Congress
should provide approval for departmental swamp land
rules. And finally, beside mentioning slight changes in
the town site law and the railroad right-of-way act, it
recommended repeal of the Preëmption Law because of its
abuse.

One of the most remarkable features of the Commission's report is provided by the contrast between the
breadth and sagacity of most of its suggestions and Congress' failure to give them any consideration. President Hayes submitted the report with the customary recommendation for consideration and on March 1, 1880 Representative Converse, presented the bill.[71] But when the
latter came up for debate it received practically no comment and no action was taken on it.[72] Meanwhile Congress
passed an amendment to the Homestead law so that entrymen who had become insane could complete requirements

69. Ibid., p. x.
70. Ibid., pp. xi-xlvi.
71. 46 Cong. 2 Sess. Cong. Rec., p. 1102. Richardson's "Messages,"
    op. cit., p. 629.
72. Ibid., pp. 1230, 2203 and 4381.

for title to their land.[73] There was no explanation for
and no discussion on this latter bill but perhaps its
passage illustrates the point that Congress could enact
trifling measures while it neglected major needs.

The failure to secure support for the Commission's proposals can be explained by a lack of leadership, certain western hostility, Congressional indifference and an apathetic public opinion. In the succeeding
Congress Representative Converse seemed to have lost interest in the reforms[74] and Mr. Hewitt was defeated for
reëlection but when he did return he gave his attention
to other problems; Mr. Hewitt did not believe in re-
stricting his usefulness by becoming attached too closely to any one proposition.[75] Furthermore popular opinion did not seem to stand behind the Commission's suggestions. Congress received petitions opposed to any
changes in the land laws but none in their support.[76]
Something of the popular attitude is doubtless reflected
in an anonymous letter sent to the Daily Pioneer Press
of St. Paul, in reply to that paper's expression of mild
approval for the proposals.[77] The correspondent felt
that in the first place there had been no widespread
backing for even a Commission and that therefore it
would not have been created if provision for its establishment had not been "surreptitiously injected" into
the appropriation bill. He also pointed out that the
absence of "western men" on the Commission detracted
from the value of its suggestions and he charged that
these suggestions were really "gotten up in the interest
of office seekers, spoilsmen and land grabbers." But
probably the best explanation for the failure to find
popular support for the proposals lies in the Commission's reference to the ease with which public land
could still be obtained. If the people did not demand
changes predatory interests did not either, for they too

---

73. Ibid., p. 4216.
74. He was placed on the Judiciary Committee and though he intro-
    duced a reform bill it was never reported out. 47 Cong. 1 Sess.
    Cong. Rec., p. 172.
75. Nevins, "Hewitt," op. cit., passim.
76. Montana was especially active in presenting petitions. Cong.
    Rec. 47 Cong. 1 Sess. Index.
77. April 5 and 19, 1880.

were securing what they wanted under an antiquated and
inefficient system.

The Commission's accomplishments are largely
confined to its reports. A. T. Britton completed the
codification of land laws and decisions and they remain
a monument to his efforts. Thomas Donaldson compiled
and then for several years added to his history, the
"Public Domain." It contains a mass of information,
part of which is inconveniently arranged. The Commissions Preliminary Report is also useful to the historian.
It is true, however, that years or decades later some of
the Commission's recommendations were adopted, though
frequently after any possibility of benefit to the land
system had vanished. It is impossible to compute the
benefits which prompt adoption of wise laws and suggestions for efficient machinery would have created for
purposes of distribution in the land rush of subsequent
decades.

Chapter V

DELAY IN ADJUSTING RAILROAD GRANTS

The American Government had been extremely liberal in donating over 132,000,000 acres of public land
to aid in constructing western and southern railroads.[1]
The gift represented an area equal to the New England
States, New York, Pennsylvania, Maryland, Delaware and
Virginia and its size alone was large enough to have
created major administrative problems. These problems
were aggravated in the period 1870 to 1890 because the
Government had originally made little provision for
supervising the grants. The result was that the roads
were able to abuse many of their privileges and evade
their obligations. Moreover they secured lawyers and
friends in the courts, administrative bodies and Congress so that they could delay or defeat attempts at
regulation. Railroad pressure on Congress, where in the
last analysis responsibility rested, brought a culpable
neglect of legislative obligations. In addition the
favors which the roads secured in the land department
were extensive. And without charging judicial bias it
is possible to note that many decisions of the Supreme
Court were decidedly advantageous to the roads and a
serious handicap to efficient administration. An examination of the requirements for fulfilling and the methods of handling grants will reveal how the railroads
were favored at the expense of public property and public welfare.

It is necessary to observe that problems arising
from railroad grants were not those which the Interstate

---

1. Sec. of Int. Report, 1934, p. 73. A revised estimate in 1880
had declared that 155,514,995 acres would satisfy all claims
from railroad granting acts. Donaldson, op. cit., p. 287. When
the grants are finally adjusted the exact amount granted, patented and retained can be known.

Commerce Commission Act of 1887 endeavored to meet. On
the contrary they represented conflicts over interpretations or abuses of the provisions of the granting acts.
All the grants contained certain features more or less
in common. The roads were given right-of-way privileges
along with a donation of from six to twenty alternate
sections of land per mile, on each side of their lines.
In some cases the land was given to a State for distribution as fast as the road was built but in other instances, notably for the Pacific roads, the grant was
given direct to the company. In order to earn these
lands the roads were required to complete their construction work within a specified time, usually ten years
from the date of passage of the act. In at least thirty-
three cases grants provided that unearned land should be
subject to forfeiture or should automatically revert to
the Government.[2] Railroad companies were obliged to pay
the cost of surveying and patenting lands before title
definitely passed. And if some of the granted land had
been taken up by the time the railroad line was definitely established, the road could receive indemnity
land as compensation, within stipulated distances of fifteen to sixty miles. In addition to these Congressional
provisions there was an Interior Department ruling that
with the establishment of the line of the road, granted
lands and indemnity limits were officially withdrawn
from occupation or settlement. All of these provisions
became subject to discussion and judicial and legislative action after 1870.

        One provision which passed through a dispute
lasting over two decades centered around forfeiture of
unearned grants. Sentiments for forfeiture developed
with the agitation to prohibit land grants in the post-
Civil War era. The cessation of grants in 1871 resulted,
according to L. H. Haney, from Granger influence and
popular hostility to the Pacific railroads.[3] The Granger
spirit was attributed to irritation over extortionate
rates and discriminatory policies of mid-western roads
while the reaction against the Pacific roads was due
chiefly to the increasing certainty that their

2. L.O.R., 1883, pp. 20-2.
3. Haney, op. cit., p. 22.

construction had been a field for stock jobbery and corruption. But before grants ceased sentiment favoring forfeiture had caused Congress in July 1870, to revoke all grants to Louisiana in aid of railroads construction if the land had not been already distributed.[4] And four years later two railroads lost their entire grants through failure to take advantage of them.

But while Congress thus acted to return small and separate areas a policy of general forfeiture was being demanded. Its advocates wanted the Government to enforce the letter of the law in all cases and recover land that had not been earned within the stipulated time. They also maintained that it was necessary for the land department only to declare the lapse and then return the land to the public domain. This contention was undermined, however, by the Supreme Court decision at its October term, 1874, in the case of Schulenburg vs. Harriman.[5] The case grew out of a dispute over the stealing of timber from railroad lands in Wisconsin. Congress had made a grant to the State in 1856 to aid in the construction of a railroad from Madison to Lake Superior. The State was authorized to sell the alternate sections along the line as fast as each twenty miles was completed and pay the money obtained to the railroad. Congress had also stipulated that after a lapse of thirteen years, or in 1869, all "the lands unsold shall revert to the United States."[6] In 1869, the State overstepped its authority and donated the land to the St. Croix and Superior Railroad Company to facilitate the construction of the last part of the road; but the company delayed its building. In the same year, however, the Wisconsin Legislature had provided State agents to protect timber on all land granted by Congress.[6]

Shortly thereafter Schulenburg and others had cut timber from districts that comprised railroad grant land. When Harriman, the Wisconsin timber protection agent, attached $16,809 worth of the illegally cut wood, Schulenburg brought suit to recover it and carried the

4. L.O.R., 1885, tables, p. 187ff.
5. 21 Wall. 44.
6. Ibid.

case to the Supreme Court. He contended that the title
to the land from which he cut the timber had not definitely or finally passed to Wisconsin; that if it had so
passed the title had reverted to the United States because of the railroad's failure to build within the stipulated time; or that if the State had received title
from Congress that title had passed to the railroad company in 1869 by the donation of the State Legislature.

The Supreme Court rule that the lands had definitely passed to Wisconsin as what was termed a grant in
praesenti, but that the State had no power to donate
them to the railroad company. Furthermore the Court
held that the lands had not reverted to the United States
because forfeiture of public grants "must be asserted by
judicial proceedings authorized by law....or there must
be some legislative assertion of ownership of the property for breach of the condition." Since it was true
that the House of Representatives had twice passed forfeiture acts which the Senate had failed to act upon,
the Congressional intent was not established; consequently title to the lands remained in the State. Schulenburg and his associates could not, therefore, recover
their stolen timber.

This decision established an anomalous type of
ownership for the States, the railroads and the Federal
Government. Since the Court had said in effect that the
lands unsold shall wait until Congress renews its declaration of forfeiture, the States held possession of the
lands without the right to use them except to spend money
to protect them. Incidentally it would seem that if the
lands had been involved in a direct grant to a railroad,
instead of to a railroad through the medium of a State,
there would have been greater reason for the Court's decision. However, railroads which had received their
grants direct from Congress also enjoyed an unusual type
of possession. The Interior Department felt that in the
light of the Schulenburg decision it could not declare
any lapsed grants forfeited even when the language was
quite explicit.[7] For instance the Illinois Central
grant had stated: "If the said road shall not be completed within ten years....the title of the residue of

---

7. Sec. of Int. Report, 1877, p. 244.

said lands shall re-invest in the United States, to have
and to hold in the same manner as if this act had not
been passed."[8] By failing to take any steps for forfeiture the Department, perhaps very properly from its own
standpoint, caused railroads to become land owners to
the extent that they could exploit, mortgage or sell
their lands and yet were not required to pay taxes on
any which they retained. Theoretically the Government
still owned the land, in the ultimate sense of the word
owned, but the railroads received full benefits from it.

The Schulenburg decision therefore placed the
responsibility of forfeiture before Congress. Secretary
Schurz recommended that Congress allow the Land Office
to take over lapsed grants after notice by publication
but Congress delayed in adopting any policy.[9] Several
more "pop-gun" forfeitures were passed during the late
Seventies yet in other cases Congress extended the time
limit for construction and in one instance it waived the
right of forfeiture. Discussion on various bills indicated that while some members favored repossessing all
lands for which the granting conditions had not been met,
others felt that since the status of many grants differed, especially because of the degree of effort which
a road might have made to fulfill its obligations, a
policy of indiscriminate forfeiture would be unfair.[10]
Some few legislators appeared to favor no action on forfeiture. In defense of those who favored only limited
forfeiture it could be shown that though only 3,543 out
of 11,686 miles of the land grant railroads had been
built within the time limits, another 4,000 miles had
been constructed by 1883, and many roads were continuing
to build.[11] It was therefore a serious question whether
or not to penalize bona fide construction work because
it had not been performed on time.

Strongly contrasting views on forfeiture can be
illustrated from two Congressional Committee reports of
the early Eighties. Substantially duplicating a previous recommendation in 1880 the House Committee on Pacific

---

8. 9 Stat. 466.

9. Sec. of Int. Rep., 1877, p. xxiv.

10. Haney, op. cit., p. 25.

11. Donaldson, op. cit., tables, p. 1269-72.

Railroads asked for the forfeiture of all unearned Pacific road grants.[12] It estimated that 106,000,000 acres could be reclaimed and it specifically urged the return of the Northern Pacific grant. The Committee confessed that it was bowing to an outraged public opinion which regarded the grants as excessive because they equaled in size the "principalities and empires of the old world." The report suggested that if railroad construction needed further assistance, money loans would be preferable to land grants. Congress, however, took no action on the Committee's recommendation.

Two years later the House Committee on the Judiciary, through Thomas B. Reed, presented an opposing view and rejected another demand for forfeiture of the Northern Pacific grant.[13] Its report stated that Section 8 of the granting act, setting a time limit for earning the grant, was qualified or limited by Section 9. This latter clause made a "further condition that if the said company made any breach of contract herein and allowed the same to continue upward for one year, then in such case, at any time hereafter, the United States by its Congress may do any and all acts and things which may be needful and necessary to insure a speedy completion of said road." In consequence of this provision the Committee held that Congress might declare forfeiture and give the unearned grant to another road if it thought such action would aid in the speedy completion of the road. But since the Northern Pacific company was bending every effort to complete its last 600 miles there was no need for Congress to act.

The Minority report upheld the right of forfeiture and stated that it opposed any qualification on Congress' power in that field. It maintained that the stipulation in Section 9 was only a "further condition" on which Congress might act for speedy completion of work if it saw fit, but it felt that Congress was not

---

12. H. Rep. #691. 46 Cong. 1 Sess. and Haney, op. cit., p. 25.
13. H. Rep. #1283. 47 Cong. 1 Sess. quoted in Donaldson, op. cit., p. 880ff. The committee divided eight to seven. Reports were submitted by the Majority and the Minority, June 6 and July 24, 1882, respectively.

bound in any way by that option. Moreover the report
demonstrated the equity of forfeiture by estimates and
statistics. For instance the Minority had calculated
that, based on the average cost of building until 1882,
the road could complete its line with a profit of
$11,000,000 despite forfeiture of all land unearned at
that date. Another estimate showed that profits would
run as high as $47,000,000 if all the land granted were
patented to the road. The report also noted that such
munificence would have no effect on the freight rate for
that was apt to continue to be whatever the traffic
would bear.

Congress failed to act on the Judiciary reports
but while the question of forfeiture was becoming increasingly debated Secretary Schurz complicated the
problem by issuing patents for land not earned within
time limits. It is true that the Land Office had delivered patents to States, where the railroad grant was
indirect, and had left their disposal in the States'
hands. In several instances the States had turned the
patents over to roads that had completed their construction after the stipulated period. Once the patents had
left Washington it is probable that the Interior Department could not have stopped the State disposal but it
could certainly have held up delivery in cases of direct
grants.

Secretary Schurz' hasty action grew out of the
construction work of the Atlantic and Pacific railroad
west of Albuquerque, New Mexico. Though completed out
of time the road applied to the Department in 1880 for
inspection of about fifty miles of track as a preliminary to securing patents.[14] Secretary Schurz hesitated
at first but in October, 1880 he decided to seek Attorney General Deven's opinion. The Attorney General advised the Secretary that it was proper to issue patents
because the grant was not in default until Congress declared forfeiture. Since Congress had not acted the
Secretary should allow the road the benefit of its
grant. Accepting this opinion Secretary Schurz had the

---

14. H. Ex. Doc. #29. 47 Cong. 2 Sess. quoted in Donaldson, op.
    cit., p. 828.

road inspected, approved its selection of land and in
January, 1881, issued patents for 23,037 acres. Meanwhile other parts of the road were completed but the
Secretary grew cautious, reversed his policy and ordered
that additional patents should be delayed until Congress
had taken some action regarding forfeiture.[15] Undoubtedly he was correct in reversing his position, even though
Congress continued a vexatious delay, because there
were increasingly strong efforts to secure a policy of
forfeiture. The character of those efforts will be tak-
en up in a subsequent chapter.

II

Meanwhile another railroad problem developed
from disputes over indemnity rights, disputes which, as
mentioned before, have lasted until the present day. In
the early period of railroad grants the roads had been
allowed special privileges through very casual Land Office procedure. In the first place the Office withdrew
the right of settlement on all lands within indemnity
limits. There was no legal provision for such a policy
and George W. Julian later showed that in fact it was
prohibited because the granting acts expressly allowed
Homestead and Preëmption settlement on all but granted
lands. In 1883 Mr. Julian wrote a magazine article entitled, "Railway Influence in the Land Office" and in
it claimed that the Office had adopted the withdrawal
rule at the bidding of the railroad.[16] He felt that the
roads wished to ensure the fact that there would be plen-
ty of good land from which to select indemnity. He declared that if the granting acts had been strictly interpreted the Northern Pacific road, for instance,
would have secured a reserved strip 80 rather than 120
miles wide through the Territories.

Railroads had also been benefited when the Land
Office assumed, without formal discussion or opinion in

---

15. L.O.R., 1883, p. 22. Secretary Teller reversed Secretary
    Schurz's last decision. Haney, op. cit., p. 26 and chap. VI,
    post.
16. North American Review, March, 1883.

any case, that indemnity was to be allowed for all land within the granted limits whether they were sold, preëmpted or reserved before or after the date of the granting act.[17] Incidentally the Office did not even require a specification of loss but seemingly granted the roads indemnity whenever they asked for it. This latter practice could be classed as both generous and unbusiness-like but the practice of permitting indemnity for losses incurred before the granting date was apparently unlawful. Most of the granting acts contained a clause similar to that in the Illinois Central grant which stated: "In case it shall appear that the United States have, when the line of said road and branches is definitely fixed....sold any part of any section hereby granted, or that the right of preëmption has attached to the same" then indemnity could be selected from land within fifteen miles of the road.

Mr. Julian pointed out that the roads had been given only that which was free and unattached public land when the grant was made. If this was true, and it seemed plausible, then the roads should not have been allowed to receive indemnity for land that had been disposed of before that time. According to the wording of the act indemnity was given only for that part of the grant which was taken up between the time of the grant and the time when the road definitely located its line; locating might be delayed for months or even years. Mr. Julian quoted a Supreme Court decision of 1840 to show that when once land had been disposed of no other act could apply to it. Consequently land that had been disposed of, but later proved to be within a railroad grant, was unaffected by any provision in the granting act.

In 1875 the Supreme Court had upheld Mr. Julian's interpretation in the case of Leavenworth, Lawrence and Galveston Railroad Company vs. United States.[18] The Court stated: "In railroad grants indemnity was not given for lands within the limits of the grant disposed of prior thereto. ....The only purpose of that clause (for indemnity) is to give lands outside the ten-mile

17. L.O.R., 1887, pp. 304-5.
18. 2 Otto 733, and see L.O.R., 1879, p. 457.

limit for those lost inside by action of the Government
in keeping the land office open between the date of the
granting act and the location of the road. This construction gives effect to every part of the act and
makes each consistent with the other."[19] At the same
term of the Court it decided the case of Newhall vs.
Sanger[20] on similar principles, the only difference
arising from a question of reserved lands of an Indian
Reservation rather than sold lands. The reserved lands
were restored to the public domain after the grant was
made, but the Court refused to permit the railroad to
obtain any part of them because the granting act had applied only to free land.

        Secretary Schurz fully accepted the principles
of the Leavenworth case when on December 26, 1877 he decided the Wisconsin Central grant dispute to accord with
it.[21] He thus overturned a departmental rule which his
predecessor had failed to modify. Since he also ordered the Land Office to adjust every grant according to
the new rule the Office began a laborious examination of
railroad grant lands, tract by tract, in order to discover which roads had received excessive indemnity. The
Acting Secretary of Interior established the peculiar
rule, however, that all patents which corresponded to
the revoked Sanger patent were "voidable" but not void
until declared so by judicial decision.[22] It therefore
became necessary to bring individual suits for all excessive patenting.

        The preparation of data proceeded so slowly[23]
because of an insufficient office force that it was not
until 1878 that suit was commenced against the Western
Pacific Railroad Company. The case was dropped, however,
when the Company showed that purchasers of the land in
dispute had not been made a party to the proceedings.[24]

---

19. Three Justices, Field, Swayne and Strong, dissented.
20. 2 Otto 761; and see Burlington and Missouri River Case, 98 U.S.
     334. Cf. Dunmeyer case, 113 U.S. 629 and N.Y. Times, March 3,
     1885.
21. H. Ex. Doc. #144. 47 Cong. 1 Sess. quoted in Donaldson, op.
     cit., p. 789ff.
22. Julian, op. cit.
23. L.O.R., 1879, p. 457.
24. Julian, op. cit.

No new action was instigated and no other suits were
started so that, according to Mr. Julian, the railroads
did not lose an acre of excess lands. He estimated that
400,000 acres were erroneously patented to the Santa Fe
company and probably 1,000,000 acres more to various
other Kansas roads.

The failure to regain any of the erroneously
patented lands was due not only to the half-hearted
court action but also to the fact that in 1880 Secretary
Schurz returned to the old interpretation of indemnity.[25]
He later explained that because there had been innumerable complaints of his original ruling, he had submitted
an indemnity case of some Minnesota grants to Attorney
General Devens for "an authoritative expression of his
views." The Attorney had then been besieged by all the
roads that could possibly be affected and on June 5,
1880, he accepted their arguments and ruled in favor of
a liberal interpretation of the granting acts. He asserted that the question of indemnity was not directly
before the Supreme Court in the Leavenworth case and
that consequently its statement on the point was merely
a "dictum entitled only to the weight which was given
the dicta of eminent judges." On the other hand he had
found an opinion of a western Wisconsin Circuit Court
which did allow indemnity for lands sold or reserved before the date of the granting acts. Mr. Devens therefore concluded that "in view of the conflicting opinions it would seem to me that the safer course for the
Department would be to return to (the) original construction of indemnity rights." This rather tenuous line of
reasoning was further weakened when Mr. Julian revealed
that the Wisconsin Circuit Court did not have the question of indemnity before it and that the section to
which the Attorney General referred was written on the
margin of the printed decision. Moreover the case was
not officially reported and evidence indicated that it
might be appealed to the Supreme Court. Nevertheless
Secretary Schurz accepted Mr. Deven's opinion and after

---

25. H. Ex. Doc. #29, 47 Cong. 2 Sess. quoted in Donaldson, op. cit.,
    p. 824ff; "Speeches" of Carl Schurz, op. cit., vol. IV, p.
    168ff.

a delay of four months ordered the Land Office to follow
it in future cases.

  This victory for liberality to the railroads
was ratified in 1884 by the Supreme Court in the Winona
and St. Peter case.[26] By deciding to permit indemnity
for land lost prior to the granting act the Court did
not exactly reverse the Leavenworth decision for it supported the Attorney General in claiming that the previous reference to indemnity was arguendo or a dictum. It
is of course entirely proper that a dictum in one case
should not bind the decision in another but the Court's
explicit statement of indemnity rights in the Leavenworth decision represents a more exact interpretation of
the granting acts than that given in the Winona case.[27]
Congress may have intended to allow the roads indemnity
for all lands absorbed within their granted limits but
the wording of the acts does not state that fact and
there is a well-established legal principle that what is
not expressly granted is withheld. The Attorney General
and the Court were therefore allowing the roads the benefit of a large doubt and interpreting the grants very
generously in their favor.

  Out of the dispute over forfeiture there developed a series of newspaper polemics between Mr.
Julian and Mr. Schurz. Mr. Julian's article of 1883 had
contained strong criticisms of the former Secretary's
vacillating policies so that Mr. Schurz printed a spir-
ited reply.[28] He not only defended his changes of policy but brought forward certain reforms which his administration established. Mr. Schurz believed that his
term was marred by only one or two small but natural mistakes. On the other hand he charged that Mr. Julian
himself was responsible for a great deal of the difficulty over railroad grants because of the vague language in
the granting acts, prepared when the latter was a member

---

26. 113 U.S. 618.
27. There seems to be a difference in the tone of the Leavenworth
  and Winona decisions as though the Court felt it was on the de-
  fensive in the latter and sure of its position in the former.
28. "Speeches" of Carl Schurz, op. cit., vol. IV, p. 168ff. and another reply, p. 184ff.

of the House Committee on Public Lands. In demonstrat-
ing that he had not been influenced by the railroads but
on the contrary had been partial to settlers Mr. Schurz
recalled that a Senate investigation in 1882 revealed
that out of 824 cases in dispute between settlers and
the railroads, 635 were decided favorably to settlers;
most of these cases were adjudicated during Mr. Schurz's
administration. In all fairness to Mr. Julian it should
be noted that he acknowledged the latter's accomplishments along that line. The former Secretary also
claimed credit as the first administrator to require
railroads to specify the location of lands for which
they sought indemnity. Unfortunately he had not followed up this reform by correcting excessive indemnity
grants which the former liberality made possible.

Mr. Schurz also called attention to his decision
in the Dudymott case where he had supported a settler
in a dispute over mortgaged lands and had thereby opened
up more millions of acres then were ever affected by an
indemnity ruling.[29] The case arose out of conflicting
interpretations of the Union Pacific land grant for
there was a proviso, common to five other grants, that
all land was liable to preëmption if not "sold or otherwise disposed of" within three years of the completion
of the entire road. Dudymott preëmpted a quarter section of granted land on which there was a railroad mortgage for he claimed that a mortgage was not a disposal
of the land within the meaning of the act. The road
contested his claim and Commissioner Williamson upheld
the road but on appeal Secretary Schurz reversed the
Commissioner and ruled in favor of Dudymott.

When the decision became known settlers swarmed
over Union Pacific mortgaged lands to preëmpt them so
the railroad hastened to bring the test case of William
H. Platt to the Supreme Court.[30] In very short order
the Court rejected Secretary Schurz's decision and held
that a mortgage was a disposal under the law.   Three

28. "Speeches" of Carl Schurz, op. cit., vol. IV, p. 168ff. and an-
    other reply, p. 184ff.
29. L.O.R., 1879, p. 459.
30. Washington Law Reporter, quoted in Copp, op. cit., June, 1879.

justices dissented on the ground that the granting act
intended to encourage settlement after the railroad had
had a reasonable time for disposal but that a mortgage
nullified the purpose.[31] Despite his defeat on preëmpting mortgaged lands Mr. Schurz's newspaper articles
demonstrated that he had supported the settler's cause
during his administration. On the other hand he might
have presented more cogent reasons to explain his failure to protect Government rights by maintaining a strong
stand on questions of indemnity and patents earned out
of time.

There is another phase of the railroad problem
that received some attention during Secretary Schurz's
term and it is connected with railroad surveys. As already noted the failure either to secure grant surveys
or to require payment for surveys performed resulted in
considerable benefit to the roads. Payment for surveys
had been made a requisite for patents by a clause in the
Sundry Civil Service bill of 1876 and was intended to
economize on Government expenditures. This provision
was actually a broad application of a rule established
previously for individual roads. The general provision
escaped notice for two years, according to the Land Office, because it was buried in the bill.[32] Perhaps the
Office meant that the roads did not discover that it
would permit them to delay patents by withholding survey
payments and thereby escape taxation of their grants. In
any case the Government's failure to secure a speedy and
accurate survey of railroad lands benefited the roads
from several standpoints. For instance most of the
grants excluded any claim to mineral lands, with the significant exception of coal and iron lands. When, however, the Government neglected to survey the grants so
as to reserve mineral land it enabled the roads to exploit the minerals until the Government successfully
contested their actions.[33] Furthermore in the absence
of surveys settlers could not be sure whether they had
located on granted or Government land and the roads took

---

31. See also the Northern Pacific Railroad's virtual violation of a
    similar provision in its granting act. Ise., op. cit., p. 252.
32. L.O.R., 1879, pp. 458-9.
33. See chap. XV, post.

advantage of the settler's ignorance and sold titles to
land which they did not possess.[34] When the public surveys did reach their lands and settlers found that they
had actually purchased public land from the roads there
was very little chance of securing the return of his
money because the roads resorted to dilatory court action.   And finally the lack of surveys benefited the
roads because their depredation on public timber could
not be redressed when the Government could not prove in
Court that the timber had actually been cut from public
land.   Secretary Schurz had pressed for a solution of
the survey problem but Congress appeared indifferent.
And unfortunately not only survey questions but questions of forfeiture and indemnity dragged along unsolved
through succeeding years.

---

34. See chap. XIII, post.

Chapter VI

THE TELLER REGIME

At the close of President Hayes' administration
the country was entering upon a period of rapid economic expansion. The depression of 1873-79 had ended and
while the East witnessed the creation of the Standard
Oil and a dozen other major trusts, the West embarked
upon an unparallelled program of railroad building.
Within a decade 73,000 miles of track were laid down,
more than three times the previous annual average.[1]
Moreover western ranching developed into an organized
business under powerful corporations; and timber and
mining companies became richer, more powerful and more
ruthlessly competitive. Population flowed into the
West faster than ever before[2] so that in the twenty
years from 1870 to 1890 the area west of the Mississippi River increased the proportion of the number of its
inhabitants from one-sixth to one-fourth that of the
entire country.[3]

Along with the economic expansion the demand
for public land rose to record heights. A temporary
drop had followed the panic of 1873, though the Land
Office attributed the decline to a grasshopper plague
and a drought rather than the economic depression. In

---

1. Statistical Abstract of the U.S., 1890, p. 273.
2. Copp's Land Owner quoted the N.Y. Tribune regarding families going West by the 1,000s where 100s went the year before. April,
   1879. Later it noted that the Immigration Board of the U.S.
   did the preliminary work of ascertaining the extent and location of Government land for prospective settlers. Nov., 1882.
3. E. P. Oberholtzer, "A History of the United States," vol. V,
   p. 592.

any case the number of Homestead entries remained fairly constant. The total amount of land absorbed in 1877
reached a low of 4,850,000 acres[4] but thereafter it
showed an almost constant rise. By 1885 nearly
21,000,000 acres were claimed under all classes of entries and 51,000 persons selected 7,416,000 acres under
the Homestead law.[5] An equal amount of land was claimed
through Preëmption filings and the number of Timber Culture entries absorbed 4,755,000 acres more. Following
the year 1885 the annual totals remained high so that
western absorption continued to account for huge areas
of land. The problems of the land department during
the Eighties must be placed against this increased activity. Under President Hayes there had been extraordinary efforts to secure what appeared to be a well-
planned system but since only a few of the projected
reforms were adopted then, the opportunity for further
changes diminished as more and more of the most desira-
ble land fell into private hands. In addition the succeeding administration showed less inclination to handle land problems so thoroughly and honestly.

The 1880 campaign to elect President Hayes'
successor was devoid of any fundamental issues and land
questions were particularly ignored. Party platforms
contained only the usual trite references to corporation grants and settler's rights[6] and candidates James
A. Garfield and Winfield S. Hancock did not refer to
any land questions in the letters accepting their nominations. General Garfield's term was so short that no
record could be established. He did appoint a promis-
ing Secretary of Interior, Samuel J. Kirkwood, a former
railroad president and the Civil War Governor of Iowa.
But when President Garfield died Secretary Kirkwood
tendered his resignation and was permitted to remain in
office only until a successor was chosen in April, 1882.
Since his administration was also brief his biographer
claims that it "was not marked by any notable activity."[7]

4. Sec. of Int. Report, 1877, p. xv.
5. L.O.R., 1885, pp. 4-5.
6. Ellis, op. cit., pp. 49 and 51.
7. D. E. Clark, Samuel J. Kirkwood, p. 363.

When Vice President Chester A. Arthur succeeded to the Presidency he met the responsibilities of his position in a manner that surprised his contemporaries. A recent study of his life has shown his desire for a reform administration.[8] Of all the problems which needed careful attention, none exceeded in importance those which grew out of the closely related facts of increased absorption and dwindling supply of available land. Railroad grants, timber and timberland, cattle-raising, Land Office requirements and extensive fraud all demanded a strong administration with well-laid policies. Judged by his message to Congress President Arthur displayed a wholesome interest in if not a vigorous attack on nearly all of these problems.[9] For instance he requested the settlement of the railroad survey and patent question so that railroad lands would afford their just share of taxes. He also expressed "serious apprehension (over) the conditions of the forests of the country and the wasteful manner in which destruction is taking place." In asking Congress to provide adequate protection for timber lands he warned that floods would result from any plan which would permit careless stripping from hillsides. The President also backed the efforts to improve conditions in the overburdened Land Office.

Unfortunately the President defeated his own reform program, especially any hope for a more satisfactory land administration, when he chose Senator Henry M. Teller of Colorado for Secretary of Interior. The reasons for this appointment are not clear. The new Secretary was not a particular friend of the President and he did not bring a strong following to his support. President Arthur had first considered Senator Sargent of California and Senator Chaffee of Colorado for the position.[10] In fact a newspaper report stated that the latter was at one time "almost in possession of the office" and that Senator Teller had worked hard to place him there.[11] But during a conference with the

---

8. George F. Howe, "Chester A. Arthur," p. 212 and passim.

9. Richardson, op. cit., vol. VIII, pp. 145-6 and 185.

10. N.Y. Times, April 7, 1882; and Howe, op. cit., pp. 163 and 212-3.

11. N.Y. Times, April 7, 1882.

President, when Senator Teller was urging the appointment of his colleague, he was asked to accept the position himself. The Senator answered, "Mr. President, I
am heartily opposed to you on the silver question, on
the Indian question and on the land question." Undis-
mayed the President made the curious reply, "That is
one reason why I insist upon having you in my cabinet
for I am well aware that you know more on each of these
questions in one minute than I could ever learn."[12] The
Senator did not accept immediately however, and it was
only after strong pressure was brought to bear that he
consented and took office in April, 1882.[13]

Secretary Teller was born in Allegany County,
New York, received a good education and then taught
school and studied law until he was admitted to the
bar.[13] Immediately thereafter he moved to Morrison,
Illinois, to practice law and engage in politics. Three
years later, at the outbreak of the Civil War, he moved
again, this time to Central City, Colorado, where he
became a staunch Union man and a Major General in the
Militia. Following the War he built up a lucrative law
practice as attorney for a number of corporations. He
also participated in various business enterprises and
served as President of the Colorado Central Railroad
for four years. His success enabled him to become a
large real estate and mine owner and in 1876 his prominence helped to secure his election as one of Colorado's
first Senators.[14]

His contacts had undoubtedly provided him with
first-hand knowledge of western needs but unfortunately
he had aligned himself with the predatory interests
which did not care for a proper solution for those
needs. While he was still a Senator Mr. Teller's law
practice had included services for Jay Gould and the
Union Pacific Railroad and this fact had caused even
the Denver Tribune to remark that he had been "on

---

12. Cleveland (Ohio) Herald, Dec. 7, 1882; quoted in N.Y. Times,
    Dec. 16, 1883.
13. National Cyclopedia of American Biography, vol. 15, p. 228;
    Dict. Am. Biog., vol. 18, p. 362.
14. N.Y. Times, April 7, 1882.

somewhat closer terms with Gould than a fine sense of
responsibility will justify."[15] The paper added however, that it believed that he would make an "entirely
honest and capable" Secretary. As a matter of fact his
association with a ruthless railroad plunger while
holding one official position foreshadowed his support
of other predatory interests while Secretary. His administration represents one of the most unusual in the
history of the Department for while he was called upon
to deal with increasingly important problems and to
plan for preventing widespread exploitation of the public domain he adopted some of the most pernicious rules
and practices ever credited to a Secretary. His record
will not stand comparison with that of his predecessor.
Where Secretary Schurz fostered timber conservation
Secretary Teller paid no attention to the subject and
on the contrary so liberalized the interpretation of
the laws as to permit their evasion. Instead of pressing for a solution of the pastoral lands problem Secretary Teller usurped legislative control of the range.
And finally though his predecessor had established at
least a partial check on railroads, Secretary Teller
seems to have allowed them practically free reign in
his office.

Before examining Secretary Teller's policies
farther it is necessary to note that his Land Office
Commissioner, Noah C. McFarland of Kansas, not only
bore a rather subordinate position in the land department, but in the light of increasing land absorption,
an onerous one as well. The Commissioner seems to have
been the moving force in seeking Congressional aid and
the Secretary could not very well ignore his official
duties when public land needs were strongly pointed out
by his subordinates. In all fairness to the Secretary,
however, it should be observed that many of his reports
sound sincere in seeking revision of particular laws
yet it is these reports combined with his biased policies which make his term so paradoxical. But to return
to the Commissioner. Information regarding his life
is scanty even in the extensive biographical collections

---

15. Quoted in **N.Y. Times**, March 29, 1882.

of Kansas. It is known however, that he originally
lived in Pennsylvania and then moved to Ohio where he
served in the State Legislature.[16] Later he took up
residence in Topeka, Kansas, and served at least one
term in the Legislature there. He was noted for his
legal ability and served for a time on the bench so
that he was popularly known as Judge McFarland. With
the full support of Kansas Congressmen, on June 17,
1881, President Garfield had appointed him Commissioner
and he continued to hold his position under President
Arthur. A contemporary described him as a "stalwart
Republican" and a "Western man (with) large and wide
experience in land matter."[17] A New York newspaper reported that he was said to be a man of decided ability
and to bear a high reputation for integrity. His honesty and legal acumen were to prove fortunate assets
during his three-year term as Commissioner.

Certainly one of the outstanding issues of the
Arthur-Teller period centered around the control timber
and timberland. It has already been shown that the
timber laws of 1878 did not provide a satisfactory solution for the timber problem and that wholesale fraud
and depredations continued. Secretary Schurz had declared that if the Government relaxed its vigilance
against trespassers or failed to amend the timber laws
conditions would grow more serious. Unfortunately his
fears proved all too accurate for Congress not only refused to modify the laws but as indicated above, Secretary Teller interpreted them quite freely. For instance though the Timber Cutting law prohibited taking
timber for commercial purposes, according to John Ise,
the Secretary allowed "lumber dealers, mill owners and
railroad contractors to cut timber for commercial purposes and for sale."[18] Furthermore because the law applied to certain States and "all other mineral districts of the United States" he permitted its use in
California and Oregon though these States were not mentioned in the act. The Supreme Court, however, reversed

16. N.Y. Tribune, June 17, 1881. (Omitted in R. and S. A. Baldwin,
      eds., "Illustriana Kansas Biographical Sketches," 1933.)
17. Copp, op. cit., July, 1881.
18. Ise, op. cit., p. 64 and note.

this rule by declaring that there was no way of determining a mineral district so that the law could not be
used outside of the Territories specifically designated.[19] Thus the Court appropriately plugged one loop-
hole which Congress had carelessly permitted and which
the Secretary had seized upon for timber interests. The
Secretary also assisted in despoiling timberland by his
remarkably liberal ruling on railroad right-of-way
privileges, a subject to be noted more fully later.

Despite this favoritism the Secretary's report
requested laws to curb the timber interests for they
were becoming constantly bolder in their illegal operations.[20] Commissioner McFarland had revealed the
abuses under the Timber and Stone Act when in 1883 he
reported, that "much of the most valuable timberland in
the possession of the Government on the Pacific Coast
is being taken up by home and foreign capitalists
through the medium of entries made by persons hired for
that purpose."[21] He felt compelled to suspend all timber entries and direct an examination "with a view to
the procurement of evidence in specific cases to authorize the cancellation of illegal entries and the prosecution of guilty parties." Investigations led to a few
indictments but no convictions so that fraud was resumed. The Commissioner also reported that he had
found forged soldiers' additional homestead certificates
turned in for valuable California timberlands.[22] The
timber had been cut and removed. Moreover timberlands
in Northern Minnesota had been so flooded with false
settlement entries that Commissioner McFarland felt compelled "to place 3,000,000 acres on the market at the
minimum price on agricultural land to avoid such wholesale criminality."[23] He did not state, however, whether
the land was surveyed or whether he had the strict right
to make the sale.

---

19. Ibid., p. 63.
20. The Secretary was principally backing or quoting the Commis-
    sioner's report. Sec. of Int. Report, 1884, p. xv.
21. L.O.R., 1883, p. 9.
22. Sen. Ex. Doc. #61. 47 Cong. 2 Sess. Serial #2076, p. 4.
23. Ibid.

The Commissioner with the Secretary's backing,
presented two solutions to the flagrant violations; increased appropriations for timber agents and withdrawal
of all timberlands until they had been examined and appraised.[24] He also recommended that Congress establish
permanent reserves before the land was all gone, especially at the headwaters of rivers. He could see no
reason why the settlement entries should be used to acquire so much timberland or why purchasers should pay
only $1.25 or $2.50 an acre for land worth $25.00 to
$100.00. In seeking larger appropriations for timber
agents the Commissioner showed that though the thirty-
six on part-time duty in 1884 had reported on 627 cases
of trespass where $7,290,000 worth of timber had been
taken, there was a surprisingly greater number of cases
that could not be reached.[25] He explained that one
reason for the increased violations was found in the
fact that free timberland was diminishing and corporations were therefore endeavoring to appropriate large
areas in order to control the product and its future
price.[26] But despite the tendency toward monopoly and
the methods used to achieve it Congress did not increase
the appropriations and enforcement continued under stag-
gering handicaps. In addition Congress ignored the
Commissioner's other recommendations.

Again in the case of pastoral lands Secretary
Teller combined usurpation of legislative right with a
commendable effort to secure the removal of illegal
fencing. Official warnings in the late Seventies that
the open range would soon vanish were practically fulfilled a half dozen years later for the expanding cattle business absorbed the most available areas. As a
result cattlemen sought to lease Indian Reservations
because such lands could be used cheaply and with a
measure of safety. Secretary Teller requested Congressional authority for regulating these leases[27] and

---

24. L.O.R., 1884, p. 18.
25. Ibid., p. 144 and 146.
26. L.O.R., 1883, p. 9. Some cut-over regions, however, were re-
    ported to possess a flourishing regrowth of timber. Special
    Report, 1879. Serial #1911, p. 444.
27. N.Y. Times, Nov. 28, 1884.

protecting the lessees but Congress failed to grant the
power. As a result the Secretary assumed it and encouraged leases even then they were contrary to Indian
treaty rights. Two days before he left office he also
opened Indian lands to grazing without receiving the
sanction of Congress and therefore presented President
Cleveland with a problem of possible hostilities which
could be averted only by revoking the leases.[28]

   While Secretary Teller was thus endeavoring to
serve the cattlemen he was forced to take cognizance of
the increasing illegal enclosures of the public domain
and to secure their removal. Prior to his term fencing
had become popular because of the exclusiveness which
it provided for ranchers. But settlers and the Government soon found that a great deal of fertile public
land was locked up and that public highways were
blocked. By 1882 the Land Office reported that illegal
enclosures had become "a matter of serious complaint."[29]
Since State or Territorial laws often provided a nominal
tax on enclosed land to ensure possessory right they
thus nullified the rights of settlers to locate on Federal property. The Land Office found that the courts
upheld these laws.[29]

   The land department had three possible methods
for redressing the evil and it used all of them. It
brought suit to secure the removal of illegal fences;
it authorized settlers to cut the fences and occupy any
public land; and it sought Congressional support for a
general anti-fencing bill so that court action would be
unnecessary. As early as December, 1882, Secretary
Teller requested the Attorney General to bring suit in
equity against Alexander H. Swan for illegal fencing in
Wyoming.[30] That every year the Land Office had requested a Congressional bill but the Department did not
wait for Congress to act. The Swan case is described
as the "first of the kind ever brought up in the courts
of the country." The Government won its suit in August,
1883, when Judge J. B. Sener declared that "unlawful

---

28. See chap. IX, post.
29. L.O.R., 1882, p. 13.
30. Quoted in Donaldson, op. cit., pp. 1174-9.

fencing of large tracts of public land constitutes first
a great public wrong and second a public nuisance"; he
therefore decreed that Mr. Swan must "discontinue the
use of the lands so unlawfully intruded and encroached
upon."

Another suit was started in 1883 when the Postmaster General complained that the Brighton Ranch Company of Nebraska had so fenced in lands as to cut off
established postal routes. The New York Times[31] later
remarked that "So defiant was this company and so notorious were its violations of the law that even Secretary Teller was induced to ask the Department of Justice to proceed against it in the courts." Something
of the company's character can be judged by the fact
that the Land Office had found that twenty of the fifty-
three entries by which it had acquired 7,000 acres,
were fraudulent.[32] In addition it had enclosed 125,000
acres of public land with fifty-six miles of fence and
a considerable part of the enclosure was fertile farming land from which settlers were frozen out. The Department of Justice sought an injunction in the District
Court to secure the removal of the fence. When the
Court granted the injunction the Company appealed to
the Supreme Court and in November, 1885, Justice Miller
delivered the opinion which upheld the District Court.[33]
It is interesting to observe that by that time Congress
had passed a bill to prohibit and punish illegal fencing and if the Court's decision had reversed the lower
court there would have been a surprising conflict of
rights.

Meanwhile on April 5, 1883, the Interior Department issued a circular to all Registers and Receivers
instructing them that fencing was illegal and that settlers who wished to reside on illegally enclosed land
could cut or destroy the fences.[34] The Government
guaranteed to prosecute any person or persons who endeavored to prevent such settlement. Gradually the land

---

31. Nov. 23, 1885.
32. Ibid.
33. Not reported, however, in the Supreme Court reports.
34. Sec. of Int. Report, 1883, p. xxxii. Osgood, op. cit., p. 192.

department collected statistics on the amount of fencing but it reported that it was unable to investigate
large numbers of complaints through "want of facilities.[35] By 1884 it had examined thirty-two cases involving 4,431,980 acres. Some reports of that time,
not necessarily referred to the Land Office, record enclosures of nearly a million acres like that of the
Arkansas Cattle Company in Colorado.[36] The Breeder's
Gazetter of May, 1884, recorded another enclosure at
the head of the Red River where there was 250 miles of
fence.[36] Such an extensive fence would have enclosed
more than 2,000,000 acres though actually in may have
included only 500,000. In still another instance the
famous partners, Miller and Lux, were reported to possess 600,000 acres in California in addition to a small
holding of 25,000 acres in Nebraska.[37]

It was impossible for settlers to challenge
such vast holdings and it would have proved costly and
difficult for the Government to bring suit against
every enclosure so the Land Office had recommended a
blanket provision making fences on the public domain
illegal. As a matter of fact a law passed in 1807 and
aimed at unlawful enclosures still existed. Under it
the President was authorized to direct the proper Federal officials to remove illegal boundaries and to call
on the military force if necessary. Although the Land
Office felt that it was only necessary to take action
under this law the Secretary doubted whether or not it
was operative.[38] The office therefore called for a law
that would stipulate penalties for illegal enclosing or
for attempting to prevent by force or intimidation entry

---

35. L.O.R., 1884, p. 17.
36. Quoted in Osgood, op. cit., p. 190.
37. Miller and Lux started as poor men and in twenty years they had
    become worth $8,000,000 and $10,000,000 respectively. Their
    irrigation canal in California was reputedly worth $1,000,000.
    Copp, op. cit., Jan. 15, 1885. Mr. Guernsey states that Miller
    possessed interests that surpassed in size and importance any
    others of similar character in the U.S., op. cit., pp. 26-8.
38. L.O.R., 1882, p. 13. For some reason Secretary Teller con-
    sidered it suspended. N.Y. Times, Aug. 18, 1885.

or settlement. A bill carrying those provisions was
reported in the House in 1883[39] but it did not pass until February 27, 1885.[40] Since its enforcement fell to
President Cleveland's administration it will be considered more fully below.

One aspect of the fencing problem was not
touched by the new law, however, because it involved
enclosing railroad lands in such a way as to include
Government sections even though there was no fence
built on Government land. This practice, too, had originated in the early Eighties when wealthy cattle companies bought great blocks of railroad land without the
exchanges which Secretary Schurz had suggested for Government and railroad holdings.[41] For instance H. L.
Osgood records that in 1882 the Union Pacific sold
750,000 acres for $1.00 an acre, along the Little
Missouri and Powder Rivers in Wyoming.[42] Two years
later the Swan Land and Cattle Company, reputedly one
of the strongest and wealthiest in the West, purchased
another 450,000 acres from the Union Pacific in Wyoming.[43] Since such purchases included only those alternate sections which the Government had granted, the
enclosures which the cattle companies erected on them
necessarily included public land. The system of fencing was called checkerboarding for the fence was built
along one side of a purchased section but terminated
just short of the corner. A slight space was thus reserved so that there would be no trespass on Government
land and the fence commenced again cat-a-corner on the
next purchased section. The intervening space was never
sufficiently large to allow cattle to squeeze through.
This system of checkerboarding not only permitted the
companies to enjoy the use of twice as much land as they
had purchased but it also presented a problem of

---

39. Quoted in Donaldson, op. cit., p. 1169.
40. 23 Stat., 321.
41. Cf. Sec. of Int. Report, 1886, p. 31.
42. Osgood, op. cit., p. 211.
43. Copp, op. cit., Oct. 1, 1884; Cf. Guernsey, op. cit., pp. 70-1.

enclosing public land which only Congress could solve. But Congress did not meet the issue by a law until the middle Nineties.[44]

While questions of timberland and pastoral lands became increasingly prominent neither of them equaled in importance the railroad problem. In the first place the time limits on the larger grants expired between 1876 and 1882 and toward the close of that period the demand for forfeiture rose steadily. Undoubtedly the demand was increased by the fact that railroads seem to have pretty consistently followed policies that made the public opposed to indulgence for breach of contract. The major transcontinental roads had received federal grants almost twice as large, proportionally, as the lesser roads, especially those smaller lines which had received their grants through the States. In addition many of the larger roads received generous financial assistance from the Government but they had almost uniformly evaded the obligations and abused the privileges which were the object of this generosity.[45] Not only did they escape the penalties for defaulted construction, defeat the purpose of paying for surveys and enjoy extraordinary favors from indemnity rights, as previously noted, but they fell far behind in their interest payments on Government loans and they neglected to establish a sinking fund for paying off the debt.[46] In addition they avoided building telegraph lines or carrying troops and supplies as required in the granting acts.[47] Meanwhile they corrupted local, State and Federal officials and charged freight and passenger rates that were grossly excessive. Other complaints against the roads included rebates, pools, stock jobbery by officials, hostility to settlers, exploitation of natural resources and excessive construction contracts[48]

44. Osgood, op. cit., p. 213.
45. Sen. Ex. Doc. #51, 60 Cong. 1 Sess., vol. II, p. 145ff.
46. Cummings and McFarland, op. cit., p. 272ff.
47. Ibid.
48. In 1881 the Auditor of Railroad Accounts estimated that the roads had spent $465,000,000 in building 5,425 miles of line. However he also estimated that it could be duplicated for $286,819,000. Quoted in Donaldson, op. cit., p. 911.

so that public opinion demanded retribution or at least
a strict construction of the granting acts where defaults had occurred.

Despite this crying need for supervision Congress procrastinated over calling the railroads to book
and the Interior Department seemed to go out of its way
to grant them further privileges and favors that bordered on the illegal. In the first place Secretary
Teller reversed his predecessor's policy in the case of
the Northern Pacific road and allowed it to secure indemnity without specifying where it had lost any of its
grant.[49] As a consequence the road flagrantly overdrew
its indemnity allowance and due to this fact and to
later developments it became one whose grant the Government struggled to adjust until 1940. Moreover Secretary
Teller reversed another of his predecessor's policies
and began issuing patents to roads for lands earned
after the grants had expired. He first favored the Atlantic and Pacific railroad,[50] the same one for which
Secretary Schurz had issued one set of patents, and then
gave patents to ten other roads. This procedure occurred while Congress continued to debate forfeiture
and while public opinion was becoming more insistent for
the adoption of some general policy. The Secretary
based his action on the Supreme Court's Schulenburg decision although there was nothing therein which required
an administrative office to complicate the Congressional
problem.[51]

Secretary Teller also assisted the railroads to
abuse their right-of-way privileges. As far back as
1835 the Government had permitted various undertakings
for internal improvements to take material from public
land for construction work. Later specific improvements
and individual railroads were granted the same privilege

---

49. Sec. of Int. Report, 1893, p. xiv.
50. L.O.R., 1883, p. 22; Haney, op. cit., p. 26.
51. He did suspend action for patents to the Oregon and California
    Railroad while Congress debated forfeiture of its grant.
    L.O.R., 1885, pp. 200-1. His policy was to issue patents if
    Congress adjourned after forfeiture debate without having
    reached a decision.

until in 1875 the Right-of-Way Act permitted all railroads to secure the necessary materials from public
lands "adjacent to the line of the road."[52]   In 1879
the Land Office complained that the number of railroads
seeking the privileges of the act was constantly increasing and that the Railroad Division of the Office
was overburdened with the necessity for approving the
applications. Congress gave the Office no assistance
and Secretary Teller made its duties more honorous by
broadening the interpretation of what constituted adjacent to the right-of-way. In individual grants the
right-of-way had been limited to either 100 or 200 feet
on either side of the line[53] but Secretary Teller entirely ignored the precedents and ruled that "adjacent
to" meant anywhere within fifty miles of the track and
even beyond the limits of the road.[54] He thus turned a
restricted privilege into license and thereby invited
wholesale abuse of the law. A flagrant case occurred
with the organization of the Union River Logging Company in Washington.[55] Though the road was ostensibly
created for the purpose of ordinary railroad business,
since it requested and received right-of-way privileges,
it built five miles of track into the thickest timber
region in the Territory and engaged in the logging business for years. There was no pretense of carrying pas-
sengers or freight except the logs stolen from Government land.

It is necessary to postpone the consideration
of Secretary Teller's policy for protecting settler's
rights of railroad lands though there can be no hesitation in summarizing it as the reverse of Secretary
Schurz's and therefore favorable to the roads. On the
other hand it is pertinent to recall that Secretary
Teller provided another privilege for railroads in the
use of certified lists. In 1857 the Land Office had
furnished railroads with certified lists of the lands

---

52. L.O.R., 1879, p. 458.
53. Cf. Union Pacific Grant. 12 Stat. 489; Atlantic and Pacific
    grant. 14 Stat. 292,
54. Ise, op. cit., p. 83.
55. Ibid. Quoting Opinions of the Attorney General. pp. 19, 547.

which they might earn, though it was expressly stipulated in a decision of the Attorney General that these
lists were for information only and carried no rights
or title. But in 1883 Secretary Teller decided that
they did carry title the same as a patent and were
therefore an established right against settlement.[56]
The Land Office had not originally made the careful
check of land that might be earned and so there might
have been many errors which should have been corrected
before the lists were used as the basis for patents.
The Secretary, however, placed the advantage with the
railroads.

Another instance of flagrant favoritism and
virtual defiance of Congressional rights is connected
with the Secretary's eagerness to issue patents for the
New Orleans, Baton Rouge and Vicksburg Railroad grant,
later called the Backbone grant.[57] This grant had been
made in 1871 as a part of the Texas and Pacific granting act and had carried over a million acres for a road
running up the middle of Louisiana.[58] But not a foot
of the road had ever been constructed; in fact the grant
became shot through with charges of bribery, fraud,
chicanery, "judicial legerdemain," and speculation.
After it had expired certain of the company's stockholders, without any authority, sold the grant for one
dollar to the New Orleans Pacific road. The latter was
constructing a line in a different location from that
called for in the Backbone grant and at first the New

---

56. L.O.R., 1885, p. 35. The Secretary based his position on the
    Leavenworth, Lawrence and Galveston Railroad Co. case decision.
    92 U.S. 733 (1875). But the statute dealing with certified
    list and the one on which the Supreme Court's decision was
    based is qualified in its approval. 10 Stat. 346.
57. The N.Y. Times denounced this grant by stating: "In all the
    history of land grant legislation there can be found nothing to
    surpass the 'Backbone' job in the way of corruption." May 19,
    1884.
58. 16 Stat. 593. The subsequent history of the grant can be found
    in House Report #678. 48 Cong. 1 Sess. Serial #2255; Sen. Ex.
    Doc. #31. 48 Cong. 1 Sess. Serial #2162; N.Y. Sun, Jan. 1,
    1883; Haney, op. cit., p. 130-33; U.S. Report, #1016. 48 Cong.
    2 Sess; and N.Y. Times, July 2, 1882.

Orleans Pacific officials had claimed they did not need
a grant to complete their work. Later however, the company had fallen under the control of Jay Gould and it
was he who arranged the purchase from the Backbone company. Gould then endeavored to secure the Interior Department's ratification to the purchase and when he succeeded he pressed for issuance of patents. The secret
arrangement made with the Backbone company at the time
of the purchase not only benefited the latter's stockholders but it also redounded to the financial benefit
of the construction company which Gould controlled.
While pressure was being exerted on the Interior Department Congress had been debating the question of forfeiting the grant but no decision was reached just before President Arthur's term expired. When Secretary
Teller saw that the bill might not pass and because he
knew that the incoming President, Cleveland, would probably reform the lax Republican policies, he set the Land
Office clerks at work on the last evening and Sunday of
the Republican term and so managed to issue patents to
over 600,000 acres for the benefit of his friend, Jay
Gould. This act matches the Secretary's secret opening
of the Indian Reservation when Congress delayed adopting a bill that would have met the problem. Both are
indefensible on any grounds of administrative obligations.

On the other hand Secretary Teller should be
credited for urging a solution of survey and forfeiture
problems. In his reports for 1883 he reviewed the injustice of permitting the roads to use their lands
without paying taxes on them and he also requested definitive action for forfeiture.[59] He had felt the press
of public opinion for he declared that it had become imperative that Congress "not only remedy the evil suggested but enable his Department to reach a finality as
to the titles to be conveyed to these corporations at
the earliest possible moment, and thus relieve an anxious and excited public feeling, already sufficiently
aroused upon the various difficult and complicated questions connected with the administration of this momentous
and important branch of public affairs."

---

59. Sec. of Int. Report, 1883, pp. xxxiv-xxxv.

In the following years he renewed his request
and presented statistics on survey deficiencies. He
estimated that there were 34,658,256 acres in grants
for completed railroad lines.[60] The owners of these
roads had paid the Government $219,715 for the survey
of a little more than 8,000,000 acres, most of which
had been patented. But that meant that out of the
total amount earned nearly four-fifths or 26,500,000
acres, remained to be surveyed at an estimated cost of
$1,000,000. The failure to secure survey and patent
for railroad lands forms a curious contrast to the accounts of railroad efforts to populate their grants.
Of course it was the Pacific roads that were most at
fault, the Union Pacific and Central Pacific being the
greatest laggards. Congress, however, resisted the demand for requiring surveys and patents until several
years after Secretary Teller's term.

Failure to secure surveys not only permitted
tax evasion but timber depredations as well. An outstanding example of brazen cutting is furnished by the
Montana Improvement Company.[61] Despite its high sound-
ing name the company was organized to monopolize timber
traffic in Montana and Idaho, along the Northern Pacific railroad. In fact it was almost entirely owned by
the railroad and rather significantly was organized in
1883 when Secretary Teller held office. Its capital
stock amounted to $2,000,000 and it secured a twenty-
year contract with the road for the exploitation of timber along the line. It seems to have concentrated on
securing timber from unsurveyed regions and the subsequent attempts at prosecution for stripping Government
timber failed largely because the Government could not
prove, in the absence of surveys, where its own lands
lay.[62] This prosecution will be noted more fully in a
subsequent chapter.

---

60. Ibid, 1884, p. xix; and Sen. Ex. Doc. #51, op. cit., vol. II,
    p. 145.
61. L.O.R., 1885, pp. 311-4 and chap. XIII post.
62. The granting act of 1864 stipulated that the road should be
    surveyed as fast as construction required. The President was
    authorized to carry out the provisions of the act but it was
    probably neglected through lack of appropriations. 13 Stat.
    365.

Secretary Teller's repeated requests for a Congressional policy of forfeiture were duplicated by suggestions from the Land Office, newspaper and magazine writers, political parties and congressmen. Yet despite an enormous amount of activity in regard to grants and forfeitures Congress delayed adopting any policy. Commissioner McFarland reported that settlers were anxious to know whether they should seek titles from the roads or from the Government. The Commissioner declared in 1883, "The public demand for a definitive settlement....is constantly pressed upon my attention."[63] He was backed by reformists papers like the New York Times which blamed the Senate for obstructing the passage of forfeiture bills.[64]

Expressions of public opinion were by no means unanimously favorable to a policy of forfeiture. Divergent view may be found in magazine articles by George W. Julian and John W. Johnston. The former favored complete forfeiture for roads whose grants had lapsed and he published a defense of his plan under the title "Our Land Grant Railways in Congress."[65] He explained that the value of the grants to the large Pacific roads was not "well known" in the 1860's but that the altered conditions of the country since that time should guide Congress in performing its duty in forfeiting lapsed grants. Mr. Julian not only believed that such action would restore 100,000,000 acres that had been unearned but that it would also bring about the return of indemnity lands. Furthermore the release of the Government's section within the granted limits, unusuable because of failure to survey them, would open up a total of 200,000,000 acres to public settlement. Mr. Julian did not have much faith in a rigorous Congressional policy but he hoped to stir up a stronger sentiment for forfeiture than Congress was manifesting in 1883.

Two years later Mr. Johnston presented a case for leniency to the railroads.[66] He felt that Congress

---

63. L.O.R., 1883, pp. 22-3.
64. Feb. 14, 1885.
65. International Review, Feb.-Mar. 1883.
66. North American Review, March, 1885.

would not deal harshly with them and that since it did
not have the time to inquire into the merits of each
lapsed grant it should allow them to be settled in
court. This view had been upheld by Senator Morgan of
Alabama rather consistently in Congress. Mr. Johnston
believed that the Government should recognize that the
Pacific roads were undertaken as national enterprises
and as such, deserved special consideration. He pointed
out that the Government itself had allowed its own sinking fund to fall behind to the extent of more than
$50,000,000 in the depression following 1873; as a con-
sequence railroads should receive indulgence for their
defaults.

Despite its continued delay in providing general treatment Congress did forfeit three more grants
in 1884-85.[67] These included the St. Louis and Iron
Mountain grant in its entirety, the Oregon Central grant
for that portion of the road which was unfinished in
1885, and all of the 13,000,000 acres tendered to the
Texas and Pacific road. It is instructive to examine
the Texas and Pacific grant in some detail in order to
explain the difficulties encountered in the move for
general forfeiture. Incidentally the jealousy with
which Congress guarded the right of forfeiture is
matched only by its indifference to the complications
which Secretary Teller added by his issuing patents.
That jealousy is well illustrated by Congressional
haste to inquire by resolution concerning the truth of
a report that the Land Office had ruled the Northern
Pacific grant in default. Even though the Office sent
a prompt denial to the Senate the House too insisted on
obtaining a similar statement for itself after the
former had been received.[68] But to return to the forfeiture of the Texas and Pacific grant. .As noted above
the grant was made in 1871 as one of the last of the
large grants and one around which charges of bribery,
preceding its passage, persisted. The road had come

67. L.O.R., 1885, p. 187ff.
68. Sen. Ex. Doc. #64 and H. Ex. Doc. #63. 47 Cong. 1 Sess.
    quoted in Donaldson, op. cit., pp. 874ff and 879ff.

under the control of Thomas R. Scott, President of the
Pennsylvania Railroad and a backer of western enterprises, though he had been unable to build it.[69]   Meanwhile C. P. Huntington of the Southern Pacific railroad
began building along much the same route as that intended by Scott.   Mr. Huntington not only pushed his
line to completion under bitter rivalry with Mr. Scott
but he also accomplished it without the aid of a land
grant.[70]   A few years later, however, when Scott had
given up control of the Texas and Pacific and had been
succeeded by Jay Gould, Gould and Huntington endeavored
to transfer the Texas and Pacific grant to the Southern
Pacific.   Since the grant had not been needed for the
construction its transfer would have represented an extremely large bonus for the Southern Pacific.[70]

While the companies sought to have the Interior
Department approve the transfer, just as Gould tried
and succeeded in the Backbone case, Congress debated
the question of forfeiting the grant.[71]   The Democratic
Campaign Handbook for 1884 asserted that the efforts
for forfeiture brought out the railroad lobby in full
force and that it endeavored to have Congress transfer
the grant to the Southern Pacific.   Metropolitan newspapers charged that corruption and bribery were used to
influence Congressmen and in truth there was a strange
delay in passing the forfeiture bill.[72]   As early as
August, 1882, the House Judiciary Committee, which was
inclined to be so lenient with the Northern Pacific
railroad, brought in an unprinted report and resolution
favoring forfeiture of the grant without assigning it
to the Southern Pacific.[73]   The House did not act on
the resolution in the few days before it adjourned but
oddly enough there was no printed copy of the resolution or report to be found; and no printed copy was
ever filed in the document room of the House.   It was
later charged[74] that Committee chairman Reed pocketed

---

69. Dict. of Am. Biog.
70. N.Y. Times, Feb. 20, 1885; Democratic Campaign Handbook, 1884,
    p. 196ff.
71. Taken up in 48 Cong. 2 Sess. Cong. Rec., p. 104.
72. N.Y. Times, Jan. 5, 1885.
73. Dem. Camp. Handbook, 1884, p. 193ff.
74. Ibid.

both resolution and report and not until two years
later did he secure permission to print them. Then in
1884 the House passed a forfeiture bill, 260-1, under
the leadership of Representative Payson of Illinois.[75]
In the Senate, however, a series of obstructionary
tactics developed.

When the bill first came up Senator Morgan of
Alabama asked for its postponement in order that the
Senate might be guided by the conference report on the
Atlantic and Pacific forfeiture bill.[76] He explained
that in the latter bill the House had demanded complete
forfeiture of the 22,600,000 acre grant but that the
Senate had provided for the return of those sections
unearned by 1884. So in order to profit by the conference report the Senate agreed to postpone consideration of the Texas and Pacific bill. This initial delay
continued for months, however, for the Atlantic and
Pacific bill conference report made no difference to
the Texas bill and each time it came up in its regular
place on the calendar Senator Blair of New Hampshire,
or a colleague, moved the consideration of some other
measure.[77] Finally Senator Van Wyck of Nebraska, described by the New York Times[78] as the only man who
"does not appear to have fallen under the influence of
Huntington and Gould," became more aggressive in efforts to secure consideration of the bill. On February
13, 1885, he secured unanimous consent to speak in behalf of debate. He remarked that "The very moment a
land grant forfeiture comes up in this body terror
reigns in some directions..... There is no question to
be considered which has not been discussed. The matter
has been considered in other bills."[79] He felt that
neither the Texas and Pacific nor the Southern Pacific
had any claim on the generosity of Congress and he referred with biting sarcasm to the famous correspondence
between Huntington and "friend Bolton," wherein bribery
and undue influence on Congress were strongly suggested.

75. N.Y. Times, Jan. 5, 1885.
76. 48 Cong. 2 Sess. Cong. Rec., p. 104.
77. Ibid., pp. 473, 1254-5, 1492, 1549 and 1570.
78. Feb. 14, 1885.
79. Cong. Rec., op. cit., pp. 1619-21.

Senator Blair made an effort to excuse the delay in considering the bill by saying that he objected
to certain of its features though he was not prepared
to discuss them. A roll call following this debate
showed that the Senate was opposed to even debating
the bill,[80] so delay continued. A few days before newspaper reports stated that a caucus of Republican Senators had voted against taking up the bill.[81] It is
curious to note, however, the Senator Van Wyck was a
Republican. Moreover a week later the latter caught
Senator Blair napping and despite all efforts to avoid
a showdown or to postpone application of the bill it
passed by a surprising vote in which only two Senators
registered opposition.[82] It scarcely seems possible
that a bill which had so little recorded opposition
should have been delayed so long but the partisans of
the land grant railroads did not always show their
colors in the open. The bill was signed by President
Arthur a few days before his term ended and he thereby
restored the entire grant to the public domain.[83]

Perhaps it is a little remarkable that the bill
passed at all for the Atlantic and Pacific bill had to
wait over until President Cleveland's administration
and Congress delayed adopting a general policy even
longer. It is evident, however, that railroad problems
were both serious and manifold and that there was apparently little likelihood of settling them under Republican auspices. Not only did the Republican Senate
and a Republican Secretary of Interior strongly favor
the roads but Congress allowed the Bureau which supervised their grants to reach a pitiable state of decrepi-
tude. It is therefore necessary to examine the duties
and burdens of the Land Office and to see that not only
the Railroad Division but every branch of the Office
contained inadequate facilities to meet increasingly
heavy responsibilities.

---

80. Cong. Rec., op. cit., p. 1621.
81. N.Y. Times, Feb. 11, 1885.
82. Ibid., pp. 1876-85; 1887-99.
83. N.Y. Times, Feb. 20, 1885; 23 State. 337. 15,000,000 acres
    were restored.

Chapter VII

THE INADEQUATE LAND OFFICE

There is an obvious need for overhauling any
Government bureau when $1,800 a year clerks can, with
the aid of the lawyer for an interested party, dispose
of cases involving property worth $1,000,000. And if
the bureau is not reorganized over a considerable period
its history warrants close scrutiny. A specific instance of this kind of neglect occurred in connection
with the General Land Office at Washington, particularly
in the years 1870-90. During those two decades the Office invariably possessed such inadequate manual and material equipment that it was not only unable to perform
a great portion of its work but it was also easily subject to baneful influences. Actually the Office's importance called for the creation of a well-staffed Department which could have been subject to the pressure
of public opinion. The justice of this remark lies in
the fact that the Bureau represented a bottle-neck
through which the distribution of hundreds of millions
of acres of agricultural, timber, mineral, pastoral and
potentially valuable desert lands passed. Moreover it
was the center for disputes which might involve title to
lands worth at least $25,000,000.[1] Consequently a study
of the Bureau's responsibilities and handicaps should
aid in analyzing the factors which kept it obscure and
neglected.

In the first place it is necessary to recall
that since its creation in 1812, the Land Office had

---

1. In 1879 Representative A. S. Hewitt of New York declared that
the Commissioner of the Land Office was "the most important law
officer of the Government if measured by the money involved in
his decisions." 45 Cong. 3 Sess. Cong. Rec., p. 1205.

experienced a haphazard growth for the new obligations which it received from time to time were not accompanied by legislative assistance. Especially after 1875 complicated laws and increased absorption brought heavy burdens. In order to meet these burdens Commissioner Williamson had called attention to the necessity for improving the pay, personnel and equipment of the Office and Congress had responded by furnishing a library, the codification of laws and the facilities for official publication of decisions. On the other hand questions of the increase in staff and pay, not to mention the establishment of a court, had been largely overlooked. In 1881 Commissioner McFarland had finally created a Board of Law Review, which as its name implies, was not a trial court but merely a three man committee for analyzing laws.[2] The Land Office judicial machinery remained, therefore, in an undeveloped state and like other branches of the Office, waited on legislative assistance.

But Congress remained indifferent to the Bureau's needs so that as its business increased its work became further and further delayed. Indeed for at least two decades the Office presents an almost unrelieved picture of steadily mounting arrears. In 1879 Copp's Land Owner recorded that the Mineral Lands Division had 3,064 entries pending.[3] The paper estimated that the entire Division would need two years to clear away these cases if meanwhile it ignored current work. Mining cases were occasionally quite complicated and in order to settle conflicting rights a clerk might have to read 1,000 or more pages of testimony. And while settlement was delayed capital investment was usually held up until patents issued.

Other Divisions in the Office were also greatly in arrears. For example the Preëmption Division had increased its undisposed cases from 454 in 1876 to 3,628 two years later. Moreover there were 9,000 cases where agricultural patents had been approved but not issued because there were not enough clerks.[4] The correspondence

---

2. Conover, op. cit., p. 29.
3. March, 1879.
4. Ibid.

of the Office was reported to have increased 30% within
a year, bringing it 50% in arrears. The most outstanding example of inadequate personnel, however, is found
in the Draughting Division. Fifty years before Congress
had authorized the Bureau to secure one Draughtsman but
by 1879 there was a need for fifteen; yet appropriations
still provided for one and an assistant.

On the threshold of the period of extensive land
absorption the Public Land Commission presented a comprehensive review of the results of Congressional neglect and offered a simple scheme for increasing efficiency and bringing the Office up to date.[5] Its report
showed that during the previous twenty years the number
of surveying districts had increased from ten to sixteen;
the District Land Offices had increased from fifty-three
to ninety-four; the amount of land surveyed had doubled
and the amount absorbed had tripled; yet the Land Office
had grown smaller. Since the Office seemed to contain
an excess of physical force and a deficiency of brain
force the Commission recommended an addition of higher
grade clerks. They would increase the number of workers
and the cost of the Office slightly, from $273,000 to
$321,000, but after the arrears were cleared up there
could be a reduction in numbers and expense below even
the previous cost. The Commission's specific suggestions included increasing the Commissioner's salary to
$6,000; establishing an office of Assistant Commissioner;
and providing for nine chiefs of Division at $2,400,
with ten assistants at $2,000, in place of the three ex-
isting chiefs at $1,800. Increasing the number of heads
of Divisions would have made it unnecessary for the Office to depend on the services of clerks to supervise
its Railroad and other important Divisions.

The Public Land Commission also called attention
to the cramped quarters in which the Office labored.
"The room allotted to the General Land Office," it declared, "is not quite the worst that it could be, nor
is it wholly inadequate, but it approximates both."[6] Because of these conditions the Commission estimated that

---

5. Report, 1880, p. xff.
6. Ibid., p. xiv.

the Government lost one-fourth of the money it appropriated for clerical force. There was little opportunity for efficient work when, for instance, filing cabinets could not be properly arranged; eight years before the Commissioner had reported that he was forced to crowd his files out into the halls of the building.[7] At a later time the offices of the Bureau was scattered in different buildings.[8]

Of course both the Secretary of Interior and the Commissioner supported the Commission's recommendations for the Commissioner had served as one of its members. Secretary Schurz called attention to the importance of securing more capable heads of Divisions for they prepared decisions "that involve property of greater value than cases decided by any State Supreme Court in the country."[9] He admitted that the Office had been well supplied with applicants during the depression years but he foresaw that with returning prosperity the Government offices "would be more and more drained of the ablest public servants," unless the Government took steps to improve their salaries and lighten their responsibilities. The Commissioner had revealed that his ablest men were "overworked days, nights and Sundays in the effort to perform properly the grave duties imposed by law" and certainly they would seek employment elsewhere as soon as opportunity offered.[10]

Despite the simplicity of the Commission's suggestions and the necessity for their adoption Congress did not respond. When the Commissioner saw that no changes would result he suggested that a joint committee of the House and Senate investigate the Office and become convinced of its needs. Why there should have been any doubts regarding the predicament portrayed by Commissioner, Secretary and Commission is difficult to explain. Incidentally the Commissioner's suggestion would seem to have cast a serious reflection on the standing committees of Congress. Though the House did not respond

7. L.O.R., 1872, p. 22.
8. Chap. XV, post.
9. Sec. of Int. Report, 1880, p. 81.
10. L.O.R., 1880, p. 415.

to the proposal for an investigation, in 1881 the Senate
authorized its Committee on Public Land to make a personal inspection of the Land Office. Consequently in
April of the following year the Committee was able to
make a report which more than verified previous reports.

The Committee found that the Bureau needed a
new building more than any other Bureau or Department in
the Government.[11]   In the first place the lack of sufficient room, light and ventilation was considered very
damaging to the health of Land Office employees. Furthermore the cramped quarters not only caused delay in work
but they were so constructed that they exposed valuable
papers to damage by fire and theft. A serious fire in
1877 had put the Office two months further behind in its
business. And finally the lack of protection for land
records had permitted their destruction by mold and de-
cay and the ravages of insects and vermin.

The Committee also found an appalling amount of
unattended cases so in order to clear them up it recommended a special appropriation of $100,000 for employing
forty-two special clerks. Because of the increase in
arrears during the previous two years, the Committee had
suggested twice the allotment proposed by the Public
Land Commission. In explaining the cause for the arrears the Committee declared that the "fault lay in the
system" of conducting business and that both Congress
and inefficient administration must share the blame. It
minimized administrative faults, however, when it noted
that Division Chiefs were generally able and efficient
and that employees performed their duties diligently and
faithfully. In fact the report claimed that clerks had
shown more ability than could be expected from men whose
salaries enabled them merely to "eke out a bare existence." The Committee provided a bit of grim humor when
it recorded that although salaries ranged from only
$1,000 to $1,800, there was little "alleged against (the
employees') honor." Certainly the Committee and Congress were responsible for failing to increase salaries
and for thereby rendering temptation less attractive.

---

11. Sen. Report #362. 47 Cong. 1 Sess., Serial #2006.

In addition to taking up the problems of poor
quarters and an insufficient staff the Senate Committee
also considered the burdens which the Land Office placed
on the Interior Department. After noting that the Secretary's time was taken up by a great variety of duties
the Committee suggested two alternatives for relieving
him: either it was the plain duty of Congress to transfer some of his Department Bureaus to another Department
or to create a Department of Public Lands. The Committee not only preferred the latter but after discussing
the benefits which it would bring, concluded: "This
fact is so patent that it needs no discussion."[12] It is
not difficult to imagine that under direct Departmental
supervision there would have been a much brighter story
of public land administration. Undoubtedly the administrative personnel would have been of a higher standard
than that which was permitted to obtain in the Land Office. Furthermore the public could have been better informed and therefore more able to exert a wholesome influence on land policies. Yet somehow the proposal for
a Department never took root. In 1870 the National Union Congress, meeting at Cincinnati, had called for a
Department and though there was increasing discussion
on the question thereafter, Milton Conover has declared
that following the Senate Committee recommendation in
1882, the proposition made "but little advance."[13] Not
only did Congress ignore that suggestion but it paid
practically no attention to the other Committee recommendations.

The increase in land absorption after 1882 meant
increased burdens for the Land Office and, increased arrears of work. In the fall following the Committee report the Secretary of Interior requested 100 additional
Land Office Clerks.[14] Office work had risen by a third
and the existing forces were able to handle only 70% of
it. Congress seems to have responded to his plea by
providing for a ten per cent increase in staff, but one-
half of the increase was assigned to the prevention of

12. Ibid., p. viii.
13. Op. cit., p. 29.
14. Sec. of Int. Report, 1882, p. xix.

frauds and therefore did not apply to routine work.[15] In
1883 the Commissioner observed that the "increase in
working force and appropriations has been doled out in
pittances and seemingly more to accommodate the Department than to meet the demands of the service." He reported further expansion of work over the previous year
and showed that instead of the 140,000 cases which the
Senate Committee had found pending the number had risen
to 600,000, and this figure did not include railroad,
swamp, mineral and private land claims. The Commissioner therefore requested 200 additional clerks for he calculated that "If but one-half of the claims should be
perfected into title it would take the present force employed upon this work three years to complete the adjustments leaving the whole volume of business that might
come up within that period unprovided for."[16]

Instead of devoting most of his time to important decisions and the formulation of policies Commissioner McFarland was forced to spend two or three hours
daily merely signing his name to an average of five hundred documents.[17] Fortunately in 1884 he was given an
assistant who relieved him of some of that burden but
Congress did not provide similar assistance to the chiefs
of Divisions. The Commissioner was able to point out in
1884 that the Office was no longer able to retain its
ablest clerks and that Congress alone could remedy the
situation. In fact he expressed a very true but not
widely held belief when he declared that "A proper protection of the public lands and provision for a speedy
adjustment of the claims of settlers appear to me to be
among the most important matters than can engage the attention of Congress at the approaching session."[18]

It is interesting to observe that instead of coöperation for the land service Congress refused the request to allot to the Office even the $8,000 a year
which it earned by copying land records for applicants.
That paltry sum would have permitted the Office to employ

15. L.O.R., 1883, p. 31.
16. Ibid., p. 32.
17. Ibid., p. 33.
18. Ibid., p. 34.

eight lower grade clerks or ten copyists but since it
was withheld, the copying continued to be performed by
regular clerks with "corresponding loss to the ordinary
business of the office."[19]

In the year before the Democrats took office under President Cleveland land officials felt the hopeless-
ness of performing their tasks. Land absorption had
reached record heights and there seemed to be no way to
stop the overwhelming number of fraudulent cases or to
handle the valid ones. In the face of these tremendous
odds the Commissioner strongly felt that the only remedy
lay in legislative action. He declared, "I have discharged my duty in presenting this subject as I have
from time to time in my annual reports and in special reports submitted to Congress as clearly and forcibly as I
could, and I leave to the higher power of that body the
responsibility of determining the course to be pursued."[20]

Reserving a discussion of the causes for Congressional neglect it is significant to note that the Land
Office was further handicapped by the inferior work of
the District Land Offices. The Public Land Commission
had endeavored to improve their efficiency by repeating
a previous suggestion for consolidating the positions of
Register and Receiver.[21] It also suggested an adequate
salary rather than the salary and fee system, and defended its proposals by claiming that they would eliminate
duplications, confusion, injustice, expense to settlers
and greater cost to the Government. But Congress failed
to make any changes, probably because two political plums
were better than one. Consequently the District Offices
continued to attract "mercenary adventurers" who could
not or would not enable the land service to work smooth-
ly.

It would be quite unfair to apply an epithet to
all local officials but it is a notorious fact that in

---

19. Ibid., p. 27.
20. Quoted in Sec. of Int. Report, 1884, p. xv.
21. Report, 1880, p. xviii. In 1879 there were 188 Registers and
    Receivers. They were paid $373,555, or an average salary of
    $1,988. Consolidation in accordance with the Commission's sug-
    gestions could have saved $91,555.

districts where frauds were the most brazen either the
officials were the only individuals unaware of what was
taking place or they were in league with the defrauders.
The California Redwood and the Colorado Coal Company[22]
cases illustrate the point and will be taken up more
fully later but there is also testimony from the head of
a large lumber company at Duluth, Minnesota.[23] The latter once stated that he, with his associates, had acquired thousands of acres of pine lands under the Preëmption act by simply filing the names of persons found
in the St. Paul and Chicago directories. He had a
standing agreement with the local land officers whereby
he could complete these entries for a consideration of
$25.00 each.

In defense of local officials it is necessary to
recall that they might suspect fraud but they lacked the
means for securing evidence to prove it.[24] Time after
time Congress was asked to authorize them to compel witnesses to testify in cases where questionable entries
had been made but Congress did not respond. Witnesses
refused to voluntarily jeopardize their lives by testi-
fying, especially when a large share of the community
might be guilty of the same offense.[25] Since the local
offices could not secure evidence they had to pass on
to the General Land Office cases in which there was no
adequate basis for a fair or accurate decision. The Office, of course endeavored to secure additional testimony in such instances but that involved extensive correspondence with a proportionate loss of time and effort;
Congress could have easily prevented the inefficiency by
granting subpoena powers to local officials.

The local offices also helped burden the General
Land Office by sending in apparently arbitrary decisions
in disputed cases. The extra work required in checking
over these decisions, however, cannot entirely be

---

22. Chaps. X and XIII, post.
23. Ise, op. cit., p. 80, quoted from "Report on the Lumber Indus-
    try," I, op. cit., pp. 260-1.
24. L.O.R., 1877, p. 32; 1886, p. 101. The power was finally given
    in 1903, 32 Stat. 790.
25. Yard, op. cit., p. 100.

ascribed to the faults of local offices because they
lacked well-established precedents; the General Land Office itself gave conflicting decisions. Evidence on
this point is found in Copp's Land Owner for June, 1885,
where the Editor states, "On our visit to Dakota last
year the land rulings were continually assailed with protests, profanity, and ridicule. Local officers from
sheer despair were compelled to rely on their own judgment without reference to the instructions received, and
attorneys on a given statement of fact never pretend to
forecast a decision."

The subject of Land Office decisions will be
taken up again but it is necessary to recall that Congress did endeavor to check up on the activities of the
local offices. In 1882 it provided three extra Land Office clerks for the purpose of inspecting both District
and Surveyor Generals' offices. Three men proved so
pitifully inadequate that in the following year Congress
responded to a special request and provided thirty.[26]
These clerks or agents were then grouped with the timberland agents to form the Special Service Division of the
Land Office. The records of the Division therefore include in an inseparable form both the activities for
handling timber violations and supervision of local and
surveying offices. Unfortunately the Division was
handicapped in a number of ways. It was always under-
staffed for the enormous areas which it was required to
cover. Its efficiency was limited by the fact that
agents could not compel submission of evidence in suspected cases. And while there is no way to assess accurately the temptations which were thrown in their way
it is a well-known fact that agents were bribed by depredators or violators, were offered profitable employment in return for favors or were so negligent or careless in their duties that frauds were perpetrated in
their presence.[27] The work of the Division was further
impaired by a constant turnover of agents, partly charge-
able to the above factors and partly due to insufficient
appropriations. For instance in 1882 the Commissioner
stated that out of the 31 timber agents employed during

---

26. Conover, op. cit., p. 29.
27. See California Redwood Co. case. Chap. XIII, post.

the year only seven remained in continuous service.[28]
Furthermore there are instances in which agents uncovered
fraud and yet since they proved uncorruptible they were
discharged through influence exerted in the land department.[29]

The fluctuations in the Special Service Division
staff characterized the entire Land Office. Secretary
Schurz had predicted a rapid turnover of clerks unless
Congress remedied their handicaps in pay and work. But
since Congress continued to permit other bureaus to offer higher salaries than those paid in the Land Office,
Commissioner McFarland found that he could not retain
his better clerks. In 1883 he cited an instance where
two valuable clerks holding positions "requiring skill
of a high order" received pay increases of $700 to $400
respectively by transfer to positions of equal rank in
another Department.[30] In fact as stated earlier positions outside the Land Office were invariably more attractive for any employee of ability. Many clerks
stayed in the Office only long enough to master the law
and technique in land cases or until they received a
favorable offer for some outside concern. The New York
World for May 23, 1885 listed fourteen former Land Office employees who had found lucrative employment with
railroads or other corporations, or had entered the
practice of law before the Interior Department. The paper stated that it was presenting only the most prominent
cases though it could continue the list indefinitely.
The list included two former Commissioners, Burdett and
Williamson, and a former Assistant Attorney General of
the Interior Department, E. M. Marble. Copp's Land
Owner also recorded the activities of former employees
and noted that ex-Commissioner Williamson was receiving
$10,000 as an attorney for the Atlantic and Pacific Rail-
road and that General E. M. Marble received the same from
the Northern Pacific road.[31]

---

28. L.O.R., 1882, p. 250.
29. Ise, op. cit., p. 75; chaps. XII and XIII, post. Further handicaps were provided when Secretary Teller ruled that entries
could not be cancelled solely on Special Agents' reports.
Furthermore agents had to be very careful of libel charges.
Copp, op. cit., Jan. 1, 1884; Oct. 15, 1884.
30. L.O.R., 1883, p. 33.
31. December, 1881.

Henry Copp, the able editor of the Land Owner, was himself a former Land Office employee. A. T. Britton's former clerkship has already been noted and his partner, Grey, had been similarly employed. Another interesting example of graduation from the Office is furnished by the case of J. R. Randall; he worked his way to the highest clerkship in four years and then resigned for private practice.[32] He joined D. K. Sickels, a former chief of the Mineral Division. The American government has frequently provided a training school for able men who were to become engaged in a business that was sometimes antagonistic to the Government itself. It is particularly unfortunate though probably quite natural that this condition obtained in the land service where every possible benefit was needed to offset a multitude of handicaps.

Still another handicap arose from the occasional fluctuation of appropriations for clerk hire. For instance during Secretary Schurz's term the Land Owner stated, "Fifty-three employees of the Land Office were furloughed on March 1, (1878), having been kept during January and February only because Congress promised later appropriate funds for them." Six months later the paper noted again, "The Land Office has been seriously crippled during the past month by the discharge of employees through lack of funds. Those who live on public lands should be most interested and should try to get Congressmen to act, Commissioner Williamson has done everything in his power....."[33]

The Land Office handicaps of rooms, staff, pay and local office deficiencies promoted inefficient procedure, the need for land lawyers, fraud and favoritism, all closely related developments. Inefficient procedure can be illustrated by examining conditions in the Railroad Division and by recounting the McBride patent case. The McBride case ultimately reached the United States Supreme Court and for the second time in its history the Court served a mandamus on a Cabinet officer.[34] The case

---

32. Copp, op. cit., Feb. 1885.
33. Ibid., March, 1878; Oct. 1878.
34. Sen. Ex. Doc. #181. 42 Cong. 2 Sess. Serial #1886.

had arisen in 1869 when Thomas McBride made a Homestead
entry in Utah. Five years later he proved up, paid his
fees and secured his certificates, usually considered
the equivalent of a patent, from the local land office.
There was a three-year delay however, in issuing his patent and during that time the authorities of Grantsville,
Utah, attempted to incorporate their town. They found
that the land which McBride claimed fell within the
town's supposed limits and their declaration to that effect February 24, 1877, before the local land officers,
initiated a legal contest over McBride's entry.

  Either because of a faulty filing system or
slovenly clerical work the General Land Office did not
record a contest. Instead a patent was issued to Mc-
Bride and sent to the Salt Lake City land office, September 26, 1877, seven months after the inception of the
contest. But before it was delivered to McBride the
Land Office discovered its error and recalled the patent.
Since it had been issued in due course McBride endeavored
to obtain it through a court order. He filed a petition
for a writ of mandamus against Secretary of Interior
Schurz in the Supreme Court of the District of Columbia.
He then carried his case to the United States Supreme
Court and obtained his right to the patent. In deciding
for McBride the Court expressed regret that Secretary
Schurz was obliged to pay the expenses of the proceed-
ings, but it is evident that greater efficiency in the
Land Office would have prevented not only the Secretary's financial loss but the entire dispute as well.[35]

  The disorganized state of the Railroad Division
in the Land Office resulted in far more serious complications than the mere struggle for a patent and was
fraught with more significance for the development of the

---

35. 102 U.S. 378. The Land Owner observed that the decision gave
 life to thousands of cancelled patents and so paved the way for
 extensive litigation. The paper also declared that the Land
 Office would have to exercise greater care in its work and that
 consequently Congress ought to provide higher grade clerks
 there. Furthermore the cancellation of a patent became mutila-
 tion of a Government record and so subjected an official to
 criminal proceedings. Jan., 1881.

country. The Division had been created in 1872 by the
Commissioner without legislative assistance. Donaldson's
Public Domain showed that during the early 1880's the
Division possessed a Chief, at a salary of $1,800, five
clerks hired for the same amount, four others who were
paid $1,000 and seven additional assistants of lower
status and pay.[36] Considering the importance and value
of the cases handled by the Division such negligence
warrants the deepest reproach. In 1884 there were 3,921
cases pending, and of these nearly one-fourth were contested cases which might involve hearings. Not only was
the Division greatly in arrears in its work but its haphazard growth had never permitted the establishment of
systematic bookkeeping. This fact was revealed in 1882
when the Commissioner was called upon for information
regarding certain land grants. He replied with some exasperation that the work of amassing the information had
required "the unremitting labor of all the available
clerks in the railroad division for the past forty days.
The delay has been caused almost entirely by the failure
on the part of this office in the past....to adopt and
perfect a comprehensive system of procuring and keeping
in a concise and convenient form all matters of information relative to each grant.[37] The Commissioner went on
to explain that for "many years past the majority of the
force....has been engaged in the settlement of contests
between settlers and railroad companies and the increase
in this class of cases has been so rapid, the rulings of
the executive and judicial departments of the government
so diversified and new legislation relative to grants so
numerous" that there was little opportunity to perform
other duties. It is clearly evident, therefore, that
the Division needed more and higher grade employees.

  The need was brought out in another connection
when it was revealed that fourteen railroads had obtained patents for more land than they had earned. The
disclosure of this fact occurred almost accidentally.
The Senate Committee on Public Lands was questioning
John W. LeBarnes, a land office clerk whose fine service
will be noted more fully later, regarding railroad grants

---

36. p. 1227.
37. Ibid., p. 811.

when he volunteered the information. Curiously enough the
Senate Committee seems to have taken no steps to investigate his statement although the House sought an explanation from the Land Office. Commissioner McFarland's
answer contained the remarkable conclusion that "The
foregoing statements must in the main be received as ex-
planatory and approximate, as I cannot undertake now to
pass upon many questions that have arisen and that may
hereafter arise, in an accurate adjustment of these several railroad grants."[38] In other words it was impossible for those in direct control to describe the status
of railroad grants or to secure readily vital information concerning them.

Land Office delay, incompetence, inefficiency
and neglect created an ever increasing demand for land
lawyers in Washington. Their opportunities broadened as
railroads, mining companies, lumbermen, private land
claimants, cattlemen and State swamp land officers found
a need for the assistance of someone in direct contact
with the Office. The Washington lawyer service could
not only secure a speedy completion of patenting but it
could also serve the predatory interests by arguing contested cases against settlers who had no such representatives and it could influence clerks either because the
latter welcomed assistance on complicated cases or because there was some obligation involved. The Land Office itself could have prevented undue influence if it
had drastically restricted two privileges the lawyers
enjoyed. One privilege permitted "special" cases and the
other allowed direct contact between a lawyer and the
clerk handling his case. The origin of permitting a
case to be marked "special" so that it could be pushed
through the Office without awaiting its turn in the
routine of business is not quite clear but the practice
apparently existed on a wide scale.[39] Lawyers were able
to charge their clients an extra fee of $50 to $100 for
securing this privilege. By just what right or rite
they obtained their help in the Office is not recorded.

There was a Departmental ruling which prohibited
a lawyer from walking into the Land Office and dealing

38. Ibid., p. 908.
39. L.O.R., 1885, p. 102.

directly with the clerk who handled his case, but it
does not seem to have been enforced. This particular
advantage for those who could afford to pay for it seems
to have fitted into the practice of the times. A Land
Office employee of the Eighties has remarked that the
farther back in our history one goes, the more open was
the work of the lobbyists with their entrée to heads of
Departments, Bureaus and Congressional Committees.[40]
Lobbyists included anyone who had a favor to seek from
a public official. Some of these lobbyists have left
quite frank letters of their talks with the Commissioner
in the Land Office files. It is impossible to say to
what extent the direct contact affected Land Office practices but there is no doubt that many cases of undue influence if not corruption occurred. One incident of the
early Nineties developed into what newspapers termed a
"patent steal."[41] The patent to valuable mineral land
near Duluth, Minnesota was held up in the Land Office
because an affidavit had been filed with a charge of
fraud on the method of entry. The attorneys for the
claimants to the patent had direct access to the papers
at the Office and rather mysteriously the affidavit and
the order to investigate the case attached thereto, were
removed. Then in the absence of the clerk who had been
handling the case the lawyers secured another clerk to
push the patent through.

There is considerable evidence to show that land
lawyers were guilty of many questionable practices either
against their clients or the Office. Periodically Secretaries were forced to disbar them from practice before
the Department. For example in the fall of 1878 Secretary Schurz staged a housecleaning and debarred 127 at
one time.[42] Later in the same year he proscribed eight
more and in succeeding years Copp's Land Owner or the
metropolitan press published lists containing from one

---

40. Author's interview with Mauchlin Nivens.
41. N.Y. Tribune, January 16, 1890.
42. Copp, op. cit., September 1878. The paper was attacked by in-
    terested parties for its support of reforms. There was an ef-
    fort to have attorneys withdraw their cards from the paper.
    September 1878.

to twelve or sixteen names.[43]   The need and the supply
constantly increased, however, for business brought
lucrative returns.   After Secretary Schurz left office
one debarred attorney attempted to sue him for breaking
up his $40,000 a year practice.[44]   This particular lawyer
had been charged with attempting to bribe a Land Office
clerk.

Any attempt to explain why the Land Office was
treated with seemingly purposeful neglect must be based
to a certain extent on circumstantial evidence and in-
ference.   There can be no doubt that Congress knew of
the limited, inefficient and distressing conditions
which existed.   There was no question of an embarrassing
Treasury deficit after 1880 and it is easy to show that
other Bureaus received increases in men and money when
requested.   The implications are, then, that there was
considerable indifference to the plight of the Office
and strong though subtle opposition to building it up.
For the most part the actual settler was not aroused to
action as long as he was sure of his land.   As stated
above it was not necessary to obtain a patent if the requirements of the settlement laws had been met and all
fees paid up.   Consequently one important group did not
unite to demand better facilities for administration.
Probably added to this group was the large majority of
the people who were unaware of or indifferent to what
was taking place.   Moreover there were outstanding though
largely irrelevant questions which sidetracked attention
from fundamental problems.   And finally, there were important predatory groups which benefited by the crippled
Bureau because they could obtain their ends more easily
through overburdened, inexperienced officials and lawyer
service.   In other words the landed interests must have
desired the Land Office to continue half equipped or
they would have improved it.   They kept an eagle eye on
its activities and protested loudly when they felt it
had infringed upon any of their privileges.

In 1879 Representative Foster of Ohio defended
the need for a larger staff and concluded, "Why western
members....have not made for years passed and do not now

---

43. N.Y. Tribune, January 10, 14, 1885.
44. N.Y. Times, March 11, 1881.

make a point of this matter, I cannot understand."[45] In
reality the Representative did not understand the interests that were largely behind not only many western members but some eastern and southern ones as well.   Such
members showed their real concern in debates on railroad
grants, or timber or pastoral land questions.   Moreover
there is a certain undefined relationship between Representative Samuel J. Randall, Chairman of the House Appropriations Committee from Pennsylvania, and Thomas
Scott, President of the Pennsylvania Railroad.[46]   Mr.
Scott was one of a group widely interested in western
land ventures as noted above, and several of these ventures could be fostered by an amenable Land Office.
Whether or not there is any direct connection between
small appropriations and Mr. Scott's desires cannot be
known unless the Randall papers are opened to the public.
Most of Mr. Scott's papers have been destroyed. And if
influence in this case is hard to prove there is also
great difficulty in explaining why a man like Representative Atkins of Tennessee, blocked an effort in Congress
to secure a larger appropriation for the Land Office
when at the same time he permitted a similar appropriation for the Pension Bureau to pass unchallenged.[47]

       Throughout this monograph are scattered refer-
ences to influence which individuals or groups brought
to bear on Congress or the Departments. That influence
in the land department is evident in Secretary Teller's
rulings and in Commissioner Williamson's action for the
Maxwell grant patent. On the whole bribery at least in
a direct form, seems to have been unnecessary for obtaining favorable action.[48]   Lax enforcement, liberal
interpretations and biased and reversed rulings gave
predatory interests all that they could wish. Not all

45. Cong. 3 Sess. Cong. Rec., p. 1175.
46. For the activities of Mr. Randall see Dict. Am. Biog.; Sidney
    Pomerantz, "Samuel J. Randall, Protectionist Democrat," M.A.
    Thesis, Columbia University; chaps. XII and XIII, post; and
    H. Dunham, "Some Crucial Years of the Land Office, 1875-91,"
    Agricultural History, April, 1937.
47. 46 Cong. 1 Sess. Cong. Rec., p. 3384 (May 14, 1880).
48. There are instances of bribery at other times than 1875-91. See
    references to John A. Benson, below.

of these items were favored by a weak Office but many of
them were. The testimony offered by the New York World
article previously mentioned, is relevant to the point.
Nearly every one of the fourteen former Office employees
which the paper lists had become connected with a railroad and the connection was reported to be significant.
The paper declared that the railroads "manipulated the
officials of the Land Office by holding out to them
tempting bribes in the way of future employment. Their
hold has grown during the years of Republican Administration to such extent that they have practically been
able to dictate decisions to the Land Office and to control to the fullest extent its actions." Better working
conditions and salaries in the Office might have offset
these temptations, at least to a considerable extent.

Another form of influence which favored corporate
interests and which made it unnecessary for them to demand an improved Office arose from family connections
between men inside and outside the Bureau. The World
charged that Britton and Grey had "been more successful
in getting favors from the Land Office than any other
firm of attorneys in the city" largely because of the
fact that Mr. Britton was the brother-in-law of Smith,
existing Chief Clerk and former Chief of the Railroad
Division. Moreover Mr. Britton was a brother-in-law of
Martin, the Assistant Chief of the Railroad Division of
the Secretary's Office.

There is also some significance in the fact that
the land department frequently changed its rulings and
failed to establish well-observed precedents. Commissioner Williamson's modification of his predecessor's
rule in order that he might secure patent to his Utah
land is an example. And evidence that inconsistent rulings were not uncommon is revealed both in a previous
quotation from the Land Owner anent Dakotans' denunciation of land decisions and in another incident which
the paper relates. On November 15, 1885 the editor had
congratulated a retiring law officer for his outstanding
legal service to the Government. The paper declared
that he had "furnished valuable precedents on all sides
of nearly every question of importance for the past fifteen years." This tribute was not intended to be

humorous or sarcastic but it apparently brought a protest from the former official because the succeeding issue of the paper apologized by stating, "No subordinate
official in the land service can be held responsible for
the decisions of his superior officers." This declaration came from a conservative, responsible paper that
was exceedingly well informed on land matters and it
therefore furnishes unimpeachable evidence on an outstanding cause for an inconstant system. There would
have been little point in this inconstancy if it had not
involved favors to those who could reach the land service.

    The story of the Land Office forms a sorry chap-
ter in the history of American government. Official indifference and favoritism were coupled with Congressional negligence to assist in despoiling the public domain.
For a few short years under President Cleveland there
was an unusually honest supervision of the land department. At the same time Congress not only failed to coöperate but even went out of its way to provide handicaps. But an examination of that unique period must
wait upon a review of the wholesale fraud which accompanied the narrowing frontier.

Chapter VIII

RIDDLING THE LAND LAWS

In his definitive study of the American forest policy John Ise declared that the possession and exploitation of immensely valuable natural resources "have given most of the distinctive traits to American character, economic development and even political and social institutions."[1] Unfortunately these distinctive traits are sometimes more to be deprecated than admired. For example the discrepancies which existed between official declarations of public land principles and policies actually adopted affords little credit to Congress. Too frequently it failed to respond to elementary obligations when confronted by hostile predatory interests. Both the Republican and Democratic platforms had repeatedly manifest concern for settlers and in January, 1884, the House of Representatives approved a resolution which favored a threefold program for forfeiting all lapsed railroad grants, framing and administering laws to secure freeholds to the largest number of citizens, and repealing all measures which facilitated speculation.[2] But meanwhile Congress was taking only the most tentative steps for carrying out this program. A few grants had been forfeited, a duplicatory law against fencing was enacted and a number of agents had been provided for checking fraud but there was little else of a positive character. On the contrary the laws which remained on the statute books fostered monopolies and speculation and Congress showed neither a desire to repeal them nor to enact others more appropriate to settler's needs.

---

1. Ise, op. cit., preface.
2. Dem. Camp. Handbook, 1884, p. 196.

In order to explain why Congress was so un-
responsive it is necessary to recall that practically
every branch of the land service was neglected. Not
only pastoral, timber, survey, railroad and Land Office
questions went unsolved, as noted above, but mining,
swamp, private claims and school land issues also
failed to receive attention. The mining law of 1872 by
which the Government sold two men "exclusive rights to
the same thing," remained unamended a decade later. The
Public Land Commission's investigations had repeatedly
revealed that under the law "two or three prospectors
camped in the wilderness, have organized a mining district, prescribed regulations....(and made) on the ace
of spades, grudgingly spared from the pack,....an entry
that the government recognizes as the inception of a
title that may convey millions of dollars."³ Careless
entry and regulations made little difference to prospectors for they usually sold out to capitalists. As
a consequence the Commission had found that "no branch
of American enterprise has ever paid to litigation, so
great and so unnecessary a share of its gross returns."
The remedy for this serious defect lay in changing the
law so that underground rights corresponded to surface
rights, but frequently the Senators, like Senator Stewart of Nevada, were lawyers who profited by mining
litigation; consequently the logical leaders for enacting a new law were opposed to change.⁴

The Public Land Commission had also called attention to the private land claims of the Southwest
where for nearly thirty years unsatisfactory procedure
had caused the claims to remain unadjusted.⁵ The

---

3. Report, 1880, p. xxxvff. The Report stated that the Comstock
   Lode had cost its owners $3,000,000 in legal fees and $10,000,000
   in underground development because of the existing laws.
4. The Commission paid little if any attention to oil bearing lands.
   L. P. Brockett devoted several pages to an account of their location, op. cit., pp. 128-9. For charges that mining operations
   fluctuated to affect the value of mining stocks see the report
   from Idaho. Sec. of Int. Report, 1879. The Nation later
   criticized the mining laws partly because they kept thousands
   of miners idle, July 2, 1885.
5. Report, 1880, pp. xli-xliii.

Surveyor's General had presented to Congress only 150
out of 1,000 claims in their files and Congress had
acted on only 71. No further claims were being sent to
Washington because Congress had long since ceased to
consider the remaining 79 and the Commission explained
that the hesitation was doubtless the result of the
judicial nature of the claims and several important errors in those already passed on. The Commission suggested that Congress establish a land court similar to
that which had been set up in California. But the bill
which the Commission submitted was amended in Senate
Committee in order to permit adjudications before the
United States District Courts.[6] There was little possibility that these courts could have handled the claims
within a reasonable time because their dockets were already crowded and because they would have found it difficult to obtain all the documents which they might
need. On the other hand the Committee had retained one
equitable feature in the Commission's bill and that was
a provision to prohibit a claimant's use of the mineral
resources on his grant unless expressly donated by the
Spanish or Mexican governments.

But unfortunately Congress failed to adopt any
new method of adjudicating claims at that time and two
years later another bill establishing a court was also
ignored.[7] In fact several bills which received Committee and Land Office approval were passed over while
territorial officials repeatedly urged action. In
1883, for example, the Governor of New Mexico denounced
the existing system as "intrinsically dilatory and....
not calculated to lead to intelligent and just conclusions."[8] He reported that his territory was largely
"plastered with grants," many of which overlapped so
that delayed adjudication had resulted in bitter disputes and even in violence. He also revealed that success in securing the confirmation of grants of doubtful
character had "so encouraged and emboldened the covetous
that it is alleged the manufacturing of grant papers

---

6. Quoted in Donaldson, op. cit., p. 1116.
7. Ibid., p. 1136ff.
8. Report of Sec. of Int., 1883, p. 555.

became an occupation and surveys have been made so erroneously as to lead to a belief that these grants are
endowed with India-rubber qualities." In the same year
the Land Office cited a typical case of expansion.[9] A
Mexican grant of less than 5,000 acres which were described by fixed, natural boundaries, reputedly "well
known and easily identified" upon assignment to other
parties, underwent a preliminary survey "purporting to
show identically the same boundaries but embracing an
area exceeding 300,000 acres." This was only one of a
score of cases the character of which caused settlers
to avoid locating near any claim.

The fact of assignment is significant for its
indicated that individuals made it a business to buy up
old claims and have them surveyed for excessive amounts.
The purchasers hoped that their claim would be confirmed
by boundary description and that the quantity of land
embraced would be overlooked. Actually the question of
confirmation did not disturb holders of invalid or excessive claims for all Mexican grants were reserved by
law from general expropriation. As a consequence
claimants were able to take advantage of their possession by renting, mining, lumbering and pasturing. Meanwhile for self-protection they exerted an unhealthy influence on the Territorial government.[10]

The Surveyor General of Arizona explained another possible use for bogus claims when in 1884 he declared that claimants intended "to allow their alleged
grants to lie dormant until towns were built upon them
and their arable and pasture lands are purchased from
the Government and settled upon, when (they will) come
forward and offer quit-claims of title or demand settlement at exhorbitant rates, usually commensurate with
the cost of improvement,....and not infrequently these
claimants are persons who in the strict eye of the old
practice would have come within the pale of punishment"
for blackmail.[11] Furthermore it was pointed out that

---

9. L.O.R., 1883, p. 12.
10. See chap. XI post.
11. L.O.R., 1884, p. 153. In 1882 this same official had made an
    interesting suggestion: he claimed that since "Manifest Destiny"
    seemed to point to further expansion of the United States south-
    ward the Government should be "vigilant in this matter of for-
    eign titles."

the construction of railroads through Arizona and New
Mexico, with the consequent influx of population, made
imperative the rapid adjustment of the claims. Yet
through indifference and neglect Congress delayed another seven years before it moved to check the continued
fraud and violence which arose from the claims. On the
other hand even such delay was prompt when compared
with the fact that private claims in Florida and
Louisiana were still unsettled in 1883 because Congress
would not appropriate funds to adjudicate them.[13]

Swamp lands were another factor in land administration which needed Congressional attention. The Land
Office reported that as the public lands became "rapidly exhausted" these grants were increasingly used "as
an investment."[14] By 1884 the amount approved or patented had reached 55,438,000 acres and indemnity totalled
another half million acres and over $1,280,000.[15] As
early as 1868 the House Committee on Public Lands had
found that one-half of the swamp grants were in the
hands of speculators. Similar interests continued to
use the law thereafter without regard for the character
of the land which they selected. In 1883 the Commissioner reported that he had been compelled to reject
the larger portions of the selections presented to his
Office.[16] He declared, "If the State agents would exercise more discrimination in presenting cases much
labor would be saved." This was probably a polite way
of saying that if they would not try to commit such
palpable frauds the Office would be less burdened.

The Office's inspection of selected lands was
particularly burdensome for there was but one agent in
the field and by 1877 the Commissioner claimed he needed forty.[17] Six years later Congress had increased the
number to four so that it continued to be impossible
adequately to inspect selections.[18] The work in the
Swamp Lands Division was likewise handicapped by a small

---

12. Omitted.
13. L.O.R., 1883, p. 11; 1884, p. 174.
14. L.O.R., 1882, p. 107.
15. Ibid., 1884, p. 9.
16. Ibid., 1885, p. 10.
17. Ibid., 1887, p. 12.
18. Ibid., 1883, p. 10.

staff. Like other Divisions it fell years behind in
its duties and such paltry aid as Congress gave was
totally insufficient. In order to remedy matters Congress could have temporarily increased the Office force
and placed a time limit on further selections. The results of Congressional inaction were shown a few years
later when A. B. Hart wrote, "It does not appear that
any great improvements have been made by the States;
and United States is now spending large sums in building levees to protect regions presented to the States
in 1850."[19]

     Because of their abundance school land reserva-
tions in the Territories also needed Congressional attention. The purpose of these grants cannot be too
highly praised but in order to achieve fully their purpose they should have been protected from a variety of
abuses. For instance there was no provision for safe-
guarding those lands which contained timber and so they
were stripped without a pretense of legality. In addition there was no supervision of arable land and as a
consequence exploiters farmed them rent and tax free.
In many instances Congress ignored repeated official
requests for permission to select arable land in lieu of
the worthless areas on which grants occasionally fell;
but on the other hand lands which contained minerals
were given to prospectors and the Territory was instructed to select indemnity elsewhere.[20] Moreover
certain types of abuse frequently developed when a
Territory achieved statehood. In requesting protection
for Dakota school lands Governor Ordway reviewed the
generous if not questionable policies that had been
adopted in California, Iowa, and Wisconsin.[21] He
showed the lands had been sold "at rates below their
value, seized by speculators and parted with by the

---

19. "The Disposition of Our Public Lands," Quarterly Journal of
    Economics, vol. I, p. 169ff.
20. Sec. of Int. Report, 1884, pp. 546-7 (Idaho); 1883, p. 511
    (Arizona); 1883, (Montana).
21. Ibid., 1881, p. 954-7. This is the Governor whom R. E. Petti-
    grew attacked for alleged corruption. Cf. "Triumphant De-
    mocracy."

State for prices below all other lands" to a favorite
few. In short he verified President Garfield's remark
that school lands were usually looked upon as "the
opima spolia--the chief booty of the new State."[22]

II

Despite the policy of neglect for school, swamp
and other lands the greatest discrepancy between official declarations and every-day practices occurred in
connection with the settlement laws. If Congress had
endeavored to carry out the principles of reserving
lands for the settler it would have tightened the requirements of the settlement laws, and either repealed
some of the laws, or provided safeguards against their
abuse. The abuse was stimulated by four factors, desire for speculation, for large aggregations, for depredations on timberlands and for inexpensive acquisition of mineral lands. Thomas Donaldson observed in
1883 that it was impossible to turn to a single state
paper or published document where public lands were mentioned without reading of fraud.[23] He justly placed
the blame on Congress and declared that "The Executive
officers can go but so far; Congress is the sole power
to stop the leaks and repeal existing useless laws."[24]
Before considering why Congress failed in these responsibilities it is significant to observe the causes for
the abuses in some detail.

The early Eighties represent one of the recur-
rent periods of fever for land speculation in the United
States.[25] Since there was a growing belief that the

---

22. Ibid., p. 957.
23. Op. cit., p. 536.
24. Ibid., p. 534.
25. Copp adds a humorous touch to the rush for land by declaring
    that "Congressmen who have been repudiated by their consti-
    tuents elsewhere arrive (in Dakota) by almost every train,"
    op. cit., Oct. 15, 1884. In 1876 the Commissioner had believed
    that there would be a gradual decline in the number of settle-
    ment entries for in "localities most accessible and desirable
    for actual settlement, lands have, to a large extent, passed
    to private ownership." L.O.R., 1876, p. 3.

best of the public domain was fast disappearing into private hands, individuals used all of the settlement laws to secure as much land as they could. Secretary Teller explained that "when the country was new and parties desiring to secure land were comparatively few....these laws were complied with in most cases where land was entered, but as the demand had increased it seems as if the people were restless under the restraint imposed upon them in securing land and they go to work systematically to defeat the very purpose of the law."[26]

Every class of persons in frontier town, for instance, exercised the right of settlement entry but without the slightest intention of living up to the letter of the law or building a homestead. Furthermore, land agents, that is those who bought and sold land in frontier regions, encouraged everyone who entered their district to take out land under as many laws as possible. Then the agents secured control of that land and endeavored to sell it to an actual settler or another speculator. Congress was well informed of this procedure for in 1882 the House Committee on Public Lands reported that in "many sections of the country the evasion of the law has become a regular organized business and offices are opened for the express purpose of preëmpting and selling land."[27] Some of the prevailing business enthusiasm can be found in the advertisement of a Kansas agent. It read, "Come all and come quick. We have deeded lands and relinquishments so cheap it will make you smile. There are also a few pieces of Government land left, but it will soon be gone. Come and see us."[28]

Speculation by agents was accompanied by the speculation that has always characterized the frontier farmer throughout American history. By taking up land a little in advance of the settled area and starting to make improvements on his claim the frontiersman soon

---

26. Sec. of Int. Report, 1883, p. xxxiii.
27. H. Rep., 1834. 47 Cong. 2 Sess. Quoted in Donaldson, op. cit., p. 679.
28. 49 Cong. 1 Sess. Cong. Rec., p. 6239; Sheldon, op. cit., p. 112.

became ready to sell out, usually at a profit, and even
before he had perfected his title. In many cases,
though, the frontiersman borrowed from a loan and mortgage company, in fact he was often encouraged to do so
by the companies and if he was unable to maintain interest payments he moved on and left the land in the
company's care. Testimony to the fact that abandoned
farms were numerous in the region west of the Missouri
is found in the reports of William G. Moody.[29] Mr.
Moody traveled extensively in the West during the
Seventies and was particularly impressed by the large
amount of mortgaged land there. He later declared that
mortgages were too large and that they placed too heavy
a burden on the settler. He declared that "one of the
most notable things that meets the attention of the observer is the great number of publications, everywhere
met with, devoted exclusively to the advertising of
small farm holdings, more or less improved that are for
sale. One is almost forced to the conclusion that the
entire class of small farmers are compelled, for some
cause, to find the best and quickest market that can
be obtained, for all they possess."

Purchaseable land of this kind, contrary to
avowed policies, formed a market for those who wished
to secure large holdings and it fostered farm tenantry.
Of course large aggregations of land, or bonzaga farms
as they were frequently called if they were used primarily for agriculture, could be secured through the
use of school scrip, military warrants and swamp and
railroad grants but as long as there was still considerable free arable land such holdings did not demand
Government action. On the other hand there was a definite obligation for preventing the engrossment of land
under the settlement laws. The abuses which cattlemen
or their agents fostered have already been noticed.
Violations of both this and other kinds were recognized
by Secretary Teller when he declared that the Government was responsible for fulfillment of its obligations
under the settlement laws even though it accepted no
responsibility for developments after it had parted
title to the land.[30] His point can be made clearer by

---

29. Moody, "Land and Labor in the U.S.," 1883, p. 85.
30. Sec. of Int. Report, 1883, p. xxxiii.

examining abuses connected with each of the important
settlement laws, omitting however, the Desert Land Act,
and noting what efforts were made to secure Congressional assistance.

After thirty years of service the Preëmption law
had become primarily a means for fraud. In 1876 the
Land Office repeated a former request for its repeal because it had found that "for every beneficial purpose
(the law) has become an obsolete statute."[31] The Office also suggested that if Congress felt that settlers
on unsurveyed land needed protection, it could amend
the Homestead law to include that safeguard. The necessity for repealing the Preëmption law was shown by the
fact that it had become "peculiarly the speculator's
law, as contra-distinction to the settler's." The Land
Office further declared that experience had shown "be-
yong all doubt," that it furnished "a means of daily
fraud." The House Committee on Public Lands reported
that, "Men are employed and paid definite amounts to
make preëmption locations, and assignments are made to
transfer lands so acquired the moment the title rests.
Agreements are made in defiance of law."[32] The Land
Office also reported that it was "a notorious fact that
under their cover large tracts of coal lands" were
gathered into the hands of single individuals.[33] In
fact throughout the succeeding years the Office revealed
again and again that not only arable and coal lands but
timber, iron and pastural lands were monopolized by
abuse of the law.[33] Perhaps one of the seven wonders
of the land system was the fact that such a flagrantly
abused law could remain unamended during two decades.[34]
Its protracted existence testified to Congressional indifference to settler's needs and honest administration.

---

31. L.O.R., 1876, p. 9. The Land Office prepared a repeal bill and
    though it passed the House in the Second Session of the Forty-
    third Congress it failed to pass the Senate.
32. H. Rep., 1834, op. cit. Quoted in Donaldson, op. cit., p. 579.
33. L.O.R., 1882, pp. 11-12; Sec. of Int. Report, 1882, p. xix.
34. See chap. XV, post.

While Congress delayed action on the Preëmption law it adopted the Land Office suggestion for extending its principle feature to the Homestead Act. In 1880 the protection for settlers on unsurveyed land became a part of the latter law so that an entryman could date his application from the time of settlement, or alleged settlement, for this provision proved a boon to defrauders.[35] The Land Office found that as soon as land was surveyed parties who desired large quantities employed men to make entries and allege residence long anterior to that date.[36] Incidentally careful surveys would have prevented much of this fraud. But the entrymen were able to make their proof within the required thirty days and thus secure a patent without waiting for five years and without paying any money but the necessary fees. Whole ranges of valuable land were obtained in that manner. The Land Office recommended that Congress amend the law to require at least six month's residence between the date of filing entry and that of final proof, "irrespective of alleged time of residence prior to entry."[37] Congress, however, ignored the request.

The Land Office also recommended extending time within which commutation could be made. As previously explained a settler was allowed to commute his entry at any time before the five years residence requirement was fulfilled if he paid the minimum price per acre.[38] The Land Office ruled that at least six months must elapse between entry and commutation but it requested Congressional authority to require a two-year residence period. The Office expressed confidence that the bona fide settler would not object to the requirement and it hoped that the capitalist employers of gangs who acquired land under the law would be checked. Such employers built houses on wheels so that they could be moved from one quarter section to another at regular semi-annual intervals to fulfill a nominal compliance

---

35. 21 Stat. 140.
36. L.O.R., 1883, p. 6.
37. Ibid., p. 7.
38. Ibid., p. 7.

with the residence requirement.[39]   But again Congress
did not attempt to check the abuse until 1891 when it
adopted a fourteen months provision.

It is unnecessary to enlarge upon abuses under
the Homestead Act for acquiring timber and mineral land
for they were similar in character to those under the
Preëmption law.   Abuses under the Timber Culture Act,
however, were apt to be confined largely to attempts at
speculation.   In 1880 Congress provided the speculator
with a golden opportunity under this law when it adopted
a separate bill which enabled an entryman to file a
written record relinquishing his entry at the local land
office.[40]   This relinquishment did not have to be sent
to Washington but the land which the entry had covered
was immediately open to a new entry.   Of course this
provision applied to all the settlement laws but it promoted the most abuse under the Timber Culture law.   The
Land Office found that when a reasonable time had
elapsed for proving up the earliest Timber Culture
entries there was very little action for presenting
proof.   Because the Commissioner suspected fraud he investigated and found that fictitious entries were
initiated "for the purpose of holding the land out of
market and selling to others the relinquishment of the
rights so acquired."[41]   He also reported that the evidence which he obtained indicated that such speculative
practices were common to Dakota, Nebraska and Minnesota
and that "as a rule as public surveys progress over the
territory subject to such entry the lands are covered
with fictitious claims and actual settlers are compelled
to pay to speculators, or persons holding the claims, a
bonus for the privilege of entering the land in a legal
and proper manner under the public land laws."

Both the Commissioner and Secretary Teller recommended repeal of the Timber Culture law[42] and reminded
Congress that it did not require settlement or even
residence within the State or Territory where the entry

39. Ibid., 1886, p. 82.
40. 21 Stat. 140.
41. L.O.R., 1882, p. 12.
42. Sec. of Int. Report, 1883, p. xxx.

was made. They also recalled that a mere record of
entry held the land for one year and "other trivial
acts" held it through another two years while the entryman endeavored to sell "at such price as the land may
command." The Secretary believed that the abuses were
inherent in the law and beyond the reach of administrative correction.

Land agents not only speculated in Timber Culture entries but they also turned their holdings to
profitable use. As quasi-landlords they farmed out
their holdings for a fifty percent share in the crop.[43]
One Chicago agent claimed that he was often able to
"turn the original price of the land over in three
years." On the other hand Timber Culture entries were
used to acquire both timber and mineral land. Secretary Teller strongly denounced the efforts to acquire
coal land cheaply and hold it for monopoly purposes.[44]
As a resident of Colorado where coal land frauds were
abundant he doubtless knew of such practices at first
hand and as a mine owner himself he represented a group
which resented competition from those who paid little
for their land.

By 1883 the abuses connected not only with settlement laws but with timber and desert laws as well
and violations of pastoral and timber lands without any
pretense of legality forced Commissioner McFarland to
propose an unusual move. He successfully requested the
President take what amounted to a dramatic step for the
land service and send a special message to Congress.
The message had been prepared in the Land Office and in
it the Commissioner summarized the tremendous amount of
fraud on the public domain.[45] He declared that the
actual settler found it "difficult if not impossible to
get to the public lands without first paying tribute to
the dishonest claimant."[46] He felt that speculators
who offered relinquishments gave "prima facie evidence
of the fraudulent character of claims to be so

43. Thomas P. Gill, "Landlordism in America." North American Re-
    view, January, 1886.
44. Sec. of Int. Report, 1884, p. xv.
45. Sen. Ex. Doc. #61. 47 Cong. 2 Sess. Serial #2076.
46. Ibid., p. 1.

relinquished." And in order to reveal the extent of speculation in a frontier region he selected Dakota and noted that 50,000 votes had been cast there only a few months before. Yet the number of agricultural entries had exceeded 150,000 and additional entries were being made at the rate of 50,000 annually.[47] The Commissioner quoted from an address of the Governor of Dakota wherein he said that "the well-intended acts of Congress allowing the entry of 160 acres of land as a tree claim have been so completely nullified by the manipulation of land sharks that our broad and fertile prairies are comparatively treeless.[47]

The Commissioner also noted that frontier regions were not alone guilty of fraud but that California presented problems of timber and desert land violations and Minnesota offered timberland frauds.[48] Moreover Alabama was exhibiting unusual abuse of the settlement laws to acquire millions of dollars worth of coal and iron land.[48] Other regions had presented charges of fraud but the Commissioner lacked the means for investigating them. In addition to these complaints the Commissioner revealed a little known fact when he declared that "appeals for protection of bona fide settlers from the exactions and oppresions of those who commit or cause these frauds to be committed, are constantly coming before this office."[49] He believed that the issue was joined: either there must be a radical change in the land laws and their administration, or there must be adequate means for enforcing penalties for fraud and violations. He added a grievous indictment of Congressional neglect when he stated flatly. "This office has never been furnished with facilities or means to secure a compliance with the requirements of the public land laws."[50] Out of the 50,000 acres embraced in individual claims before the Office the Commissioner asserted that "a very considerable portion" were believed to be

---

47. Ibid., p. 3.
48. Ibid., p. 4. He asserted that "A flood tide of illegal appropriations seems to be sweeping over the new States and Territories, threatening to engulf the entire public domain."
49. Ibid.
50. Ibid., p. 4.

without validity or merit yet unless Congress provided
assistance they would have to be treated as valid and
passed to patent because there was no possibility of
investigating them.[50]

The Commissioner suggested several possible
methods of assistance. In the first place, if Congress
allowed the Office to use the money it collected from
timber depredations it could materially check fraud and
violations of all kinds. Or if Congress provided an
appropriation of $150,000 the Office could place a spe-
cial agent in every Local Office and hire a sufficient
force in the General Land Office to supervise their
work.[51] Then of course, there was an alternative of
amending the laws. The Commissioner's report concluded
with fifty finely printed pages, containing two or
three letters to the page, each of which illustrated
some phase of the abuses which he wished to remedy.

For one of the few times during the period
1870-90 a major Land Office request was speedily granted and within a month Congress appropriated $100,000
for special agents. The Office was therefore able to
hire thirty men[52] to replace the three clerks previously employed and it formed the Special Service Division.
It is significant that Congress provided money rather
than repeal of abused laws. The causes for the failure
to secure such repeal will be considered below but the
lack of success from the work of the special agents has
been touched on previously. Additional evidence on
this latter point may be found in the Land Office report for 1884. It recorded that there were 3,531 cases
of alleged fraudulent entry investigated in the previous
year and yet 5,000 more were suspended only because
there were an insufficient number of agents to assign
to them.[53] There were also 627 cases of timber trespass
acted upon, with many others in abeyance, and investigations of illegal fencing on 5,000,000 acres. The Commissioner sent a special letter to the Senate declaring
that "the proportion of fraudulent entries found to

---

50. Ibid., p. 4.
51. Ibid., p. 6.
52. L.O.R., 1883, pp. 28 and 203.
53. L.O.R., 1884, p. 144.

exist is so large that if it be the intention of Congress that the remaining public land shall be protected from indiscriminate absorption through illegal and fraudulent appropriation more adequate legislative measures will need to be adopted."[54]

The land department's helplessness was manifested in the final reports of both Commissioner McFarland[55] and Secretary Teller. The latter favored not only repeal of many laws so that the Homestead law would serve all needs for acquiring arable land, but he also requested the enormous appropriation of $400,000 in order "to suppress the fraudulent acts going on."[56] The Commissioner suggested an extra $60,000 so that Registers and Receivers could hold hearings in fraudulent cases. Moreover he requested assistance for the Attorney General in handling cases of illegal fencing.[57] Congress, however, continued to ignore such suggestions.

III

Congress' failure to protect the public domain for settlers' use can be explained partly by the fact that the tremendous increase in abuse had developed over a comparatively short period. Furthermore according to authorities such as Secretary Teller and Thomas Donaldson, the public was not aware that the policy of allowing those nearest the public lands to prescribe legislation, was outmoded.[58] In addition despite

---

54. Quoted in Sec. of Int. Report, 1884, p. xv.
55. See also L.O.R., 1883, p. 207; Cummings and McFarland, op. cit., passim.
56. Sec. of Int. Report, 1884, p. xvff.
57. L.O.R., 1884, p. 76. Copp urged Congress to pass a liberal appropriation for special agents and claimed that their services had already checked fraud covering millions of acres. Op. cit., March 15, 1884.
58. Donaldson also claimed that it did not seem to know that constantly thousands of acres were being entered "with cash in unlimited quantities by the favored few who have money, lands which should be reserved for the actual settler." Donaldson, op. cit., p. 533.

notable exceptions in the West, there was still no general knowledge that the supply of the best land was
diminishing. And finally one of the most important
reasons for the neglect is found in the pressure exerted by powerful vested groups. Nevertheless Mr. Donaldson declared that because the press and official reports had presented "many startling statements as to
frauds" the public lands had received "much attention."[59]
Yet he felt that more publicity and leadership were needed to achieve reforms.[60]

Mr. Donaldson also believed that by allowing
representatives of frontier regions to propose laws in
a time when railroads and quick communication existed,
Congress had adopted "much legislation dictated or proposed by in some cases single persons and he (being)
sometimes an interested party, or a friend of such
parties." For example he cited the 1876 law permitting
public sale in the South rather than entries under the
Homestead Law.[61] He maintained that the law was passed
by an explanation which was actually a "cunning device"
intended to secure a cash sales law when "hardly a member of Congress could or can be found who would intro-
duce a bill to sell public lands outright for money and
in unlimited quantities." Though he did not cite the
timber laws of 1878 nor the methods used for establishing survey changes he did point to the deposit survey
provision of 1879 as a "shrewd and cunning" change in
the deposit law.[62]

If interested parties were able to obtain laws
which were favorable to themselves they were also able
to block the repeal of obnoxious laws. For instance in
1882 the House had received a favorable report on a
bill for repealing the Preëmption law.[63] Immediately
opponents attacked the bill in order to save the law
which Mr. Donaldson described as "the hope of the land

---

59. Ibid., p. 534.
60. He regretted, however, the false publicity of steamship and
    railroad companies to gain immigrants. Ibid., p. 535.
61. Ibid., p. 544.
62. Ibid., p. 548.
63. Ibid., pp. 678-70.

grabber and the land swindler's darling." Their attack
was unsuccessful for the repeal bill was defeated. But
the advocates of land reform then tried a more subtle
method and inserted a repeal clause and several other
land amendments in the sundry civil expenses bill on
February 19, 1883. These amendments would have prohibited attorneys from filing entries for land seekers;
required two and one-half years residence on a Homestead claim; restricted the use of the Timber Culture
law; and repealed the relinquishment act. But again
the opponents of reform protested and Mr. Donaldson described their efforts in a satiric fashion. He stated,
"At once....the mails and telegraphs were burdened with
letters, petitions and messages demanding that these
items be not enacted into law. Indignation meetings
were held in some localities and stirring resolutions
passed denouncing the attempt of Congress to thus de-
prive speculators and grabbers of the splendid chances
under existing laws of fraudulently gathering in the
little remaining agricultural lands of the West.[64]

In spite of these remonstrances the bill passed
the House and by February 24 it was placed before the
Senate Committee on Appropriations. Mr. Donaldson
claims that then protests "poured in tenfold in number"
so that the Committee struck out the land clauses. The
day before the end of the session the bill passed the
Senate and then rather than hold up appropriations the
House agreed to the Senate changes so that the reforms
were lost.[65] In the face of the well-organized protests, which could hardly have come from bona fide settlers because their rights were not infringed, it was
impossible to duplicate the coup for the National
Academy's proposals.[66]

---

64. Ibid., p. 681.
65. Ibid., pp. 682-5.
66. Ise suggests that since the Appropriations Committee was domi-
    nated by Easterners it was easier to obtain an appropriation
    like that of 1883 than it was to secure abused settlement law
    repeal which must be sponsored by Public Land Committees domi-
    nated by Westerners. The above discussion partly refutes that
    explanation. The latter committees frequently sponsored re-
    peal bills and Finance Committees restricted appropriations.
    See chap. XII below.

        While Congress failed to meet its obligations
and thereby placed tremendous burdens on the land department judicial decisions occasionally added to the
burdens. There are, of course, many instances in which
decisions filled in legislative gaps but there were
others which defeated law enforcement or effective administrative control. The Schulenburg decision has already been described as one which complicated the railroad question and a few years later the case of Atherton vs. Fowler resulted in a decision which produced
handicaps for enforcing settlement rights.[67] The case
arose in California where Atherton had enclosed 800
acres of public land to which he could not obtain title.
Fowler later attempted to preëmpt a quarter section of
the enclosure and in the litigation which ensued the
case was brought to the Supreme Court. The Court held
that by enclosing the tract Atherton had the right to
its exclusive use and Fowler would have to get out.
Three judges dissented but the decision served to protect those who enclosed any tract despite the Land Office offer to assist those who wished to settle on illegally enclosed land. Following another decision of a
similar character Secretary Schurz had requested a law
to protect "settlers in good faith,"[68] but it was not
until the anti-fencing bill of 1885 that such settlers
were protected.

        The Supreme Court was not always consistent in
its opinions on land cases and when one of its decisions was adopted by a lower court in such a manner as
to practically justify fraud the Court became more
cautious. For instance in the case of United States vs.
Throckmorton the Court upheld a Mexican land grant to
which fraud had been attached; the basis of this decision was that though fraud had been used to obtain the
grant from the Mexican Government it had not been
brought into any action before the California Board of
Private Land Claims.[69] The Court asserted that there

---

67. 6 Otto 513. Quoted in Donaldson, op. cit., p. 539; and L.O.R.,
     1879, pp. 417-9.
68. Hosmer vs. Wallace, 7 Otto 575; Sec. of Int. Report, 1879,
     p. 26 and Donaldson, op. cit., p. 539.
69. 91 U.S. 61.

would be greater "mischief in retrying every case"
where false testimony of witnesses or documents was
concerned than "any compensation arising from doing
justice in individual cases."

The Throckmorton case was cited by the Circuit
Court in California to uphold a decision of jesuitical
character.[70] According to the evidence George E. White
and others were guilty of fraud and perjury in connection with Preëmption entries in Humboldt County, California. The Government brought suit against the offenders for violating the clause of the act which stated that if any person took the oath that he was not
seeking his land on speculation and was later proved to
have sworn falsely he should forfeit both the land and
the money paid for it. The Circuit Court declared that
it considered the forfeiture "highly penal" and as a
consequence seemed to pay no more attention to it. On
the other hand the Court admitted that the defendants
could be tried for perjury but since such a trial required a jury it could not be held in the Circuit Court.
Because it was extremely difficult to convict a man of
perjury in acquiring western lands it is reasonable to
conclude that the Court believed that no punishment
should be inflicted on those who were apprehended for
land frauds. Indeed one sentence from the decision supports this view. The Court stated, "In view of the
notorious liberality in favor of purchasers, not to say
looseness, with which the preëmption laws have, ever
since their adoption, been administered all over Western States, to relax the rules referred to in the
authorities cited, especially where no pecuniary damage
or injury has resulted either to the Government or to
private parties" and to retry all such cases, would
"open a Pandora's box of evils....to the great detri-
ment of the public peace and prosperity." When a similar decision citing the Throckmorton case was appealed
to the Supreme Court it was reversed with a certain
show of indignation.[71]

---

70. Pacific Coast Law Journal, July, 1883; quoted in Donaldson,
    op. cit., pp. 1171-4.
71. U.S. vs. Union. 114 U.S. 233. (1885).

Irrespective of these decisions the Courts
could not reform the land system--the responsibility
rested squarely on Congress. Of course its problems
were increased by such irresponsible administrators as
Secretary Teller but in any case the failure of Republican control was apparent. A comprehensive plan for
surveys and another for an adequate system of distribution had been too readily dropped. Individual questions of desert lands, timberlands, surveying needs,
land-department facilities, railroad grants, private-
land claims, swamp and school donations and an increasing amount of engrossment were also neglected while
abuses and injustice were augmented. Observers were
usually pessimistic over the prospects for improvements.
In 1871 Henry George had asserted, "A generation hence
our children will look with astonishment at the recklessness with which the public domain has been squandered. It will seem to them that we must have been
mad."[72] More than ten years later another writer summed
up his feelings in the assertion, "After us the deluge."[73]
Nevertheless there was hope in a change of officials and
since a Democratic administration was brought into power
by the election of 1884 it becomes necessary to examine
its policies and leaders.

---

72. H. George, Works, op. cit., I, p. 11.
73. E. T. Peters, Century, Feb., 1883.

Chapter IX

REFORM UNDER CLEVELAND

When President Grover Cleveland took office in
1885 public land issues were again among the most important which the Government faced. During the previous
year a record absorption of over 27,000,000 acres[1]
caused the faults of an unregenerated system and lax administration to become increasingly apparent. In several
respects, however, the opportunity for reform seemed to
match the urgency for it. In public discussion and
Congress the partisan sectional issues which had arisen
from the Civil War were giving way to the consideration
of more fundamental economic problems. The westward
push of population and the growth of business enterprise
following the depression of 1873-79, meant that questions
of strikes, trusts, cattle companies, immigration, tar-
iffs, railroads, timber, Indians and land could no longer be ignored or subordinated to privileged control.[2]
The significance of third party movements was not lost
on the members of the two major parties. Furthermore increased publicity for both land abuses and new policies
indicated a growing public concern for the adoption of
reform measures.

Publicity was provided through a great variety
of newspapers, magazines and books. Certain papers, such
as the New York Times, had been demanding reform for
years.[3] The labor press had also taken an advanced

---

1. L.O.R., 1884, p. 4.
2. D. R. Dewey, "National Problems," p. 3.
3. After 1885 it averaged an editorial on land affairs every week
   for three years. Its program as stated May 11, 1886, accompanied
   praise for President Cleveland and his day and night efforts for
   justice and good government. The Times urged the President to
   secure sufficient equipment for the Land Office; repeal of abused
   laws; keep thieves out of the public domain and uncover past

165

position and after 1885 labor papers and the Times increased their efforts. Labor's demands were exemplified
by the Knights of Labor program which called for the return of all unearned grants, full taxation of all land
whether under cultivation or not, the removal of all
fences on public lands, repurchase of all lands held by
aliens, prohibition of foreign acquisitions and the reservation of the remaining public domain for actual settlers.[4]

Moreover in 1885 the New York Herald delegated
special reporters to study western developments at first
hand and these investigators sent back stories of frauds
that filled columns and even whole pages of the paper.
Newspapers from all over the country applauded the
Herald's policy.[5] Not to be outdone the New York World
printed long accounts of land grievances.[6] Moreover the
North American Review sent Thomas McGill, a member of
the British Parliament, as an impartial observer to investigate land-lordism in the Mississippi Valley. He
reported that America was on the same road to "latifun-
dia" which Pliny claimed had killed Italy and he condemned the landlord and tenant laws of the western States
as representing the most "one-sided scheme of legislation....(in) the history of constitutional government."[7]
Harper's Monthly published an article which explained
how subtly corporations secured large blocks of land to
the bewilderment of the public. The author, V. P. Paine,
pointed out the assistance which the land department
gave and observed that "The wanton and wholesale plunder
of our public lands furnishes material for the most astounding chapter of American History."[8]

Academic centers became interested in the necessity for land law reform. Herbert B. Adams of Johns

(footnote continued) thievery; have the Department of Justice pun-
　　ish "rascals" who had violated laws; reclaim great tracts from
　　corporations; correct private land claims, and defeat specula-
　　tors.
4. Fine, op. cit., p. 120.
5. See list of papers in the Herald, April 17, 1886.
6. See the seven-column story on "Great Land Steals" in the World,
　　May 23, 1885.
7. Op. cit., January, 1886.
8. October, 1885, p. 742.

Hopkins University wrote several articles on the subject
and urged the press to stir the land question.[9] He declared that because the issues were largely economic
there was no "occasion for socialistic alarm"; Americans
were "neither communists nor fools." An extension of
his efforts is found in Shosuke Sato's timely "History
of the Public Land Question in the United States." Mr.
Sato had been sent to America as a special commissioner
of the Colonial Department of Japan and he spent several
years as a fellow at Johns Hopkins. His research under
Mr. Adams lead to his book in which he declared that the
Knights of Labor program was neither extreme nor radical.
He summed up a proper land policy in two phrases: Reform
of legal abuses, and, Recovery of public land from the
railroads.[10]

The increased publicity for land questions and
the enhanced opportunity for official consideration of
basic economic problems were accompanied by the inauguration of a Democratic administration for the first time
in thirty years. The election of 1884 was not fought
over any fundamental issues, it is true, for the major
parties did not take definite positions on any major
question, but both the Republicans and the Democrats included in their platforms the usual statements about corporation grants and homesteaders.[11] The platforms of
both parties also contained a new plank which called for
a prohibition on alien, absentee ownership. Yet if the
party declarations appeared similar the records of the
presidential candidates manifest divergent attitudes
toward the functions of government. The Democratic
candidate, Grover Cleveland,[12] had experienced a remarkable rise from an obscure position in Buffalo to the
Governorship of New York State and his reputation for
honesty, hard work and courageous conduct were well established. He opposed groups who sought special privileges and he refused to submit to the leadership of the
notorious Tammany machine. His integrity and independence

---

9. Galley proofs in Columbia University Clipping Bureau.
10. P. 181.
11. Ellis, op. cit., pp. 55-8; 64.
12. A. Nevins, "Grover Cleveland," chaps. VI-VII.

indicated a wholesome attitude toward party and official
responsibilities. On the other hand the Republican
candidate, James G. Blaine of Maine, had established an
unfortunate record of opposition to civil service reform,
addiction to partisanship and sectionalism and very
questionable relations with land grant railroads.[13] After a campaign marked by personal villification of both
candidates Governor Cleveland was elected by a close
vote.

The new President immediately showed his interest in the land question by referring in his inaugural
address to the necessity for protecting the public domain from purloining schemes and unlawful occupation.[14]
In his first message to Congress he elaborated his views
and first called attention to the manner in which the
settlement laws were perverted to foster monopoly.[15] He
declared that he was opposed to the concentration of
land ownership whether it resulted from fraud or not and
he believed that Congress could materially check the
practice. He also believed that the days of plentiful
free land were gone and that in order to safeguard the
remainder Congress should adopt the very comprehensive
changes suggested in the Secretary of Interior's report.
The President was soon called upon to take a hand in
settling land disputes and as later discussion will show
he furnished forthright leadership. By continued contact with land problems he became better acquainted with
the urgency for reform and he occasionally stepped into
the work of the land department to support its policies
or he strongly urged legislative assistance.

Unfortunately, however, the President was handicapped in fulfilling the promise of his election and his
wholesome views. In the first place his own party was
split on important issues such as the tariff. Furthermore leading Democrats like William M. Barnum and Cabinet members like William F. Vilas were connected with
land operations which were antagonistic to reform.[16] The

---

13. D. S. Muzzey, "James G. Blaine," chaps. V-VI; XI-XII.
14. N.Y. Tribune, March 5, 1885.
15. 49 Cong. 1 Sess. House Doc., vol. I, p. xxxix.
16. Mr. Barnum was Chairman of the Democratic National Committee,
    1876-1889; Biog. Direct. of Am. Cong. He was instrumental in

Senate retained a Republican majority and it continued
to support partisan, sectional and special interests.
And finally public opinion was divided because of many
newspapers' hostility, not only to Democratic policies
in general but to land reforms in particular. These papers abandoned all standards of legitimate criticism and
also played up cases in which the Administrations' laudable reform efforts failed. For instance the New York
Tribune and the New York Sun[17] which had been at least
mildly critical of lax administration and had delighted
in exposing certain notorious operations where fraud occurred, reversed their policies when the Democrats took
office. The Tribune[18] called individual Democratic officials "cheap reformers seeking a pinchback reputation"
and "communists of the most pronounced type, thoroughly
reckless, thoroughly irresponsible, vindictive and
malicious." Its obvious bias led to a strenuous newspaper feud in New York wherein charges of "bought" and
"liar" were bandied about.[19] Criticism was not confined
to the eastern press for mid-Western and Far Western papers also attacked officials and policies with a venom
or subtlety that frequently betrayed an ulterior motive.

As a result of the various handicaps the Democratic opportunities for reform were largely restricted
to administrative measures and it was in that field that
the greatest accomplishments took place. If it was difficult to change the land laws the Democrats nevertheless checked cattlemen in their abuse and violations of
laws and the domain; railroad grants were supervised
with greater care than ever before; timber depredations
were halted and prosecution for past offences was pushed;
surveying and private land claims frauds were uncovered
and prosecuted; manipulation of settlement entries was
discouraged; and successful efforts were made to reclaim
large areas for general use. While the President deserves

(footnote continued) manipulating the Backbone grant. Sen. Ex.
   Doc. #31, 48 Cong. 1 Sess. Mr. Vilas is discussed in chap. XIV,
   post. Attorney General Garland probably belongs in the same
   classification. Nevins, "Cleveland," op. cit., p. 198. The Attorney General's office produced a poor record in prosecuting
   frauds, chap. XIII, post.
17. For comment on the Sun see N.Y. Times, December 14, 1885.
18. Dec. 6, 1885.
19. N.Y. Times, Jan. 2, 1886; Aug. 22, 1887.

a large share of the credit for fostering or backing
these reforms it is also necessary to notice the particularly able assistance which he received from his subordinates.[20]

For his Secretary of Interior President Cleveland turned toward the South and selected Lucius Q. C.
Lamar of Mississippi. Ex-Senator Lamar had served the
Confederacy during the Civil War in both a military and
diplomatic capacity.[21] He had later taught law at
Mississippi University, and returning to the national
legislature, earned widespread respect for his eulogy of
Senator Sumner in 1875. His cabinet appointment in 1885
met with some hostility, though the New York Times stated that "Secretary Lamar's original and thoughtful mind,
conservative habit and sobriety of judgment" would make
him "a good advisor and an administrative officer."[22]
The paper noted that he had a distaste for confining and
routine work and that he was something of a dreamer but
these defects were reputedly counterbalanced by "a lik-
ing for doing well anything he undertakes."

There is no doubt that Secretary Lamar was an
able and honest if somewhat temperate official for a reform administration. The contrast between his policies
and those of his predecessor, Secretary Teller, stands
out vividly for his first duty was to the Government and
not to special interests. Perhaps a great deal of Secretary Lamar's administration is characterized by his
handling of the Backbone grant case. A previous chapter
has related how Secretary Teller on the last day of his
term began rushing patents through the Land Office for
Gould's Backbone railroad grant. When Mr. Lamar became
Secretary he found the Office machinery running "full
blast." And because the company's rights to the patents
were extremely questionable the Secretary stopped further
work on them. Yet instead of exposing the whole case he

---

20. Ise truthfully remarks that President Cleveland's first adminis-
    tration "marks out a separate period in the history of public
    lands." Op. cit., p. 87.
21. Wirt A. Cate, "L. Q. Lamar," passim.
22. March 6, 1885, also quoted in Cate, op. cit., p. 425. Senator
    Lamar was also reported to be forgetful. N.Y. Times, Feb. 27,
    1885.

merely requested Congress to pass a measure which would settle the company's claim and so end a long dispute. Furthermore he protected Secretary Teller by asserting that his haste had revealed "nothing inconsistent with the strictest good faith and honest administration."[23] If this was accurate it would seem that there should have been no necessity for adopting a law which would quiet the title to the lands for which the patents had issued.

Like all the Democratic officials Secretary Lamar was plagued by office seekers because there was a strong demand to turn the Republicans out in favor of the long suffering Democrats. Nevertheless at first the Secretary removed only the heads of the nine Bureaus in his Department and later, whenever possible, he is said to have allowed subordinate clerks to complete their term in office undisturbed.[24] During his first months as Secretary he conducted a full investigation of every activity and every Bureau under his control and he presented the results in five volumes accompanying his first report.[25] According to a recent biographer the investigation led to many reforms and served as the basis for important legislation.[26] Not much of this legislation applied to the land service but his suggestions in that field represent in the main a thorough study of its needs. Since these suggestions received the President's express approval they merit brief notice.

Several of the recommendations duplicate those which had been presented many times before.[27] In fact in offering his plan for timberland disposal the Secretary himself remarked that perhaps the "frequent

---

23. Ed. Mayes, "L. Q. Lamar," p. 499. Senator Teller reported falsely when he said that there was nothing in the Interior Department to show that Jay Gould was interested in the grant. 49 Cong. 1 Sess. (Special Session of Senate) Cong. Rec., p. 13.
24. Mayes, op. cit., pp. 434, 426.
25. Cate, op. cit., p. 442ff. See a brief analysis of the duplicated and overlapping functions in N.Y. Times, March 2, 1885.
26. Cate, op. cit., pp. 459, .461.
27. Sec. of Int. Report, 1885, p. 38ff. He did not, however, take up ranchers' problems.

repetition" of the subject had "rendered it a common-
place as a part of the routine report."[28]   Nevertheless
he emphasized the necessity for survey and appraisement
of timberland and then he proposed that the Government
reserve one quarter of each section and sell the remainder to the highest bidder at not less than appraised
value. He also sought amendments to the Timber Cutting
Act in order to safeguard it from abuse.[29]   The Secretary repeated former recommendations for the repeal of
the Desert Land Act and the Timber Culture law and for
the adoption of some new method that would adjust private
land claims.[30]   Furthermore he sought the repeal of the
Deposit Survey law and the payment of a salary in place
of fees to District Land Officers.[31]   In order to assist
in the removal of illegal fences he requested for the
Department two special agents who would have no responsibility to the Land Office.[32]   And finally in order to
protect the remaining fertile land for settlers he recommended that Congress increase the minimum price for
the public lands[33] and then provide a more efficient
method for checking up on the character of the improvements which were made to fulfill the requirements of the
settlement laws.

    In support of this last proposal Secretary Lamar
quoted from a western letter which declared: "There
ought to be some way to distinguish between a fireguard
of a few furrows plowed around a quarter section and a
cornfield; some way to determine whether a description
of a house '14 by 16' referred to inches or feet square;
whether the floor was bored or board; and whether 'shin-
gle roof' meant more than two shingles, one on each
side."[34]   Although the Secretary's suggestions received
slight attention he nevertheless continued to press for
Congressional coöperation as he, like the President,

28. Ibid., p. 45.
29. Ibid., p. 40.
30. Ibid., pp. 38-9.
31. Ibid., pp. 41-2.
32. Ibid., p. 43.
33. Ibid., p. 51.
34. Ibid., p. 52.

became better acquainted with the practical operation of
the land service.[35] Before he left office as the result
of his promotion to the Supreme Court in January, 1888,
Secretary Lamar confessed that "the most difficult and
important duty of the Department was the administration
of the public lands."[36]

Whatever the Secretary lack in zeal and drive
was compensated for by his Land Office subordinate. Just
three weeks after the inauguration President Cleveland
appointed William Andrew Jackson Sparks Commissioner of
the Office.[37] Mr. Sparks had grown up in Illinois, received a college education, studied law and for a brief
period held a position in a local land office at Edwards-
ville, Illinois. After serving in the State Legislature
he had been sent to Congress for several terms. There
he became a member of the Military Affairs Committee and
was given the sobriquet of General. He was a staunch
advocate of Federal regulation of railroads and as his
name implies, an opponent of Civil Service policies.[38]
When Mr. Sparks became Commissioner his friends asserted
that the combative qualities which he had displayed in
Congress would be turned against any "crookedness" which
he might discover in his office.[39] He was noted for his
great firmness of character and his stubborn honesty.
Copp's Land Owner observed that the Commissioner impressed a visitor as a man of great mental power and

35. The two agents which he requested were provided and he praised
    their work in his last report. Sec. of Int. Report, 1887, p. 13.
36. Ibid., p. 3.
37. N.Y. Times; N.Y. Tribune, March 25, 1885; and Dict. Am. Biog.
    The Tribune claimed that beside support from the Illinois dele-
    gation, Mr. Sparks had been strongly recommended by Representa-
    tive S. J. Randall, "a warm friend" of the former.
38. His reputation on this score may, however, be the result of the
    unfavorable barrage of propaganda to which he was submitted.
    See his own statement on the slight changes in the land depart-
    ment. N.Y. Tribune, June 1, 1885. For attempts at ridiculing
    the Commissioner see ibid., April 20, 1885 and May 10, 1885.
39. N.Y. Times, March 25, 1885. The Washington Post called him "an
    excellent and capable gentleman." March 25, 1885.

rare physical energy and strength. He was also said to
have built up "a liberal fortune" through his extensive
law practice in Illinois and his well-chosen investments.[40]

Not only the Commissioner's financial security
but his training as a lawyer, his honesty and combative-
ness, and his robust health were necessary for his management of the Office. He quickly began one of the most
vigorous and remarkable efforts to improve the land system that the Office ever produced. John Ise describes
him as the "great moving force in the department"[41] and
the manner in which the Commissioner shouldered the
burdensome and complicated business of the Bureau and
then proceeded to revise rules, expose fraud and begin
prosecutions in great numbers, amply bear out that description. It is obvious that he aroused strenuous opposition but he was particularly fortunate in the support which he received from his superiors for most of
his efforts and in the fact that the Secretary was both
courteous and tolerant. The full scope of the Commissioner's work, however, must be reserved for later consideration.

Commissioner Sparks received valuable assistance
from his Law Clerk, Colonel John W. LeBarnes. In fact
Colonel LeBarnes was so well informed on public land
questions and so keen in his knowledge of law that he
was consulted by Secretary Lamar, Congress and even the
President.[42] Colonel LeBarnes later asserted that he
had been interested in preserving the public land for
settlers and in seeing that corporations lived up to the
letter of the law. As a result of his efforts along
those lines he was denounced by critics like the New
York Tribune though they also had to acknowledge his
talents.[43] It was somewhat unusual to find a man of
outstanding ability preferring a minor Government position when he undoubtedly could have made a success in
private law practice.

---

40. April 1, 1885.
41. Op. cit., p. 87.
42. N.Y. Herald, January 13, 1888.
43. December 6, 1885.

Colonel LeBarnes had first been employed in the Land Office in 1875 and five years later he had been promoted to the position of Law Clerk.[44] He had antagonized railroad interests in 1882 when he testified before Congress regarding excessive patents for railroad grants and it is to Secretary Teller's credit that he did not discharge Colonel LeBarnes when pressure was exerted for that purpose. The latter had also been threatened with dismissal twice at the outset of the Democratic administration because he was a Republican but both times Commissioner Sparks, friends in Congress or Assistant Secretary of Interior Jenks interceded and he was retained. The coöperation between the Commissioner and Colonel LeBarnes is illustrated by the critical attitude of a colleague who claimed that the Law Clerk "took Commissioner Sparks by the hand and went out of the way to show his chief how to play the devil."[45] If the Commissioner entered the service with the idea that it was permeated with fraud his subordinate was said to have met him halfway. The Law Clerk is also said to have "fed his ideas" to the Commissioner and to have given him information on various members of the Office. It is important to note, however, that the Commissioner undertook at least one reform on his own initiative and without the approval of his Law Clerk who knew not only when reforms were legal but when they had a tenuous basis.

II

One of the first administrative reforms which the Democratic officials undertook arose from the Teller-Arthur policy regarding Indian lands. Before his term was six weeks old President Cleveland issued a proclamation ordering all settlers who had gone on the Crow, Creek and Winnebago Indian Reservation in Dakota Territory to depart within sixty days.[46] Furthermore all cattlemen were required to depart within forty days. What had been the necessity for such an order? In the

44. N.Y. Herald, January 13, 1888.
45. Judge S. V. Proudfit, author's interview.
46. Nevins, "Cleveland," op. cit., p. 228ff.

early 1880's when the Interior Department recognized
that the Reservation belonged to the Indians by treaty,
it had endeavored to buy or exchange the land. Apparently in an effort to facilitate the Department's plans
the Senate passed a bill permitting an exchange.   The
bill had received President Arthur's backing but the
House delayed action on it. When toward the expiration
of the President's term the House seemed unlikely to approve the bill Secretary Teller prepared an executive
order or proclamation opening up 500,000 acres of the
Reservation to settlers without, as a newspaper reported, any "compensation or the least regard for the Indian's treaty rights."[47]

Though dated February 27, 1885, the proclamation
was not made public until March 2. Strangely enough,
there was no previous knowledge of it by the Indians,
Congress or even the Commissioner of the Indian Bureau.
Yet despite this official secrecy advance notice of the
proclamation had reached a Dakota politician through
"inside" telegraphic communication from the Interior Department.[48] The politician, whose name was not revealed, was president of a bank in Chamberlain, near the
Reservation and since he received news of the progress
of the proclamation from the time of its drafting until
it was approved he was prepared to take advantage of it.
As soon therefore, as the proclamation was signed several hundred of his followers began moving onto the Reservation. It is impossible to tell whether or not the information leaked out with high official knowledge but in
any case those who were ready to move obviously obtained
the best locations.

The Indians naturally protested against the in-
vasion and the proclamation and so President Cleveland
was forced either to reconcile them to the remainder of
their Reservation, reported to be the most unfertile
part of it, or order the preëmpters and cattlemen off.
He chose the latter course when Attorney General Garland
pronounced President Arthur's proclamation illegal.[49]

---

47. N.Y. Times, August 11 and 31, 1885.
48. Ibid., April 11, 1885.
49. Ibid., April 11 and 18, 1885.

The Governor of Dakota wrote to the President that because of the hardships and harm to innocent settlers he regretted forcing them off but at the same time he acknowledged that the policy was correct and he did his part to urge them out.[50]

President Cleveland was also called upon to intervene in the disputes which grew out of grazing leases on Indian lands. As the demand for grazing land increased with the growth of the cattle business ranchers or speculators secured leases, or as they were often called 'licenses', for large blocks of various Reservations. In some cases speculators were able to sublet their rights to cattlemen or settlers at a handsome profit.[51] But according to law no lease was valid unless it had been made by treaty or in convention with the Indians. Instead of upholding this provision Secretary Teller assumed the right to protect the leases. He wrote one lessee that while the Department could not recognize his lease to "the extent of approving of the same," it would nevertheless "see that parties having no agreement with the Indians" were not allowed to interfere with those who had.[52]

Though many leases benefitted the Indians because they provided a steady income the lease for the Cheyenne and Arapahoe Reservation caused a great deal of unrest.[53] Prior to 1885 ranchmen, with the aid of the Indian Agent, had secured control of about nine-tenths of the Reservation, or nearly 4,000,000 acres. The resulting Indian dissatisfaction caused President Cleveland, soon after he took office, to send General Sheridan to investigate. When the latter made his report it was considered at a Cabinet meeting and the President decided

---

50. Ibid., April 30, 1885.
51. N.Y. Times, August 18, 1885; R. Haynes, "Life of J. B. Weaver," pp. 236-8. General Weaver revealed a 500% profit on releasing part of the Cherokee strip for a total income of $500,000. Companies were the Dominion Cattle Co. of Canada, the N.Y. Cattle Co. and the Standard Oil Co.
52. N.Y. Times, July 6, 1885. Cf. Nevins, "Hewitt," op. cit., pp. 229-30; and Times, July 25, August 6, 1885.
53. Ibid., September 6, 1885. Incidentally it was also subleased at five times the amount paid the Indians.

to issue a proclamation ordering the ranchmen to leave
the Reservation within forty days. Dated July 23 the
order also reflected the seriousness of the situation
when it placed the Indians temporarily under the control
of the War Department. Since ex-Secretary Teller had
resumed his seat in the Senate he was called upon to explain his policy in regard to leases and he endeavored
to show that a lease on grass was not a lease on land.[54]
The New York Times ridiculed the distinction and asserted: "According to this interpretation the ranchmen who
have enclosed vast tracts in the Indian Territory with
wire fences and who maintain possession of this land by
means of armed cowboys have been merely enjoying a lease
on grass. It was not his (Teller's) duty to try to find
holes in the law."[55]

The cattlemen who were affected by the proclamation sent a delegation to Washington to interview the
President and to persuade him to revoke it or modify the
time for their departure. They prepared a memorandum,
hired counsel to argue their case and, it is said, even
planned to seek an injunction against the order if necessary.[56] On August 4 the interview took place and the
delegation presented some cogent arguments.[57] They related that the order affected about 250,000 cattle which,
with fences and other improvements, were valued at
$7,000,000. They claimed that if their lease was unlaw-
ful they had at least made it with the knowledge and implied sanction of Secretary of Interior Teller. Moreover they had paid their rent until November so that the
order to leave by the first of September would cost them
two months occupation. There was a very great problem
in endeavoring to secure the 1,000 experienced men and
the 5,000 horses which were needed for removal. And
finally the delegation maintained that there was no place

---

54. See also his explanation to a N.Y. Herald reporter. August 13,
    1885. He had made the same distinction in his last report.
    N.Y. Times, November 28, 1884.
55. Ibid., July 25, 1885.
56. Cf. Ben Butler visited Justice Miller for the purpose. Ibid.,
    September 1, 2, 1885.
57. N.Y. World, August 5, 1885. Senator Cockrell and Representative
    J. M. Glover of Missouri were present.

to take their herds except on a long trek to the North
because the quarantine statutes of Kansas, Colorado and
New Mexico forbade crossing those regions before December.[58]

The President, however, feared that the restlessness of the Indians would bring disaster to near-by
settlers so he refused to compromise and told the delegation: "On the one side we have public peace, public
security and the safety of lives. On the other side are
your interests. The former, gentlemen, must be considered though private business suffered."[59] The cattlemen finally accepted the President's decision and by
September they reported moving off the Reservation.
Eastern newspapers rejoiced in the President's firmness
and claimed that "the ranch lessees made the mistake of
assuming that the old methods and the old influence
would prevail with the present administration." The
press also pointed out that the State Land Board of Texas
had recently leased 1,250,000 acres in the Panhandle district at six cents an acre. Moreover there were still
an estimated 24,000,000 acres of school lands available
at the same rate but that rate was three times what the
ranches had paid on the Reservation.[60]

A third proclamation which the President issued
early in his term was not an attempt to correct former
Republican policies but a result of the February 27 law
against unlawful enclosures.[61] The proclamation served
notice August 10, that since fences on the public domain
were illegal they should be removed or Government prosecution would follow. The results of the order were summarized by the Governor of Wyoming when he claimed that
it "was looked upon as a joke at first, then denounced
as an act of tyranny on the part of the Democratic

---

58. N.Y. Times, September 4, 1885.
59. Ibid., September 4. Senator Plumb is reported to have been in-
    terested in Indian land leases. Ibid., August 3, 1885.
60. Ibid., September 6, 1885.
61. Ibid., August 11, 1885, and 3 columns in N.Y. Herald, August 14,
    1885. President Hayes had issued a proclamation April 26,
    1879, authorizing the removal of all who illegally occupied In-
    dian Territory west of Arkansas, with military force if neces-
    sary. Copp., op. cit., May, 1879.

administration and then they (the fences) came down; not
willingly but through the vigilance, perseverance and
intelligent labors of the Government agents."[62] The
Governor also reported that the cattlemen had found out
for themselves that their mania for large bodies of land
and fences did not always pay[63] but the Government nevertheless faced a difficult task. Secretary Lamar spoke
of the vastness of the public domain and the powerful
combinations of capitalists, who "by delays and evasions
and other well-known methods defeat the ends of justice,"
as factors which made it difficult to execute the law
and the President's proclamation.[64]

        The attitude of some of the ranchers who resent-
ed the Government's efforts is exemplified by the views
of ex-Senator S. W. Dorsey. In a letter that reached
Secretary Lamar, Mr. Dorsey declared that there were certain things essential to the conduct of the cattle business.[65] A ranchman must have pasture and in securing it
he simply did what the necessities of the case demanded.
Mr. Dorsey considered it a lamentable fact that the land
laws were such that the fencing of the public domain became unavoidable. Secretary Lamar found it impossible
to accept this viewpoint and the New York Times declared
that the dire necessity was "simply the necessity that
certain capitalists should own great herds of cattle and
make large sums of money."[66] The paper considered that
Mr. Dorsey's code of morals was unchanged since the necessities of the case demanded generous expedition of his
Star Routes.

        Statistics reveal that the Government was able to
reduce materially the amount of illegal fencing. By 1887

---

62. Sec. of Int. Report, 1887, p. 1059. For a list of illegal en-
    closures see N.Y. Tribune, August 13, 1885.
63. Sec. of Int. Report, 1887, p. 1020.
64. Ibid., 1886, p. 30. See also the difficulties from encroach-
    ments on Indian Reservations. Chicago Tribune, March 26, 1885;
    N.Y. Herald, April 6, 1886.
65. Sec. of Int. Report, 1886, p. 32.
66. December 24, 1886. Mr. Dorsey possessed one fraudulent Mexican
    claim and he had acquired another ranch through fraudulent use
    of the land laws. N.Y. Times, April 10, 1887 and Surveyor Gen-
    eral Julian's reports from New Mexico.

465 cases involving nearly 7,000,000 acres had been
brought to the attention of the Land Office[67] and in the
following year it reported that 4,500,000 acres were
restored to the public domain.[68] The Office claimed
that the practice had been "very largely broken up and
the larger enclosures have either been removed or suits
to compel removal are now pending in the courts." It is
necessary to observe, however, that if the Democratic
administration was able to break up the practice of illegal fencing their achievements were not permanent.[69]
A. E. Sheldon relates[70] that subsequent and less strict
administrations permitted the return of aggressive cattle raisers in Nebraska and the evidence presented in
President Theodore Roosevelt's Public Land Commission
Report of 1904-5, indicates that illegal fencing continued to be widespread.[71]

In the middle Eighties cattlemen faced not only
the problems[72] of a crowded range, removal of illegal
fencing and cancellation of leases on Indian lands but
many other handicaps as well. In the first place western
courts, such as those in New Mexico, witnessed more vigorous action against land law violators. The blizzard
of 1886-87 had severe effects on a large area and since
there was a simultaneous drop in the demand for beef,
many companies went bankrupt. And finally Commissioner
Sparks enforced a more strict compliance with the provisions of the settlement laws, particularly the Desert
Land Act. His efforts produced strong protests such as
that found in the Cheyenne, Wyoming Daily Sun for February, 1887.[73] In mock solemnity the paper stated: "Thou

---

67. L.O.R., 1887, p. 457.
68. Ibid., 1888, p. 17.
69. Secretary Lamar declared that only where corporate "connivance
    and prodigal railroad grants came to their assistance have cat-
    tlemen defied the law and rendered powerless the efforts of this
    Department to correct this abuse." Sec. of Int. Report, 1887,
    p. 13.
70. Sheldon, op. cit., p. 178.
71. Osgood, op. cit., p. 192.
72. Many difficulties are discussed in Webb, op. cit., p. 237.
73. Quoted in Osgood, op. cit., p. 207. The Commissioner's policy
    according to one account, helped to bring about a migration of

shalt have no other gods than William Andrew Jackson
Sparks and none other shalt thou worship. Thou shalt
not raise cattle upon the land, neither sheep nor any
living thing but only corn the same as in the State of
Illinois."

At the same time there were conciliatory requests for an appropriate ranching law. The Wyoming
Stock Growers Association which had opposed Major
Powell's stock-raising homestead plan in 1880, passed a
resolution stating: "Resolved--That this Association
would welcome any legislation which would lead to a fair
and equitable adjustment of this question and would secure to all stockmen a legal tenure of the land they
use."[74] Yet there was no law enacted and the reasons
would seem to lie in the fact that manifold misfortunes
had so weakened the cattle business that there was no
great necessity for a law. Furthermore as previously
explained, there were many ranchers who did not need legislative assistance and so did not join with others to
urge a new measure. And finally because it opposed land
monopoly and favored settlers, many of whom were filling
in the cattle country, the Democratic administration did
not press for a grazing land act.[75]

Despite the failure to solve the cattle question
under President Cleveland the Democrats had removed

(footnote continued)   certain cattle raising interests to Canada.
    Land could be leased there reasonably. Cf. Letter of Prof.
    C. E. Lowrey of the University of Michigan; on November 21,
    1886 he wrote from the descrted Powder River Cattle Company
    ranch in Wyoming to the Buffalo Express, (New York).

74. Quoted by the Governor of Wyoming. Sec. of Int. Report, 1886.

75. The Governor of New Mexico explained that he preferred to see
    1,000 men owning one cow each rather than one man owning 1,000
    cows. Sec. of Int. Report, 1885, p. 1009. By a resolution
    Congress authorized the Secretary of the Treasury to investi-
    gate the cattle industry. It therefore received the Nimmo Re-
    port. At that time the industry was valued at $340,000,000.
    The Nation, July 2, 1885. For comment on the report see suc-
    ceeding issues of the Nation. It was not until 1916 that Con-
    gress authorized stock-raising homesteads of 640 acres.   39
    Stat. 862. Nevertheless on August 9, 1888 it permitted Wyoming
    to lease its school lands. 25 Stat. 393.

threatening disturbances and had replaced favoritism to
cattle interests by vigorous efforts to uphold Government rights and obligations. These early reforms in one
field were paralleled in other branches of the service.
It will therefore be interesting to examine the new spirit which animated the work of the Land Office from 1885
to 1887.

Chapter X

COMMISSIONER SPARKS' NEW RULES

Commissioner William Sparks has already been described as the moving force in the reform of the land
service. He unconsciously worked to raise the General
Land Office to the position which it deserved, that of a
department. With the backing of his superiors he made
it a powerful instrument in caring for the public domain.
There were, of course, intra-departmental conflicts, but
reserving a discussion of them until later, it is important to notice that the Commissioner made vigorous attacks on survey, railroad, timberland, private land
claim, swamp land and settlement land abuses.   He revised regulations, enforced laws strictly, attempted to
punish violators and sought Congressional assistance
through exposing the variety and amount of fraud which
was depriving the Government of huge areas of land.

The Commissioner was not only seeking Congressional support but popular support as well and although
his reports carry what a colleague has termed stump
speeches, they nevertheless present a more complete picture of corruption, violations and lax administration
than can be found in any other official documents. Commissioner McFarland had done yeoman work while he too
sought legislative coöperation. Commissioner Sparks'
contribution lay in the broader scope of his exposures
backed by copious illustrations, frequently containing
the names of the persons involved. When he published
his first report, after only seven months in office,
Copp's Land Owner observed that it was a "valuable document" which would surprise even land men who were supposed to know how the land system had been administered.[1]

1. Dec. 15, 1885.

In this report the Commissioner recalled that his material had been furnished by officers and agents of the previous administration. He then issued his oft-quoted statement: "I found that the magnificent estate of the nation in its public lands had been to a wide extent wasted under defective and improvident laws and through a laxity of public administration astonishing in a business sense if not culpable in recklessness of official responsibility. The widespread belief of the people of this country that the land department has been largely conducted to the advantage of speculation and monopoly, private and corporate, rather than in the public interest, I have found supported by developments in every branch of the service. ....I am satisfied that thousands of claims without foundation in law or equity involving millions of acres of public land, have been annually passed to patent upon the single proposition that nobody but the government had any adverse interest."[2]

The Commissioner referred to the long-standing handicaps which the office had faced and noted that his predecessor's efforts to check fraud by suspending the issuance of patents for several States and Territories had been thwarted in the closing days of the previous administration by an official order.[3] Consequently a flood of suspected entries was passing to patent when Commissioner Sparks took office. Subsequently he had received applications for instigating suits to set aside patents on the ground of fraud, where the patents had been issued as late as March 3, 1885. Furthermore the reports of special agents, registers and receivers, inspectors of Surveyors General and Local Land Offices, and communications from United States attorneys and private citizens throughout the country, all "revealed one common story of widespread, persistent public land robbery committed under guise of the various forms of public land entry."[4]

Solutions for this astounding condition were considered by the Land Office staff. A proposal to close

2. L.O.R., 1885, p. 3.
3. Ibid., p. 48-9.
4. Ibid., p. 49.

the Local Land Offices was rejected because prospective
settlers arriving in the various districts would find
themselves unable to locate.[5] A suggestion to shut up
the Land Office in Washington, temporarily, was also
considered inadvisable.[5] The Commissioner finally decided that since fully half the patents issued were
fraudulent he would not issue any more until he had had
time to investigate conditions more fully. With the approval of the President and the Secretary[6] he therefore
published his famous April 3 order which suspended final
action on all entries, except private cash and scrip,
of the public lands in western Kansas, western Nebraska,
all of Colorado, Dakota, Idaho, Utah, Washington, New
Mexico, Montana, Wyoming and Nevada; the order also suspended final action on all timber entries under the Timber and Stone Act and all desert land entries.[7]

Part of the testimony on which this action was
based was given in fine print in the 1885 Report and
some of the letters of approval which poured in from
every quarter were presented in the succeeding Report.
Of course there was also much protest against the ruling
from a variety of sources.[8] Because Secretary Lamar
came from Mississippi the New York Tribune charged that
it discriminated in favor of the South.[9] The paper also
asserted that the order was based on the assumption that
every man who had taken up or intended to take up a
homestead claim was to be regarded as a scoundrel until
one of Commissioner Sparks' detectives had had a chance
to investigate.

Against charges of this kind and others that
arose the Commissioner returned complete answers.[10] For

5. Copp, op. cit., June 15, 1885.

6. Testimony of Representative Payson. 49 Cong. 1 Sess. Cong.
   Rec., p. 6229.

7. L.O.R., 1886, p. 43. Papers like the Washington Post gave their
   approval. April 6, 1885.

8. Another result is found in the fact that scrip increased in value. A quantity calling for 5,000 and held in Washington increased in value from $13 to $17 an acre. N.Y. Tribune, April
   27, 1885.

9. April 21, 1885; and see the Nation, July 2, 1885.

10. A. T. Britton made a strong attack on the Commissioner in the
    Chicago Interocean, June 6, 1885.

instance he showed that only four Southern States had
Land Offices and that many more than that in the North
were not touched by the order.[11] He acknowledged that
fraud existed in both of those regions but he believed
that the most of it could be found in the West. He
promised that other districts would receive care and attention as soon as possible.[11] The order was also made
the excuse for attacks inspired by other reasons. The
Commissioner had aroused the antagonism of Washington
attorneys when he cut off lucrative sources of wealth
and influence. On April 13 he ordered that all cases
marked "special" should be returned to the docket and
await their turn in the routine of business.[12] And
thereafter no cases were to be hurried through unless by
written order of the Commissioner. Lawyers naturally
resented their loss for they could no longer secure fees
ranging from $25 to $100 on special cases.[13] Furthermore lawyers were prohibited from visiting clerks and
employees of the Office during business hours.[14] And the
rule that no former employee could practice before the
Bureau until he had been out of office for two years was
revived and enforced.

        Undoubtedly these changes aided in the organized
effort to have the Commissioner ousted for, the movement
began in Washington. The Commissioner declared that
circulars were issued and sent broadcast to local attorneys and money brokers advising them to cause letters
to be written to Congressmen in protest against suspending patents.[15] This scheme fitted in well with the
grievances of western land dealers. In the first place
the Commissioner had aroused great dissatisfaction in
the West by limiting every entryman to the use of one
settlement law.[16] This had especially handicapped

---

11. Copp, op. cit., June 1, 1885.
12. L.O.R., 1885, p. 102.
13. These lawyers were frequently backed by official or political
    influence. L.O.R., 1886, p. 48. The $100 fee was the charge
    for handling a suspended case.
14. N.Y. Times, Jan. 11, 1886. The paper welcomed the opportunity
    to restrict "inside" information.
15. L.O.R., 1886, pp. 48-9. For the attitude of western attorneys
    see also N.Y. Herald, April, 1886.
16. Ibid., p. 81.

ranchers and land agents who had hired entrymen to take
out land under the Homestead, Preëmption, Desert Land
and Timber Culture Acts simultaneously. Secretary Lamar
partially modified the Commissioner's order but it was
still effective in checking unnecessarily rapid absorption. Although it had formerly urged every entryman to
use all the laws possible Copp's Land Owner gave hearty
approval to the Commissioner's policy and regretted its
modification.

Furthermore Commissioner Sparks disrupted the
profitable business of mortgaging. Western loan companies and banks which invested heavily in mortgages
were well established by 1885 and they were frequently
connected with financial houses or capitalists in Boston, New York, Philadelphia or Europe. An interesting
sidelight on these connections as well as on the business of mortgaging is found in a pamphlet by an English-
man, Alfred Fryer. Mr. Fryer had become the British representative of the Philadelphia firm, Jarvis, Conklin
and Company and he had come to America, traveled nearly
ten thousand miles in the West and then written a report
for private distribution in England.[17] He entitled it
"The Great Loan Land" and the brochure proved so popular
that he issued a public edition in 1887. While boosting
mortgages as a form of investment Mr. Fryer declared
that the western States were "plaistered over with mortgages," yet these plasters were eagerly sought because
they were soothing and strengthening and they greatly
relieved a little "painful tightening of the chest." Just
what he meant by the tightness he did not explain. He
estimated that £3,120,000,000 was invested in farming in
the United States and he felt sure that interest rates
on this investment would probably never drop below six
percent. Money placed in mortgages was safe; for example
the oldest loan firm in Kansas had lent £2,000,000 and
not one of its clients had ever lost a penny in interest
or principle. Mr. Fryer also noted the rapid turnover
in land ownership and declared that nevertheless the

---

17. He did not reveal the names of its members but one Director was
a former Secretary of War and a judge; another was Superintend-
ent of the Kansas Southern Railroad; and a third was a Director
of the Provident Life Company of Philadelphia. Copy in N.Y.
Public Library.

price of farms was constantly increasing. He maintained
that although the land policies of the country aimed to
discourage tenantry, the transfer of land was as simple
as the sale of a horse; consequently when capitalists
acquired land through default on a mortgage they could
easily keep it and secure tenants to farm it. One form
of this transfer, however, was attacked by Commissioner
Sparks.

     Banks and loan companies provided entrymen on
the public lands with funds in return for a mortgage.
But if the entryman did not fulfill the requirements for
a patent and left his entry before it was completed, as
he frequently did, the title to the land reverted wholly
to the Government and the mortgage was of doubtful value.[18] Nevertheless loan companies had maintained that
in such cases they had the right to a patent. Apparently their claims had been allowed but when Commissioner
Sparks took office he refused to acknowledge that they
had any better title than the entryman had acquired. He
felt that a prior mortgage on an unpatented entry placed
a great burden on the bona fide settler who endeavored
to secure the land.[19] Consequently he sought to discourage the practice just as he endeavored to discourage
the sale of relinquishments.

     Loan agents twisted the Commissioner's position
by stating that he prevented mortgaging or selling settlement claims. He replied to this charge by showing
that of course any man could sell or mortgage his property but that he could give no better title than he possessed.[20] The Commissioner believed that a man who took
up land under the settlement laws in order to sell or
mortgage it was committing a fraud.[21] He did not deny

---

18. In many cases the applicant never even saw his land but merely
    signed the necessary papers in an attorney's office. Attorneys
    could and did practice fraud on their clients through the meth-
    od of entry and sale. L.O.R., 1886, p. 71.
19. Ibid., p. 81. The alliance between "fictitious" entries and
    land brokers partly accounted for the growth of bonanza farms.
20. He also denied that he prostrated the land business of the coun-
    try, Copp, op. cit., June 15, 1885.
21. Ibid., p. 46.

that a settler often needed money to begin working his
claim and he felt that despite the new official policy
any settler could borrow on his incompleted entry. According to the Commissioner all that the first class
loan and trust companies of the East demanded was that
the borrower should be a bona fide settler and therefore
entitled to patent.[22]

Nevertheless western land agents were not slow
in adopting the suggestion of Washington attorneys and
writing to protest the April 3 order. One letter, addressed to Senator Charles F. Manderson of Nebraska, was
sent by William Coleman, a loan agent and influential
citizen of McCook, Nebraska. The Senator handed the
letter to Commissioner Sparks for an answer.[23] Mr. Coleman had lamented the "wonderful amount of suffering"
which the suspension order had caused. He cited cases
of entries made in 1885, where needed loans or sales
were held up because there was no possibility of obtaining patents. Commissioner Sparks showed that there must
have been a mistake somewhere for since the Land Office
was nearly two years behind in its work, patents for the
cases cited could not have issued for another year under
any circumstances. The special New York Herald correspondent in Nebraska reported that the real suffering
had been caused by the fact that the Commissioner had
"raised cain with business" by refusing to recognize
vested rights created through the transfer of entries as
described above.[24] The Commissioner's answer to Senator
Manderson also stated that there should be no great hurry for patents for only "the knave wants his patents
rushed through in twenty-four hours."[25] The eagerness
of the Backbone grant owners in seeking patents was offset by the fact that the Land Office held nearly 300,000
other completed patents which were uncalled for because
their owners' claims were valid.[26]

In addition Commissioner Sparks showed that he
had not suspended patents for regular Homestead entries

---

22. Copp, op. cit., June 15, 1885.
23. L.O.R., 1886, pp. 45-9.
24. April 16, 1886.
25. Copp, op. cit., June 15, 1885.
26. Donaldson, op. cit., p. 1227; and L.O.R., 1886, p. 47.

but chiefly for commuted Homestead or Preëmption cases.
He reported that very few of these latter were found to
be genuine upon investigation and that he had received
no complaints from bona fide entrymen over delay in issuing patents.[27] On the contrary he had found that it
was the universal testimony of men of "disinterested observation" that the great body of people in the public
land States and Territories approved of his course. The
November, 1886, elections gave evidence of that approval
by the increase of western Democratic votes.[28] The Commissioner also reported that the same universal testimony indicated that the whole array of persons engaged
in the promotion and procurement of illegal and fraudulent entries, were just as bitterly opposed to his course
as settlers were heartily in favor of it. He added that
from the outset he had not expected that the clutch of
speculation could be loosed from the public lands without a struggle.[29]

After a breathing space of eight months Commissioner Sparks modified his April order by the creation
of a Board of Review, consisting of the Assistant Commissioner, the Chief Clerk and the Chief Law Clerk.[30]
The Board's duties were to pass on contested cases where
the rights of successful parties had been established;
cases where examination was made by Government agents
and no fraud appeared; and cases where Homestead entries
were completed according to law. Meanwhile western interests sent George S. Engle of Dakota to Washington in
order to have the order revoked. Mr. Engle made no head-
way with the Commissioner and so he appealed to Secretary Lamar. It was reported that a Cabinet meeting considered his testimony and planned to mollify western dis-
content.[31] The bitterness of feeling toward the Commissioner was shown by the remark of a Nebraska Representative who stated: "It is my honest belief that if General Sparks should visit Nebraska the people would mob
him before he got out of the State."[32] Similar antagonism

---

27. L.O.R., 1886, pp. 47-8.
28. Copp, op. cit., Dec. 1, 1886.
29. L.O.R., 1886, p. 49.
30. N.Y. Times, Dec. 23, 1885.
31. Ibid., April 8, 1886.
32. Ibid., Dec. 7, 1886.

appeared in Dakota and in fact westerners are said to still resent the manner in which the Commissioner checked up or restricted their land activities.[33]   In 1885 westerners held meetings in various localities to denounce Commissioner Sparks and his rulings.[34]   Yet it is possible to discount much of this protest even when raised under the banner of farm groups because there is evidence that in many instances land attorneys and speculators were the instigators.   The New York Times[34] raised a pertinent question when it declared that "no one has ever heard of an indignation meeting held in that region for denouncing the thieves and perjurers who have fraudulently taken possession of so much land in the Territory..... What do the worthy settlers of Dakota think of these scoundrels?"

Nevertheless in order to placate western hostility Secretary Lamar wrote a letter rebuking the Commissioner and directing him to "proceed to the regular, orderly and lawful consideration and disposal" of all claims.[35]   At least one eastern newspaper considered the Secretary's language was "intentionally severe and even offensive" and it claimed that the Board of Review was accomplishing all that the Secretary could desire.[36]   It showed that the Commissioner's order had suspended 24,541 cases for examination.   Of this large number 3,941 were later sent to patent but 18,777 were canceled as fraudulent, thereby saving the Government about 3,000,000 acres.   The statistics for the entire year 1885 showed that patenting was proceeding at the normal rate despite the order and cancellations.   From 1882 to 1885 inclusive the annual number of patents was 57,501, 45,702, 66,601 and 64,936.[37]   The eastern newspaper felt

---

33. Ise, op. cit., p. 88.
34. N.Y. Times, Dec. 19, 1885.
35. 49 Cong. 1 Sess. Cong. Rec., p. 6231.
36. N.Y. Times, April 10, 12, 1886; The New York Herald suggested that instead of revoking the order the President might have addressed a solemn and urgent special message to Congress "revealing conditions and asking for proper legislative remedies." April 12, 1886.
37. They fell materially in 1886, however. See chap. XV, post.

that the Commissioner should be upheld in the course he
was pursuing and it declared that appeals from Dakota
where Commissioners of both parties had believed 75% of
the entries to be fraudulent, should not cause the Administration "to yield to the clamor of scoundrels whose
rascality is blazoned upon thousands of pages of official reports."[38]

As a result of the Secretary's letter on April 9,
1886, the order was entirely rescinded and the Board of
Review was increased to twenty.[39] Its duties were enlarged to embrace the examination of all entries before
the issuance of patents. Copp's Land Owner observed:
"This will disappoint the ring attorneys who hoped for
the opportunity to complain that the (Secretary's) order
was not being carried out in good faith."[40]

Among the many charges flung at Commissioner
Sparks' administration there was one which claimed that
the alleged frauds on the public domain rested wholly on
the loose and confidential opinion of special agents.[41]
The agents were said to have derived their information
from hearsay or from observations made through the win-
dow of a palace car while traversing the country.[42] The
Commissioner denied this allegation in a letter of June
19, 1886, to Representative L. E. Payson of Illinois.[43]
He showed that special agents had more incentive to favor entrymen than the Government because of tempting
bribes or the possibilities of dismissal through wealthy
influence if reports were unfavorable. Special agents
were required to obtain and transmit to the Land Office
affidavits of parties cognizant of the facts in a case.
If the agents could secure affidavits of fraudulent actions from entrymen themselves, they did so; in one

---

38. N.Y. Times, April 10, 1886.
39. L.O.R., 1886, p. 49 and Copp, op. cit., May 1, 1886.
40. May 1, 1886.
41. Cf. The Nation, July 2, 1885 and L.O.R., 1886, p. 71.
42. 49 Cong. 1 Sess. Cong. Rec., pp. 5734-5.
43. Chairman of the House Committee on Public Lands; a strong de-
    fender of Commissioner Sparks and the April 3 order; and a man
    who considered the land question non-partisan. The letter is
    in L.O.R., 1886, p. 71ff.

instance one agent obtained eighty-three such confessions.

When a claimant's entry had been investigated and fraud was found he was notified of the charges and given sixty days in which to answer them. In a period of little over ten months ending in June, 1886, more than 500 entries had been canceled because the entrants had declined to defend them after proper notice.[44] These were the most flagrant and indefensible cases and the entrymen allowed them to go by default because they feared subjecting themselves to prosecution for perjury. In the first year of Commissioner Sparks' administration agents had reported upon 2,591 cases and because fraud was proved in 2,223 of them they were canceled. Many of the rest were subjected to further investigation. The Land Office estimated that in 95% of the instances in which hearings were held on agent's reports the charges of fraud were sustained and that in the other 5% failure could usually be attributed to the inability to secure the proper witnesses.[45]

Every sort of expedient was resorted to in order to defeat the Government at its hearings.[45] In the Estes Park cases in Colorado where a large quantity of public land was fraudulently entered by agents of the Earl of Dunraven, not a witness could be produced at the day of hearing, although the testimony previously obtained by the affidavits of numerous citizens was overwhelming in character.[45] In Nebraska witnesses had been warned by "regulators" and in California an important witness for the Government was murdered by employees of parties whose entries were questioned.[46]

An attack on Commissioner Sparks and special agents had broken out in Congress on June 15, 1886 when the House was considering appropriations for the agents.[47] Representative James Laird of Nebraska vehemently denounced the work of the Land Office. In florid language he maintained that the Commissioner was "running a

---

44. L.O.R., 1886, p. 71.
45. Ibid., p. 72.
46. Ibid., pp. 72-3.
47. 49 Cong. 1 Sess. Cong. Rec., p. 5734ff.

vendetta against the best interests of all the territory beyond the Missouri River." His indignation mounted as he termed the Commissioner a public enemy[48] who was driving peaceful settlers "forth from their homes, to the end that he may pose as a reformer, and drink the paid flattery of his gang of spotters, spies and poisoners of the tenures of the settlers of the West."[49]

Such a wild outburst suggested ulterior motives. It was perhaps natural that as a representative of the disgruntled State of Nebraska Mr. Laird might feel that it was necessary to make a stump speech in behalf of some of his constituents. But Congressmen and the press soon revealed that there were also personal reasons for his attack. In 1883 when a District Land Office was opened in McCook, Nebraska, settlers were reported ready to make entry along the Stinking Water Creek.[50]   These entrants were pushed aside, however, by "the Laird party" which filed in a bunch entries covering land for twelve or thirteen miles along the stream; it was obvious that the firm of Kelley and Laird had planned a stock ranch. The General Land Office investigated the entries in the following year and found that not only were the charges of high handed registration true but that one of the partners of the company was a brother of Congressman Laird.[50]   It was not until Commissioner Sparks took office that there was an opportunity to handle the case properly and while the Commissioner was planning what steps to take he refused to allow Representative Laird to inspect the agent's report.[51] He believed that it was contrary to public interest to open these reports because of possible threats or violence to witnesses before the Government could arrange a hearing.

---

48. Ibid., p. 5734.
49. Representative Payson made an excellent reply defending the Commissioner and attacking exploiters of the public domain. Ibid., p. 6236ff. Representative T. R. Cobb also defended the Commissioner and Mr. Laird told the latter that he was welcomed to all the dignity he could get "by scattering the contents of the Commissioner's garbage cart in this House." Ibid., p. 6231.
50. N.Y. Times, June 21, 1886.
51. 49 Cong. 1 Sess., op. cit., p. 5734.

Probably the Representative's family interest and his
feelings after the rebuff from Commissioner Sparks go a
long way toward explaining his denunciation of Land Office officials. It is true that Representative Laird
disclaimed any participation in the activities of his
brother's company but nevertheless he had secured the
Register his position at McCook.[52] It is difficult to
say whether or not a sense of obligation permitted the
Register to accept the obviously illegal entries of the
Laird company.

Not all criticism of the Commissioner's policies
came from groups or individuals who were personally affected. The Governors of Wyoming and Montana, for instance, declared that a strict compliance with the settlement laws that were framed for use on fertile soil
was almost impossible.[53] Either an entryman had to supplement his income from some outside source and so not
live on his claim all the time or he had to be able to
secure a sufficiently large amount of land to attract
the capital which would enable him to irrigate and work
it. Each Governor estimated that by far the largest
share of the land in their Territories was arid or poor
land. Yet oddly enough both ignored the possibility of
requesting new and appropriate legislation. Instead
they recommended that the land department adopt a broad
interpretation of existing laws. Furthermore in an apparent effort to discourage Congress from modifying the
laws which enabled one man to make entry for large tracts,
the Governor of Wyoming claimed that the rapid decrease
in the public domain should not cause Congress to be-
grudge the settler his portion of land. He unhesitatingly
charged that the decrease was largely the result of extravagant subsidies to railroads and States.

Over against the bitter or temporate criticism
of the Commissioner's course there were several sources

---

52. Ibid., p. 6235.
53. Sec. of Int. Report, 1885, p. 1203ff. and 833-4. The Governor
of New Mexico, however, claimed that pasture land could be
farmed and that therefore only the Homestead law should remain
on the statute books. Ibid., 1887, p. 874.

of unqualified support. Not only visitors, letter-
writers and the pro-Democratic press assured the Commissioner that they approved his program[54] but even an anti-
Administration paper like the Cincinnati Commercial Ga-
zette gave a measure of support by attacks on the past
record of the Land Office.[55] The paper remarked that
"It is notorious that the General Land Office has been
corrupt as long as men can remember." Individuals who
supported the Commissioner outright were quoted to the
same effect. For instance, E. B. Washburne, a former
minister to France, declared that the Office had been
"the most corrupt department that ever existed in any
government on the face of the earth."[56] He also attacked a Chicago editor who had denounced Mr. Sparks'
policies through the press and suggested that the logical way in which to correct an erroneous policy or decision was by appeal to Secretary Lamar not by personal
denunciation. Former Supreme Court Justice David Davis
indicted the great corporations and other monopolies
which had been able to steal millions of acres through
collusion and coöperation with officials in the land department.[57] In a letter to the Commissioner he suggested that the predatory groups would combine to break down
any attempt at crushing the venal system but he encouraged Mr. Sparks to continue his good work.

The Commissioner's exposure of fraud and his revised rules were accompanied by strong recommendations
for the repeal of all the settlement laws except the
Homestead Act; and he added that the latter should be
safeguarded by lengthening the time for commutation. In
1886 he was supported by President Cleveland, though
formerly the President had supported the less severe proposals of his Secretary. The President's second message
to Congress praised the purpose of the settlement laws
but then declared that "through vicious administrative

---

54. The letters include some from land brokers who especially approved the April 3 order. L.O.R., 1886, p. 60.
55. Quoted in the N.Y. Times, August 24, 1885.
56. Ibid., January 29, 1886.
57. 49 Cong. 1 Sess. Cong. Rec., p. 6245. Henry D. Lloyd wrote
   to express his approval. L.O.R., 1886, p. 61.

methods and under changed conditions of communications
and transportation, (they) have been so evaded and violated that their beneficent purpose is threatened with
entire defeat."[58] He also deprecated their abuse to secure large holdings and he felt that the best solution
for the whole problem lay in the repeal of all but the
Homestead law. Secretary Lamar ultimately took the same
position. In 1887 he stated that at first he had hoped
to see a gradual change but that after much thought he
had reached the conclusion that immediate and total repeal was necessary.[59] He went so far as to suggest, that
if Congress felt that the problem was too heavy, control
of the public lands should be given to the States.[60]

     Although a dozen repeal bills had been intro-
duced at the opening of the Forty-ninth Congress and
though some of them were similar to those which had
passed one House or another in the previous session, it
was not until April 15, 1886 that the House of Representatives received a bill containing the Commissioner's
recommendations.[61] While for nearly two months this
bill waited debate the number of entries, particularly
Preëmption entries, rose surprisingly. At the Land Office in Denver, Colorado, several counties reported an
increase amounting to 400 or 500% over the previous
year.[62] Because he believed that this rise was largely
speculative Commissioner Sparks received the Secretary's
consent to suspend further entries under the settlement
laws. When the Secretary's attention was called to the
doubtful legality of such an act he quickly reversed himself though not in time to avoid a Congressional resolution of inquiry.[63]

     Shortly thereafter, in June, 1886, with strong
support from Representatives Cobb of Indiana and Payson

---

58. H. Ex. Doc., vol. I, 49 Cong. 2 Sess., p. xxx-xxxi.
59. Sec. of Int. Report, 1887, p. 3.
60. Ibid., p. 7.
61. 49 Cong. 1 Sess. Cong. Rec., p. 3514; N.Y. Times, April 18,
    1886; the vote was 183-40.
62. Ibid., June 8, 1886; presented in debate, Cong. Rec., op. cit.,
    pp. 5370-80.
63. Author's interview with Judge Proudfit.

of Illinois, the House took up the repeal bill. Representative Cobb, as Chairman of the Committee on Public
Lands, submitted statistics showing the recent efforts at
speculation and quotations from Commissioner McFarland's
reports showing previous evidence of fraud. After a
moderate amount of discussion the bill then passed the
House by a vote of 184-42.[64] The Senate, however, substituted an almost entirely new bill, one which made
fundamental changes in the system of distribution.[65] In
fact the Senate amendments were a bald attempt to protect defrauders and to assist speculators and monopolists. The Senate bill ratified all Preëmption entries
where land had been sold to "bona fide purchasers"; it
confirmed all "final entries hereafter made under the
Preëmption and Homestead Act"; it gave a blanket approval to all Timber Culture entries and allowed entrymen to
prove up without planting any trees; it provided for the
private sale of, rather than settlement entry on, released military reservations; and it allowed mountain
homesteads of 320 acres, without requiring any cultivation. Moreover the Senate attempted to protect existing
and future titles by providing a five-year time limit
for suits to annul patents. By request both Commissioner Sparks and Secretary Lamar commented on the bill and
they registered strong disapproval.[66] The former felt
that no honest entry needed confirmation and that only
corporations, syndicates and mortgage firms would benefit by such a provision.

On the other hand the Senate had attempted to
treat the problem of desert lands more realistically. In
the first place it provided for the transfer of desert
land entries. It also definitely abandoned the fiction
that the Desert Act was intended for the typical settler
for it required an expenditure of nearly $2,000 on an

---

64. 49 Cong. 1 Sess., op. cit., p. 5380.
65. Ibid., p. 6006. On June 29, 1886, the Senate indefinitely postponed a bill to repeal the Preëmption and Timber Culture laws.
49 Cong. 1 Sess. Cong. Rec., p. 6266. On February 1, 1886, it
had done the same to a bill that also repealed the Desert Land
Act.
66. Ibid., pp. 6011-2; 7158-9; L.O.R., 1886, pp. 74-9.

entry within three years.[67] The House refused to adopt
the Senate amendments so the bill went to conference.[68]
A first and a second conference both failed to reconcile
the differences and in the following Session a third conference found the representatives of the two Houses con-
ferring through written rather than personal discussion.[69] Feeling had apparently run high for they were
able to agree on all but one point: the Senate insisted
on protecting entrants accused of fraud by providing a
series of appeals from the Commissioner to the Attorney
General and even the courts if necessary. It was obvious that only wealthy individuals possessing entries
which had been made without adhering carefully to the
letter of the law, would be benefited by such circumlo-
cution. The House conferees opposed it because it removed the control of the public lands from the hands of
the land department. It might be recalled that Congressmen who were friendly to the land grant railroads also
endeavored to shunt questions of forfeiture into the
courts. But when the repeal bill conferees failed to
adjust their final difference the bill was withdrawn,
March 3, 1887.

Observers had pointed out that the question was
non-partisan because Secretary Teller and Commissioner
McFarland had favored repeal. Furthermore the opposing
views on the conference committee were championed by
Representative Payson on the one side and Senators Dolph
of Oregon and Plumb of Kansas on the other, and all three
were Republicans. The New York Times[70] denounced the
Senate for adding another count to its repeated opposition of the popular will but the National Republican of
Washington raised the party flag. It asserted: "One of
the most comprehensive and perfect systems to secure
homes for the people ever found or suggested by any

---

67. In the preceding Congress the Senate passed a bill which con-
     tained a clause validating all sales made within withdrawn rail-
     road limits even though Congress forfeited the land. This at-
     tempt was more flagrantly generous to corporations than the
     above bill. N.Y. Times, February 3, 1885.
68. Cong. Rec., op. cit., p. 6446ff; N.Y. Times, July 26, 1886.
69. Cong. Rec., op. cit., pp. 7158-74; ibid., 2 Sess., pp. 2743-5.
70. July 22, 1886.

country is that passed by the Republicans--the preëmption, (sic!), timber culture and homestead laws."[71] But
if the Democratic recommendations were adopted the paper
claimed that they would prevent "the poor men of the
country from securing homes on the unoccupied lands of
the government." In view of the fact that the Homestead
law was not to be repealed such an inaccurate statement
could have had only the same political purpose as that
of waving the bloody shirt.

Because the system of land distribution was not
revised by Congress the Commissioner continued to expose
the manifold types of land abuses and to request various
forms of coöperation. An Interior Department law clerk[72]
who was a contemporary of Commissioner Sparks told the
author that he could talk for hours on the means used to
secure land illegally or to defraud the unwary entrymen
and the Commissioner has provided abundant illustrations
of these methods. Beside the widespread abuses of the
cattlemen throughout the region west of the Missouri
and the timber frauds in the Far West there were the
frauds for securing farming lands in the semi-arid country. An extreme though somewhat typical example which
the Commissioner cited as true for several districts, occurred in the Garden City region of Kansas.[73] Several
land firms there were reported for disbarment because of
their "illegitimate practices and unprofessional conduct." They all advertised relinquishments for sale, in
many cases specifying the lands and the prices asked for
the relinquishments. The prices of these latter varied
from fifty to more than five hundred dollars. They also
employed "Rustlers" to induce or force settlers to purchase relinquishments. If a prospective settler endeavored to "contest" a claim rather than purchase a relinquishment his success would be doubtful yet there was
no legal way in which to thwart the speculators.

One firm hired a half dozen rustlers and clerks
and placed a bed or cot in front of the Land Office door
so that one of them could sleep on it each night in

71. Quoted in ibid., December 3, 1887.
72. Judge S. V. Proudfit.
73. L.O.R., 1886, p. 85.

order to be the first in line when the Office opened.[74]
On one occasion the firm held possession of the door for
thirty days and intimidated all actual settlers who attempted to make entries and defeated them in every effort to do so. During this period the company brought
in an applicant for a tract which they had relinquished
before a notary public in their own office. The Register
attempted to question the applicant but the latter was
warned by the head rustler to answer no questions and
he was immediately afterwards hurried away to prevent a
Government agent from interviewing him. The same firm
also appeared as attorneys of record for two different
contestants against the same entry, the same grounds of
contest being alleged in both cases.[75]

In order to illustrate another form of speculation Commissioner Sparks had an agent investigate the
entries made upon the opening of the Fort Dodge military
reservation, near Garden City, Kansas.[76] The agent
found that out of seventy-five settlement entries eighteen were made by gamblers, saloon keepers, bartenders
and sporting women engaged in business or plying their
vocation at Dodge City. Twenty-five entrymen were engaged in other businesses of various kinds in the same
town, or were working there during the day. Four were
represented to be widows, generally living in Dodge, but
claiming residence on the land by reasons of visits
thereto of more or less frequency. Six were railroad
employees working for the Santa Fe railroad. Five were
unknown and no improvements could be found on their
claims. In fact the agent reported that "Actual evidences of a home....are not to be found, except in less
than a dozen cases."[77]

Commissioner Sparks believed that a great deal
of the fraud which he pictured could be thwarted if Congress would provide for a sufficient protective force.
He declared that the Special Service staff of twenty-five

---

74. Ibid., p. 86.
75. See also the examples of obstructionary or violent tactics such
    as shooting at a Government witness. Ibid., p. 90.
76. Ibid., p. 96ff.
77. Ibid., p. 97.

or thirty agents who were responsible for 111 land districts was "a force so utterly inadequate as to be almost a mockery of effort."[78] Without the repeal of the
laws which were so grossly violated he felt that there
was an absolute need of not less than one hundred capable and efficient men in the field. Moreover the Commissioner urged the necessity for empowering Registers
and Receivers to summon witnesses in suspected cases.
Minnesota had passed a law giving that power to United
States land officers there but the Commissioner believed
that Congress should make a similar provision for all
States and Territories.[79] He also requested a special
appropriation in order that the Office might clear up
its arrears of work. The only one of these requests
which was answered was found in the $10,000 increased
appropriation for the Special Service Division, an
amount large enough to employ only a few additional
men.[80]

In 1887 despite the lack of legislative coöperation Commissioner Sparks continued his work of reform
and exposure. His report referred to the previous
year's discoveries of "Bold, reckless and gigantic
schemes to rob the government....in every state and territory containing public lands."[81] It appalled him that
"Men of high intelligence and high standing in the community, in many cases millionaires, were leaders in these
unlawful transactions" and that public officials did not
exercise ordinary diligence in thwarting them. Many
legal papers dealing with entries or proofs for entries
could be executed before State and Territorial officers
over whom the Land Office had no control. The Office,
however, supervised its own officials as carefully as
possible and also prepared its first regulations for the
admission of attorneys and agents who wished to practice

---

78. Ibid., p. 100.
79. Ibid., p. 101.
80. In 1885 Congress had appropriated $90,000 for protecting the
    public lands against illegal and fraudulent entry. Commission-
    er Sparks requested $300,000. L.O.R., 1885, p. 236. The total
    appropriation for the Special Service Division in 1886 was
    $175,000. $75,000 was for timber protection. L.O.R., 1887,
    p. 379.
81. L.O.R., 1887, p. 54..

before the Local Offices. The use of unprofessional
methods by attorneys was made a cause for refusing permission to practice before the department and according
to reports that provision had a most beneficial effect.[82]

One of the outstanding examples of fraud which
the Commissioner cited merits consideration in some detail because titles to a part of the land involved had
been attacked by the Government in 1880. Seven years
later, or at the time of the Commissioner's report, the
case was decided by the Supreme Court and the decision
illustrates the fact that Congress was not the only
agency which blocked reforms. Commissioner Sparks related how several groups in southern Colorado fraudulently secured over 600 patents for nearly 100,000
acres.[83] One-third of this amount was valuable coal
land estimated to be worth from $50.00 to $100.00 an
acre. The coal land had been chiefly obtained when
those interested had hired competent mining engineers to
prospect for them. Then they followed the usual procedure of securing deposit surveys and fraudulent entries
under the Homestead or Preëmption laws. Incidentally
forty-two entries were filched from some of the conspirators when a resident of Colorado discovered what
was taking place and secured a contact with the General
Land Office so that the moment patents were issued he
made out and filed with the proper officials in Colorado
deeds of sale to himself.[84] If the victims of his fraud
had attempted to regain their patents it would have
meant exposure of the entire scheme so they apparently
acquiesced in his plot.

Another batch of entries, those which the Government later attacked, were secured in the first instance
by ex-Governor Alexander T. Hunt.[85] Mr. Hunt made use

---

82. Ibid., p. 53.
83. Ibid., p. 56.
84. He sold the entries to the Cincinnati-Colorado Coal, Coal, Coke
    and Iron Co. L.O.R., 1887, pp. 500-2. The Government brought
    suit for them in 1888.
85. U.S. vs. Colorado Coal and Iron Co. 123 U.S. 307. Transcript
    of the Record, #46, pp. 1667-8. Commissioner Drummond tried to
    secure the removal of the officials without success. Craig vs.

of the Preëmption law for sixty-one entries and he paid
$12,000 for the land chiefly in agricultural college
scrip. The Register and Receiver at Pueblo, Colorado,
where he filed his entries could not have been unaware
of the fraud but they issued warrants and allowed the
entire block of about 10,000 acres to pass to patent
with their approval. There was one brief hitch in the
procedure when a lawyer at Trinidad, Colorado, warned
the Land Office in Washington of "Most gigantic frauds
in coal lands in southern Colorado."[86] The Commissioner, Willis Drummond, replied that he would suspend issuing agricultural patents for that area until he could
secure an investigation.[87] But whatever action the Land
Office took it did not succeed in thwarting the fraud
and from 1873 to 1875 patents were delivered to Mr. Hunt.
He sold them and they came into the possession of the
Colorado Coal and Iron Company, a Rockefeller concern.

In 1879, however, acting from causes which are
not quite clear, Secretary of Interior Schurz requested
Attorney General Devens to bring suit for the cancellation of the sixty-one patents.[88] Consequently on January 22, 1880 the Attorney General brought in a bill
charging that Mr. Hunt, the Register, the Receiver and
others were guilty of a conspiracy to defraud the Government and that the entire transaction from entry to
sale was fraudulent. The evidence submitted showed that
the entries lay along the Denver and Rio Grande Railway
line and that the principle persons involved in the suit,
except the Register and Receiver, were officials of the
Road. Mr. Hunt and General William J. Palmer[89] were the

(footnote continued) Leitensdorfer, 123 U.S. 189. Transcript of
    the Record. Secretary Delano may have been involved in the
    frauds. Cf. A. Nevins, "Hamilton Fish," p. 765. A brief ac-
    count of Mr. Hunt's romantic and tragic life is in Nat. Cyclop.
    of Am. Biog., Vol. VI, pp. 447-8.
86. Transcript, #46, op. cit., pp. 1667-8.
87. Ibid., pp. 1504-5.
88. In January, 1879, Copp's Land Owner reported that special agents
    were investigating settlement law entries on coal lands. This
    investigation may have led to the suit.
89. Sketch of his life in Dict. Am. Biog.

founders of the railroad company and Mr. Hunt had been
in charge of laying out its line.[90] He had sold the
warrants for his entries, in most cases before patents
had issued, to William S. Jackson, the Secretary and
Treasurer of the railroad and Mr. Jackson sold out to
General Palmer. A year after he received the last of
the warrants or deeds, Mr. Jackson and two other men incorporated the Southern Colorado Coal and Town Company
and both Mr. Jackson and General Palmer became Directors
of the concern.[91] Furthermore General Palmer was made
President of the Company and Mr. Hunt became a stock-
holder and General Manager. The Company held the property originally acquired by Mr. Hunt.

     The Government had begun its suit against the
Town Company in the Colorado Circuit Court and on the
day following its introduction the Company was merged
with two other concerns to form the Colorado Coal and
Iron Company.[92] Consequently judicial action was continued against the latter. The Iron Company had almost
immediately mortgaged the property in dispute for
$3,500,000.[93] For three years the Court heard arguments
on the case and then in 1883 Judge McCrary gave the decision.[94] He ruled against the Company largely on the
ground that the legal title to the lands had never
passed from the Government because there had been no
person who could legally receive it. The sixty-one
patents were therefore declared void and the Company's
plea of innocent purchaser was rejected.

---

90. Nat. Cyclop. of Am. Biog., Vol. VI, pp. 447-8; William F. Stone,
"History of Colorado," Vol. I, p. 163.
91. The office of the Secretary of State in Colorado has written
the author that since the two names are very indistinct on the
articles of incorporation it is forced to guess whose they are.
92. The Court records showed that the merger took place two days
before suit was commenced but a letter to the author from the
Colorado Department of State gives Jan. 23, 1880, one day after
suit was filed. The merger probably resulted from the fact that
the Maxwell grant patent, issued May 19, 1879, covered some of
Town Company's lands. See Chapter XI post.
93. February 1, 1880. Louis H. Meyer of N.Y. was trustee.
94. N.Y. Times, Nov. 10, 1883.

The case was then appealed to the Supreme Court but it was not acted upon until four years later. Meanwhile the Court decided another suit of almost exactly the same character. While this latter case, United States vs. Moffat,[95] involved only two settlement entries, they had been made on coal lands and patents had been obtained in the same manner and at the same time that Mr. Hunt secured his, with the approval of the same Register and Receiver. In delivering its opinion against Moffat the Supreme Court upheld the Circuit Court by supporting the principle that no title had passed because there was no one to receive it legally. In fact the Court declared:

> "The patents being issued to fictitious parties could not transfer the title, and no one could derive any right under a conveyance in the name of the supposed patentees. A patent to a fictitious person is, in legal effect, no more than a declaration that the government conveys the property to no one. There is, in such case, no room for the application of the doctrine that a subsequent bona fide purchaser is protected."

In the Colorado Coal and Iron Company case, however, the Supreme Court, speaking through Justice Stanley Matthews, reversed the Circuit Court and ruled in favor of the Company.[96] In the first place the Court held that the Company was an innocent purchaser. In order to arrive at this position and to demonstrate what the Company had purchased the Court was forced to evade its pronouncement in the Moffat case. Consequently it raised a subtle distinction as to the type of fraud which had been committed. The Court declared that the Government had proved its charge of fraud against those perpetrating it, or those claiming under them with notice; but it was "not such a fraud as prevents the passing of legal title by the patents." This legal title which under a former decision was null and void, was now valid and had been secured by Mr. Jackson without any knowledge of the fraud used in securing patents. The Court therefore rejected the charge of collusion between

95. 112 U.S. 24.
96. 123 U.S. 307.

the railroad officials. While it is true that the evidence is not conclusive it is difficult to explain how
Mr. Jackson could buy unpatented land from a man who did
not own it without exercising the ordinary caution of
any purchaser who was using funds in trust. Mr. Hunt
did not own the land until he had secured the patents
for it and by fictitious deeds of sale transferred the
title to himself. Mr. Jackson bought from Mr. Hunt before this procedure had taken place.[97]

        The Court also ignored the strong evidence found
in General Palmer's reports to his stockholders of the
Town Company.[98] For instance in 1879 he referred to the
fact that "in the early days....the founders" of the
railroad had acquired the property which the Town Company owned. Since the railroad company was formed in the
latter part of 1870, the period about 1873 when Mr. Hunt
was securing his land is more apt to be classed as "early
days" than 1876 when the Town Company was formed. And
it has been pointed out above that the "founders" of the
railroad company were Messrs. Hunt and Palmer. In short
it is difficult to accept the Court's analysis[99] that the
other railroad officials were ignorant of the fraud. At
its best the decision was the recognition of a fait ac-
compli which the Court did not wish to disrupt because
of the construction work and commitments that were involved. The decision might also be considered an encouragement to other defrauders. The New York Times was
amazed by it and devoted three editorials to condemning

----

97. He paid for his purchases with $45,000 furnished him by about
    fifty speculators from the East and the West but he was curi-
    ously vague in testifying concerning his agreement with this
    group.
98. Transcript #46, op. cit., pp. 1507-10; Stone, op. cit., p. 348.
99. See also its claim that the Government had not proved that all
    the patents were issued to fictitious persons and its reversal
    of its position as given in the Moffat case, regarding the cul-
    pability of the local officials. There was also the curious
    suggestion that the Government should have secured testimony
    from the Washington firm, Britton and Gray. The firm had ob-
    tained the patents from the Land Office for Mr. Hunt but it
    was in no position to testify as to the validity of the en-
    tries or the charge of collusion.

it.[100]   The Baltimore Herald, a Republican paper,
claimed: "We are not able to understand the grounds on
which this decision was made....Some technicality serves
the evasion of the law.....   The stealing of the people's land is a more atrocious offense than stealing a
man's horse."[101]

But to return to the exposures in the Land Office report of 1887.   The latter showed that in the
previous year 1,153 entries were cancelled with 2,312
held for cancellation.[102]   It also stated that these
figures represented but a small portion of the number of
entries actually annulled because, as usual, a great
many were voluntarily released upon investigation.   Furthermore many persons who had taken part in frauds
sought to rectify the wrong which they had done.   Such
actions, along with a more wholesome effort in many
western regions to punish violations, reflect the moral
effect of the administration in Washington.   One instance of an attempt to rectify fraud occurred at a
trial in California where over one hundred entrymen voluntarily testified that they had been persuaded by
agents of land syndicates to make illegal entries.[103]
One of these entrymen, while on the witness stand, was
assaulted by the attorney for the defendants and cruelly
beaten because he reported that the attorney had endeavored to bribe him not to appear as a witness.

In his continued attack on speculation the Commissioner cited statistics for the use of the Preëmption
and Timber Culture laws.   For the three years ending in
1887, in the States of Colorado, Kansas and Nebraska,
there were 73,908 Preëmption filings.   During the same
period there were only 25,558 Preëmption entries, a second step toward securing patent.[104]   Regarding this discrepancy the Commissioner argued: "It is presumable
that bona fide locations may sometimes be abandoned.   It

---

100. Nov. 22, 23; Dec. 12, 1887. One editorial was truthfully head-
     ed "Fraud Triumphant."
101. March 19, 1888, quoted in "Public Opinion."
102. L.O.R., 1887, p. 51.
103. Ibid., pp. 53-5.
104. Ibid., p. 56.

is not presumable that 48,350 out of 73,908 actual settlers would abandon claims made in good faith. Hegiras
of this kind are unknown."[105] He therefore concluded
that nearly two-third of the filings were speculative
and not for the purpose of securing homes.

An examination of entries under the Timber Culture Act in relation to the number of relinquishments
revealed an astonishing amount of speculation and what
may be classed as an earlier form of racketeering. The
Commissioner showed that in many sections of the country
Timber Culture entries were filed, later released and
then filed immediately again in some cases on five successive occasions.[106] As a consequence the land so
entered remained uninhabited, unimproved and uncultivat-
ed until a settler who was willing to buy off the speculative entry came along. The total number of relinquishments for one year, whether for immediate re-entry on
speculation or purchase by a settler, proved enlighten-
ing. In Dakota, Kansas and Nebraska for the year ending
June 30, 1887 there were 26,780 relinquishments for an
area totaling 4,284,800 acres.[107] It is plausible to
suppose that one-half of the entries were released for a
bona fide settler at an average of $100 each. If that
were true it would mean that $1,339,000 was paid to land
racketeers in three States or Territories during one
year. Such a sum obviously added a considerable burden
to farming.

To finally clinch his point that the public domain was subject to unwarranted appropriation, on April
28, 1887 Commissioner Sparks directed his special agents
to select representative townships in Minnesota, Nebraska, Kansas, Oregon, California, New Mexico, Montana,
Dakota and Washington, examine the records and discover
what actually happened to land absorbed under the settlement laws. The agents chose thirty-six townships,
scattered throughout the designated areas. They reported that out of 1,416 agricultural entries embracing over
225,000 acres of land taken up under the Homestead and

---

105. Ibid., pp. 56-7.
106. Ibid., p. 57.
107. Ibid., p. 61.

Preëmption laws, the requirements of the laws were fulfilled in only 268 instances.[108] Nearly one thousand
of the tracts entered had been transferred or mortgaged.
The mortgages had generally been foreclosed and the
title of the land passed out of the hands of the entryman. The agents also reported that out of 732 Timber
Culture entries, 600 had been relinquished and cancelled. Some of the settlement entries may have been
abandoned to mortgagors due to the restlessness of fron-
tiersmen but in any case they represent a violation of
the spirit if not the letter of the law.

The Commissioner had accompanied the exposures
of his last report by a request for $50,000 additional
to aid in protecting the public lands and he also sought
an additional grant for timber land protection. These
increases were denied but before they were considered
the Commissioner had left the Land Office. The cause
for his departure as well as further analysis of the
problems which the land department attacked will be considered later. Yet only by reading all of his three reports is it possible to comprehend fully the Commissioner's work and his handicaps. Though his term was relatively brief his record stands unmatched.[109] The Commissioner had his faults and it is obvious that much of
the reform work which he accomplished depended on the
support from his superiors. Nevertheless he honestly
and energetically struggled with the evils of a system
that was denying elementary rights to the very people in
whose name it had been created and by his success he
aided the cause of democracy.

---

108. Ibid., p. 82.
109. Gustavus Myers calls him "one of the very few incorruptible
     Commissioners of the Land Office." "Great American Fortunes,"
     p. 263, (rev. ed.).

Chapter XI

THE MAXWELL LAND GRANT FRAUD

One of the early reforms credited to the Democrats resulted from their efforts to check corruption
in New Mexico. The Republicans had found the Territory
subject to disorder and violence. Murders by despera-
does like Billy the Kid, feuds like the Lincoln County
wars,[1] and brazen thefts like the Star Route manipula-
tions were examples of unsatisfactory conditions. There
were also extensive land frauds both in connection with
private land claims and in ranchers' abuses of the settlement laws. One effort for improvement was undertak-
en by President Hayes when he appointed General Lew
Wallace Governor with instructions to leave no stone un-
turned in achieving order.[1] Nevertheless the General's
three-year term, 1878-81, did not correct basic faults.
Later in a vain effort to check frauds Commissioner
McFarland had suspended land patenting there for two or
three years.[2]

Under President Cleveland, however, the Democrats adopted more thorough-going measures. They removed judicial and administrative officials, attempted
to prosecute those guilty of malpractices and saw to it
that land frauds were adequately exposed and impeded if
not halted. The President appointed George W. Julian of
Indiana to the post of Surveyor General at Santa Fe.[3]

1. R. E. Twitchell, "Old Santa Fe," p. 396.
2. L.O.R., 1886, p. 47.
3. All of the appointments did not turn out successfully. Representative Springer of Illinois, who reputedly had investments in
   the Territory, and Attorney General Garland, who was favorable
   to corporate interests secured the appointment of Judge Vincent
   to be Chief Justice of the Supreme Court of New Mexico and ex-
   Senator Ross to be Governor. The President soon removed Judge
   Vincent when he learned that he was connected with land frauds.
   N.Y. Tribune, Oct. 17, 1885; Nation, Oct. 22, 1885.

The office needed a dependable occupant because of the
important role it played in determining the validity of
private land claims. By his lengthy reports to the Land
Office and by magazine articles and speeches, Mr. Julian
supplemented the testimony of the New York Herald's special correspondent[4] and helped to make New Mexico a by-
word for land law violations. But because the Government could not convict the alleged guilty, with juries
that were largely sympathetic to them, because the Supreme Court upheld certain land titles, and because
eastern newspapers vigorously attacked Democratic efforts it was difficult to find out the truth of conditions at that time.[5]

There is no doubt of abuses, however, and New
Mexico offers an interesting case study in public land
administration. It was probably more malodorous than
most Territories, yet it reveals certain characteristics
that were common to the West. Its story can be told
best by concentrating on one Mexican grant. There are
several that might serve: The San Pedro and Canon del
Agua grant whose owners endeavored to secure General
Grant as president of their company (fortunately for
him he refused and the Supreme Court later annulled the
grant);[6] the Peralta grant, representing an enormous
claim based on pure fabrication, and one which years of
research finally cancelled;[7] the Una de Gato grant exploited by S. W. Dorsey until it too, was found to be
fraudulent;[8] William R. Hearst's grant, which was finally patented for an amount greatly reduced from his

---

4. April, 6 to 14, 1886.
5. Even R. E. Twitchell has displayed a curious animosity. He
   states that with the Cleveland administration "an assault on
   land titles to lands in New Mexico was inaugurated which for
   virulence of action and incapacity of management" had never been
   equaled. He appeared glad to report that the efforts failed and
   that few violators were convicted. "Leading Facts of New Mexican History," vol. II, p. 498.
6. 4 N. Mex., 405-602; 146 U.S., 120; and Twitchell, op. cit.,
   pp. 182-4.
7. Report of the Attorney General, 1895, pp. 17-8.
8. L.O.R., 1879, p. 458.

original claim;[9] or the Maxwell grant, possessing a
record as unique and discreditable as any in American
history.

The scope of the Maxwell grant makes its story
particularly significant; it affected thousands of settlers and miners, the Land Office, politicians, Congress
and the Supreme Court. The grant involved nearly
2,000,000 acres, an area equal in amount to the States
of Delaware and Rhode Island. It contained some of the
richest coal lands in America; gold, iron, timber and
other resources were also extensive. In 1887 it was
valued at $25,000,000.[10] The grant affected high of-
ficials or prominent business men in America, England
and Holland. It produced guerilla warfare in New Mexico and wild scrambles on the Amsterdam stock exchange.
It attracted considerable attention in the United
States when Commissioner Sparks urged renewed court action to set aside its patent. This brought into prominence several outstanding Democrats and Stephen B. Elkins, Blaine's campaign manager in 1884.

Only an outline of the story from 1840 to 1890
is possible here. There are innumerable thorny problems that hang over the grant: irreconcilable dates,
conflicting and contradictory testimony, questionable
documents and a general suspicion of fraud from start
to finish. It originated in 1841 from a petition by
two Mexican citizens, Guadaloupe Miranda and Charles
Beaubien, to the civil and military governor of New
Mexico, Manuel Armijo.[11] At that time, New Mexico was
practically independent of Mexico and General Armijo
exercised despotic powers.[12] The Beaubien and Miranda
petition requested a tract of land which was described
as "below the junction of the Rayado with the Colorado,"
the present Canadian River, northeast of Taos. The
authors claimed to be interested in growing sugar beets
and cotton and in raising cattle. The Governor granted
their request "in conformity with law" so that they
might use it as "the law allows." Two years later the

_____

9. Report of the Attorney General, 1904, p. 109.
10. N.Y. Herald, May 23, 1887.
11. H. Rep., #321. 36 Cong. 1 Sess., p. 246.
12. Twitchell, op. cit., p. 207.

grantees were given formal possession by Justice of the
Peace, Cornelio Vigil.[13] He accompanied them from Taos
to the grant, circumvented it in about six days, and
set up seven stones to mark its limits. He then gave
them a sketch map called a diseno, and a certificate of
juridical possession describing the boundaries in approximately the same manner as the original petition.[14]
It is possible that he attempted to give them all the
land in what were considered "out-boundaries"[15] instead
of just a tract within them. Yet according to Mexican
law no man could receive more than eleven square leagues
or about 48,000 acres. This would have allowed about
97,000 acres to the two grantees, although the out-
boundaries covered perhaps fifteen times that much.[16]

---

13. He later acquired part of the Vigil and St. Vrain grant north
    of Beaubien and Miranda's claim. The former supposedly covered
    100 square leagues. H. Rep. #321, op. cit., p. 271ff.
14. H. Rep. #321, op. cit., pp. 247-8.
15. Later in arguing a case for the grant owners their lawyer re-
    ferred to the "out-boundaries" as the limits of the grant which
    the American Government patented. U.S. vs. Maxwell Land Grant
    and Railway Co. 121 U.S. 325. Transcript of Record, October
    term, 1886, vol. 27, p. 709. Hereafter referred to as "Tran-
    script."
16.   In discussing the origin of the Maxwell or Beaubien and
    Miranda Grant it is chiefly necessary to follow the official
    documents under which it was confirmed by Congress. It has
    been stated above that many documents seem of questionable
    validity. Furthermore the evidence based on verbal and other
    testimony for the Government's suit against the Maxwell Company
    or for other suits which affected the grant, conflict. What
    actually was granted legally or even illegally, if such a grant
    can be made, cannot easily be determined. For instance there
    is no doubt that Charles Bent, of the famous brothers who built
    Bent's fort on the Arkansas River, had an interest in the grant.
    He helped to obtain the grant when he was Secretary and confi-
    dential advisor to Governor Armijo. (H. H. Bancroft, "History
    of Nevada, Colorado, and Wyoming," vol. 25. Complete Works,
    1890, note p. 594.) In a suit which was later brought to the
    Supreme Court the Bent heirs claimed that Charles Bent had ob-
    tained a third interest in the grant. They later changed their
    claim to demand one-fourth interest. (Cf. Thompson vs. Maxwell

When in the following year Beaubien and Miranda
began to make use of their grant they were confronted

(footnote continued) Land Grant and Railroad Company, 168 U.S. 451
and the Transcript of the Record for the case.) The changed
claim of the Bent heirs suggests that there was a fourth member
who profited by the grant. This fourth member was doubtless
Governor Armijo himself. There is an untranslated letter which
the Governor wrote in May, 1846 and which is included in the
Transcript of the Record for the Maxwell case. 121 U.S. 325.
How the letter got there and why it was not translated is difficult to say for it was never used and is certainly antagonistic to the claims which the Company was making. The letter
stated, "a mi nombre resiba la posesion de terreno....del
rincon del Rio Colorado," which may be translated "the possession of the (grant at the) bend of the Red River resides in my
name." Transcript, p. 240.

The grant was later patented by the United States Government as related in the present chapter, for even more than
the out-boundaries or the illegal boundaries called for. The
largest district included by the patent lay in Colorado and included part of the land over which the Maxwell Company and the
Colorado Fuel and Iron Company struggled. Furthermore the
heirs of Beaubien brought suit after the patent issued because
they claimed that they had been misled on the amount of land in
the grant and so had not been paid enough for their share of
it. This would appear to be a legal way of stating that they
knew that the grant had not been as large as that for which the
Government gave patent and so they felt they should share in
the fraud.

Practically the same conditions of a grant which had more
behind it than appeared on the face of important official documents existed for the Vigil and St. Vrain grant. Charles Bent
and Governor Armijo both held an interest in this grant according to the records produced in a law suit when the United
States had taken over the Southwest. Craig vs. Leitensdorfer,
123 U.S. 189. Transcript of the Record. This grant, the
Beaubien and Miranda grant, the Sangre de Christo grant and
the Nolan grant gave Armijo, Bent, Vigil and St. Vrain control
of about 7,000,000 acres. These men made up the center of a
"Mexican" Santa Fe ring and their greed, aggrandizement and
harsh treatment of the Indians in addition to the fact that
some of them were appointed Territorial officials when the
United States took control, probably accounts for the Taos
Massacre of 1847. Cf. N.Y. Herald, May 23, 1887.

by an official decree of suspension.[17]   The government
had acted upon a petition from a priest of Taos, A.
Jose Martinez, and some of the Pueblo chiefs. They had
asserted that the use of the land belonged to them
under an agreement with Charles Bent, an American who
had a claim on the land. Senor Beaubien answered the
petition by a decree at bar filed before the Governor,
temporarily not Armijo. The former's written petition
is of the first importance as evidence regarding the
size of the claim.[18]   He explained that he and Miranda
had received a grant at El Rincon (bend, elbow) del Rio
Colorado, but that it had no connection with Mr. Bent's
lands. In fact it seemed to Senor Beaubien "that the
curate Martinez and his associates do not know to whom
these lands belong, nor their extent, as he states that
a large number of leagues were granted, when the grant
does not exceed fifteen or eighteen, which will be seen
by the accompanying judicial certificates."

This declaration was subject to contradictory
interpretation when the grant was again in dispute. One
view held that Senor Beaubien referred to his own grant
as "fifteen or eighteen" square leagues and the opposite
interpretation claimed that he was speaking of Mr.
Bent's lands under which the Curate was claiming rights.
There is little doubt that the documents concerned and
the wording of the statement are confusing but it is
most probable that in presenting judicial certificates
to support his statement, Senor Beaubien was referring
to his own claim. If the Curate was claiming rights to
land under Mr. Bent, Senor Beaubien would not have presented certificates to show where the Curate's lands
were but where his own lands were. However, the Governor turned the whole question over to the Departmental
Assembly, (of whose existence there is some doubt), and
that body placed Beaubien and Miranda again in possession of their land.[19]

---

17. H. Rep. #321, op. cit., p. 248.
18. Ibid., p. 249.
19. In another part of Beaubien's reply he speaks of the fact that
    he is submitting his own documents and he asks for their return
    when the Governor has examined them.

According to subsequent testimony of Kit Carson, the famous scout, the grantees began scattered settlements on their claim.[20] In 1844 he and Lucien B. Maxwell had passed through the grant region. Maxwell was the man for whom the grant was later named.[21] He was also a scout and frontiersman, one who had been a native of Kaskaskia, Illinois. He had first come to Taos when about twenty years old. Then he had met Senor Beaubien and his six daughters. He soon fell in love with one of the latter and married her. He did not abandon scouting immediately but in 1848 he and Carson agreed to settle on the grant.[22] Starting humbly Maxwell became prosperous and finally built himself the remarkably conducted ranch house which became so well known to travellers along the Santa Fe Trail.[23]

After the United States acquired New Mexico, Congress had passed the law for settling titles to claims derived from the Mexican government. A previous chapter has noted that the plan for Congressional confirmation of claims which the Surveyor General had examined did not prove at all satisfactory. One of the first titles submitted to the Surveyor General however, was that of Beaubien and Miranda. In the spring of 1857 they presented their papers and evidence that the grant contained at that time about 200 acres under cultivation and about 1,500 head of stock.[24] When the Surveyor General forwarded the grant papers, with those of a dozen other grants, to the Land Office for transmission to Congress, he presented his opinion on them. For the Beaubien and Miranda claim he stated in part: "The grant having been confirmed by the departmental assembly and been in the constant possession of the grantees from the date of the grant to the present

---

20. Ibid., p. 254.
21. See the sketch of his life in the Dict. of Am. Biog.
22. D. C. Peters, "Kit Carson's Own Story of His Life," p. 93.
23. Henry Inman, "The Old Santa Fe Trail," chap. xviii.
24. H. Rep. #321, op. cit., p. 254. For evidence that there is a question regarding the reliability of some papers from the Santa Fe office see "History of New Mexico. Its Resources and People." Pacific States Publishing Co., 1907, vol. I, p. 185.

time,....it is the opinion of this office that it is a
good and valid grant, according to the laws and customs
(!) of the Republic of New Mexico and the decision of
the Supreme Court of the United States as well as the
treaty of Guadaloupe Hidalgo of February 2, 1848, and
it is therefore confirmed to Charles Beaubien and
Guadaloupe Miranda, and it is transmitted for the action of Congress in the premises.[25]

It was not until three years later that Congress
found time to consider the claims.[26] In April, 1860,
the House accepted a report from the Private Land
Claims Committee and approved sixteen grants.[27] The
Committee had asserted it gave approval from a sense of
justice to the people of New Mexico. It freely confessed the want of time to examine the grants fully and
admitted its own ignorance of the amount of land claimed
in most of them. The Committee also recognized the Surveyor General's inability to do justice to his work and
it suggested that a special board or commission be
formed, similar to that for California, to pass on all
New Mexican grants. There seemed to be some doubt that
Congress would adopt this suggestion but the Committee
hoped that if there was any chance, the commission
would "finally determine" all claims.

Six weeks later the Senate Committee on Private
Land Claims, through Judah P. Benjamin, reported on the
grants.[28] It had examined them more carefully than the
House Committee and had found one for which the grantees
had requested one hundred square leagues, or nearly
450,000 acres. The Committee believed that that was
"too extravagant for words" so it reduced the claim to
five square leagues. By examining the diseno of another claim the Committee had estimated that it too

---

25. Ibid., p. 254.
26. In a pessimistic mood R. E. Twitchell declared that every
    claimant had to spend considerable time in Washington, organize
    a lobby and buy "the army of official and non-official cormo-
    rants which have always infested the Capital." "Leading
    Facts," op. cit., vol. II, p. 467.
27. H. Rep. #321, op. cit.
28. Sen. Rep. #228, 36 Cong. 1 Sess. Cong. Rec., p. 2750.

covered one hundred square leagues or possibly much more. In addition to its indefinite extent there was an irregularity in the method of procuring the grant.[29]

Consequently the Committee declared it would be guided by the colonization law of 1824 and allow the claimants the legal amount of eleven square leagues to each. It believed that confirmation for that amount would be all the claimants could "fairly expect" and it "would be not only a fair but a liberal compliance with the obligations" imposed by the peace treaty.

The Senate accepted the Committee's report with no discussion, June 8, 1860, and two weeks later the House approved the Senate amendments.[30] On the same day President Buchanan signed the bill which thus "confirmed" certain land claims, "as recommended for confirmation by the Surveyor General," with two exceptions.[31]

Then the Civil War intervened so that the Land Office made no effort to have the Maxwell claim surveyed or patented. Senor Beaubien had bought out the interest of Miranda in 1846[32] and when he died in 1864, Maxwell, who had been a great favorite of his father-in-law, inherited control of his wife's share in the grant. Maxwell then purchased the claims of the other children, paying not more than $3,500 for each share.[33]

---

29. This was the Vigil and St. Vrain or Las Animas grant.
30. Ibid., pp. 2750 and 3216.
31. The bill also stated: "The foregoing confirmations shall only be construed as quit claims or relinquishments on the part of the United States, and shall not affect the adverse rights of any other person or persons whomsoever." 12 Stat. 71.
32. Among other curious records are two deeds of sale from Miranda to Maxwell, one dated 1858 and the other 1868. Transcript, p. 396 and pp. 399-400. See also R. E. Twitchell, "The Military Occupation of the Territory of New Mexico," pp. 267-9.
33. Transcript, op. cit., p. 396ff. There is some doubt, however, about the legality of the purchases. Cf. N.Y. Herald, May 23, 1887 and the "History of New Mexico," op. cit., vol. I, p. 188. The latter claims that Beaubien's wife never sold her interest in the grant. The suit which the Herald refers to is not recorded in the New Mexico law reports prior to 1895, at least.

He also bought off certain other claimants, who need not
be considered here, and thus became apparently, sole
owner of the grant. Hereafter it will be referred to
as the Maxwell grant. A close friend of Maxwell's reported that in 1866 the latter was willing to sell the
entire "ranche" for $75,000.[34] Fortunately he did not
find a buyer for in the following year gold was found
in the vicinity. It is said that Maxwell then extended
his claim to include the mining section. The possibilities of the grant must have attracted considerable
attention for in 1869 Maxwell gave an option bond to
Jerome B. Chaffee, later Senator from Colorado. Then
Maxwell sought a Government survey and a patent.

On May 30, 1869 the Surveyor General forwarded
Maxwell's survey application together with a surveying
contract to the Land Office.[35] The Office however,
withheld approval until it obtained more definite information on the extent of claim. The Surveyor General
then mailed certain statements by Maxwell and a diseno
which purported to be a copy of the original map given
in 1843. It was not a true copy and the shape of the
grant was materially altered. But since the original
had not been forwarded to the Land Office in 1857, the
latter was unaware of the discrepancy. At any rate,
the map showed that Maxwell was claiming nearly
2,000,000 acres. The Commissioner reported the case to
Secretary of Interior, Jacob D. Cox, because he realized
that its interpretation would be a precedent for
others.[36] After discussing the origin and subsequent
history of the grant the Commissioner gave such clues
as he could to the amount of land which it might contain for he did not believe that the 2,000,000 claim
was correct. His opinion was based on the colonization
laws of Mexico, the claimants' estimation that the
grant did not exceed eighteen (square) leagues, the Surveyor General's opinion that it was a valid grant under
the laws of the Republic of Mexico, the repeated

34. Leon Noel, "The Largest Estate in the World," Overland Monthly,
    Nov., 1888.
35. L.O.R., 1885, p. 126.
36. Ibid., pp. 125-7.

decisions of the Supreme Court on similar cases in California, and Congressional restriction of a grant approved in 1860 to eleven square leagues.

Secretary Cox's reply of December 31, 1869 accepted the Commissioner's arguments.[37] He ruled that the grant should be limited to eleven square leagues for each claimant. He added that all future cases should be treated in the same manner if they had been confirmed without measurement of boundaries or distinct specification of the quantity contained. Regarding the "eighteen" leagues in Beaubien's 1844 petition, the Secretary said: "It would be, in my judgment, a gross fraud upon the Government to allow it to be extended to the enormous quantity of 450 leagues or upward....after obtaining the grant upon so explicit a statement of the amount claimed." He also ordered the Commissioner to run the public surveys over the claim if his rule was rejected.

Since there was no appeal from this decision it would seem that Maxwell would have had to accept twenty-two square leagues, 97,000 acres. But trusting to better fortune from a change in Cabinet officers, Maxwell, and those who were by that time interested in the grant with him, refused to accept the decision. Consequently on July 27, 1871, when Mr. Cox had been replaced by Columbus Delano, another appeal was made. After hearing the appeal, the Secretary refused to reverse his predecessor's decision on the ground that under departmental rules he lacked authority to do so.[38]

When Maxwell's backers refused to accept the limited area of twenty-two square leagues, the land department carried out Secretary Cox' order and in 1874 extended the public surveys over a large part of the district which they claimed. The township plats were filed in the local Land Office and entries were allowed under the federal settlement laws.[38] Though notice of this action was forwarded to Senator Thurman of the Public Lands Committee and did not provoke a protest it

37. Ibid., pp. 127-9.
38. Ibid., p. 129.

did not settle the case and the story must shift to activities in New Mexico.

It has been pointed out that Maxwell gave an option bond to Jerome Chaffee. With the latter were associated George M. Chilcotte, later another Colorado Senator, and Stephen B. Elkins and Charles F. Holly of New Mexico. They engineered the purchase from Maxwell and his wife, April 30, 1870.[39] At first Maxwell retained about 1,000 acres surrounding his ranch but later this too, was sold. The supposed purchaser was the Maxwell Land Grant and Railroad Company of New Mexico, though actually the company was not organized until two weeks after the purchase. The company's officials included: William A. Pile,[40] Governor of the Territory; T. Rush Spencer, Surveyor General of New Mexico; John S. Watts; John Pratt; and Miguel A. Otero.[41]

Despite Secretary Cox' rejection of their claim Mr. Chaffee's associates contracted privately for a survey in January, 1870, before the company was organized.[42] Shortly thereafter the survey was executed by United States Deputy Surveyor, W. W. Griffin. He, of course, surveyed the 2,000,000 acres. A copy of this survey, approved by the Surveyor General, was sent to the Land Office to be placed in its files for reference. Meanwhile the Company sent representatives, including Wilson Waddingham of New York, to London to sell the tract there. After making several false representations[43] the agents succeeded in selling the grant for about $1,350,000 and then the English purchasers mortgaged the grant to some Hollanders for £700,000.[44] The Company issued $5,000,000

---

39. Transcript, pp. 425-6. The price was $1.00.
40. Governor Pile had been recommended by Carl Schurz. Cf. A. Nevins "Hamilton Fish," p. 120.
41. A letter to the author from the State Corporation Commission of New Mexico omits Mr. Spencer's name though the Supreme Court Records include it with that of Messrs. Pile and Watts.
42. Transcript, p. 595.
43. Philadelphia Press, June 7, 1887.
44. The mortgage deed listed Thomas A. Scott, President of the Pennsylvania Railroad, and Samuel M. Felton, a director of the road, as trustees. Maxwell was paid $750,000. Transcript, p. 430. N.Y. Sun, Sept. 1, 1884.

worth of stock and chose General Palmer its first president and Stephen B. Elkins the resident director and local attorney.[45]

In order to assure their foreign friends that the grant really contained 2,000,000 acres and not 97,000 which the Secretary of Interior had ruled, the company secured opinions as to the validity of title from some of the leading lawyers of the country. How these men were supposed to know the amount of land involved with any precision is a matter of doubt. The lawyers were George F. Curtis, William M. Evarts, Senator Thomas F. Bayard, Chairman of the Committee on Public Lands, and Judah P. Benjamin, Chairman of the same Committee in 1860 when the grant had been confirmed. In 1870 Mr. Benjamin was one of the leading lawyers in London and he had been retained as the London representative of the company.[46]

All of these gentlemen upheld the rights of the company to the amount of land described in the original petition for the grant. They uniformly asserted[47] that Congress had confirmed the grant for the enclosed area and they assumed or inferred that the claim to 2,000,000 acres was valid. The most informing opinion should have been and in some respects was, Mr. Benjamin's. He upheld the company's claim in vigorous style but at the same time he was in a dilemma. His Committee in 1860 either knew or they did not know that the Beaubien and Miranda grant covered a vast area. Mr. Benjamin claimed that the Committee did know it and that therefore Congress approved the large amount. But he could not explain why his Committee made an exception for that grant when it had reduced one claim to the lawful amount and had explained that 100 square leagues were too extravagant for words. If, therefore, the Committee did not know that the Beaubien and Miranda claim covered nearly 450 square leagues it could not have intended to approve that amount. In fact Mr. Benjamin gave his case

---

45. N.Y. Tribune, June 30, 1885.
46. Dict. of Am. Biog.
47. Opinions on file in Land Office under Maxwell Grant. Mr. Bayard is quoted in N.Y. Tribune, June 30, 1885.

away when he criticized the Land Office for not warning
the Committee regarding the size of large grants. His
opinion in 1870 may have been influenced by his connection with the company which scarcely seems to have
sought the truth.[48]

In addition to these opinions and time the Maxwell company had a third source of strength in the iron-
clad political control which its members held over the
Territory of New Mexico.[49] Republican rule there arose
shortly after the Civil War and continued almost un-
broken throughout the remainder of the Nineteenth Century. Its most brilliant representative while he lived
in the Territory, and even long after he had moved east,
was the company lawyer, Stephen B. Elkins. His law
partner was Thomas Catron, later a Senator. Associated
with them in a business capacity was W. W. Griffin, the
surveyor. These three and others made up what became
known as the "Santa Fe Ring," and they controlled appointments, elections and legislation with a ruthless
hand. They finally planned to defeat Secretary Cox' decision through Congressional aid. Consequently in 1872
they managed to elect Mr. Elkins, "Smooth Steve Elkins"
as his fellow Senators later called him, Territorial
delegate to Congress.[50] He was to press for favorable
legislation. The very year in which he took his seat
he was chosen president of the company, though he later
publicly denied that he had held any such office. Then
while he was in Holland on business for the company he
was re-elected to Congress by a fraudulent count of
votes.[51] He failed, however, to obtain the adoption of
any of the bills which he sponsored.

Meanwhile the company and its English representatives ruled over their pretended empire in lavish and
reckless style.[52] They frequently clashed with settlers

---

48. In 1872 Attorney General George H. Williams held that the Mexican law of limitations had no effect on the grant since Congress
had confirmed it by metes and bounds. C. F. Coan, "A History
of New Mexico," vol. I., pp. 482-3.
49. R. E. Twitchell, "Old Santa Fe," p. 394ff.
50. Ibid., p. 394.
51. Transcript, p. 456.
52. N.Y. Tribune, Sept. 22, 1879.

and miners and feeling in the district ran high. Many
residents sought assurance from the Land Office that
they had a legal right to the land and the Office usually replied by enclosing a copy of Secretary Cox' order.[53]
Nevertheless the settlers were uneasy for they feared
the power of wealth. In 1870 a local newspaper had
said: "On the one side is a company of capitalists of
great wealth and unlimited audacity, pushing a policy
of proscription toward free labor and independent enterprise. On the other the entire community of miners,
settlers, merchants, and mechanics with no ally but
justice and no capital but nerve. Who shall win?"[54]

It was a portentous question. The Government
seemed to be on the settlers' side. Moreover the depression of 1875 plus the failure to secure a patent,
brought the company into a bankruptcy which also seemed
to favor them. Yet the "Ring" was able to keep the
claim legally alive irrespective of depressions and official decisions, through tax assessments. When in
January, 1877, the Company became penniless the grant
was sold to cover an alleged tax debt.[55] Ostensibly it
was bought by a member of the New Mexican Legislature
and then transferred to Thomas B. Catron, Elkin's law
partner and at that time United States Attorney for the
Territory.

Meanwhile the efforts to secure a patent for the
large claim had taken a new turn. The New York attorneys
for the Company found in the Colorado courts a case
which involved a Mexican grant similar in several respects to the Maxwell grant, and one which they felt
could be appealed to the Supreme Court for a favorable
test.[56] The case had arisen from a dispute between a
John Tameling and the United States Freehold and Immigration Company. Tameling had attempted to settle on
a part of the 500,000 acre claim which the Company had

---

53. Land Office Files under "Maxwell Grant."
54. Railway Press and Telegraph, Sept. 17, 1870. (Land Office
    Files.)
55. "History of New Mexico," op. cit., vol. I, p. 186; H. Report
    #1253. 52 Cong. 1 Sess.
56. N.Y. Tribune, June 30, 1885.

derived from the Sangre de Christo grant.[57] He maintained that since the Mexican law had restricted grants
to eleven square leagues to a person the Company's
claim was illegal and that he had, therefore, settled
on public land. The case reached the Supreme Court in
its October term, 1876, and the Court decided in favor
of the Company. It stated that Congressional confirmation passed title as effectively as though a patent had
issued. But in taking this stand the Court refused to
construe the highly ambiguous confirmatory act and
evaded a re-statement of previous decisions upholding
the Mexican law.

Contrary to expectations, however, the Maxwell
Company did not use the decision as a basis for an appeal in the Interior Department. Instead Commissioner
James Williamson began a series of suspicious moves
when he wrote to Secretary of Interior Zachariah
Chandler, March 10, 1877, and called attention to the
Tameling decision.[58] He noted that it appeared to be
opposed to the decision Secretary Cox had laid down in
the Maxwell case. In the light of this conflict the
Commissioner concluded his letter: "I have the honor
to request that I be instructed how I shall proceed in
the adjudication of like cases in the future."

Less than a week later Secretary Schurz, who
had succeeded Secretary Chandler, replied:[59] "The decision of the Supreme Court must be taken as the construction of the law by which the rights of parties are
to be determined. You will hereafter be governed by

---

57. The grant was patented for about 1,000,000 acres in 1881. The
   Freehold Company claimed half of it. The Sangre de Christo
   grant has an amazing history. It was given by Governor Armijo
   to Louis Lee and a son of Charles Beaubien. The son was twelve
   years old at the time and probably away at school. He and Lee
   were killed in the Taos massacre. Charles Beaubien therefore
   inherited his son's share and bought the other half of the
   grant for $100. Beubien sold it all to William Gilpin, one
   time Governor of Colorado, though the date of the sale is two
   months after Beaubien's death. 93 U.S. 644.
58. L.O.R., 1885, p. 129.
59. Ibid., p. 130.

the rule laid down by the court in said case in all similar cases and patents will issue for the tract recommended by the Surveyor General and confirmed by an act
of Congress, notwithstanding it may exceed 11 square
leagues of land."

What followed this letter is uncertain. It is
probable that since Mr. Chaffee and Mr. Elkins were frequent visitors at the Land Office[60] they had kept in
close touch with developments. They doubtless learned
of the Secretary's instructions and one or the other may
have caused Washington attorneys to write the letter
which requested a patent for the Maxwell company. Incidentally the letter was written on Land Office Sta-
tionery.[61] The Commissioner answered it, thereby indi-
cating that he felt he had authority to open a case
which a former Secretary had refused to open.[62] He
could not have been unaware that Secretary Schurz' letter applied to unadjudicated cases. He stated that the
grant had not been surveyed under the authority of the
United States and that a request for survey would have
to originate in New Mexico. When a proper survey had
been made then an application for patent would be considered.

Seven weeks later the Surveyor General of New
Mexico forwarded a contract for the survey which was to
be performed by W. W. Griffin and C. Fitch.[63] But someone advised Secretary Schurz from New Mexico that Griffin was physically unable to perform surveying work and
that he was not a disinterested party.[64] The Land Office therefore called for a new contract. In so doing
the Commissioner pointed out certain errors, based on
the diseno of the grant, in Griffin's survey.[65] He also

---

60. Indicated by references to such visits in their letters to the
    Land Office.
61. Transcript, p. 833.
62. Ibid., p. 834.
63. Ibid., p. 835.
64. Letter from F. M. Cazin in Land Office Files.
65. A short time before the first contract arrived Mr. Elkins asked
    that the Griffin survey be accepted. He characterized Mr. Grif-
    fin as "a man of high character as a surveyor and a citizen and
    I believe," he added, "his survey is entirely correct." Land
    Office Files.

called for a "capable and disinterested deputy" in draw-
ing up a new contract, but obtained neither requiré-
ment.[66] The Surveyor General contracted with R. T. Marmon and John T. Elkins.[67] The latter's experience seems
to have been confined to surveying a few questionable
private land claims and the former later admitted that
he had had little to do with the Maxwell survey. Furthermore John Elkins was a brother of Stephen and
Stephen was one of the bondsmen for the surveyors.[68]
Nevertheless the Land Office accepted the new contract
and within twenty-two days the survey was completed.
Careful work probably would have required two months but
three weeks forms an interesting contrast to Cornelio
Vigil's six days in 1843.

The residents of the surveyed area naturally
protested strongly when they learned that the work was
official.[69] They felt that their trust in the Government was betrayed. The Surveyor General of New Mexico,
however, allowed public hearings on the survey. He then
brushed aside the protests which came from settlers, accepted Elkins' work and forwarded it to the Land Office,
December 20, 1878.[70] He reported to the Office that the
protests related chiefly to statements of Beaubien as to
where his boundaries ran. This testimony he considered
valueless because a member of the original party which
accompanied the Justice of the Peace in 1843 also accompanied Elkins and Marmon and identified the old mounds.
The Surveyor General ignored the obvious fact that he
was setting the testimony of a witness who had been a
mere boy in 1843 against that of one of the original
owners of the grant. The reliability of this witness
will be noted later.

The Elkins' survey had included a large section
of Colorado as well as New Mexico. Consequently twenty-
five citizens of Las Animas County, Colorado, wrote

---

66. Transcript, pp. 722-3.
67. L.O.R., 1885, p. 131.
68. Ibid., p. 131.
69. In 1888 the population of Colfax County, half covered by the
    grant was 3,398. H. H. Bancroft, "History of Arizona and New
    Mexico," p. 781.
70. Transcript, p. 767.

Secretary Schurz in protest.[71]   They estimated that over
2,000 residents of the County were bounded by the survey.
Many of them had entered their lands at Pueblo, and had
received patents.   There does not seem to have been any
response to this petition.

          For four months after the Land Office received
the Elkins survey Commissioner Williamson continued to
write residents in New Mexico that the survey had not
been received so that he was unable to tell whether or
not their fears or protests were justified.[72]   He assured these settlers, however, that their interests
would receive proper attention.   On May 9, 1879 he also
prepared a letter for the Surveyor General of New Mexico
and pointed out certain gross errors which had been
found in the survey while preparing the patent.[73]   These,
he said would have to be corrected before completing the
patent.   But for some reason best known to the Commissioner this letter was never sent.   A note on its margin
states that the Commissioner decided to issue patent.   On
May 19, 1879, he therefore signed and delivered a patent
for 1,714,764,094 acres which were inaccurately surveyed.[74]   The company had won.

          Obviously the Commissioner's actions from the
time he sought modification of Secretary Cox' decision
to the time he issued patent are subject to suspicion.
No direct evidence involving him in corruption is available, but when a short time later he visited New Mexico
it was openly charged that he was directly interested in
some of the private land claims and that he had become
so by pushing them to patent.   There is no doubt that

---

71. Transcript, p. 760.   The Jicarilla Indians had felt that they
    owned the land but since Maxwell was their friend they let him
    use it.   An Indian agency at Cimarron was abolished in 1872 and
    the Indians were forced out.   Bancroft, op. cit., Vol. 17, p. 738.
72. Transcript, p. 786.
73. Land Office Files under Maxwell Grant.
74. On May 8, 1879 the Commissioner ordered a deputy surveyor in
    Colorado to extend the public surveys to the Maxwell Grant line.
    This was supposedly already done, however, for the Commissioner
    complained in his unsent letter that the Elkins and Marmon sur-
    vey did not show existing Government survey lines.   Transcript,
    p. 285 ff.

he lacked authority to reverse a Secretary's decision
and it is evident that he betrayed his office by making
false statements to settlers and issuing what he knew to
be an erroneous patent. Proof of complicity in a fraudulent act has not been found.

There had been something of a struggle to secure
possession of the patent between representatives of the
company, the receiver in bankruptcy (though supposedly
the company's property had been sold for defaulted taxes), the trustees of the bonds, and foreign bondholders.
Judge Lucien Birdseye of New York represented the foreigners and after an agreement with Stephen Elkins, attorney for the receiver, he received the patent by mail.
Then all the interested parties went to New Mexico where
the affairs of the company were to be straightened out.
In the fall of 1879 a foreclosure suit[75] was brought before Chief Justice Prince, a member of the Santa Fe
Ring.[76] Two other suits were begun at the same time and
the conflict of claims seemed particularly involved. The
case had attracted the leading men of the bar from Colorado, New Mexico and New York. Mr. Birdseye finally
staged a coup d'etat on the last afternoon of the last
day of the court term when, by consent, he had all the
motions dismissed and then brought a new motion.   Three
seconds before midnight the decree of foreclosure was
signed by the Judge to complete what seemed like a rascally piece of judicial legerdemain.

During the following spring the foreclosure sale
was held. A Mr. Frank R. Sherwin, acting for himself
and the foreign bondholders, and his counsel, Judge
Birdseye, bid in the entire property under the first

---

75. N.Y. Tribune, Sept. 22, 1879.
76. Miguel A. Otero asserts that Prince was a member of the Ring.
    M. A. Otero, "My Life on the Frontier," Vol. II, pp. 4-5.   In
    the San Pedro and Canon del Agua case Chief Justice Prince
    hastily reversed his original decision and thereby aroused gen-
    eral suspicion of bribery. New Orleans Times, Oct. 8, 1881.

mortgage for the small sum of $1,000,000 and under the
second mortgage for $100,000.[77] It is said that the
aggregate worth of the two mortgages and interest was
about $8,000,000.[78] Frank Sherwin was a Wall Street
plunger of unfortunate reputation, who had become interested in the grant when in 1877 he learned that an official survey was to be made.[79] He went to Holland and
speculated in certificates for the bonds. He later
testified that at that time they were worth five cents
on the dollar in the Amsterdam financial market. When
the Elkins survey became known certificates began to
rise in value and extensive trading took place. Within
one hundred days the grant was said to have changed
hands several times. Sherwin claimed that it "was the
leading speculative feature on the Amsterdam market."[80]
Certificates advanced as high as sixty cents on the dollar but Sherwin secured majority control.

On May 31, 1878, a year before patent issued,
Sherwin had also made an agreement with the company's
stock and bondholders protective committee, though the
nature of the agreement was not fully divulged.[81] Sherwin, however, profited handsomely when a new company was
organized in Holland about a month after the foreclosure
sale.[82] The company was called the Maxwell Land Grant
Company, the Railroad part of the old name being dropped.
Sherwin was given £813,000 worth of stock in the new
company and £150,000 worth of income bonds. He was also
made one of the American directors, along with N. K.
Fairbanks, George Pullman and George B. Carpenter.

The company was not permitted to enjoy its possessions in peace, however. When President Garfield
succeeded President Hayes in 1881 the settlers on the

---

77. N.Y. Times, March 24, 1880.
78. The nominal capital had been £1,975,000. Of this £1,647,740
    had been received in cash or its equivalent. Cf. "Proposal of
    John Collinson to the Stock and Bondholders of the Maxwell Land
    Grant and Railway Company," November 20, 1874.
79. His record can be found in N.Y. Times, August 1883 - November
    1884, passim.
80. Transcript, p. 598 ff., especially p. 652.
81. Ibid., p. 610.
82. Ibid., pp. 598-600 and 610-1.

grant made a new appeal to the Interior Department. They
interested Secretary Kirkwood in their case and he sent
to the Land Office for the papers involved.[83] After
studying them and without recommendation from Commissioner McFarland, the Secretary concluded that the patent had been issued too hastily and that the Government
should seek annulment. On August 16 he therefore requested the Attorney General to bring suit for cancellation. The Secretary regretted the fact that the matter
had been placed beyond the power of his Department to
correct. "It may be," he said with great truth, "extremely difficult to so bring the subject before judicial
tribunals as to enable a thorough sifting and intelligent action to be had upon the whole matter.[84]

He summarized his reasons for seeking cancellation in the statement that sufficient consideration had
not been given "the protests and complaints of settlers
and inhabitants whose possessions were involved and
covered by the claims of the grantees. The testimony of
the witnesses who profess to have identified and pointed
out the calls of possession is in the highest degree
loose and contradictory, besides being meager and unsup-
ported, and the alleged plat or diseno (of 1843) fails
to indicate any approach whatever to the Purgatory or Las
Animas River." This river ran through Colorado, paral-
leling for fifteen or twenty miles, the northern boundary
of New Mexico, though it was about twelve miles north of
the boundary. The Elkins and Marmon survey had run
along the edge of the river for many miles and had then
crossed to its north bank, dipping still deeper into
Colorado.

The Department of Justice undertook the case,
secured considerable testimony at Trinidad, Colorado,
and in August 1882, filed charges in the Eighth Circuit
Court of Colorado.[85] The Government claimed that officials of the company had practiced fraud on the land
department so as to secure 300,000 acres in Colorado
that were never included in the out-boundaries of the

83. L.O.R., 1885, p. 133.
84. Ibid., p. 134.
85. U.S. vs. Maxwell Land Grant and Railway Co., 121 U.S. 325.

grant. It attacked particularly the north and east
boundary lines. During the following year the Government amended its bill to include the proposition that
under Mexican law only 97,000 acres could have been
granted. The Maxwell Company denied both charges and
in 1884 Judge Brewer gave a preliminary decision that
contained some points favorable to both sides.[86] He
also allowed for further presentation of argument.

In the meantime, the Democrats took office.
Commissioner Sparks undertook to press the case and his
efforts brought publicity.[87] Secretary of State Bayard's
name cropped up as one of the attorneys who had furnished
an opinion favorable to the company in 1870. Republican
newspapers therefore made political capital of the fact
that two members of a reform administration disagreed.[88]
Stephen B. Elkins' name was mentioned as the probable
owner of the grant but he denied he had ever been connected with the company except as a local director and
attorney in New Mexico and an attorney to receive patent.
The Democrats never attempted to refute him by publishing the evidence that he had been president in 1873.

The Government secured additional testimony on
the case in Colorado, made further argument and received
a final decision from Judge Brewer.[89] He declared the
Mexican law limiting a grant to about 48,000 acres to a
colonist did not apply to the Maxwell grant in view of
Congressional confirmation of the large boundaries. He
also disagreed with Secretary Kirkwood on the nature of
the survey. His concluding words will suffice to indicate his points. He remarked:

> "I leave the case with the final observation that after
> the fullest inquiry and observation by the government

---

87. L.O.R., 1885, p. 135; N. Y. Times, June 13, 30 and July 1, 1885.
    Mr. Sparks wanted the Government to start a new suit in New
    Mexico.
88. N.Y. Tribune, June 30, 1885.
89. 26 Fed. Reporter 118. Congress received a resolution of in-
    quiry at the time but did nothing about it. 49 Cong. 1 Sess.
    Cong. Rec., p. 4594.

with all the means and facilities at its command, the officers of the government, (deputy surveyors and the Surveyor General), and the claimants stand without a stain
upon the rectitude of their conduct, and the boundaries
of the grant as finally surveyed and patented, if not
proved to be absolutely accurate and correct are at least
shown to be as nearly so as any known testimony can determine."

Space forbids an analysis of some of the interesting points the court handled, such as the false copy
of the diseno sent to the Land Office in 1869. The Government appealed the case to the Supreme Court and
though its docket was extremely crowded[90] the Court
heard argument in March 1887. In the following month
the Court, through Justice Miller, upheld the Circuit
Court and dismissed the bill against the company. Again
the company had won.[91] The Government's points had been
ably presented by Mr. Maury and Mr. J. A. Bentley, former
Pension Commissioner. They attacked again the north and
east boundaries of the grant and presented a large number of cases in which the Supreme Court had held that
the Mexican Government was empowered to grant only eleven
square leagues to a colonist. They did not attempt to
implicate the General Land Office in the fraud so that
evidence like Commissioner Williamson's unsent letter
had not been presented in Colorado, or, of course, before the Supreme Court.

Mr. Frank Springer of New Mexico, presented the
main argument for the Maxwell Company.[92] He denied that
there had been any fraud; he upheld the accuracy of the
surveys, defended the claim against limitations of the
Mexican law and made a strong plea for a finality to attacks on the company's rights and property. His points
were careful, clever and bold to a high degree--thorough-
ly able. It is said that he received the thanks of the

90. N.Y. Times, Oct. 26, 1886.
91. 121 U.S. 325. By estimate the grant had cost the company
    $12,000,000 including $2,000,000 spent in litigation. N.Y.
    Herald, May 23, 1887.
92. Transcript of Record, op. cit., and Twitchell, "Leading Facts,"
    op. cit., Vol. II, p. 453.

Court for the ability with which he presented his case.
But an analysis of the testimony shows that he was guilty of false statements, that he contradicted himself materially, ignored important points and skillfully con-
fused the question of boundaries. An example of his
methods and personal veracity is found in his handling
of the survey question. The Griffin survey was reputedly based on the identification of the original boundary
marks by Jesus Silva, supposedly a member of the 1843
party which set the marks. When Elkins and Marmon were
ready to begin their official survey in 1877, Mr. Springer was present and he argued that they ought to follow
Griffin's lines.[93] The deputies refused to do so, however, and they proceeded to omit about 100,000 acres
that Griffin had included. But strange to relate Elkins
and Marmon also professed to rely on the personal identification of boundary by Jesus Silva. Despite this confusion in identification and despite his earlier efforts
to have Elkins follow the Griffin survey Mr. Springer
argued before the Supreme Court that the Elkins survey
was correct.[94] In fact he claimed that the Government's
arguments could be hurled in vain, against Silva's
identification of the boundaries. Since Mr. Silva could
not have been right in both instances it seems that Mr.
Springer tempered his views of what constituted established boundaries according to the exigencies of the moment. As a matter of record parts of Silva's testimonies
not only contradict themselves as between 1870 and 1877
but they contradict themselves several times in 1877, (he
explained one discrepancy by stating that he had answered
a question in a high wind and rain storm!); they contradict testimony of friends of Beaubien and the records of

---

93. Transcript, pp. 709-10.
94. Mr. Springer also claimed that the Alcalde had selected the
    wrong mountain for a boundary mark; that his crude drawing of
    a straight line excluded the 100,000 acres that should have
    been included, (this was, of course, impossible if Silva identi-
    fied the original boundary marks); and that Maxwell did not
    know where his north boundary ran for he could have obtained
    300,000 acres more there, according to the method of Congres-
    sional confirmation. This latter claim also ignored Silva's
    testimony. Transcript, passim.

1843; and they contradict testimony of the famous frontiersman, Richens Wooten. Incidentally, the latter contradicted himself. On this sort of testimony the boundaries had supposedly been run.[95] Rather curiously, the
map which is incorporated in the Supreme Court's printed
decision is materially incorrect for the corner of the
grant which the Government attacked.

The Supreme Court's analysis of the case has
some interesting features. Justice Miller listed three
questions which he felt should be answered. First: Do
the colonization laws render the grant void notwithstanding its confirmation by Congress? The Justice answered, "No." He noted that Congress had limited certain grants in its confirmation act of 1860 but that it
had not limited others. On the basis of the Tameling
decision he refused to analyse the seemingly more appropriate question of what Congress had confirmed in the
Maxwell case.[96] Second: If the grant was valid was
there a mistake in surveying which would justify setting
the patent aside? Again the answer was "No." But the
analysis presented indicated that the Justice concluded
that the land department was the best institution for
ruling on that point and since it had approved the survey he would accept it too. Such a position threw out
half of the Government's argument and neatly evaded the
astounding testimony on which the survey purported to
rest. Third: Was there actual fraud in securing this
survey to justify setting the patent aside? For the
third time the Justice answered in the negative. While
he indicated that the case was not above question he
laid down the rule that fraud must be established by satisfactory and conclusive evidence.

The New York Times was frankly incredulous at
the decision.[97] It believed that the Government's case
must have been inadequately presented for it felt that
the boundaries could not have been accurate.[98] The New

---

95. Ibid.
96. The confirmation had included the evidence regarding the eigh-
    teen leagues.
97. April 19, 1887.
98. The Philadelphia Press of June 7, 1887 printed a dispatch from
    Raton, New Mexico and observed: "Probably no greater outrage

York Tribune, allegedly the oracle of Stephen Elkins and
S. W. Dorsey, used the decision to berate Commissioner
Sparks, though of course he had not instigated the suit.
The paper declared: "Certain cheap demagogues among
whom Land Commissioner Sparks is conspicuous have for
years sought a pinchback reputation for filling the air
with charges of fraud against officials, against law
makers, against corporations and against settlers.....
It is time that this carnival of slanders should come
to an end."[99]

The land department was taken back by the Supreme Court's position. On May 12 it filed a petition
for rehearing, because it believed the Court had wrongly
interpreted certain points and because there was new
evidence available.[100] Since the department manifested
such a great interest in the case the Court considered
the petition but refused to allow a rehearing. The department believed the Court had misinterpreted the "fifteen or eighteen" league statement by Beaubien in 1844.
But in denying the rehearing the Court again maintained
that Beaubien was referring to the Bent lands rather
than to his own. This point has been considered above
and need not be repeated. It is interesting to note,
however, that even Commissioner Williamson had declared
that the grantees referred to their own grant as fifteen
or eighteen leagues. No officials but the Court placed
a contrary interpretation.

Unfortunately the Government's additional evidence did not see the light. It was to have been based
on the testimony of the manager of Maxwell's ranch. When
he learned of the decision he wrote the Land Office,
from Colorado, stating that he had been notified but
never summoned as a witness when the Government was taking

(footnote continued) was ever perpetrated on a people than that
    which is involved in the colossal fraud by means of which a
    grant" of 100,000 acres became 2,000,000. Settlers were re-
    ported to have lost faith in the courts. Columbia Clipping
    Bureau.
99. April 22, 1887. For comment on the paper see N.Y. Times,
    Aug. 22, 1887.
100. 122 U.S. 365.

testimony.[101] He declared that the Government had been
swindled and that if a new trial was granted he would
give some interesting information as to the boundaries
of the grant. Perhaps his testimony would have made
little difference. In the middle Sixties, before gold
had been discovered, Maxwell had had a survey made[102]
and although the record of it had been mysteriously lost,
witnesses had testified that it had not included nearly
so much territory as the Elkins and Marmon survey. But
this testimony had been largely ignored in judicial actions.

Perhaps Maxwell's manager was purposely kept
from presenting testimony. New Mexican and grant officials were reported to have interfered with mail and
other forms of communication. They did not hesitate at
murder. The mysterious death of the Reverend Mr. Tolby,
a man who sympathized with settlers, has been attributed
to Ring instigation. And on the margin of the copy of
the Griffin survey in the Land Office, opposite the name
of the flagman who accompanied Griffin, are written the
words, "Slain by Ring influence."

Space does not permit an account of the subsequent history of the grant. Thousands of settlers could
not accept the Supreme Court decision. At first they
resorted to violence.[103] Many hoped that President
Cleveland would aid them as he had Guilford Miller but
the President only wrote a letter advising peaceful measures and declaring that the law would "protect every
right of the citizen."[104] Consequently groups of settlers sent innumerable petitions in the effort to secure
every form of official aid possible. A former minister,
O. P. McMains, was tireless in seeking to have the land

---

101. Letter in Land Office Files.
102. "Hist. of New Mexico," op. cit., Vol. I, p. 184.
103. Clipping from unrecorded paper in L.O. Files; sent by E. H.
     Boggs to President Cleveland under date Sept. 11, 1888. The
     clipping was headed "Fighting for their homes" and it showed
     that troops were required to combat settlers. See also "Hist.
     of New Mexico," 1907, p. 188.
104. Philadelphia Press, June 7, 1887; N.Y. Times, Oct. 12, 1887.

department carry out Secretary Cox' order of 1869[105]
for it had never been legally revoked.[106] The settlers
in Colorado, especially those who had already obtained
patents from the Government, brought suit and carried
their case to the Supreme Court.[107] Though they represented a group with prior property rights based on official action, a condition which the Court held in high
esteem, the Court decided against them and in favor of
the company. A later Governor of Colorado enlisted on
the side of the settlers and forwarded a petition to
Washington because he believed that the grant was "a
fraud from the ground up."[108] Congress finally inquired
into the case and though the committee report was entirely favorable to the settlers no action was taken on it.
As late as Theodore Roosevelt's administrations settlers' petitions were received by the Government, particularly the President.[109] And in the 1920's efforts
to obtain some of the land adjacent to the grant were
rejected by the Land Office because Mr. Springer advised
the Office that the survey should have included that
area![110]

  The success of this tremendous fraud apparently
encouraged other efforts along the same line[111] but on
the other hand it was undoubtedly a factor leading to
the efficient Private Land Claims Court of 1891. The
Court was notably successful in clearing up maladjust-
ments of half a century and it rejected nearly
33,500,000 acres of claims out of 35,500,000 presented

---

105. **N.Y. Times**, March 30, 1884; L.O. Files, Petition dated June 22,
  1890.
106. The Supreme Court has held that "Public Officials cannot bind
  the government beyond the scope of their lawful authority."
  Leavenworth, Lawrence and Galveston Railroad vs. U. S., 92
  U. S. 733 (1875).
107. Russell vs. Maxwell Land Grant Co., 158 U.S. 253.
108. **Philadelphia Press**, Sept. 29, 1893.
109. Land Office Files under Maxwell Grant.
110. 48 L. D. 87 and letter dated Oct. 19, 1927 to H. R. Haynes,
  Land Office Files.
111. Cf. Interstate Land Co. vs. Maxwell Land Grant Co., 139 U.S.
  569.

to it.[112] Furthermore the Supreme Court upheld at least
fifty-eight of the seventy-two claims which were appealed to it[113] from the Claims Court. The Supreme
Court did not always show toward private land claims the
carelessness, to characterize it no stronger, which it
manifest in the Maxwell case. It did, of course profess
a tremendous respect for property rights, particularly
when a land patent was involved, but in 1888 it over-
threw the claims of the owners of the Canon del Agua
grant.[114] In short its record shows a motley of decisions, occasionally quite favorable to corporate interests whether private land claims,[115] railroads or timber
companies and occasionally favorable to poorer individuals or the Government. The Maxwell case is unhappily a
score for ruthless corporate interests, in fact its entire story illustrates the unfortunate conflict between
private enterprise and official responsibilities.[116]

---

112. Attorney General's Report, 1904, p. 95.
113. Ibid., p. 98 and Twitchell, "The Spanish Archives of New
     Mexico," Vol. I., pp. 492-502.
114. 146 U.S. 120.
115. The Court's decision on John C. Fremont's claim in California
     could be considered highly favorable to him. Cf. Cummings and
     McFarland, op. cit., pp. 130-2.
116. The conflict of interest between two ruthless corporate inter-
     ests produced a special problem for the Court. The Maxwell
     Company, however, won all the principal suits brought against
     it. The Colorado Coal and Iron Company may have been behind
     the Russell suit which was mentioned above. In the 1890's the
     Colorado Coal Company also brought suit to void the Maxwell
     Company claims in Colorado but again the latter was successful.
     These differences were later reconciled for the Colorado por-
     tion of the Maxwell grant came into the possession of the
     Rocky Mountain Coal and Iron Company which was owned and con-
     trolled by the Colorado Fuel and Iron Company. Cf. Moody's
     "Industrials" under the latter title, 1908.

Chapter XII

REFORM IN THE SURVEYING SERVICE

Government surveys have already been described as a very important function of public land administration. Correct surveys were essential to the settler, miner, corporation or State in securing titles and to the Government in assessing its resources. Yet long before 1885 the contract and deposit methods had proved not only inefficient and inadequate but frequently corrupt as well. A decade of official requests had brought no improvements which benefited the land department yet Commissioner Sparks took up the chorus as he too urged legislative assistance. In addition he uncovered an amazing amount of corruption and gross administrative laxity. When he considered the general features of administration in his first report the Commissioner began with the problem of surveys[1] and after devoting several pages to detailing careless and fraudulent work, particularly in the Far West, he observed: "I thus found this office a mere instrumentality in the hands of 'surveying rings'."[2] He promised that it would not be so during his term and consequently some of his most strenuous efforts for land reform were directed toward improving the surveying service. He was met, however, by a determined resistance which was manifested in subtle and devious ways both in Congress and in the Departments of Justice and the Treasury.

The Commissioner discovered and reported anew the results of official carelessness in the West when he

---

1. 969,245,192 acres in the public land States and Territories were surveyed by June 30, 1885 and 478,288,796 were listed as unsurveyed. L.O.R., 1885, pp. 159-160.
2. Ibid., p. 14. The Coast and Geodetic Survey seems to have been subject to abuses and inefficiency too. Applet. An. Ency. 1885, p. 759.

learned that the Government had never collected from the bonds of a deputy who was proved guilty of fraudulent work.[3] But he believed that more serious abuses resulted from the liberal regulations which the land department had drawn up for the deposit system. For instance applications for deposit surveys uniformly ignored the law's requirements for "settlers" because the department had allowed one settler to a township.[4] Moreover the fact that the bulk of deposit surveys originated in timber and grazing land districts and accrued to the benefit of speculators and syndicates was explained by the regulations which permitted deposits for lands where the "larger portion" was "not known to be mineral," desert or timber lands.[5] The Commissioner remarked that the system of procuring survey and making illegal entry was so thoroughly organized that agents and attorneys had "been advised of every official proceeding and enabled to present entry applications for the land at the very moment of filing of the plats of survey in the local land offices."[6]

The departmental regulations were too liberal in other respects. They allowed connection lines, that is standard and base lines, to be run, whereas the law had been restricted to township lands "within the range of the regular progress of the public surveys." The law had authorized the assignment of certificates issued after March 3, 1879, the regulations allowed those issued before as well. And it was also reported that through Land Office carelessness duplicates of certificates were obtained, thereby "opening the door to a double redemption or two payments by the United States for one deposit."[7] Consequently Commissioner Sparks thoroughly revised departmental regulations.

Many irregularities in connection with the deposit system were traced to a Surveyors General Convention at Salt Lake City in 1880. One recommendation of

---

3. Ibid., p. 12.
4. See the Commissioner's letter to the Surveyor General of New Mexico, June 6, 1885, Ibid., pp. 163-5.
5. Ibid., p. 14.
6. Ibid., p. 15.
7. Ibid., p. 14.

that group had urged every possible facility for surveying under deposits. Then shortly after the meeting a
report had reached Washington that a syndicate had been
organized in San Francisco. With strong financial assistance the group "undertook successfully to control
all special deposit contracts principally on the Pacific slope."[8] The Land Office believed that it was
largely this syndicate and its accomplices that formed
a powerful lobby which defeated repeal of the special
deposit law in 1882 after it had passed the House of
Representatives. The lobby was not able, however, to
prevent repeal of the amendment making certificates as-
signable.[9] Yet according to the Commissioner during the
month in which the repeal bill was under consideration
the syndicate put forth great efforts so that the number
and estimated liabilities of special contracts "far exceeded those of any prior period of time equal in
length."

It was later revealed that John A. Benson was
head of the syndicate but even by June 10, 1885 the Land
Office had obtained sufficient evidence to warrant suspending for examination all contracts under his name.[10]
These with others suspended June 20 covered an area of
more than 1,150,000 acres. Upon investigation some contracts were found to have been "floated" to cover two to
twenty times the amount of surveying work originally
contracted for. An example is found in that awarded to
Edward F. Stahle for work in Wyoming.[11] In fact the
manipulation of his contract illustrates several abuses
in the surveying service.

---

8. Ibid., p. 161 ff.
9. Commissioner Sparks declared that the special deposit law was
   an "unmixed evil." He added that,"It has promoted unnecessary
   and improvident expenditures, premature and worthless surveys,
   the corruption of public officers, and the unlawful appropriation of vast bodies of the most valuable unsettled public
   lands." Ibid., p. 15.
10. Ibid., pp. 165 and 183-4. The copy of the Land Office Report
    given the author by the Land Office has Benson's name written
    in on p. 165.
11. Ibid., pp. 166-7.

The contract, dated September 21, 1880, had originally called for $6,000 payable from special deposit funds. Five years later, July 7, 1885, Commissioner Sparks wrote the Surveyor General at Cheyenne, Wyoming: "Up to the present date the aggregate amount of surveys returned and paid for under said contract is $128,943.88, added to which you state that Mr. Stahle has returned to your office field-notes of thirty-three additional townships (estimated cost $20,000) which await platting. Nearly $150,000 worth of returns under an original contract for $6,000!" This expansion had not been based on additional settlers' applications, after 1881, though they were an "absolute and indispensable requisite in all special deposit contracts"; it was a self-imposed expansion. It had been facilitated through the official adoption of a new form of "detached bond" early in 1881.[12]

During the last three years of the contract's existence it had allowed $3.00 per mile more than the maximum rate. This was contrary to the stipulation that was required to be written into every contract. Deputy Stahle had sublet parts of his work though that, too, was unlawful.[13] The Land Office estimated that through Stahle and others, three-fourths of Wyoming was surveyed, an amount far beyond current needs and of course some of it was fraudulently or carelessly done. The Office learned that Stahle's "India rubber contract" was well known throughout the surveying district of Wyoming, yet when John W. Meldrum took office as Surveyor General in July 1884, he made no effort to correct it. At a later period it was revealed that Stahle was connected with the Benson"ring." Stahle appealed his case, when halted, to the General Land Office through Benson lawyers in San Francisco![14]

Another Democratic improvement in the surveying service concerned office examination of survey plats.[15]

---

12. Ibid., p. 172.
13. L.O.R., 1886, pp. 276-7.
14. Ibid., 1887, p. 252.
15. He also revised the surveying instructions. See circular issued April 8, 1887. L.O.R., 1887, pp. 514-15. Some deputies guilty of fraudulent work were debarred from further government contracts. Ibid., p. 515.

After 1881, when Surveyors General ceased inspections of
field work their examination of notes and plats had become merely perfunctory. They could not judge the character of the work performed. And the half dozen deputies which the Land Office employed for field inspection, did not perform their inspection until _after_ the
plats and field notes had been accepted, _after_ the plats
had been filed in the District Land Offices and _after_
the contracting deputy had been paid in full.[16] In 1885
Commissioner Sparks reversed the order so that the Land
Office could have some knowledge of the quality of work
performed as a basis for acceptance and payment. Probably excess of duties had prevented preceding commissioners from establishing this businesslike procedure.[17]

Commissioner Sparks' administrative reforms were
only the first steps toward improving the surveying
service. He requested Congressional coöperation through
complete repeal of the deposit system; more permanent
methods of marking; and penalty for the return of false
and fraudulent surveys as well as for the removal of
survey markings.[18] In 1885 he reduced the estimates for
new surveys to $250,000 though he sought the former
amount of $50,000 for inspection. Congress appropriated
only $80,000 for surveys and inspection and ignored the
other requests. An analysis of this lack of coöperation
will be given later.

The Commissioner continued to seek support after
1885 by citing examples of widespread fraud and the consequent urgency for legislative changes. In 1886 he declared:[19] "the reports, statements and affidavits

---

16. _Ibid._, pp. 178-81.
17. In 1883 Congress made a special appropriation of $15,000 for a
    resurvey of land in Kansas, originally surveyed in 1871. Com-
    missioner McFarland paid for the resurvey but was unable to ac-
    cept the field notes and plats because of settlers' protests on
    the work. L.O.R., 1886, p. 183.
18. In 1888 Appleton's Annual Encyclopedia stated: "The necessity
    for enduring monuments of iron and stone to mark corners and
    lines....is obvious and has been repeatedly urged on Congress.
    The deficiency is serious," p. 467.
19. L.O.R., 1886, p. 269. Secretary Lamar's Report spoke of the
    "painful exhibit" of western reports and he felt that the

received from special agents, contracting deputies,
county surveyors and other relative to the condition of
public surveys as found on actual observation in the
surveying districts of Arizona, California, Colorado,
New Mexico, Washington, and Wyoming not only corroborate
the statements made in the last annual report regarding
fraudulent surveys, but indicate the extensive and systematic operations by which mere purported surveys were
extended--extended on paper only."[20]

Nearly twenty pages of the 1886 Report contain
extracts from special agents or deputy surveyors of the
Rocky Mountain or Pacific Coast regions. A few of the
cases which they related are worth recounting. A deputy
surveyor of Colorado[21] was unable to locate certain
lines that were essential to his work and he later
learned that the deputy who had reputedly performed the
earlier survey defended himself by claiming that he was
"a Teller man."[22] His surveying had included very little field work but he had scaled the large maps of the
Geological Survey to secure false notes and plats for
the Land Office.[21] In other words the lack of coördina-
tion in the surveying service made it possible for deputies to defraud the Land Office. There is evidence that
this system was not uncommon in the Colorado region for
the Kansas City Times related that both Colorado and adjoining districts gave signs of similar methods.[23] The
paper described how surveys were made from the tops of
moving trains with the survey maps later filled out by
sketches from Professor Hayden's explorations. The
field notes were constructed to indicate ravines, gulches

(footnote continued) "resurvey of a considerable portion of sev-
    eral States and Territories is becoming a matter of urgent
    necessity." Sec. of Int. Report, 1886, p. 25. He called for
    a law providing punishment for false and fraudulent surveys.
20. Poor surveying work was also reported from Florida.
21. One agent referred to a Colorado surveying "ring" which was as-
    sociated with certain Californians. He did not mention any
    connection with Benson but he did report that its members were
    seeking contracts in Washington Territory. L.O.R., 1886, p. 274.
22. Ibid., p. 270.
23. Quoted in N.Y. Times, March 5, 1888.

and "old ruins," a favorite land mark in such cases, so
that they were readily accepted in the Surveyor General's office when backed up by affidavits. The Times
also claimed that the Star Route swindlers made profits
that were "narrow and stingy" when compared with survey
profits.

In the neighboring Territory of New Mexico a
special agent made an inspection tour of 650 miles and
reported to the Land Office: "During the entire trip I
was unable to find a post, mound or pit made by deputy
United States surveyors."[24]   A great many surveys which
were performed in New Mexico were unofficial but served
to protect cattle ranchers from trespass.

From Wyoming a county surveyor reported that
section and quarter section lines were omitted from
Government surveys and that township lines were poorly
marked, if marked at all. Consequently settlers who
wished to have their lands properly located were obliged
to pay deputies for resurveys of the larger divisions as
well as for their own smaller ones.[25] The expense was
therefore triple the amount it should have been if Government surveys had "been according to notes."

The Land Office learned that Oregon surveyors
"extracted money from settlers as an addition to....com-
pensation from the United States, a corrupt practice believed to have been largely followed."[26]   A year later
the Surveyor General of Arizona reported that "without
specially searching for defects" there were "hardly any
existing evidences of work executed as late as 1883."[27]
He had also found that a large block of land, about 80
miles in width and 100 miles in length, surveyed under
the deposit system for the Atlantic and Pacific Railroad
had been "carelessly done if not criminally instigated.
It was notoriously commented upon by settlers on this

24. L.O.R., 1886, pp. 271-2.
25. Ibid., p. 275.
26. Newspaper reports asserted that frequently settlers in the
    Colorado district were forced to pay $13.00 a day for a sur-
    veyor to retrace a line five to twenty miles to their claims.
    N.Y. Times, March 5, 1888; L.O.R., 1886, p. 16.
27. Ibid., 1887, p. 11.

tract during the past year that the watering places are almost entirely on the railroad sections." John Benson contracted for a substantial part of the surveys, though other names were used as dummies. The Surveyor General concluded: "The field was open for crooked work, the evidence of which is plainly visible, and that the government was the victim it is easily to be inferred."[28]

Other neighboring States and Territories revealed similar "crooked work." Sometimes the field notes were found to differ so greatly from actual topography that they bordered on the ridiculous. Streams were omitted or shown flowing in the wrong direction; mountains which were covered with snow from six to twenty feet deep or tremendous gorges were allegedly traversed by some dauntless deputy.[29] Too many notes have evidence of pure fabrication and a large number of cases showed some connection with Benson and Company in San Francisco.

In 1887 the Land Office thoroughly exposed John Benson and his ring though his frauds had long been a public scandal in the West. From material collected then and from additional information published during the muck-raking period of the early 1900's it is possible to sketch something of his history.[30] Mr. Benson was born in New York and later became a deputy surveyor in Iowa. After five years service there he moved to California and for a short time taught school. But soon he took up surveying again and embarked upon the career which led to the domination of western surveying. He began by securing as many contracts as possible. On September 9, 1873 he was awarded a contract for $1,814.61 and this was followed by six others in the same year, all to himself.[31] Gradually the number was

28. Ibid., p. 12.
29. Ibid., p. 19.
30. Cf. Oscar K. Davis article in N.Y. Times, September 8, 1907. A full page is devoted to Mr. Benson though some of the information seems inaccurate. Bailey Millard, "The West Coast Land Grabbers." Everybody's Magazine, May 1905. See also N.Y. World, Oct. 25, 1889.
31. L.O.R., 1887, p. 258.

increased. It was possible to fulfill the contracts because actual survey work was kept at a minimum. In several counties no townships were visited at all. The
field notes were faked in Mr. Benson's office where a
county map and imagination for details constituted the
equipment.

The field of operation was broadened to include
States and Territories controlled from the base at San
Francisco. Nevada, Oregon, Idaho and Washington were
visited by a travelling corps of surveyors and assistants.[32] These men were hired to visit the district and
do such field work "as was deemed absolutely indispensable." Further enlargement brought in regions like Colorado, New Mexico, Montana, Utah and Wyoming where the
ring secured the services of resident and "reliable
parties" like Edward F. Stahle. The New York Times reported that Benson's control brought him $150,000 to
$200,000 annually.[33]

It is important to note that the ring's work was
not merely a matter of frauds which benefited a group of
surveyors or alleged surveyors. Mr. Benson assisted
corporations and the San Francisco Bank of Nevada. The
latter stood behind the ring and supplied the money for
fraudulent deposit surveys. When in 1887 the fraud was
exposed the Bank held powers of attorney for surveying
claims amounting to $500,000. Corporations like the At-
lantic and Pacific Railroad Company, mentioned above,
had also profited by the very favorable type of survey
which the Benson Company performed. In addition the
Central Pacific and the California and Oregon Railroads
had deposited $56,000 and $60,000 respectively for surveys and Mr. Benson obtained the contracts. The San
Francisco Chronicle claimed that his influence in the
Surveyor General's office enabled him to learn what
others bid for deposit surveys so that he was able to
bid just under their figure.[34] It became notorious that
railroad lands which Mr. Benson surveyed in California,

32. Ibid., p. 252.
33. Quoting the San Francisco Chronicle, April 4, 1887.
34. Quoted in N.Y. Times, April 4, 1887.

contained 1,000 to 1,400 acres per section rather than
the standard 640. Obviously, therefore, there was a
sizable group of beneficiaries who wished to protect Mr.
Benson and his work.

The Land Office investigation occurred during
February and March, 1887, and it was conducted by a
shrewd special agent, Charles F. Conrad.[35] According
to an official report agents who had previously been assigned to the task were moved if they came "too close
to smelling a rat." Fortunately Mr. Conrad began his
work under a Secretary and Commissioner who could not be
influenced. His research enabled him to depict with
proof the complete process which the ring used, from
making fictitious applications for surveys to fraudulent
powers of attorney for receiving payment. Consequently
on April 2, 1887 a Federal Grand Jury returned indictments on sixty-five counts against Mr. Benson and thirty-four alleged deputies.[36] Further investigation showed
that three of thirty-four were dummies. Most of the
others were relatives, partners or associates of Mr.
Benson.[37] Two were intimately associated with Theodore
Wagner who for several years was Surveyor General of
California. Mr. Wagner had approved 113 out of nearly
250 contracts which were credited to the ring. There
is some evidence, however, that Mr. Benson dealt primarily with Mr. Wagner's chief clerk, Theodore Reichert.[38]

Mr. Benson was arrested along with many others
who were indicated, but he was released under a $17,500
bond which two directors of the Nevada Bank signed. His
indictments were carelessly drawn by an Assistant District Attorney who was reported to be the paid attorney
of the Bank. The indictments were therefore quashed in

---

35. L.O.R., 1887, p. 247.
36. N.Y. World, Oct. 25, 1889 and L.O.R., 1887, p. 249.
37. One of Mr. Benson's partners, John McNee also held a contract
    from the War Department for filling in the Potomac flats in
    Washington, Newspapers suggested that that work should be in-
    vestigated. N.Y. Times, April 4, 1887.
38. One employee was said to have committed suicide when he found
    that he had been engaged in fraudulent work. N.Y. World,
    October 25, 1889.

August on technical defects and errors.[39] About the
same time Mr. Benson walked out on his bond and departed for the East. Detectives trailed him but failed to
find him before he left for Europe. According to one
account Mr. Benson was mistakenly arrested in Copenhagen
by British police; after they discovered their error and
learned that he was wanted in America they turned him
over to American authorities for extradition.[40]

Meanwhile new indictments had been drawn and
the Nevada Bank, whose President was ex-Senator James G.
Fair of Nevada, then hired Senator W. M. Stewart,[41] also
of Nevada, as Mr. Benson's attorney. The Bank again
went surety for the bonds that were set after the judge
mysteriously reduced them by half. Through various
means the date for Mr. Benson's trial was postponed until 1889 and though Special Agent Conrad had spent the
intervening time in further investigation he was dismissed just before it was to take place. There is undoubtedly, a relation between the fact that he was the
most informed person on the fraudulent surveys of the
ring and the fact that under the Republican administration which had replaced the Democrats, his dismissal was
largely the result of a demand from Senators Stewart and
Jones of Nevada and Senator Stanford of California.
Senator Jones was an intimate friend of Bank President
Fair and Senator Stanford was influential in the control
of the Central Pacific Railroad, a company which Mr.
Conrad had antagonized on several occasions. A fuller
account of the dismissal will be taken up in a subsequent chapter.

---

39. N.Y. Times, August 31, 1887.
40. O. K. Davis attributes his arrest to a street brawl. N.Y.
    Times, Sept. 8, 1907. In 1888 the Times claimed that Mr. Ben-
    son need not fear new indictments. Jan. 15, 1888. See also
    ibid., Dec. 13, 1887.
41. Senator Stewart was a noted mining lawyer associated particular-
    ly with the Comstock Lode. A Congressional committee also ex-
    posed him as "a Sharper." A. Nevins, "Hewitt," op. cit.,
    p. 301 and Dictionary of American Biography. For the connec-
    tion between the Nevada Bank and the Comstock Lode see Dict.
    Am. Biog. sketch of James G. Fair.

Perhaps Mr. Conrad's release assisted in continued postponements of the trial until 1892. A jury
then found Mr. Benson not guilty on the first charge
brought against him and three years later the last of
the seven charges "fizzled out" and he went free.[42]
Within a decade, however, he was once more indicted for
land frauds which were connected with school lands and
on this occasion he was convicted.[43] His later manipu-
lations lie outside the period covered by this monograph
but it is instructive to observe that like his earlier
influence in securing the removal of special agents, Mr.
Benson was found to have bribed Land Office Clerks in
Washington.[42]

Another unfortunate aspect of Mr. Benson's story
is connected with payment for his work. Aside from the
fact that he received double payments occasionally, he
was able to secure a sizable sum over Commissioner
Sparks' veto. On the basis of the testimony submitted
by Agent Conrad and other agents the Commissioner had
refused to approve many surveys which he had suspended
early in his term of office. For this stand he became
subjected to "every form of indignant abuse."[44] The
Commissioner claimed that those who were seeking compensation resorted to "every expedient known to legal
chicanery." They finally appealed to Comptroller Durham
of the Treasury Department for payment on $48,950. The
attorney for their appeal was William S. Bissell, President Cleveland's former law partner. It is reported
that Mr. Bissell came to Washington, secured a letter of
introduction from the President to Comptroller Durham
and "with very little delay" secured payment despite
Commissioner Sparks' protests.[45]

---

42. Millard, op. cit.
43. Mr. Benson had also been interested in manipulating school
    lands in the 1880's though little was made of it. L.O.R.,
    1887, pp. 252-3.
44. L.O.R., 1886, p. 17.
45. N.Y. World, Oct. 25, 1889. The fact of payment without the
    necessary consent of the Commissioner was noted in the Land
    Office Report of 1889. Commissioner Stone called for Congres-
    sional investigation of the transaction without any result.

The breakup of the surveying ring was only an
incident in Land Office affairs. Prosecution of the indicted group had been carried on under the Attorney General's office, though with continued assistance from
the Land Office's special agent. Meanwhile the surveying service faced greater problems. It fell into
straightened circumstances because Congress continued to
reduce its appropriations. From 1880 to 1885, nearly
$8,000,000 had been appropriated for regular and special
deposit surveys; $5,813,000 was required to repay spe-
cial deposits and the remainder, averaging nearly
$350,000 annually, was spent for regular surveys. But
for each of the fiscal years beginning June 30, 1886 and
1887 only $50,000 was appropriated.[46] This covered the
cost of the regular surveys only; there were no special
deposits so that the official work was decidedly restricted.[47]

Commissioner Sparks received the full support of
the Secretary for his requests and he pointed out that
the needs for surveys were still as great, if not greater, than formerly.[48] He felt keenly the discrepancy between the former large appropriations for work which was
carelessly and fraudulently performed, and his own totally insufficient funds. There was an urgent need for
surveying railroad lands and in 1887 Surveyors General
were requesting a total of $518,640 for regular work.
A previous chapter has brought out Governors' and Surveyors Generals' demands prior to 1885 for surveys in
rapidly filling regions. To a large extent these demands

(footnote continued) L.O.R., 1889, p. 44; Sec. of Int. Report,
    1889, p. xxxii. John W. Mackay of the Nevada Bank of Cali-
    fornia held survey certificates worth $500,000. N.Y. Times,
    March 17, 1887.
46. L.O.R., 1887, p. 92.
47. It is fairly evident that poor settlers could not readily ad-
    vance cash for surveys, particularly since they often needed
    to borrow for their homes, implements, livestock and tools. It
    would seem that the law scarcely benefited poor settlers but
    only those who had wealth and those who speculated. See Chap-
    ter IV, ante and Applet. An. Ency., 1888, p. 468.
48. L.O.R., 1887, p. 92; Sec. of Int. Report, 1886, p. 25.

had not been met. When appropriations were reduced to
one-sixth of the former amount, frontier needs rose
proportionately.[49]

The Commissioner reduced Surveyor Generals' requests in 1887 to a minimum of $300,000 for Congres-
sional appropriation. He described his estimate as
"barely sufficient for immediate" needs.[50] Yet Congress
continued to provide only $50,000.[51] The Commissioner
had run into another snag when he sought to secure bids
for surveying heavily timbered regions to provide information in a timber trespass suit amounting to
$1,100,000.[52] Yet no one would bid for the work because
the rates were said to be too low.[53] The Commissioner
had allowed the highest rates permitted by law and when
he failed to secure bids he asked Congress to restore
former maximum rates. This request was also refused.[54]

It was even more serious that the Land Office
lacked sufficient funds for examination of surveys.
Hundreds of thousands of dollars were involved in claims
for survey work which the Office suspected was fraudulent but there was no adequate staff to examine the
field work and check up. Furthermore the Government
could not protect itself against fraudulent deposit survey of mineral, especially coal, land which had been returned as agricultural. This fact was also true for
timber land. From 1881 to 1885 Congress had provided
$50,000 annually for special examination. Commissioner

---

49. The neglect of surveys is also indicated by the fact that more
    than 1,665,000 acres in Louisiana had never been surveyed.
    L.O.R., 1885, p. 159.
50. L.O.R., 1887, p. 92.
51. Occasionally deputies conspired to prevent bids so that they
    could force higher rates. Cf. Commissioner's letter to Sur-
    veyor General of Nevada. L.O.R., 1887, pp. 238-39.
52. L.O.R., 1887, p. 235.
53. Congress continued to appropriate large amounts ($248,000) for
    the Coast and Geodetic Survey. 50 C. 1 S. H. Ex. Doc. #154.
    Army surveys of the upper Mississippi continued. H. Ex. Doc.
    #158.
54. Secretary Lamar was refused a special request for $200,000 with
    which to survey the land along the three largest Pacific Rail-
    roads. Sec. of Int. Report, 1887, p. 15.

Sparks believed that even that sum was "wholly insufficient for the broad and multiform purposes of appropriation."[55] But after he had exposed the laxity and fraud
of previous years Congress cut the appropriation in
half. The following year brought further reduction to
$10,000. Whether intentionally or not Congress was aid-
ing rascally deputy surveyors and designing exploiters
of the public domain. It is significant to note that
in 1888 the Government was faced with a surplus of
$140,000,000[56] and Commissioner Sparks was asking for
only $75,000 to protect the Land Office and the Govern-
ment from fraud. He did not obtain it.[57]

The Land Office was also seeking a meager sum
to secure the proper survey of private land claims in
Louisiana, California, New Mexico and Arizona. It was
necessary to settle disputed boundaries and reduce the
greatly augmented claims of districts like New Mexico.
Surveyor General George W. Julian, of the latter Territory, estimated he could save 4,000,000 acres for the
public domain if Congress would provide him with a special fund of $27,000. He felt strongly the need for
settling the claims and stated: "If the country was
worth fighting for and adding to the territory of the
United States, it is worth governing and caring for by
decent and civilized means."[58] The Surveyor General of
Arizona also requested $27,000. Commissioner Sparks re-
duced these figures in his estimates for Congress but
he was unable to obtain any funds for that year. In
1885 and 1886 the appropriations had been progressively
diminished and in 1887 they were, as noted, cut off altogether. Even the sum appropriated annually to provide
for survey, appraisement and sale of abandoned military
reservations was withheld, except for $2,000 to care for
the lands.[59]

---

55. L.O.R., 1887, pp. 93-4.
56. J. F. Rhodes, "History of the United States," Vol. VIII,
    p. 306.
57. The Office was able to hire only one inspector, Special Agent
    Conrad, and he was fully occupied with the San Francisco Ring.
    50 Cong. 1 S. H. Ex. Doc. #152.
58. L.O.R., 1887, p. 94.
59. Ibid., 1885, pp. 237-9; 1886, pp. 367-9; 1887, pp. 384-5.

It is difficult to be certain of the cause for this parsimony in the light of a Treasury surplus. The most obvious explanation seems to be that it was a subtle attempt to embarrass Democratic reforms or an indirect means for protecting culprits and special interests. The evidence offered by committee reports and debate on a general appropriations bill is only tentative.[60] Appropriations Committees wielded extensive power and when they desired to reduce any appropriation they did so, frequently with no explanation.[61] In the haste of passing the bill Congressmen might neglect to inquire as to the Committee's reasons. Occasionally, though, statements in Congress were particularly revealing. In 1886 a Committeeman was explaining to the House why the estimates for the Labor Bureau were reduced. He declared: "I think, without mentioning any names, that the view of some statesmen upon that Committee is, that it is, well, where they do not agree to the policy of the law, to regulate it by refusing appropriations or giving small appropriations."[62]

This policy may also have applied to surveying work. At times the Senate Committee showed hostility to increases for Land Office needs. The New York Times, however, placed heavy blame on House Speaker Samuel Randall who reputedly treated Land Office requests with contempt.[63] He was admittedly in control of appropriations bills and, as stated previously, his reasons for stringency can be better known when a study of his papers is permitted.

The surveying service was also handicapped greatly through the failure to secure full salaries for

---

60. Cf. Legislative, Executive and Judicial Approp. Bill. H. R. #8974. 49 Cong. 1 Sess.

61. In 1886 the Senate Appropriations Committee refused to allow the House increase for ten instead of three principal clerks in the Land Office. During the discussion of the appropriations bill no one questioned the move.

62. 49 Cong. 1 Sess. Cong. Rec., p. 5422.

63. April 7, 1888. In December, 1887 the Times declared that "the influence of shrewd and tireless jobbers and the stupid stubbornness of Mr. Randall" Congress had persisted in crippling the Land Office. Dec. 5, 1887.

Surveyors General and full appropriations for their office work. In the case of salaries Congress continued
a policy in times of prosperity that had originated ten
years before during the depression. Congressional debate brought out some protest against this practice but
the reductions continued.[64] For the fiscal year beginning June 30, 1887, for instance, every surveyor general
but two received from $200 to $700 less than the salary
stipulated by law.[65] There may have been some justifi-
cation for the practice where work had practically
ceased but in any case it was a slip-shod way of handling official business. In some instances it brought
strong and justified protest. One surveying officer declared, "With the same justice salaries of the President
and other high officials could have been cut down as a
matter of economy."[66]

The policy of cutting appropriations for surveying office clerks proved even more harmful to the service. In 1885 Congress had provided $156,600 for the
salaries of Surveyors General and their assistants.
Commissioner Sparks reduced the estimates for the following year to $122,750 because some offices were ending
up their work.[67] Congress, however, allotted about half
the amount requested and when in the following year the
Commissioner sought $112,450 Congress appropriated
$69,550.[68] The Land Office had reduced Surveyor Gen-
erals' requests in the usual economy move but Congress
far out-did the Office. The needs of the service and
the effects of small appropriations are well expressed
by the Surveyor General of Arizona. He despairingly
stated, "Unless Congress in its wisdom increases this
amount I would respectfully recommend that no apportion-
ment be made to this Territory for the survey of public

---

64. 49 Cong. 1 Sess. Cong. Ref., pp. 5422-37; 5525; and 5732-3.
65. See Representative Hermann's attempt to secure $2,500, instead
    of $1,800 for the Surveyor General of Oregon. He claimed Ore-
    gon stood fifth in the number of Homestead entries and there-
    fore owed its officials full salaries. He won applause but
    lost his motion. Ibid., pp. 5779-80.
66. L.O.R., 1887, p. 96.
67. Ibid., 1886, pp. 363-5.
68. Ibid., 1887, pp. 375-7.

lands. It avails nothing either for the Government or
the parties interested to have public land surveys made
if the work cannot be prosecuted to a close..... Congress might as well try the experiment of running a
steam engine without fuel as to require this office to
perform work without suitable assistance. The clerical
work in this office is daily increasing and much time is
consumed in searching the records to give information
solicited by settlers in order to ascertain the location
of their lands, which, owing to defective work heretofore in the field, they are unable to do."[69]

          After Commissioner Sparks left office groups in
the west made a concerted effort to secure larger survey
appropriations. California, Washington, Oregon, Montana
and Idaho wrote the Land Office to plead for more
money.[70] Their petitions were sent on to Congress. One
request from Colorado was signed by twenty-nine State
and Federal officials including the Governor, the Secretary, Treasurer, Auditor, Attorney General, Chief Justice of the Supreme Court and others.[71] This group
sought additional surveys and resurveys because of the
great influx of settlers. It spoke of great hardships
that had resulted from absence of surveys, though the
hardship was not described. It also mentioned a need
for additional office clerks. In transmitting these requests through the Secretary of Interior, the Land Office sought $360,000 in addition to the regular appro-
priation; $100,000 was to be distributed to the several
surveying districts and one-fourth of it was to go for
inspection of past and future work; and $200,000 would
be used for surveys within grant and indemnity limits of
railroads. The Office also requested an increase in
maximum rates per mile.

69. L.O.R., 1887, p. 12; see also p. 573.
70. The Surveyor General of California spoke of 3,398,000 acres of
    surveys suspended for examination with no action likely. There
    were also 1,212,260 acres of surveying that had been rejected
    by the Land Office and these needed resurveys. 50 Cong. 1 S.
    H. Ex. Doc. #132. Citizens of Nebraska and Dakota sent peti-
    tions directly to Congress. 50 Cong. 1 Sess. Cong. Rec.,
    pp. 1840, 2133, 2240.
71. H. Ex. Doc. #180. 50 Cong. 1 Sess.

Congress did allow $10,000 for survey deficien-
cies on March 30, 1888 and in the following fall it ap-
pripriated $100,000. By 1889 survey appropriations ap-
proached former totals, for in that year $200,000 was
provided, four times the amount set aside under Commissioner Sparks.[72] And as though old times were returning in more ways than one the Commissioner in 1889 reported that survey work of recent date in seven States
was badly done or unfinished.

In conclusion, there does not seem to be any excuse for inferior and fraudulent surveys unless the Government intended to benefit some of its most undesirable
citizens. Blame for the situation has been placed chiefly on Congress. Even though interested groups and the
technique for appropriation hampered intelligent action,
the Commissioner's reports should not have been ignored.
If the reports were unsatisfactory a Committee could
easily have secured the necessary information for formu-
lating a feasible policy. Probably the surveying service suffered because it was tied up with the general
system of land administration. Thorough revision of one
would have required thorough revision of the other.
Railroads, timber and cattle companies, land lawyers and
brokers, private land claimants and others were determined to thwart any radical improvement. As a consequence the surveying service wasted money or was de-
frauded for the benefit of deputies and land exploiters.
The government and the settler paid the bill.

---

72. L.O.R., 1890, p. 33. See Chapter XV post.

Chapter XIII

TIMBER COMPANIES AND RAILROADS UNDER FIRE

The strong administrative reforms which Democratic authorities applied to speculation, surveying,
cattle enclosures and private land claims were equally
evident in the correction of timber and railroad grant
abuses. It seems extraordinary that executive action
could accomplish so much in the face of Congressional
indifference or hostility. During President Cleveland's
term, however, legislative coöperation for checking the
railroads was more apparent than formerly; yet on the
other hand there was little assistance in handling the
timber problem. Public timber lands increasingly required not only vigorous control but a well planned system of reservation along the headwaters of rivers and a
system for judicious disposal to prevent monopoly.
Secretary Lamar and Commissioner Sparks first attacked
the timber question by revising Secretary Teller's regulations.[1] For instance because the Timber Cutting Act
had confined cutting to "domestic purposes," in 1885 the
Department revoked the former rule which permitted cutting for export. In addition it revised the regulation
for the Right-of-Way Act so that railroads could no
longer remove timber from what Commissioner Sparks described as "practically anywhere in the United States."[2]
Under the "Licence to Timber Thieves" bill of 1880 Republican regulations had permitted a person to enter at
private cash sale land on which he had unintentionally
trespassed. Secretary Lamar restricted this right to
lands which were legally open to private cash sale, a
right which did not exist widely in the West. He also
revoked a rule which extended the same law's protection

1. L.O.R., 1885, pp. 82-3.
2. Subsequently upheld by Judge Moses Hallett of the Colorado District Court in U.S. vs. The Denver and Rio Grande Railroad Co.
   L.O.R., 1887, p. 85.

to intentional trespassers.[3]

In suggesting legislative changes both the Commissioner and the Secretary favored repeal of the 1878 timber laws and the sale of timber land at its assessed value. The Secretary had also recommended that the Government reserve one quarter of each section it sold but the Commissioner presented more comprehensive plans.[4] He felt that it was necessary to withdraw all entry rights on forest lands until a satisfactory plan for permanent forest reservations could be worked out. He included the program which Representative Atkins had supported in 1879 and suggested that the question of reservations should be considered along with those of river navigation, irrigation and flood control. The Commissioner called attention to the number of "thoughtful persons, scientific bodies and patriotic societies throughout the country"[5] which were in favor of such a comprehensive program. In addition his first report requested a $15,000 increased appropriation for timber protection.

The Senate took up only a portion of these suggestions when by a resolution of March 17, 1886, it asked the Commissioner what, if any, legislation was needed to protect public timber. The Commissioner's reply repeated the recommendation for the repeal of the two timber laws and then added a statement calling for the repeal of the Preëmption law and the commutation feature of the Homestead law. He also suggested the repeal of the first two sections of the 1880 protection law, but added that in order to meet western needs he felt that there should be a new measure which would allow reasonable cutting privileges to bona fide settlers.[6]

Because the Senate had not adopted any of his suggestions in his last report the Commissioner called attention to the fact that public timber land was

3. In 1885 the Commissioner declared: "depredations upon public timber....(are) universal, flagrant and limitless." Ibid., 1885, p. 81.
4. Ibid., p. 73 ff.
5. Ibid., p. 83.
6. L.O.R., 1886, p. 441.

"disappearing at a rate that excites grave apprehension..... The struggle to accumulate great private fortunes from the forests of the country has reduced forest areas to a minimum." He then repeated his former suggestions and somewhat prophetically noted that the remaining forests deserved protection because they were of "infinite importance and value for climatic effect, the natural regulation of the flow of waters, and to prevent the relapse of large agricultural districts to a desert condition." He referred to the establishment of several State Commissions for forest protection and reported that the Forest Commissioners of California, Colorado and other States favored the idea of reservations.[7] Nevertheless it was not until several years after Commissioner Sparks left office that Congress almost unwittingly provided for their establishment.

The Commissioner was fortunate in the fact that while his appropriations for timber protection never exceeded $75,000, as he requested, they never fell below that amount. In 1887 he was able to show that the land department had recovered more than $128,000 from trespassers in the previous year so that the department was returning a profit to the Treasury.[8] Excessive costs could not, therefore, account for refusing him an increase. And while the appropriations were not sufficiently large to prevent considerable depredation nor prosecute all of the offenders who were apprehended they did permit extensive exposure of fraud and violation.

Some of the most notorious instances of fraud which the Land Office uncovered and sought to correct occurred in the magnificent redwood district of California. Timber operators had used the settlement laws or the Timber and Stone Act to acquire large tracts for sale or exploitation. An outstanding example is furnished by the case of the California Redwood Company According to official reports, in the summer of 1882 Charles H. King and James D. Walker of San Francisco planned to acquire a large block of timber land in

7. Ibid., 1887, pp. 87-8.
8. Ibid., 1887, p. 379.

Humboldt County, California.[9]　After securing an expert
to examine a likely tract Mr. Walker went to Edinburgh,
Scotland, and arranged with certain unnamed capitalists
to secure 50,000 acres for $7.00 an acre.[10]　A contract
was signed October 23, 1882, and in the following year
the Scotchmen formed the California Redwood Company in
Edinburgh.　They chose Mr. Walker president and Mr. King
and David Evans, a former business partner of Mr. Walker's, business managers.

　　　The managers employed locators and surveyors
and then secured agents in Eureka, California, to hire
a large number of entrymen.　One of the agents was
Charles E. Beach, described as "an old experienced land
sharp" and another was M. P. Roberts, a brother of the
Receiver of the Land Office at Eureka.[11]　The agents
made no effort to keep their activities a secret.　They
advertised for 400 men, or as Californians styled them,
"dummies," to make entries under the Timber and Stone
Act.　Some citizens of Eureka refused to be hired but
according to Land Office reports the agents were determined to obtain the quota so that "farmers were stopped
on the way to their homes (and) merchants were called
from their counters and persuaded to allow their names
to be used to obtain land."　In addition sailors were
secured from "Coffee Jack's" boarding house and escorted
to the County Court House where they filed their first
citizen's papers.[12]　Then they were aided in making out
timber filings and a blank deed of sale and were paid
off with a sum varying from $5.00 to $50.00.　The deeds
were executed and the filings completed at the agent's
headquarters at the back of a "notorious saloon," near

9. L.O.R., 1886, p. 95; 1887, p. 81.　H. Ex. Doc. #282.　50 Cong.
　　1 Sess. Serial #2561.
10. S. A. D. Puter claims that Edward Everdeen went to Scotland and
　　that the Company paid $25.00 an acre for the land.　The N.Y.
　　Times asserted that 96,000 acres were involved, April 20, 1886.
　　Cf. Puter, "Looters of the Public Domain."
11. L.O.R., 1887, p. 81.
12. 309 first papers were filed in Humboldt County from November,
　　1882 through 1883.　Only 37 had become citizens by 1887, yet
　　all except 37 had allowed their names to be used for entries.
　　L.O.R., 1887, pp. 81-2.

the Land Office. The agents presented the applications
to the Register and Receiver in bunches of twenty-five
at a time.[13] They later completed the requirements for
title with the aid of "cronies" willing to swear to anything.

In order to speed up patents the Company sent an
attorney to Washington. But after some patents had been
issued the Land Office became suspicious and sent a special agent to investigate in California. He was "picked
up" by the timber agents but later in 1883 the Office
sent another investigator, W. T. Smith. He was offered
a bribe of $5,000, which he refused and reported to the
Land Office.[14] His investigations led him to estimate
that nearly 100,000 acres had been fraudulently entered.
He secured an affidavit from ex-Surveyor General Gardner,
implicating the local Land Office.[15] Another affidavit
from a Mr. McLaughlin revealed that he had furnished the
agents with more than 100 men at $5.00 each and that
these men, whose names he listed, had made entries.

Evidently Mr. Smith's investigations resulted
in the grand jury indictment against David Evans,
Charles Beach and others on the charge of fraudulent acquisition of timber land.[16] They escaped prosecution in
1884, however, though special agent Smith was suspended
and afterwards dismissed from the service. Commissioner
Sparks testified later that the dismissal occurred "at
the instance, it was understood in this office, of great
influence brought against him from the Pacific Coast and
in Washington."[17] The Commissioner also reported that
the case showed ramifications of fraud in the Land Office for the clerk having charge of the case ignored the
special agent's report and in a letter to Commissioner
McFarland recommended 157 entries for patent. The latter accepted his subordinate's word and issued patents
to an additional 22,000 acres valued at $440,000.

---

13. Ibid., p. 95.
14. Ibid., 1886, p. 94.
15. N.Y. Times, Apr. 20, 1886.
16. N.Y. Times, Nov. 22, 1886.
17. L.O.R., 1886, p. 94.

After the Democrats took office the case attracted particular attention in the East, both because
the Land Office thoroughly exposed it and because the
ensuing publicity revealed that a brother of Postmaster
General W. F. Vilas[18] was implicated. In December, 1885,
Commissioner Sparks appointed a fourth special agent to
investigate entries in Humboldt County. The new agent,
B. F. Bergen, could not be bribed and his superiors were
not amenable to pressure from interested politicians.
Yet every effort was made to hinder the investigation.[19]
The Land Office reported:

> "Some of the witnesses were spirited out of the country,
> others were threatened and intimidated; spies were em-
> ployed to watch and follow the agent and report the names
> of all persons who conversed with or called upon him; and
> on one occasion two persons who were about to enter the
> agent's room were knocked down and dragged away."[20]

The local Land Office officials could not assist
the investigation for they still lacked the power to
summon witnesses. Furthermore the Company defeated attempts to secure subpoenas under the State Code. Agent
Bergen was able, however, to secure evidence from the
former Receiver of the Local Office when he testified
openly at the Office. Mr. Bergen also obtained affidavits from ninety entrymen and several other company
employees. His evidence was used to indict again David
Evans, Charles King and six others.[21]

Within a month, on May 4, 1886, the men were
freed when the Federal Court quashed the charges. The
New York Times recalled the former indictments and observed that probably the men would again "resume business at the old stand." It then raised the embarrassing
question, "But cannot the Department of Justice hold

---

18. See below.
19. The magazine Conservation reported a case where a special agent
    was invited to a dinner in his honor but an attempt was made to
    poison him by putting rough-on-rats in his coffee. Quoted in
    Ise, op. cit., p. 76.
20. L.O.R., 1886, p. 95.
21. N.Y. Times, Apr. 5, 1886; Apr. 20, 1886.

someone responsible for such shameful failures to enforce the laws?"[22]   The Land Office, however, did not
give up. Those entries which had not been patented
were cancelled or held for cancellation, pending further investigation. The Office also recommended that
the Secretary request the Attorney General to bring suit
for the annulment of 151 patents for which fraudulent
entry had been found.[23] For some reason Secretary Lamar
delayed the request until seven months after the Office's suggestion.

Meanwhile in order to protect their investment
the Scotch owners had formed a new company called the
Humboldt Redwood Company. It purchased the property of
the California company and then in answering the Government's charges in Court claimed that as an "innocent
purchaser" it should not be deprived of its property despite fraud by others.[24] But since the stockholders
were the same in both companies and since the American
representatives were also the same the plea was somewhat
specious. The cases then dragged along. Finally Congress adopted a resolution requesting the Secretary of
Interior to submit any information which he possessed
regarding the company.[25] On April 27, 1888, Secretary
of Interior W. F. Vilas, who had succeeded Mr. Lamar,
presented[26] some of the evidence from the Land Office
files. The Secretary was placed in an embarrassing position for in the preceding year when the Land Office
agents were exposing the timber frauds, a dispatch from
Milwaukee, Wisconsin, reported that Mr. Vilas' brother,
Joseph, was an owner of a large timber tract in Humboldt
County, California. Joseph Vilas was said to have gone

---

22. It also observed with some asperity that since the laws seemed
    unenforceable the Land Office should be abolished "so that the
    thieves may be free to fight among themselves for what is left
    of the public domain," May 5, 1886.
23. In March, 1887, suit for all patents was commenced. Some en-
    tries had never been approved because they covered mineral land.
    Ibid., Nov. 22, 1886; H. Ex. Doc. #282, op. cit.
24. L.O.R., 1887, pp. 496-9.
25. 50 Cong. 1 Sess. Cong. Rec., pp. 1151; 2371.
26. Ibid., p. 3436.

west with H. C. Putnam[27] to invest $150,000 in Redwood
lands; the latter secured a tenth interest in the California Redwood Company, and according to later reports
both men bought land adjoining the Company's from the
same agents and reportedly secured in the same fraudulent manner.

Irrespective of a possible family connection
Secretary Vilas' report denounced the company's "well
concocted scheme" which was "boldly carried out" but he
presented no indication that the Department of Justice
was making any effort to recover the patents or punish
the conspirators.[28] He did recommend a law empowering
Registers and Receivers to summon witnesses in suspected
cases and that request would indicate that the Government had been unable to carry through its prosecution.
In any case the eastern papers and Congress do not seem
to have carried any further news of Government activities. S. A. D. Puter claims that the company lost a
large share of its investment when its patents were cancelled. It is probable that he was thinking of entries
though he may be accurate. He also claimed that 30,000
acres of the same land were taken up again at a later
time in practically the same manner and turned over to
a "notorious" American lumberman.

Another case involving fraudulent entries was
prosecuted under President Cleveland though it came before the Supreme Court for adjudication after his first
term was completed. The Court's decision was highly
significant for it materially aided concentration of
timber control and for all practical purposes made it
unnecessary for timber companies to seek any change in
the Timber and Stone Act. In July, 1882, David E. Budd
had entered 160 acres under the latter act at the Van-
couver, Washington, Land Office.[29] Less than six months

---

27. See his statements to a newspaper reporter; his protests are
    perhaps a shade too ingenious. **N.Y. Times,** Apr. 16, 1887. He
    was refused a hearing at the Land Office but Secretary Lamar
    ordered hearings in Eureka on the ground that Mr. Vilas was an
    innocent purchaser.
28. See comment of, ibid., April 28, 1888.
29. 144 U.S. 154.

later he conveyed the land to James B. Montgomery, though he did not receive patent until May 5, 1883. The transfer would indicate an illegal prior agreement to sell, particularly when the deed listed the purchase price at $1.00. The price which he had to pay the Government was $400 though the land was worth about $5,000. Montgomery secured 10,000 acres at about the same time through other entrymen. A link between them was established when it was learned that one witness served in twenty-one cases of entry. Another witness had been engaged in examining the lands entered and had reported them to Montgomery.

After an investigation under the Democratic administration the Government brought suit to have the Budd patent set aside on the grounds of prior agreement for transfer. The case passed to the crowded docket of the Supreme Court and in 1892 was decided in favor of Budd. In the decision Justice Brewer held that there was no absolute proof of prior agreement so that there was no ground for cancellation. The Justice also added what seemed like a gratuitous dicta when he declared: "Montgomery might rightfully go or send into the vicinity and make known generally or to individuals a willingness to buy timber land at a price in excess of that which it cost to obtain it from the Government." Undoubtedly Justice Brewer presented a logical method for filling in deficiencies of timber legislation but he thereby placed a curious interpretation on the provision which required an applicant to swear: "that he does not apply to purchase the same on speculation."

Justices Brown and Harlan issued a strong dissent. They held that Montgomery's acquisition, "however it may have been done (was) a practical defeat of the intention of Congress." They continued:

"It certainly demands, and in this instance received, a searching investigation. When we see the most valuable portion of an immense domain which has been reserved by the beneficence of Congress for the benefit of actual settlers, being gradually absorbed by a few speculators, we are forced to inquire whether there is not a limit beyond which even a land patent of the United States begins to lose something of its sanctity."

The Budd decision made it possible for capitalists to bring train loads of individuals who were to
enter timber land in the public land regions.[30] Concentration of control therefore advanced apace. John
Ise notes that ultimately not over a fraction of one
percent of the area acquired under the Timber and Stone
Act could be found in the hands of the original entrymen and patentees.[31] Even before the Budd case, of
course, monopoly and trustification of the timber industry was well started. In 1887 the Milwaukee Sentinel
reported that Frederick Weyerhauser was "the controlling
spirit of lumber corporations in Wisconsin, Minnesota,
Iowa and Missouri." His companies possessed an aggregate capital of $70,000,000 and produced over a billion
feet of lumber annually.[32] A great many companies, however, including at least some of Mr. Weyerhauser's,
owned timber land purchased from railroads, not from
speculative entrymen.[33] The Supreme Court, because of
Congress' failure to modify the law, merely hastened the
time when practically all timber was concentrated under
the control of a few individuals.

If the Government encountered difficulty in
checking manipulation of timber entries it found it
practically impossible to prevent timber depredations.
Vigorous action by Democratic officials was largely nullified by the strength of the corporations prosecuted;
by insufficient numbers of timber agents; by the ease
with which offenders could skip to other States; and by
the conflicting methods and red tape in the Department

---

30. National Conservation Commission Report, 1909, p. 389.
31. Ise, op. cit., p. 226. Quoted from "Lumber Industry," op. cit.
32. Quoted in N.Y. Times, Oct. 3, 1887. American capitalists were
    also reported to be buying the pick of the timber and coal land
    of British Columbia. Copp, op. cit., January 15, 1885.
33. Mr. Weyerhauser purchased a great deal of timber land from the
    Northern Pacific Railroad. He also secured some of the in-
    demnity land along the Chicago, Minneapolis and Omaha Railroad
    and a departmental dispute over some of this land led to Mr.
    Sparks' dismissal. See Chapter XIV post.

of Justice. H. C. Cummings and C. McFarland have explained in their work "Federal Justice" something of the
"rising tide of timber depredations" which reached its
flood in the 1880's and the difficulties of successfully
attacking corporations.[34]

One interesting case which they take up but
which is also discussed in Democratic official reports
was furnished by the attempt to prosecute the Sierra
Lumber Company of California.[35] The company was formed
in 1878 but its depredations on public timber were not
fully reported until after a Land Office investigation
in 1884. Later Secretary Lamar requested Attorney General Garland to bring suit for about 64,000,000 feet of
cut timber,[36] valued at $2,240,000. Such suits fre-
quently did not cover the full amount of the depredation
but only so much as the Government felt reasonably sure
of prosecuting successfully. The Secretary recommended
a Mr. Oates as special counsel in the case and the Attorney General accepted him. Before instituting suit
Mr. Oates had proposed that the Government compromise
with the company for $15,000 but the Government refused.
Suit began in April, 1886, and by January, 1889, the
Government obtained a favorable verdict for $41,000.
Since the prosecution could not prove the depredations
willful, the indemnity was small.[37]

The victory was incomplete, however, and further
action by the company lead to a compromise in favor of
the Government, for $15,000 and costs. The case was
marked by an expensive resurvey of land because the
original survey had been incorrect. Furthermore the
Land Office agent's report was inaccurate and there was
considerable friction between subordinate officials.
And finally there were charges of misconduct on the part
of the California District Attorney and the Special
Counsel, Mr. Oates. Whether these facts influenced the

---

34. Op. cit., pp. 262-4.
35. L.O.R., 1885, p. 82; and Cummings and McFarland, op. cit.,
    pp. 264-5.
36. This was enough timber to build over 4,000 five-room houses.
37. Yet meanwhile its depredations continued. Copp, op. cit.,
    Jan. 1, 1888.

settlement is not recorded.[38]

Another prominent company which was indicted
for timber trespass, was the previously mentioned Montana Improvement Company, a subordinate of the Northern
Pacific Railroad.[39] One of the company's officials
claimed that it had obtained verbal permission from the
Secretary of Interior, when the Montana delegate to
Congress was present, to cut all the timber required in
building the road, "from Government land--at least
where the land was not surveyed"! The Secretary who
gave this permission must have been Henry M. Teller,
the same official who allowed the railroad to select
indemnity land without specifying the basis therefore.[40]

The Democratic administration carefully prepared
its suit against the Montana company but by 1887, when
the case was ready for trial, the Government had exhausted its funds for securing witnesses and postponement was
necessary.[41] The Land Office complained bitterly of the
delay. It believed that when the time for trial recurred
many witnesses would have disappeared, much evidence
would have been destroyed and the Government would have
to prepare its case anew, thereby wasting time and money.

---

38. In Idaho, the District Court granted a writ forbidding the local
    Register and Receiver to investigate an alleged fraudulent en-
    try. The District Attorney, however, successfully appealed for
    release of the writ. Occasionally District Attorneys were very
    active against offenders for small depredations but this was in
    order to collect fees. N.Y. Times, Oct. 26, 1886.
39. The Montana Company supplied all the timber used during the con-
    struction of about 925 miles of the railroad. It controlled
    all timber on the railroad's lands and claimed control of all
    timber on adjacent Government lands. Cummings and McFarland,
    op. cit., pp. 265-6; L.O.R., 1885, pp. 311-2.
40. The company also obtained official permission to erect saw mills
    on the Flathead Indian Reservation and to use the timber there
    until the railroad was completed to Portland, Oregon. Though
    finished prior to 1885, the Land Office found the mills running
    day and night. L.O.R., 1885, p. 312.
41. Preliminary action is noted by Cummings and McFarland though
    they present erroneous or confused names and dates, op. cit.,
    p. 266.

The new investigation would prevent the Office from taking up other and flagrant cases of trespass which had been reported.[42]

While the case was held up the company did continue its trespass and did endeavor to destroy evidence of former offences.[43] As a matter of fact the case never came to trial and in 1891 the suit was dismissed. Cummings and McFarland explain that failure was due partly to the difficulty in finding witnesses; partly to the fact that some of the timber was cut for lawful purposes (?); but principally to the Government's inability to show that timber was cut from the public domain.[44]

The Government also instigated a number of suits against the Northern Pacific Railroad Company, itself. The cases dragged along until the Department of Justice changed its strategy, dismissed all the suits and brought one action in Minnesota to cover trespasses for the entire line. There was no success[45] and ultimately Commissioner of the Land Office Carter, from Montana, suggested that the Government and the company consider joint action against individual depredators.[46] One suit which had been brought against the railroad failed because the land involved had not been surveyed. The Land Office made a special allotment of $15,000 for surveying part of the region where depredations occurred but owing to the low maximum rates which the law permitted there were no bids for the work.[47] John Ise notes that the

---

42. In the same year trial of the Sierra company was postponed for the same reason. Two agents had worked nearly a year gathering evidence. L.O.R., 1887, pp. 83-4. The Land Office needed about $4,000. N.Y. Times, Apr. 7, 1888. The Office probably referred to the annual appropriation of $20,000 marked for summoning witnesses on cases of fraudulent entry. In 1887 the Commissioner requested $30,000. L.O.R., 1887, p. 379; 1885, p. 236.
43. Ibid., p. 84; 1888, p. 45.
44. Cummings and McFarland, op. cit., p. 266.
45. The N.Y. Times claimed that the statute of limitations protected the company, Apr. 7, 1888.
46. See Chapter XV, post.
47. L.O.R., 1887, p. 246.

decision in this case, given in a Montana court,[48] provides strong evidence of railroad domination of the
court. In view of the many failures in the Northwest
it is interesting to observe that in Alabama, where
there were vigorous officials, unprejudiced judges and
apparently certain opportunity for prosecuting depredators and recovering stolen property, the timber operators appealed to Congress and obtained relief after all
else has failed.[49]

Despite the discouraging results of Democratic
timber administration there is some evidence that it
succeeded in discouraging timber law violations.[50] The
western demand for law observance, that is that part of
the West which made such demands, the effectiveness of
special agents' work and the attempted prosecution of
outstanding depredators resulted in a "feeling of depression" until 1888. By that time Commissioner Sparks
had left office and timber activities had begun to increase. Very shortly timber-grabbing was booming. Mr.
Puter testified that in Oregon "every hotel in the timber section was crowded with timber land speculators,
cruisers and locators" and "the woods were alive with
men." Consequently in the following decade the "muck-
rakers" were able to disclose a new set of scandals.[51]

II

Congress' unfortunate failure to establish a
suitable timber policy[52] or provide for law enforcement

48. Ise, op. cit., pp. 84-5.
49. Cummings and McFarland, op. cit., pp. 268-9.
50. In Washington Territory, however, the Governor continued to
    show that lumbering was increasing. The San Francisco Journal
    noted that 200,000,000 feet of timber were sent to California
    from Puget Sound alone in 1886. Sec. of Int. Reports, 1885,
    p. 1078; 1886, p. 863; 1887, p. 952. For evidence of fraud see
    L.O.R., 1886, p. 93. For continued violations in Alabama and
    Florida see Copp, op. cit., Jan. 15, 1888.
51. Puter, op. cit., p. 20.
52. The provisions of an act of October, 1888, permitting with-
    drawal of lands for irrigation purposes will be taken up in
    the following chapter.

were not altogether duplicated in the handling of land
grant railroads. Through executive action the Cleveland
administration reversed policies and regulations that
had ignored a strict interpretation of law. It restored
21,000,000 acres of indemnity land withdrawals to the
public domain and began an adjustment of grants in which
careless supervision had permitted excessive patents.
Surprisingly enough these reforms were matched by Congressional efforts to check railroad license. For example despite the presence of railroad lawyers in the
legislature as partly revealed in the debate over the
Railroad Attorney bill,[53] the Interstate Commerce Commission Act was passed in 1887. Another law of the same
year gave the Interior Department full authority to adjust all grants in accordance with Supreme Court decisions. And a third act passed the year before permitted
States to tax surveyed grant lands to which the roads
had delayed taking patents. In short, great strides
were made toward meeting railroad problems which had
arisen prior to 1885. On the other hand there was a
noticeable failure to adopt a policy of forfeiture of
lapsed or unearned grants, although several more individual forfeiture acts were passed. No special steps
were taken to secure survey of railroad grant lands and
an inadequate staff in the Railroad Division of the
Land Office continued to face an overwhelming task.

        In addition to various requests for improvements
Commissioner Sparkers' reports contained a severe indictment of railroad policies.[54] He proposed to hold
the roads to strict accounting, particularly when recti-
fying mistaken claims and erroneous patents. Without
mentioning any names the Commissioner also indicted
former departmental methods. He asserted: "It is the
history of this office and department that lawful claims

---

53. See comments in N.Y. Times, June 2, 1886 ff.
54. He reported that 100,000 miles of road were built without land
    grants and only 17,631 miles with them. The former were as
    frequently constructed through isolated country as the latter
    were through settled areas. L.O.R., 1885, p. 26. Secretary
    Lamar also devoted considerable space to railroad policies and
    benefits. Cf. Sec. of Int. Report, 1887, p. 9 ff.

of settlers to lands within railroad limits that were
not granted to the railroads from express terms of exception in the granting acts have gone down under official decisions as grain before the reaper's scythe."[55]
He had found that especially after 1881, "the antagonism
to settlers' rights is shown in printed as well as in
unpublished decisions to have amounted to a crusade."
The Commissioner also reported that occasionally the Supreme Court had corrected departmental decisions. Yet
even when contested cases resulted favorably for a settler and he had received a patent it was reported that
some railroads "systematically" pursued the patentees
to the courts. There with "vexatious, dilatory and expensive proceedings" the companies often forced a second
purchase.[56] According to one authority Commissioner
Sparks almost stopped deciding cases brought up against
railroads favorably to them. An examination of many of
his decisions, nevertheless, reveals that he always held
closely to the law.[57]

       The Commissioner also supported many of the
charges which George W. Julian had made earlier. He
showed that the department had evaded the requirement
for withdrawal of lands when the line of the road was
definitely established by permitting roads to file maps
for only part of their routes or to file one map which
cut off settlement and then later a second.map which
definitely established the line. As a result there had
been many changes of location. The Commissioner declared that "problematical lines (were) run over nearly
all portions of Washington Territory and widely divergent lines (were) made the basis for withdrawals in
Minnesota, Dakota, Montana and Idaho."[58] Settlement

---

55. L.O.R., 1885, p. 35.
56. Ibid., p. 45.
57. Another side of the picture is shown by the testimony that set-
    tlers purposely located in the railroad lands in a spirit of
    bravado. Proudfit interview.
58. .L.O.R., 1885, p. 29. The Leavenworth, Lawrence and Western
    Railroad line had been located for reservation on a problemati-
    cal route by "pencil lines drawn across a territorial map by an
    unaccredited attorney" before the company had filed its ac-
    ceptance of the grant. Ibid., p. 26.

rights had also been restricted when the Office allowed
railroads claims to date from the time the roads were
making preliminary surveys or from other premature
dates. Many of these rulings seemed to be intended to
allow the roads the first chance for establishing speculative town sites but in any case the Commissioner remarked that the "various instances of false construction
of law, erroneous rulings and mistaken decisions have
been in favor of the corporations."[59]

The amount of lands withdrawn had occasionally
exceeded that which was granted. The Alabama and Florida Railroad was overdrawn 245 acres per mile for 113
miles in Alabama. The Winona and St. Peter Railroad had
about 480 acres per mile excess in Minnesota. Investigation of the withdrawal for the Atcheson, Topeka and
Santa Fe road in Kansas alone served as a basis for es-
timating that total overwithdrawals would amount to
300,000 acres. The Missouri, Kansas and Texas Railroad
and the Kansas Pacific road also had excess reserves.
The Commissioner estimated that the total for all roads
would reach 10,000,000 acres.[60]

There were still other ways in which the department had favored land grant railroads. According to
a law of 1874 when a settler's entry had been permitted
and the Office later found that it rested on land to
which a railroad had a prior claim, the road could sell
the land to the settler and then select indemnity.[61]
Such a provision was extremely generous but official
regulations had applied it to indemnity lands as well as
granted lands. The department had also ruled that railroads were entitled to an amount of land which accorded
with their total length in mileage rather than the mileage between two points. In other words those roads
which had curves and sinuosities were theoretically
straightened out in calculating the number of sections
that the companies were to receive. Patents had issued
under this rule but Commissioner Sparks believed that it

59. Ibid., p. 27.
60. L.O.R., 1885, p. 32.
61. Ibid., p. 28, (18 Stat. 194).

was legally unwarranted.

In order to recover land for which patents had erroneously issued the Commissioner requested the Government to bring suit.[62] Consequently in 1886 action was started against the Burlington and Missouri Railroad, The Missouri, Kansas and Texas road, the Central Pacific and the Southern Pacific.[63] Where patents had not yet issued the Land Office itself undertook the correction. An example is found in the case of land reserved for the Atlantic and Pacific railroad in California.[64] The granting act had provided for a line from Colorado "by the most practicable and eligible route to the Pacific." The company had run its line to San Buenaventura in the southern part of the State but had then made an extension 380 miles northward to San Francisco. In 1874 the Attorney General ruled that the road was entitled to a land subsidy for the extension and the land department made a withdrawal for it. The California legislature had protested the withdrawal and a Circuit Court decision, involving the land, had declared there was no grant for the extension.

The withdrawal stood, however, until 1885 when, in a disputed case, Commissioner Sparks agreed with the Circuit Court decision and ruled that the company had no claim to the land. This decision was appealed to the Secretary of Interior and he called for a report from the Land Office. In order to discredit the Commissioner a report was immediately telegraphed over the country that his decision had been reversed. On the contrary the Secretary set a date for a hearing and March 23, 1886, decided the withdrawal was illegal. He therefore

---

62. Bills were immediately introduced in Congress in an attempt to protect the roads against loss for excess lands which they had sold. L.O.R., 1886, pp. 34-5. Later, however, settlers who had bought such land were partly protected.
63. The N.Y. Times lamented the lack of careful and honest management which had made suits necessary. It felt, however, that there was no point in restoring the land since they would soon be acquired by "land grabbing individuals who thrive upon fraud," May 7, 1886.
64. L.O.R., 1886, pp. 30-1.

ordered the Office to restore the reserved 1,500,000 acres to the public domain.[65]

Another outstanding adjustment affected the Northern Pacific Railroad in Oregon and Washington. According to a strict construction of the granting act and subsequent laws affecting it, the company received no subsidy for a branch line from Portland, Oregon to Puget Sound.[66] Nevertheless the land department had withdrawn lands along the branch but without citation of authority. While reviewing a settler's claim to a portion of the area, Commissioner Sparks ruled against the railroad. On the very day he wrote his decision for the local office at Olympia, Washington Territory, President Robert Harris issued to the stock and bondholders of the company a letter in which he declared: "There is no foundation in law or reason for such decision."[67] He intended to appeal the case to the Secretary and the courts, if necessary. He did appeal but apparently was defeated. Newspapers estimated that the land in dispute was worth $25,000,000.

Additional adjustments affected 800,000 acres for the Southern Pacific,[68] 12,000 acres for the St. Joseph and Denver City, and 30,000 acres for the Oregon Central Railroads.[69] The latter endeavored to secure a Circuit Court injunction restraining the Register and Receiver from allowing entry on the land it claimed but the Court refused for want of jurisdiction.[70]

The opposition which the Commissioner met in this work caused him to recommend that Congress provide the office with full authority to proceed along the line already mapped out. He also recommended forfeiture

---

65. California land was becoming quite valuable. Only three counties were rated at $2.00 an acre. The remainder were valued much higher.
66. L.O.R., 1886, pp. 333-5.
67. N.Y. Times, Jan. 13, 1886.
68. Ibid., August 16, 1885.
69. Reform newspapers carried many notices of adjustments. See the N.Y. Times caustic comment May 2, 1886.
70. L.O.R., 1886, p. 32.

of all grants unearned at the expiration of their time
limit, speedy survey of all grants and taxation of all
earned land to which railroads had neglected to take
title.

Congress confined its attention to forfeiture
of individual grants rather than to the question of
general forfeiture. The Northern Pacific and the Atlantic and Pacific concessions received considerable
debate. In July, 1886, that portion of the grant to
the latter road along the unfinished portions of its
line, was forfeited.[71] A few days later four lesser
roads were also deprived of their land subsidies.[72]
The Northern Pacific case, however, dragged on in a dispute among those who wished to hold the company to
strict accounting, those who agreed to partial forfeiture and those who endeavored to protect the road
from any loss.[73]

There was no particular response to the recommendation for a complete survey of railroad lands but
the request for the right to tax unpatented grant lands
was adopted after the Supreme Court placed the responsibility squarely before Congress. Trail County, Dakota,
endeavored to tax Northern Pacific lands but the railroad resorted to the courts. It claimed immunity under
the law which required railroads to pay the cost of surveying and patenting before receiving title. Since the
company had not yet paid these costs and received patents, title to the lands remained in the Government.
The State Supreme Court ruled against the company but
the United States Supreme Court reversed the decision.[74]
The latter acknowledged the abuse which resulted from
the principle thus upheld but it asserted: "The remedy
lies with Congress. If that body will take steps to enforce its lien for these costs of survey by the sale of

---

71. 24 Stat. 123.
72. 24 Stat. 140.
73. N.Y. Times, May-June, 1886, passim.
74. 115 U.S. 600; N.Y. Times, Dec. 8, 1885. See similar previous
    decisions, Kansas Pacific Railway Co. vs. Prescott. 16 Wall.
    603; Haney, op. cit., p. 181. Railroad Co. vs. McShane.
    22 Wall. 444. Donaldson, op. cit., pp. 1264-5.

lands or by forfeiture of title, the Treasury of the
United States would soon be reimbursed by its expense
in making these surveys" and States and Territories
could levy taxes.

Within three months Congress began debate on
one of many bills which permitted States to tax the
grants of the major Pacific roads.[75] Representative
Crisp of Georgia presented a lucid explanation of the
privileges which railroads enjoyed under Court decisions
namely that the roads were permitted to mortgage or sell
land on which they did not have to pay taxes. The bill
passed the House in March, 1886. Four months later
Senator Van Wyck of Nebraska offered a substitute which
applied to all land grant railroads. Since the Senate
had already spent considerable time debating similar
bills the Nebraskan's measure passed in short order.
After conference the House accepted his bill and on
July 10, President Cleveland signed it.[76] The new law
provided that States, Territories and municipalities
could tax railroad grant lands if surveyed and in organized counties, irrespective of patenting. The Secretary of Interior could require roads to pay the expenses
of surveys and patents and if they refused after 30 days
notice the Attorney General could bring suit for the
money. The Governor of Wyoming described the measure
as "another long stride along the highway of reform."[77]

The fourth Land Office recommendation, that for
legislative authority to adjust grants, was enacted into
law March 3, 1887.[78] Though such legislation would seem
to have been unnecessary the first section authorized
adjustments. Another section specifically required

---

75. 49 Cong. 1 Sess. Cong. Rec., pp. 3718-21; 4953-8; 5018-28;
    5140-53; and 5190-6.
76. 24 Stat. 143. The N.Y. Times severely criticized Senator Blair
    of New Hampshire for attempting to load the bill with amend-
    ments, May 27, 1886. See also ibid., June 4, 1886.
77. He reported that about one-half of the railroad land grants in
    the Territory had already been sold, some for many years. It
    was thought they were largely held for speculation. Sec. of
    Int. Report, 1887, p. 1017.
78. 24 Stat. 556.

the railroads to return all lands erroneously certified
or patented. If the roads refused to comply with a departmental request the Government was authorized to
bring suit. Certain other sections of the law dealing
with settlers' rights were not completely protective for
although they insured patents for those who had erroneously purchased from the roads they required the settlers to sue the roads for the purchase price of their
lands. But perhaps the most unusual provision of all
was found in section seven which declared that no more
lands were to be certified or conveyed to a railroad if
it appeared to the Secretary of Interior that the road
was securing more than it was entitled to. In any case
the department was able to proceed without legal objections even though it was handicapped in other ways.[79]

In addition to its efforts to correct grants the
Democratic administration, with the special assistance
from President Cleveland, was able to make some fundamental changes in the control of indemnity lands. Land
Office withdrawal of this type of land had formerly
brought sharp criticism from George W. Julian. Commissioner Sparks was able to show officially that the railroads greatly abused the privilege which withdrawals
created. He stated that they used indemnity rights:

> "To compel settlers to purchase railroad waivers or relin-
> quishments in land to which the company had not or might
> never have any color of legal right; to appropriate the
> products of coal and other valuable lands; to dominate
> town sites and monopolize water privileges; (and) to deva-
> state forests of their timber."[80]

---

79. Adjustments did not proceed rapidly. By the end of the year
    nine grants had been checked over, thereby prospectively saving
    3,000,000 acres but the Secretary modified the basis for adjust-
    ment. By 1891 five roads had been dealt with and seventeen
    awaited the Secretary's approval. L.O.R., 1887, p. 46; 1891,
    p. 37. And see the difficulties recorded by Samuel J. Crawford,
    special Kansas Agent for adjusting claims. Report to the Gover-
    nor of Kansas, 1892. The Attorney General's analysis of the
    act received newspaper praise.
80. N.Y. Times, Oct. 29, Nov. 23, 1887.

In a previous chapter it was pointed out that
Secretary Schurz had first required railroads to specify areas for which they sought indemnity. This rule
had not been followed by careful inspection of areas selected. The roads were reported to have used areas for
which they had already obtained indemnity, for a second
indemnity.[81] Such selections were not checked probably
because the Office had been handicapped by its inadequate staff. The extent of excess selections was first
revealed when Commissioner Sparks reported that preliminary examination for the Winona and St. Peter Railroad showed 300,000 acres overdrawn. Further inspection
was expected to reveal twice that figure. The Atcheson,
Topeka and Santa Fe had overdrawn a similar amount.[82]
The Northern Pacific was reported to have chosen 380,000
acres more than it lost, in Washington Territory alone.[83]

Departmental rules had segregated land covered
by indemnity selections and on the basis of this pre-
sumptive title the roads had sold quitclaim deeds or
evicted settlers.[84] The Democratic administration revised the rules for selections and instructed Registers
and Receivers to require railroads to be specific in locating lands for which they sought indemnity.[85] All
previous selections without specification of loss were
to be corrected to date before additional lists were submitted. And the new regulations stipulated that future
selections could be made only in the area nearest the
lost sections, not in another State or Territory.

The Commissioner began to modify rules for indemnity before the departmental regulations were distributed. One of the earliest cases is that which involved Guilford Miller's settlement entry in Washington
territory,[86] on what became Northern Pacific indemnity
land. Miller settled on his claim two years prior to
the indemnity withdrawals but he had not made entry at

81. L.O.R., 1885, p. 30.
82. Ibid., p. 31.
83. Ibid., p. 34.
84. Ibid., p. 33.
85. Ibid., p. 34 and N.Y. Times, Aug. 6, 1885.
86. L.O.R., 1885, p. 201 ff.

the land office until 1884, a year after the railroad
had selected his quarter section as indemnity. The
local officials felt that his entry should be disallowed
and they forwarded it to the Land Office for final action. On July 13, 1885, the Commissioner decided in
favor of Miller.[87] In a lengthy opinion which considered the legality of indemnity withdrawals, the Commissioner held that they were valid for information only.
Miller's settlement, irrespective of entry, gave him
prior claim.

The company appealed to Secretary Lamar and he
listened to "argument at great length." He sought the
advice of Attorney General Brewster and eventually submitted the case to President Cleveland, at the latter's
request. Most of the land department, including the
Attorney General, were opposed to the Commissioner's decision.[88] In 1887, however, the President ruled in
favor of Miller and upheld the Commissioner.[89] He noted
that indemnity withdrawals kept millions of acres beyond
the reach of citizens and that such a condition was contrary to the avowed policy of public land distribution.
He also noted that there was no evidence of how much
land would be necessary for indemnity and no time limit
placed on selections Fifteen years had already passed
in the case of the Northern Pacific road and it did not
appear that the company would need all that had been reserved for it.

The President believed that "such a condition of
public lands should no longer continue. So far as it is
the result of executive rules and methods these should
be abandoned; and so far as it is a consequence of improvident laws these should be appealed or amended."
The President concluded that it was possible to allow

87. The N.Y. Times applauded the decision and expressed the hope
    that Secretary Lamar would uphold it. Ibid., July 14, 1885.
    For a similar decision see the case of John Walton.
88. Author's interview with Judge Proudfit.
89. The original copy of the decision in the President's handwrit-
    ten "boiler plate" was, until recently at least, hanging framed
    on the Land Office walls. Copy in L.O.R., 1887, pp. 42-4.

the company to select alternate land that did not include Miller's claim, without calling into question the
legal proposition set forth by the Attorney General.

Since indemnity withdrawals were the result of
departmental rules Secretary Lamar adopted the President's suggestion for abandoning them.[90] He ordered
hearings for twenty-two railroads to show why withdrawals should not be revoked. After the hearings, the
Secretary ordered restoration of about 21,000,000 acres
of reserved land.[91] Democratic and Independent newspapers, such as the New York Herald, the New York Times,
the Boston Times and the Philadelphia Times, praised the
administration's stand. Some Republican papers like the
St. Paul Press derived the President's decision or
termed it a "strictly political move." The Chicago
Inter-Ocean, the Omaha Bee and the Baltimore American,
other Republican papers, praised the President moderate-
ly. The Italian and German press of New York gave unqualified approval.[92]

The Northern Pacific made a new appeal to Secretary Lamar's successor, Secretary Vilas. But in August,
1888, the latter upheld Miller's claim.[93] Among other
reasons which he assigned for the decision was the fact
that the company had failed to show a basis for selecting Miller's land. The Northern Pacific's entire land
policy was open to severe criticism. It had not only
vigorously battled settlers but it had employed men to
enter grant lands that were worthless and date their
time of residence prior to the location of the line so
that the road could demand indemnity.[94] Newspapers
credit the road with a radical change in policy after
Henry Villard took charge. Thereafter various officials

---

90. Yet his report indicates that he also acted under the authority
    of the March 3, 1887, adjustment law. Sec. of Int.' Report,
    1887, p. 12. The Nation approved the action even though it
    meant reversing a previous decision, Aug. 25, 1887. And see
    L.O.R., 1887, pp. 44, 46-9.
91. N.Y. Times, Dec. 5, 1887.
92. Cf. Public Opinion, Vol. III, #4, 1887.
93. N.Y. Times, August 3, 1888.
94. L.O.R., 1886, p. 33.

were removed from office and settlers were encouraged.[95]

      The promising start which Democratic officials
had made on railroad grants was not consistently pursued. The question of indemnity rights was undoubtedly
complicated by the long period over which they had been
carelessly handled. Perhaps this accounts for the fact
that within a few months after establishing a rule for
indemnity adjustments Secretary Lamar modified it in
favor of the roads. There may be other reasons for this
reversal, however, as discussed below. In any case it
is gratifying to note that for more than two years railroad influence in the land department had been effectively checked.

---

95. A newspaper dispatch from St. Paul, Minnesota, read: "The land
ring of the Northern Pacific, which Mr. Villard proposes to utterly wipe out is one of the most corrupt concerns that ever
fastened its fangs on the throat of a Territory..... Immigrants
have been prohibited from settling along the line of the road
in order to provide large tracts for speculation, impossible
booms, and town sites without the echo of a town. Many papers
charge it with corrupting cheap legislators, courts and juries.
It is charged with levying toll on immigrants and with all
manner of swindles. Mr. Villard is said to grow more indignant
every day as he....finds to what an enormous extent the road
has been cheated out of a continuous population."
N.Y. Times, Oct. 14, 1887. The Railroad's Land Commissioner,
C. B. Lamborn, had remarked that he saw no reason to object to
timber cutting by the road, on indemnity land. The Company
nevertheless sought to prevent others from cutting by means of
injunctions. N.Y. Times and Tribune, Jan. 11, 1886; Times,
Nov. 18, 1887.

Chapter XIV

SECRETARY VILAS HINDERS REFORM

It would be entirely misleading to imply that
President Cleveland was responsible for thwarting the
Democratic land reform program. He does, however, have
to accept the responsibility for transferring his close
friend Attorney General Vilas to the Interior Department
when Secretary Lamar was promoted to the Supreme Court.
The price which the President paid for his new Secretary
was a partial surrender to the railroads on the indemnity question, a more liberal interpretation of the settlement laws and the dismissal of two faithful subordinates, Commissioner Sparks and Law Clerk Le Barnes.
This accusation should in no way diminish the importance
of the President's contributions to progressive measures: his outspoken recommendations to Congress, his
eagerness to curb ranching and railroad indemnity license and his support of aggressive land officials for
more than two years.

Before taking up the methods of changing officials it is necessary to present further evidence that
the most powerful check on reform was found in Congress.
This evidence can be found by examining again the conditions of the swamp land grants and the needs of the
Land Office. By 1887 State selections of swamp land had
totalled 77,407,273 acres and of this amount two-thirds
had received patents.[1] The Government had also paid
$1,500,000 and allowed absorption of 570,000 acres as
indemnity. Yet there still was no time limit for selections and because the Land Office had an insufficient
staff and field force the States took the opportunity
for considerable speculation. Commissioner Sparks, however, was able to establish administrative checks on
certain abuses, throttle many claims and secure the

---

1. L.O.R., 1887, p. 57.

indictment of several individuals for forgery.

Some of the fifteen States which secured swamp grants resorted to a system of contracts whereby an agent was allowed 10 to 50% commission on whatever he could secure from the Government.[2] The Land Office complained that it was "these contracting agents, or their attorneys, armed with the authority of the state," who appeared before the department in the character of State agents and made selections in the name of the State. They arrayed the influence of state representations in support of the demands of what thus had become "corporate and private speculation."[3]

Such groups were able to obtain dry arable land as well as timber and mineral land.[4] The misrepresentations which they used are well illustrated by the oft-quoted reference in the Land Office Report of 1885;[5] the Office had found a desert land and swamp land entry side by side in Oregon. The Commissioner had not been able to determine which, if either, was valid. He felt, however that in any case both claims were speculative.

In order to secure ungranted lands State agents corrupted Government inspectors. For example Oregon agents had selected 90,000 acres in 1882. The Land Office agent reported that they were swamp and overflow lands, but patents were held up by allegations of fraud. Commissioner Sparks directed another agent to investigate and he found that the selections covered fertile agricultural areas.[6] He also learned that the preceding agent had been physically incapacitated when he was reputed to have made his inspection and that he had a written agreement with the State agent to receive a

---

2. For other methods States used in disposing of land see L.O.R., 1886, p. 39; 1887, p. 37; 1891, pp. 60-1. It is also significant to note that out of 386 contests between settlers and agents, over 300 cases were decided in favor of the settlers. The land could not, therefore, have been swampy.
3. Ibid., 1886, p. 39.
4. Ibid., p. 38, 1887, p. 38.
5. Ibid., p. 47.
6. L.O.R., 1886, p. 41.

generous sum for his favorable report. The Commissioner found that that type of case was by no means exceptional.

The effort to secure swamp land indemnity produced equally unfortunate results. The Commissioner investigated an Iowa claim for $21,000 of indemnity and
found that the affidavits on which it rested and the
special agent's report were largely false. Several similar instances in Illinois were cited. One case in particular was entirely false and the agent withdrew the
claim after Land Office inspection. The Commissioner
declared: "It is humiliating that the necessity exists
for the expenditure of money by the government to obtain
evidence to protect the Treasury from such schemes.
The obstacles thrown in the way of a full and fair investigation of those claims by interested parties and
their attorneys have materially increased the expense
of the work."[7] He estimated that $500,000 had been
saved the Government in two years but that an increased
appropriation was necessary "to properly carry on the
work." He also requested a limitation on the time for
further selections and authority to withhold land from
any State that illegally secured either land or indemnity, until a proper adjustment had been made. His requests were not granted.

Considerable space has already been devoted to
official requests for a larger and more adequately paid
Office staff. They had been based on a progressive arrears of work that had accompanied increased absorption.
There is little point in repeating the similar requests
which Secretary Lamar[8] and Commissioner Sparks presented
through regular and special reports. In his final report the Commissioner stated: "I have asked for the
minimum increase which increased work and increased
arearages render absolutely necessary." Because he had
not obtained them he added that it was "absolutely
essential that more adequate provision be made."[9]

---

7. For instance California contested his right to question the
   validity of survey returns for swamp land. Ibid., 1887, p. 39.
8. Sec. of Int. Report, 1887, p. 7.
9. L.O.R., 1887, p. 107.

The need for these provisions were fully set
forth in the report of a special Senate committee which
was appointed to inquire into the causes of delays in
transacting public business. By a resolution of March
3, 1887, the Senate provided for a group of five, headed
by Senator Cockrell of Missouri, whose inquires were to
extend to all the executive offices of the Government.[10]
The Committee uncovered a chaotic condition in the Land
Office.[11] It reported that on August 20, 1887, there
were 276,670 individual cases pending in the Public
Lands, Preëmption, Review, Contest and Mineral Divisions
of the Office.[12] In addition there were 14,000 unan-
swered letters, an unknown volume of private land claims
and nearly the entire work of railroad grant adjustments.
And finally there were swamp, school, internal improvement and other Congressional grants, Indian allotments
and the work of fraudulent entry and timber trespass ex-
aminations, all accumulated from years past.[13]

In reporting these conditions the Committee
seemed to be more concerned with the system than with
officials, that is, it did not blame Commissioner Sparks'
administration. It did give high praise for some of the
Office reforms which had been recently inaugurated, such
reforms as the Board of Review.[14] On the other hand the
Committee believed that the principal reason for the
chaos was to be found in the "want or lack of plain,
correct, business methods" for the local Land Offices
and the central office. As a result of this deficiency
the Committee reported that there had been: heavy expenses for bona fide entrymen and occasional loss of
their homes, encouragement to blackmailers and

---

10. The other members were: Senators I. H. Harris of Tennessee;
    J. K. Jones of Arkansas; O. H. Platt of Connecticut; and S. M.
    Cullom of Illinois. The Democrats were in the majority. 49
    Cong. 2 Sess. Cong. Rec., pp. 2662-3.
11. Sen. Rept. #507, Vol. I. 50 Cong. 1 Sess. Serial #2521.
12. As an indication of Congressional interest in settlers the Land
    Office reported that the Preëmption Division was five and one-
    half years behind in its work. L.O.R., 1887, p. 101.
13. Ibid., p. 143.
14. Ibid., p. 232.

corruptionists to institute contests against uneducated, poor claimants; encouragement to speculators and spoilators to sieze lands; and the necessity for entrymen to employ attorneys in Washington to attend to their cases. In some instances Washington attorneys were reported to have sent out circulars stating that they had special facilities for hastening action in the Department, "thus creating the suspicion of collusion between such parties and employees in the Office."[15]

The Committee then elaborated its account of conditions and offered a few inadequate suggestions for improvement.[16] It was appalled at the manner in which the local land officers disregarded the laws and the regulations of the Department.[17] It believed that new and simplified circulars and the replacement of officials who refused to carry out their duties would materially speed up work. The Committee found that inefficiency in the General Land Office was most pronounced in the method of handling finances.[18] The Commissioner had testified that he had attempted to mitigate red tape by a general order but that he had lacked the time to take up many such problems in detail. For further deficiencies the Committee made only minor suggestions such as that for increasing the hours of work.[19] The official working day for many departments of the Government was seven hours, but the Committee felt that the Land Office employees should work eight. The longer hours would, in effect, increase the force by one-seventh. The Office was also directed to dispense with every incompetent employee, every drone. There was to be no forbearance toward "inefficient, incompetent employees,

---

15. Ibid., p. 228.
16. For instance it found that the tract books which should have contained complete information on each subdivision of land had not been properly filled in or kept up since 1832.
17. Committee members knew personally of many instances in which two patents for the same bit of ground had been issued to two separate individuals. This type of error developed largely from inefficient methods in the local offices. Ibid., pp. 225-6; 229-30.
18. Ibid., pp. 33-91.
19. Ibid., pp. 229-33.

on account of age, sex, condition or influence." The
Committee observed with questionable accuracy, "This is
not a pension office."

In another part of its report the Committee admitted that inadequate room for clerks and storage accounted for considerable delay in work,[20] and it believed that the stream of new laws, grants and forfeitures added further burdens.[21] But it was flatly
opposed to an increase in clerks or salaries, though
Commissioner Stockslager showed that work was continually increasing.[22] For instance the office handled
132,000 letters in 1885, 150,000 in 1886 and 158,000 for
1887.[23] The Commissioner noted that there was an improvement in efficiency for the past year but that the
arrears was too heavy to be cleared up without assistance.

There seems to be little doubt that the investigation was beneficial. On the other hand the Committee's approach and solutions were too incomplete, too
divorced from reality. It failed to take into account
laws which permitted abuses in administration, such as
the fee system in local offices, or to realize influences which were brought to bear on officials. An
analysis that came closer to actualities was presented
by Secretary Vilas and it will be noted later. But
among other points he suggested increased salaries.
This increase was both a matter of good business and of
justice. The Land Office was the only Bureau in the
Government where chief clerks were paid less than
$2,000. Most bureau chiefs received $2,250 to $3,500
annually.[24]

---

20. Ibid., p. 120.
21. The Committee made only two insignificant recommendations to
    Congress. One concerned the disposal of useless paper and the
    other, letters patent of the United States. Neither became
    law. They form an interesting contrast to the 1881 recommenda-
    tion for a Department. Senate bills #2304, #2305. 50 Cong.
    1 Sess.
22. The Committee declared that there already were "honest, intelli-
    gent and worthy employees....in positions earnestly sought for
    by other honest, intelligent and competent (!) applicants."
23. Report #507, op. cit., p. 221.
24. H. Rep. #4001. 49 Cong. 2 Sess. Cong. Rec., p. 1522.

It is curious to note how first one House then the other blocked appropriations for improvements in the Office. In 1884 after an investigation, the Senate had provided equal rank for all heads of Land Office Divisions and had also voted them $2,250 annually.[25] The House refused to pass this measure though in 1886 it was the Senate which refused a similar House bill.[26] Again in 1887, Senator Teller put through the Senate a bill to raise the status of division heads and to pay them $2,000 but with obstructionary tactics and levity the House neglected it.[27] The discrimination against the Land Office indicates a failure to comprehend its importance or a willful attempt to cripple it.

A comparison of the Office staff, and its duties, in 1887 with that of 1931 will indicate something of the fallacy behind Senator Cockrell's Committee report. In the former year there were 377 employees. The Commissioner estimated that they could clear away the arrears of work in three years if there were no new entries or claims.[28] But more than 25,858,000 acres were sold, entered or selected in the year ending June 30, 1887.[29] On the other hand in 1931, 5,200,000 acres were entered or selected.[30] There was practically no arrears but the Office employed 318 persons.[31] The comparison therefore shows that a staff 16% smaller than that in 1887 was provided for handling only one-fifth as much current work and practically nothing else. In 1931, the Office was housed in a commodious, modern building, instead of a cramped, inflammable structure which had once suffered fire. It is impossible to calculate the benefits which the country would have derived from a properly equipped

---

25. Ibid., p. 1590.
26. The Senate Committee on Public Lands issued a favorable report on such a bill, January 1886. 49 Cong. 1 S. Sen. Rep. #1580. The Finance Committee blocked the other bill. Ibid., Sen. Rep. #1387; 49 Cong. 2 Sess. Cong. Rec., p. 1284.
27. Ibid., pp. 1589-91; 1822.
28. L.O.R., 1887, p. 106.
29. Ibid., p. 5.
30. Ibid., 1931, p. 1.
31. Ibid., p. 40.

land administration in the 1880's.[32]

      In his last report Commissioner Sparks presented a detailed account of the needs of the Office. The responsibilities and burdens of the higher officials as well as the work of each Division were carefully analysed in terms of assistance which Congress could provide. The account was part of a series of recommendations which the Commissioner compiled for an "entire reformation of existing laws." He felt piece-meal measures or amendments would no longer suffice. His list was not so comprehensive as that of the Public Lands Commission, but from the administrative standpoint it represents an outspoken, dispassionate and cogent analysis. It should be read by anyone who desires first-hand information on the public land system.[33]

      While it ignored practically every one of the Commissioner's recommendations Congress should receive credit for enacting into law two requests which came chiefly from other sources. Scientists and land officials had long proposed reserving the headwaters of rivers for irrigation projects. And popular indignation toward large scale, particularly foreign large scale, holdings had produced demands for their restriction. The method by which great aggregations were obtained has already been described in discussing the growth of cattle ranches. Railroads, private land claims, college grant scrip, purchases in Texas or other States, and

---

32. Other offices, bureaus or departments were greatly neglected too, as the Cockrell report showed. See also Cummings and McFarland's "Federal Justice." In 1887 Commissioner Sparks felt 159 more permanent and 112 temporary clerks would be able to clear up arrears, though he reduced his requests to 48 permanent and 125 temporary clerks. L.O.R., 1887, pp. 106-7. These would have made additional office space obligatory. For an amazing attitude toward the Land Office see the bill favorably reported out in the Senate after Senator Stewart introduced it in September, 1888. It provided for a Committee to investigate whether there was fraudulent acquisition of land, illegal use of money for protection, and collusion with law breakers by Office chiefs. 50 Cong. 1 Sess. Cong. Rec., pp. 8280, 8603.

33. Important new suggestions included prevention of dummy mineral entries for monopolists; and special Government counsel in land suits. L.O.R., 1887, p. 86 ff.

fraud, were the mediums through which extensive tracts
were collected.   In 1879 William G. Moody's trip through
the West had shown him a large number of farms of from
10,000 to 100,000 acres each.[34]   And although A. M.
Schlesinger reports scores of sizable tracts by the
early Eighties, it was the enormous holdings that created concern.[35]   A ranch of 90 square miles in Sacramento
Valley, California, and one of 115 square miles in
Dakota were small when compared with a 3,500,000 acre
holding in Texas or 4,000,000 acres belonging to Hiram
Disston in Florida.   By 1883 the Standard Oil Company
held 1,000,000 acres.   A short time later Henry George
was quoted to the effect that there were 200 men in two
western States, who held 100,000,000 acres.[36]

In addition to these holdings, though possibly
overlapping somewhat, there were the extensive possessions of foreigners and these in particular aroused
antagonisms.   Foreign money was invested in railroad
lands, mining ventures, cattle raising, timber lands,
cotton plantations, settlement undertakings and broker-
age company mortgages.   Publicity for investments like
that of the Maxwell Land Grant and Railway Company were
later followed by more frequent notices of other undertakings.   In 1882 a European company headed by a resident of Liverpool, England, purchased 100,000 acres of
cotton lands in Arkansas.[37]   About the same time the
Dundee Land Company of Scotland acquired 44,000 acres of
timber land from railroads in the same State.[38]   The
Danish Consul General purchased 55,000 acres in Minnesota for $5.00 an acre from the Chicago, Milwaukee and
St. Paul Railroad.[39]   These lands were reputedly to be
used for settlement purposes.   A short time earlier the
same railroad had sold 100,000 acres to an English syndicate for the same purpose and at a similar price.   A

---

34. 49 Cong. 1 Sess. Cong. Rec., p. 6002.
35. A. M. Schlesinger, "Rise of the City, 1878-98," pp. 31 and 41-2.
36. Cong. Rec., op. cit., p. 6002.
37. Quoted in W. G. Moody, "Land, Labor and Capital," p. 78.
38. Copp, op. cit., Dec. 1882.
39. Ibid., Nov. 1882.

Scotch concern paid $2,500,000 for the Swan Cattle Company and residents of the same country founded the California Redwood Company, mentioned above.

In 1883 Copp's Land Owner recorded that $30,000,000 in British capital had gone into Texas and Wyoming during the previous year. The same paper also reprinted from the Troy Times a list of large scale land owners who were aliens.[40] Prominent in the list were titled Englishmen. Sir Edward Reed was credited with 2,000,000 acres. Philips Marshall and Company of London held 1,300,000 acres and the Duke of Sutherland reputedly possessed 400,000 acres. The Democratic Handbook for 1884 contained another list with some additional names; the size of the holdings varied from 4,500,000 acres downward. In addition to English[41] and Scotch owners there was a German syndicate owning 1,100,000 acres and an individual from Nova Scotia who held 600,000 acres. It is important to observe that these aggregations were not confined to the Territories where most of the new land was being taken up but they included holdings in Florida, Mississippi, Arkansas, Kansas, West Virginia, and Texas.

As the result of a Congressional request the Secretary of Interior also compiled a list of foreigners' possessions in America.[42] He found twenty-nine companies or individuals who owned a total of about 20,000,000 acres. While it is impossible to estimate the value of foreign holdings a Scotch firm, Tait, Denman and Company, with offices in New York, claimed that the Scotch alone had invested $25,000,000 in American Territories.[43] This concern classed itself as "Cattle Ranche and Land Brokers" and asserted that it had nine agencies and numerous correspondents throughout the West.[44]

---

40. Op. cit., Oct. 15, 1883.
41. The London Telegraph bought 50,000 acres of desert land in the Southwest reputedly for the sake of cactus pulp. N.Y. Times, Aug. 16, 1885.
42. Sen. Ex. Doc. #181. 48 Cong. 1 Sess.
43. 48 Cong. 1 Sess. Cong. Rec., p. 369.
44. The Wyoming Cattle Ranch Co. and the Prairie Land Co. of Colorado, in addition to the Swan company were Scotch concerns. The Prairie Company was attacked by Commissioner McFarland. N.Y. Times, May 24, 1886.

The increasing number of large scale holdings aroused public opposition particularly because many of them were charged with land law violations. Abuses were most common in connection with securing cattle ranches and frequently the ranches were secured by or for Britishers. During President Arthur's term there were numerous bills and resolutions which aimed to investigate or thwart further aggregations. When no legislation resulted both of the major political parties incorporated planks in their platforms, calling for a curb on alien holdings. But even before the Democrats had been inducted into office the House received a favorable report on a law to prevent aliens from holding any land in the United States.[45] The bill did not pass but the New York Times[46] took the Committee to task for its "ignorance and narrowness" in believing that the exclusion of foreign capital would not hurt anyone in the country. The paper did approve of the idea of endeavoring to keep the Dakota wheat fields and the Colorado cattle lands out of the hands of the British aristocracy but it felt that foreigners should be allowed to own homes in the United States. It reported that Englishmen were said to own one-sixth of the cattle on the western plains but it particularly favored restrictions on alien possessions because they were frequently held for speculation without any effort to develop them or they were subject to tenantry. Furthermore the paper feared that foreclosure suits against railroads, where foreigners had invested millions of dollars, would place a large share of the 100,000,000 acres of land grants in their hands.

The first Congress in President Cleveland's administration received scores of petitions demanding action against alien owners.[47] Knights of Labor bodies were particularly active in sending in demands. Again there were a variety of bills introduced but in April, 1886, the House Judiciary Committee reported unfavorably on a bill limiting alien possessions in the Territories.[48]

---

45. H. Rep. #2308. 48 Cong. 2 Sess.
46. Jan. 22, 24, 1885.
47. 49 Cong. 1 Sess. Cong. Rec., see "Alien Land Owning," in Index.
48. Ibid., p. 3883.

Three months later, however, the House Committee on Public Lands presented a report which was favorable to the limitation.[49] Although it listed many foreign holdings, largely duplicating the former enumeration, the Committee declared that it had not included them all. It estimated that the total amount of land involved would reach 30,000,000 acres. It also observed that American lands were becoming more valuable yearly and it believed that in foreign hands they would be subject to a system of "landlordism and conditions totally un-American." The Committee was particularly opposed to enriching foreigners at the expense of Americans. The bill which it had brought in with the report passed the House with little discussion.

A short time before, however, the Senate had adopted a more comprehensive alien land holding bill.[50] For several years it had been considering limiting all future large holdings whether American or foreign. Senators Plumb of Kansas and Van Wyck of Nebraska had both sponsored measures aimed to accomplish that purpose in 1884. Then in 1886, as Chairman of the Committee on Public Lands, Senator Plumb,[51] had pushed his bill and he secured its passage in the Senate.[52] When the House bill came up for consideration he again spoke briefly on the subject and declared that American lands should be held for Americans. He believed that his bill was only an experiment in obtaining that end. Without much discussion his measure limiting alien holdings and all holdings over 5,000 acres in the Territories was substituted for the House bill. The House then refused to accept the substitution until the Second Session so that it was not until February, 1887, that the bill passed. It was signed by the President on March 3.[53]

---

49. Ibid., p. 7830-2. H. Rep. #3455. The N.Y. Times criticized the Committee for presenting the same old list of twenty-nine corporations, May 24, 1886.
50. 49 Cong. 1 Sess. Cong. Rec., p. 5108.
51. Senator Plumb had acquired part of his wealth from coal and cattle land ventures in Colorado. Dict. Am. Biog.
52. Cong. Rec., op. cit., pp. 7954-6.
53. Ibid., 2 Sess., pp. 2435 and 2319. 24 Stat. 476.

In its final form the bill prohibited for the future, alien persons or corporations from holding land in the Territories except by inheritance or the lawful collection of debts. It also forbade any corporation or association of which 20% of the stock was held by individuals or corporations who were not citizens to hold land thereafter acquired in the Territories. A third section prohibited future holdings of over 5,000 acres in the Territories, by any but railroads, canal companies and turnpike companies. It is evident that in applying only to the Territories and to future acquisitions it did not remedy existing monopoly aggregations.

Public opinion seemed to favor the bill, especially since it affected the British.[54] It was criticized, however, as too mild to prevent evasion. And although Representative Payson told a reporter of the Engineering and Mining Journal that the law was not directed against mining property the principal objections to it came from the Territories possessing foreign investments in mining or desiring to attract foreign capital.[55] The Governor of Idaho claimed that "Several large and important mining transactions were about to be consummated by mine owners of Idaho with foreign capitalists" and that negotiations were suspended upon passage of the bill.[56] He believed that it was acceptable for all classes of lands except mineral. The Governors of Montana and Utah took the same position. The Governor of Dakota, however, suggested an amendment to permit foreign loans on all classes of lands, with adequate protection for mortgage forfeitures.[57]

The Philadelphia Press substantiated the Governor of Idaho and reported that the law brought a check to the ambitions of mining companies, most of which it seemed to feel were questionable ventures, in Frankfort, Amsterdam and London. The law also blasted the hopes of a variety of American promoters in London.[58] One great

---

54. Cf. "Public Opinion," Vol. III, Apr.-Oct., 1887.
55. Ibid., quoted in the Philadelphia Press.
56. Sec. of Int. Report, 1887, p. 850.
57. Ibid., pp. 869, 881, 807.
58. N.Y. Times, Apr. 10, 1887.

"City" speculator estimated that it knocked in the head not less than 300 big American land schemes. For years London was said to have been full of Americans, ranging all the way from millionaires to needy adventurers, seeking to sell mines, ranches and estates. The "swarm of American sharpers" who had become destitute borrowers would be driven home, for the law had "scared the hitherto credulous English" from touching American investments. Perhaps this report was intended as a clever piece of financial propaganda but it furnished an interesting sidelight on western development. It also remarked how Stephen W. Dorsey was among the Americans who were "left." He had previously given a "great and ostentatious dinner" and then had departed for Amsterdam to negotiate there. London dispatches also referred to the satisfaction in American States such as California and Nevada, because they were not affected by the law. There were other results from the bill but they will be taken up in the consideration of later demands to strengthen it.[59]

The other measure which Congress adopted before the close of President Cleveland's administration dealt, as indicated above, with plans for a more comprehensive system of irrigation. Commissioner Sparks had emphasized the fact that the Desert Land Act had "conspicuously failed" to meet western conditions.[60] The statistics for the law bear out this statement. In 1886 the Wyoming delegate, J. M. Carey, stated on the floor of Congress that in the nine years of its existence the Desert law had been used in entries covering about 3,000,000 acres.[61] Yet less than 500,000 acres had been patented. This did not mean that one in six entries was fraudulent or for the purpose of speculation because a considerable part of the entries might still be pushed to patent. But since the figures presented in the Land Office report for 1931, covering the entire period of the law, bear the ratio of about four entries to one patent it is evident that either the law was subject to

---

59. Ibid., April. 10, 1887.
60. L.O.R., 1885, p. 75.
61. Quoted in Sec. of Int. Report, 1886, p. 1014.

more abuse than use, or that men found it impossible to fulfill its requirements.[62]

The evidence indicates that both of these conclusions are true but the important point for the present discussion lies in the fact that westerners and officials after 1885 continued to ask for a more liberal interpretation of the law than the land department permitted or for some new provision for large scale enterprises. The Governor of Idaho, for instance, favored Government construction of irrigation facilities and he estimated that such a method would add only $1.00 per acre to the purchase price of the land.[63] He believed that Idaho alone could then provide the opportunity for 100,000 homes. Continued suggestions brought a Congressional joint resolution in March, 1888, authorizing the Secretary of the Interior, by means of the Geological Survey, to investigate the practicability of constructing reservoirs for the storage of water in arid regions.[64] Since the plan was reported to be practical, in the Sundry Civil Service bill of October, 1888, Congress appropriated $100,000 for the "investigation, segregation and selection" of sites for reservoirs, and all such sites were to be reserved from settlement or appropriation.[64] The policy thus inaugurated was continued on a broader scale, in the following year so its further development will be considered in the succeeding chapter.

II

The Commissioner's last report was written a few weeks before he, followed shortly by Law Clerk Le Barnes, was forced out of office. The report contained a statement that might have been intended as the Commissioner's valedictorian address. He said: "I have no word to recall that has hitherto been uttered touching aggravated misappropriation to which public lands

62. L.O.R., 1931, p. 17.
63. Sec. of Int. Report, 1886, pp. 849-51.
64. Ibid., 1889, p. xxiii.

have been subjected through improvident laws and inefficient administration and to which they are still exposed under present wasteful methods and fraud inspir-
ing systems of disposal..... There is no regret to express, or apology to offer."[65]　Six weeks later the
break which brought his resignation occurred.

　　　　　The break arose ostensibly from a dispute over
the adjustment of the grant to the Chicago, St. Paul,
Minneapolis and Omaha Railroad. Actually it can be
traced to the death of Supreme Court Justice William B.
Woods, May 14, 1887.[66]　A short time thereafter Secretary Lamar was mentioned as a possible successor, and
in August the President let the Secretary know that he
wished to appoint him. The Secretary then wrote Attorney General Vilas that he and the President wished the
Attorney General would take over the Interior Department.[67]　Out of this effort must have come the under-
standing that Mr. Vilas would consent if Mr. Sparks was
removed from the Land Office. There were official
denials that Mr. Vilas was responsible for the Commissioner's removal but the Interior Department and newspaper reporters understood that he had requested it.[68]
His reasons may have been reported correctly as based
on a dislike for working with the insubordination which
the Commissioner had reputedly displayed. But there may
also have been other reasons. Newspaper accounts recalled Mr. Sparks' hostility to Joseph Vilas' possessions in California and Secretary Lamar brought about
the break with the Commissioner over the Omaha indemnity
grants which were partly in Wisconsin, Mr. Vilas' home
State.[69]　Whether or not this was a coincidence is

---

65. L.O.R., 1887, p.
66. Cate, op. cit., p. 469.
67. Ibid., p. 472.
68. S. V. Proudfit Interview and N.Y. Evening Post, Nov. 12, 1887.
　　For denials of Mr. Vilas' part, see N.Y. Times, Nov. 15;
　　Dec. 9, 1887.
69. In 1886 the Commissioner had recommended to Secretary Lamar
　　that the Attorney General bring suit against the Omaha Railroad
　　and several timber companies for cutting timber from Government
　　land. The railroad had sold land which it had selected within

difficult to say until Mr. Vilas' papers are made public.

In any case during August, 1887, Secretary Lamar requested the Commissioner to adjust the Omaha railroad grant under the law of March 3.[70] The Commissioner had already received approval for his adjustment of another road so he followed the same interpretation of the law for the Omaha grant. On October 7, however, the Secretary rejected the Commissioner's adjustment. He then returned to an abandoned interpretation of indemnity lands and allowed the road about 70,000 acres formerly reserved within its grant limits. Since the Commissioner had not duplicated his citation of authorities for the second, or Omaha, case he believed the Secretary had been misled.[71] He therefore requested a review of the Secretary's decision because he knew it would affect all other grants. The Secretary suggested allowing the matter to rest for a while so the Commissioner acquiesced. But he did draw up his opinion with great care and detail.[72]

A month later, the Secretary sent a note requesting the Commissioner's opinion. The latter, therefore, changed the date on his paper to November 10 and signed and sent it to the Secretary. Newspapers reported that Secretary Lamar and Attorney General Vilas called on the President on the day following the reception of the Commissioner's letter and discussed it.[73]

(footnote continued) its indemnity limits, to the companies whose
    president was Mr. Weyerhauser. Since the Office had not yet
    adjusted the railroad grant and particularly had not given the
    road patents for its land it was cutting timber from and sell-
    ing property to which it had no title and might never have un-
    der an adjustment. Mr. Lamar refused to ask the Attorney Gen-
    eral for action. The Omaha road had taken over the Northern
    Wisconsin Railroad Company and it was on the lands of the lat-
    ter that the official differences arose. L.O.R., 1887, p. 311
    and pp. 489-94.

70. N.Y. Times, Nov. 13, 1887.
71. Ibid., Nov. 16, 1887.
72. L.O.R., 1887, pp. 303-15.
73. N.Y. Evening Post, Nov. 12, 1887.

On that same day the Secretary gave to the press his
answer to the Commissioner.[74] The answer was so framed
as to make the Commissioner's opinion seem rebellious
and it asserted that either the Secretary or the Commissioner must resign because such subordination could
no longer continue. The Secretary also referred to his
subordinate's "elementary citation of legal maxims" and
his "entirely irrelevant" opinions.[74]

Faced with the necessity for defending his position or resigning the Commissioner delayed action over
a week-end. Some observers felt that he might fight the
issue and endeavor to force the President to choose or
appoint the Secretary to the Supreme Court.[75] But when
the Commissioner learned the President backed the Secretary, on November 15 he wrote a letter of resignation
defending his views and concluding with cordial wishes
to the President.[76] He stated that the Secretary's answer diverted "the issue from one of legal construction
to one of authority and insubordination." This was a
"substitution of force for argument, a diversion of the
public mind from the merits of the case." He felt that
if the administration was going to change its policy
toward the railroads, his sense of duty would not allow
him to remain in office.[77]

The President accepted the resignation by a letter which was cordial though somewhat ambiguous.[78] It
referred to the point at issue as one on which two men
might differ. But later it lectured the Commissioner
on the necessity for following the law, limited and controlled by the courts, which were not to be resisted!

---

74. The New York Times and the Chicago Tribune were unable to un-
    derstand the Secretary's rule for indemnity. The latter re-
    ported that one railroad in Kansas alone, was expected to re-
    ceive nearly 850,000 acres which the State had come to regard
    as public land, Dec. 12, 1887.
75. Washington Post, Nov. 13, 1887.
76. N.Y. Times, Nov. 16, 1887.
77. Osgood believes that the resignation was due to an excess of
    zeal, op. cit., p. 207. Ise says, "perhaps he (Sparks) was too
    vigorous or too undiplomatic, or it may be that he was fighting
    a hopeless fight," op. cit., pp. 87-8.
78. Washington Post, Nov. 13, 1887.

The President gave assurances that the policy of saving
the public land for settlers in good faith would continue. He added, "I desire to heartily acknowledge the
value of your services in the improved administration
of the Land Department which has been reached and to assure you of my appreciation of the rugged and unyield-
ing integrity which has characterized your official conduct."

There is some testimony to the fact that Mr.
Sparks was not an easy subordinate. His personal qualities made him eager and perhaps hasty in establishing
reform. He occasionally made decisions which the Secretary later reversed as in his attempt to restrict every
entryman to one settlement entry. The Secretary was
more "practical" minded and often did not desire to
overturn well established rules even for the benefits
reform would bring.[79] He lectured the Commissioner on
the necessity for observing the principle of res
adjudicata though he broke the rule himself and was
therefore twitted by newspapers for his preaching.[80]
The Commissioner was not as tactful toward the Secretary
as he might have been;[81] according to former colleagues
he overstepped the bounds of departmental etiquette.
Newspapers supported this charge. Nevertheless some
stories at the time of the Commissioner's resignation
have an "inspired" sound, as though there was an effort
to uphold the Administration.[82] On the other hand the
leading papers of New York and Washington praised the

---

79. On the other hand the Secretary did not always uphold the Com-
    missioner when he should. "A notorious rascal who....swindled
    his client" was suggested for disbarment to the Commissioner.
    For at least one and one-half years the Secretary ignored the
    request. Copp, op. cit., Vol. XIV, April 1, 1887.
80. N.Y. Times, May 31, 1886.
81. N.Y. Evening Post, op. cit., N.Y. Times, Apr. 8 and 12, 1886;
    N.Y. Tribune, Dec. 6, 1885.
82. N.Y. Post, Nov. 16, 1887 has a different tone in two dispatches
    sent on the same day; and N.Y. Times, Nov. 15, 1887; Washington
    Post, Nov. 13, 1887.

Commissioner's zeal and integrity.[83] Even the New York
Tribune did not gloat over a fallen foe but indirectly
acknowledged that his reform work had been necessary.[84]
The New York Times felt that the Commissioner might have
been retained, despite his peculiarities, because of his
fine work.[85]

Secretary Lamar's nomination was not submitted
to the Senate until three weeks after the Commissioner's
resignation. It then dragged along for more than a
month and the President became anxious to have it settled. He felt that nothing was being done in the Interior Department and he wanted "someone on duty"
there.[86] Finally the Secretary resigned, the resignation to take effect January 10. On that last day he
ordered the dismissal of Law Clerk Le Barnes.[87] But
rather than accept dismissal Colonel Le Barnes wrote out
his resignation with the Secretary's order on his desk.
The New York Herald protested under the title, "Not Well
Done Mr. Lamar."[88] It also obtained testimonials from
leading Congressmen, regarding the character of Colonel
Le Barnes' work. General Weaver of Iowa was asked
whether the Law Clerk was discharged at the request of
corporations. He replied that he could not tell but he
trusted that "the character of the votes which Mr. Lamar
may receive from the Republican side of the Senate would
set that matter at rest and render the conclusion impossible." Unfortunately the vote did not have that
effect.

The opposition to Secretary Lamar had seemed to
be largely sectional and partisan.[89] The Judiciary Committee reported unfavorably on his nomination yet on
January 16, he was confirmed by the close vote, 32-28,
in which Republican Senators Riddelberger, Stanford and

---

83. Cf. N.Y. Herald, Nov. 12, 1887; Washington Post, Nov. 13, 1887.
84. Nov. 16, 1887.
85. Nov. 12, 1887.
86. H. J. Ford, "The Cleveland Era," p. 112 quoting S. M. Cullom.
87. N.Y. Times, Jan. 12, 1888.
88. Jan. 13, 1888.
89. Cf. "Public Opinion," Vol. IV.

Stewart voted in the affirmative.[90] To the San Francisco Chronicle, a Republican paper, the votes of Stanford and Stewart "looked suspiciously like a trade."[91]
It felt that they had been given in return for Mr.
Sparks' dismissal. The Pittsburgh Dispatch, an Independent paper, believed that Mr. Le Barnes' dismissal
was involved too. It feared that the removal of Sparks
and Le Barnes indicated a change of policy with regard
to corporations and public lands and that corporations
were likely to have their own way in the Department
under William Vilas.[92]

     It is impossible to say how much of this sus-
picion is justified.[93] Perhaps Secretary Lamar dismissed Mr. Le Barnes at Mr. Vilas' request, though he
denied that charge. There was no official reason given
for the dismissal and Mr. Le Barnes' ability and service were widely acknowledged. Copp's Land Owner expressed regret over the loss of both Sparks and
Le Barnes.[94] Of the former it said that beyond question
he had accomplished much good "and like pioneers generally he has prepared an easy road for his successor."
The Land Owner also testified that, "Next to Commissioner Sparks, Colonel Le Barnes was the best or worst
abused man connected with the late administration of the
(land) office. Yet his enemies were never able to deny
his keen intellect, wonderful industry and powerful
will. His retirement is a serious loss."[95]

     Congressmen who were interested in the welfare
of public lands were full of praise for the Colonel.[96]

---

90. Cate, op. cit., p. 485.
91. Jan. 28, 1888 quoted in "Public Opinion."
92. "The Boston Journal (Republican) believed, however, that the
    President bargained with Senators Stanford and Stewart for
    votes in return for easy recommendations regarding the Central
    Pacific Railroad in the Pacific Railroad Commission Report,
    submitted January 17. Quoted in "Public Opinion."
93. The New York Times declared that there his dismissal was dis-
    cussed with animation as having a bearing on Secretary Lamar's
    nomination, Jan. 12, 1888.
94. Copp, op. cit., Dec. 1, 1887.
95. Ibid., Jan. 15, 1888.
96. N.Y. Herald, Jan. 13, 1888.

They described him as "a walking encyclopedia on all
subjects pertaining to land laws," "a source of information that was absolutely necessary to the public welfare" and "invaluable to the government." Colonel
Le Barnes said that since he had been accused "apparently by authority" of entertaining views not orthodox he
felt free to defend himself. He was unaware of any
dereliction of conduct or duty. He had not changed his
views since he had prepared part of the Secretary's report and the public land portion of the President's message. He knew that many attempts had been made to remove him because he stood for the Government. He had
"found that land robbery was respectable and generally
successful and that those who were in the way were likely to be crushed." In reports to Congress or in the
Commissioner's reports he had occasionally exposed the
legislative scheme in which influential gentlemen were
interested. Poor men never came to Congress with "jobs"
and he stated that he "scarcely ever knew a measure"
for the relief of settlers on the public lands that was
not as General Butler once expressed it, a bill "to relieve settlers of the public lands."[97]

Newspaper reports had charged that occasionally
there were anonymous articles criticizing decisions of
Secretary Lamar and placing him in sympathy with "plun-
dering corporations." Colonel Le Barnes was suspected
of writing some of them.[98] If this was true it seems
strange that the Secretary waited until the last day to
discharge him. Perhaps nothing, however, equalled the
vehemence with which Mr. Le Barnes himself was attacked
in the press. For instance he was vituperously denounced by the New York Tribune, a paper which would
have welcomed his discharge earlier.[99]

Considerable space has been devoted to Sparks'
and Le Barnes' resignations because of the time and conditions under which they occurred. Both men were outstanding workers for the protection of Government interests during a reform administration. They were forced

---

97. Ibid., Jan. 13, 1888.
98. N.Y. Times, Jan. 12, 1888.
99. Dec. 6, 1885.

out of office for reasons that will not bear examination. After them the Land Office was to fall back into comparative obscurity. The amount and importance of its work still remained great but its prominence diminished. Occasionally some significant development would bring it into the lime-light as under President Theodore Roosevelt or President Taft. But the prominence was short lived and subordinated to larger issues.

Comment on the obscurity of the Land Office should not belittle the work which later Commissioners performed. Mr. Sparks' successor, his former Assistant, S. M. Stockslager of Indiana, endeavored to carry out his policies though without the militancy and domination of the Office which Mr. Sparks had shown. This was partly due to the fact that Secretary Vilas assumed greater control than Secretary Lamar had done. Mr. Stockslager, a boyhood friend of Mr. Sparks,[100] endeavored to ascertain the effect of his predecessor's administration by questioning Government agents and officers. Forty-six of the fifty-seven replies to the questionnaire of June 6, 1888 reported "marked improvement"[101] in the service. Copp's Land Owner also testified to improvements in the Land Office. It felt called upon, however, to issue a warning in 1888 that the Office should take "no steps backward," reforms of the previous two years "should not lightly be set aside." And then the paper presented one of the most significant comments on the Office ever offered by a reliable authority. It stated: "The day should be forever past when a few attorneys stalked through the General Land Office, leading the Commissioner by the nose, bulldozing clerks, ordering their cases made special and dictating decisions therein."[102]

It has been intimated that the change in administrative tone was due to Secretary Vilas' policies. In fact his short term does not altogether bear out the promises which President Cleveland had given Mr. Sparks.

---

100. Copp, op. cit., Oct. 15, 1885.
101. L.O.R., 1888, p. 56.
102. Jan. 1, 1888.

There is doubtless some connection between this fact
and Mr. Vilas' background. He had been born in Vermont
but he spent most of his life in Wisconsin.[103] In the
latter State he had become noted as a lawyer, soldier
and professor at the University of Wisconsin. He had
taught law for seventeen years though in the meantime
he became wealthy through speculation in land and timber. Furthermore he had served land grant corporations
in a professional capacity.[104] These extra-curricular
activities caused him to be subject to attack when he
entered political life. He had been permanent chairman
of Democratic Convention in 1884 and President Cleveland later appointed him Postmaster General. The efficiency and economy which he established in that Department won him the respect of business firms and Congress.[105]

The President doubtless hoped that he could
achieve a similar improvement in the Interior Department.
One of his earliest reforms for the land service may or
may not have been in the cause of efficiency but it involved relieving his Assistant Secretary of the responsibility for land decisions and taking them under his
own supervision.[106] As a consequence Secretary Vilas
modified the rules for issuing patents and during his
first week in office 3,633 patents were issued.[107] This
compares curiously with the 16,324 turned out in the
preceding three and one-half months under the improved
methods praised by Senator Cockrell's report. Secretary
Vilas also set a rapid pace for deciding appealed cases
and in one year he handled as many as his predecessor
had in three.[108]

---

103. Dict. of Am. Biog. It is interesting to observe that he was
     a close friend of Charles Van Hise, President of Wisconsin
     University and a noted supporter of the conservation movement.
     Mr. Vilas left his estate to the University.
104. N.Y. Times, Dec. 7, 1887.
105. Nat. Cyclop. of Am. Biog., Vol. II, p. 410.
106. Washington Critic, Jan. 20, 1888.
107. Ibid., Jan. 23, 1888.
108. Nat. Cyclop. of Am. Biog., op. cit., p. 410.

Despite the more liberal interpretation of laws which his policies indicate the Secretary discovered that no amount of official speed and efficiency could overcome the deficiencies of the General Land Office. He emphatically declared that he knew of "no branch of government administration which appeals so cogently in every respect of wisdom and justice for intelligent, thorough and effective Congressional action for its relief as the Land Office."[109] His analysis of conditions warrant extended quotation. He stated:

"When one reflects upon the almost incalculable value of the records and documents of the Land Office, the importance of a prompt and efficient disposition of its business and then contrasts its present condition, involving so heavy injustice and injury to the vast numbers who are rightly entitled to beneficent consideration, the cost of providing safe and commodious quarters, in which it will be possible to efficiently re-organize the Bureau so as at least to approximate the objects of its existence, becomes so insignificant as only to intensify the reproach justly due the neglect of such action..... As it is, a backward glance over the long course of time through which its business has become more and more entangled and involved, gives little promise for the future. The inadequate salaries paid its responsible officers and chiefs of divisions, their brief and uncertain tenure, the opposition of private interest to public duty and the wants of adequate cooperative legislation so many times recommended without avail, constitute elements of weakness, which cannot but tend hereafter, as heretofore, to render the performance of the office unequal to the demands upon it."

The Secretary found[110] that the judicial functions of the Commissioner and Secretary "had developed into a strong resemblance of the court of chancery with much of the machinery, methods and peculiarities, mutatis mutandis, of that venerable tribunal; a likeness not lost in its consequences of expense and delay. The variety of contests and causes is naturally great and the ingenuity of the seekers of the landed wealth of

---

109. Sec. of Int. Report, 1888, p. viii.
110. Ibid., p. ix.

the Government and their counsel, provokes seemingly
limitless enlargement." He added that "few cases can
safely proceed now without counsel." His specific recommendations for the Office and the service were largely a repetition of those of his predecessors.

Although the President had permitted the removal of some of his able lieutenants, in his Congressional message of 1888 he still urged remedial land
legislation.[111] He berated Congress for failing to repeal laws which were grossly violated and for continuing to make further grants to States and individuals.
He felt that Congress should have learned from foreign
examples that large aggregations, acquired through
"rapacious seizure by a favored few" could not be "too
severely condemned." Nevertheless the President was
able to point with satisfaction to the fact that something had been done at last "to redress the injuries to
our people and check the perilous tendency of reckless
waste of the national domain." He was referring to the
fact that although a larger amount had been unfortunately lost, his administration had recovered 83,000,000[112]
acres from railroads, other grant recipients and fraudulent entries.

In analyzing this claim it is possible to review the major accomplishments of the President's first
term.[113] Figures on recoveries cannot, of course, indicate the value of strict administration of cattlemen's
encroachments, survey frauds or timber violations. Nor
can they portray the significance of other efforts like

---

111. H. Ex. Doc., Vol. I, 50 Cong. 2 Sess., p. v ff.
112. See also L.O.R., 1888, p. 17.
113. The Democrats also abolished the private entry and sale of
    land. This ended a policy that had favored the wealthy but it
    also abolished the accepted method of acquiring southern tim-
    ber land. 25 Stat. 854-5. Ise, op. cit., p. 101. They also
    extended a law which penalized timber depredations on military
    and "other" reservations to include Indian Reservations spe-
    cifically. 25 Stat. 166.

those to limit alien holdings or establish reservations
for irrigation purposes. On the other hand the amount
of land recovered in some instances cannot be entirely
credited to Democratic efforts.[114] For example the
above total included 4,500,000 acres recovered from illegal cattle enclosures. This achievement was based on
the anti-fencing bill passed under Republican auspices.
Nevertheless the largest amount of land recovered was
due to the Democratic attempt to check the land grant
railroads. Both administrative action and legislation
accounted for the return of 51,685,367 acres. Over
2,000,000 acres of this amount had been recovered from
excess lands within railroad grants limits. More than
28,000,000 acres were restored as the result of Congressional acts of forfeiture.[115] And finally 21,323,000
acres were returned to the public domain from former
indemnity limits. A greater part of these indemnity
lands would have been restored ultimately for they had
never been granted to any railroad and were not needed
to complete the amounts granted. Special credit, however, is due the Democratic administration for taking
action on a matter that had been too long delayed.

Over three-quarters of a million acres were restored at the expense of private land claims, though
that figure scarcely represents the value of Democratic
efforts in that field. Nearly 1,000,000 acres were re-
captured through rejection or cancellation of invalid
State selections, particularly swamp lands. And in the
last place more than 25,000,000 acres were reported
saved through the cancellation of settlement, mineral
and timber entries after examination by Federal agencies. While this was an example of what vigorous administrative policies could do it was not necessarily a
permanent saving for less strict control would permit
new fraudulent entries. Incidentally a still more

---

114. The figures themselves may not be entirely accurate. The Land
     Office Report for 1887 shows some larger and some smaller
     amounts for identical classifications, p. 4.
115. The Atlantic and Pacific Railroad had received an estimated
     22,000,000 acres and as mentioned above its grant had been
     forfeited in 1886.

impressive amount of land might have been recovered if
Congress had responded to recommendations for the forfeiture of 65,000,000 acres, 84% of which comprised unearned railroad grants. Later Congress did provide for
forfeiture but not under a strict interpretation of the
law, as the succeeding chapter will show, so that only
5,500,000 acres were returned.

Before reviewing the manner in which the Republicans under President Harrison reversed the Democratic procedure and returned to lax administration,
with however, outstanding legislative accomplishments,
it is proper to apportion praise for Democratic achievements. Aside from certain leaders in Congress, where
some of the most effective work came from Republicans
like Representative Payson and Senator Van Wyck, considerable credit goes to President Cleveland for his
high purpose, integrity and support of his subordinates.
Secretary Lamar's interest and aid in reform work and
his good natured coöperation with Commissioner Sparks
also played an important part. And finally the honesty,
militant sense of duty and zeal of the Commissioner were
matched only by the keenness, usefulness and laudable
aims of John Le Barnes in providing the land department
with one of the most remarkable chapters in its history.

Chapter XV

REPUBLICAN REFORM AND REACTION

The close of President Cleveland's first administration seems to mark off a distinctive period in public
land history because it ended outstanding executive efforts for reform. Yet the legislative enactments in the
early part of President Harrison's term, representing
Congressional reform efforts, call attention to a more
satisfactory dividing line. For it was in the years
1890 and 1891 that Congress took perhaps its second major step in meeting the problems which were raised by
settlement in the trans-Missouri region. The first step
was taken with the "introductory" mining, desert and
timber land laws and the establishment of the Public
Land Commission. The second step brought more adequate
provision for western and national needs and the repeal
or amendment of laws that had become a source of serious
abuse. The most outstanding of these legislative measures was the Omnibus Land Reform bill of 1891 and its
passage at that time is no little cause for wonder. In
the first place the party in control of both Houses of
Congress and the Presidency was the Republican Party,
one which was dominated by men who usually opposed reform. Moreover the Fifty-first Congress faced an array
of important issues--tariffs, pensions, trusts, silver
--that seemed to preclude any attention to public land
affairs. And finally the bill passed a "lame-duck"
House that had been overwhelmingly replaced by a Democratic majority in the election of 1890.

Nevertheless the factors which militated against
the Omnibus bill and the other nearly contemporaneous
measures, were matched by more imposing factors which
had long been held subordinate by indifference, neglect
or special interests. These latter factors could no
longer be denied. For instance the increasingly evident
disappearance of free arable land in humid regions

315

necessitated a revision of the settlement laws. Some
of the latter were completely outmoded. Furthermore
the effort to provide reservoirs for irrigation was
manifestly only a step toward revising the unfortunate
policy created by the Desert Land Act. Timber and
timber land problems also needed more forthright handling. The lamentable measures which the Government
had provided for disposing of timber had resulted in so
much fraud or evasion of the laws that trespassers demanded Congressional protection for their acts. In addition, regions to which the timber laws did not apply,
requested the right to tap the Government's forest
wealth. And on the other hand the failure to protect
forest lands against depredations and monopolization,
along with the desire to prevent floods and soil ero-
sion, produced a strong demand for Government forest
reservations. The notorious abuse of private land
claims, typified by the action over the Maxwell grant,
required the speedy adoption of a new procedure for adjudication. The admission of six new States in the period 1889-1890, reduced the area to which the prohibition on alien holdings was confined, since it applied
only in the Territories, and so necessitated a new method for checking the evils of foreign landlordism. The
continued increase in the number of other types of large
holdings suggested restrictions on the size of both entries and holdings. And finally, more than a decade of
failure to settle the status of lapsed railroad grants
increased the urgency for action in that field.[1]

In considering the Government's response to the
foregoing problems it is important to call attention to
two facts: first, the apparent coöperation manifested
during President Harrison's term between the executive
and legislative branches of the Government and secondly,
the character of Republican leadership. In regard to

---

1. This is not a complete list of demands for improving the land
   service for, with one exception, it contains only those which
   found Congressional response. The exception is the demand for
   further curbing alien land holding; it became the subject for
   discussion in the press and Congress but only State Governments
   took action upon it. See below, p. 332ff.

the first point it would be easy to overemphasize the
significance of the coöperation because the urgency for
land law reform undoubtedly played a large part in securing the adoption of new measures. Moreover it is
evident that many important executive recommendations
were almost entirely ignored by Congress. Incidentally
the recommendations were chiefly those of the Secretary
of Interior, not the President. And some reforms may
have been adopted more by chance than legislative de-
sign. In regard to the second point, the character of
Republican leadership, while the land department played
its part in fostering legislative reform measures, it
also followed several policies that are open to grave
objection. For instance public land officials were
guilty of flagrant subservience to ruthless exploiters.
They also displayed a careless disregard for the spirit
as well as the letter of the land laws. And they made
unwarranted attempts to discredit Democratic reforms by
using the old political trick of confusing a vital issue with partisan feelings. These criticisms and the
character of the reforms noted above will bear more detailed analysis.

        The election of 1888 was not centered on any is-
sues arising from public land policies but rather on another field that fostered favoritism and privilege,
namely the field of tariff protection. Party platforms,
however, made sure to include public land planks, even
though neither party was entirely accurate in its claims.
For example the Democrats pointed to a reversal of Republican methods of granting lands to, or permitting
them to be acquired by, corporations and syndicates.[2]
Yet large grants like those to railroads had ceased
seventeen years before. The Democrats also called attention to the restoration of "nearly 100,000,000 acres
to be sacredly held as homesteads for our citizens." As
mentioned in the preceding chapter not all of this
amount could be credited to Democratic policies. The
Republican Party, on the other hand, claimed credit for
the homestead policy which had "brought our great western domain into such magnificent development."[3] If,

2. Ellis, op. cit., p. 67 ff.
3. Ibid., p. 67 ff.

unlike the Desert Land Act, that policy had been translated into an appropriate law for semi-arid regions
there might have been a more legitimate reason for
boasting. The party also somewhat inaccurately denied
that the Democrats had restored an acre to the people,
but claimed that about 50,000,000 acres of unearned
grants had been returned through the efforts of both
parties. And finally the Republicans charged the Democrats "with failure to execute laws securing to settlers
title to their homesteads and with raising appropriations made for that purpose to harass innocent settlers
with spies and prosecution under the false pretense of
exposing frauds and vindicating law." This misleading
assertion was intended to secure the vote of dissatis-
fied western elements.

Benjamin Harrison, the Republican nominee, said
little in his letter of acceptance except to approve
the party platform.[4] President Cleveland, however, referred to the necessity for "the protection of our national domain, still stretching beyond the needs of a
century's expansion, and its preservation for the settler and the pioneer."[5] This estimate should be born
in mind as an offset to the 1890 Census report which recorded the end of the frontier line of settlement. The
election of Mr. Harrison brought to the presidency a
man whose knowledge of the West qualified him to lead a
movement for reforming the public land laws.[6] As an
Indiana lawyer he had been appointed by President Hayes
to the Mississippi River Commission in 1879. In the
following year he was elected to the United States Senate where he served as Chairman of the Committee on
Territories. Yet despite this valuable experience President Harrison's restrained personality and his belief
that the Chief Executive should never take the initiative, prevented him from championing any measures for
land reform.

His failure to assume the position of a leader
was revealed by his inaugural address and his first

4. N.Y. Tribune, Sept. 12, 1888.
5. Ibid., Sept. 10, 1888.
6. Dict. Am. Biog. There is no complete biography of Mr. Harrison.

message to Congress. In the former he referred to the
equity of adjusting titles to settlers and confirming
by patent their honest entries.[7] He thus adopted a
rebuke from his party's platform for Commissioner
Sparks and his April 3 order. The President repeated
the same sentiment to Congress in December by suggesting that no doubt should be thrown on honest titles.[8]
He felt that the laws should be "so administered" that
fraud would be checked and land and timber grabbers
punished. His only specific recommendation dealt with
the need for settling private land claims in the Southwest.

Such indifference to important issues was followed by a failure to appoint subordinates who would
"so administer" the laws as to achieve his avowed ends.
In part this criticism applies to his cabinet officer
for land affairs. The President selected a westerner,
John W. Noble of Missouri, for his Secretary of Interi-
or. Mr. Noble had been a soldier, a lawyer, and then a
United States District Attorney in St. Louis for three
years.[9] Upon returning to private law practice in 1870
he had secured as some of his principle clients, large
corporate and railroad interests in the Southwest. And
he had invested in mining ventures which, incidentally,
aided him financially after 1893. The new Secretary
was, therefore, like the President in a position to
know considerable about western land conditions at first
hand. This fact may help to account for his broad and
uncompromising recommendations to Congress as well as his
creditable support of the movement to secure forest reservations.

Temporarily postponing adverse criticism it is
worth noting that in his first report Secretary Noble
practically demanded that Congress declare forfeited
21,000,000 acres of railroad grants that had not been
earned by completion of the lines within the stipulated

---

7. N.Y. Tribune, March 5, 1889.
8. H. Ex. Doc., Vol. I. 51 Cong. 1 Sess., pp. xxii-xxiv.
9. Dict. Am. Biog. Public Opinion prints no important comment on
   the Secretary, though the N.Y. Times was critical of the entire
   cabinet. Public Opinion, Vol. 6, p. 483.

time limits. He minced no words in stating, "There
should certainly be found somewhere the moral courage
to give the evidence of title to the railroads as it is
given to the individual if it is intended that any possible forfeiture will not be insisted upon. The obligation....fairly rests on Congress."[10] Meanwhile, despite his party's stand on Democratic suspension of
land laws, Secretary Noble, himself, suspended action
on the grants in order "to await legislation for forfeiture." Fortunately the Secretary had only about a
year to wait until Congress took action. In the fall
of 1890 both Houses passed a measure declaring forfeited all lands granted to any State or corporation
for the construction of a railroad and situated along
any portion of the road which was uncompleted and not
in operation at the date of the act's passage. Instead
of returning a large amount of land to the public domain this law forfeited only a little over 5,000,000
acres claimed by twelve railroads. It enabled the Land
Office, however, to go ahead with the adjustments of
grants and endeavor to settle the disposition of a much
greater area.[11]

      Secretary Noble did not meet with the same leg-
islative response when he called for an investigation
of railroad grants which were suspected of containing
mineral lands.[12] As previously mentioned, mineral lands
had generally been exempted by the granting acts but in
the absence of Government surveys the method of determining the character of the land was left to the railroads. Occasionally certain roads secured private surveys of their land but railroad officials did not have
to divulge the results and so could conceal any knowledge of the mineral character of the land they were to

---

10. Sec. of Int. Report, 1889, pp. xxix-xxxi.
11. It affected over 29,000,000 acres. Railroads which had re-
    ceived grants had practically stopped building for only forty
    miles of line were constructed in the previous year. Sec. of
    Int. Report, 1891, p. iv. R. F. Pettigrew's account of the
    passage of the forfeiture bill seems to be in error. Compare
    his account in Triumphant Democracy with that in L.O.R., 1891,
    pp. 37-9.
12. Sec. of Int. Report, 1889, p. xxxi.

receive. The Secretary realized that Government surveys would be costly but he deemed them worth the price.
He felt that it was necessary to pay particular attention to the Northern Pacific grant, a large part of
which was believed to cover mineral lands.

Despite his inability to secure action for such
surveys the Secretary moved vigorously to care for the
lands which had been withdrawn for prospective irrigation projects.[13] The policy inaugurated in 1888 was
continued in the following year when Congress appropriated $250,000 for further selections by the Director
of the Geological Survey. As a consequence Secretary
Noble, following the Director's advice, selected
547,000 acres in California, Colorado, Utah, Idaho,
Montana and New Mexico. In carrying out the provisions
of the law the Secretary included in his selections
sites for reservoirs, irrigation works, ditches, canals
and all lands that might be irrigated by these devices.
Furthermore he cancelled all entry filings made on these
cites since the passage of the law, October 2, 1888.
This latter step was taken after the Assistant Attorney
General had given it his approval, but such forthright
action aroused strong western protest. Apparently the
cancellations affected certain private undertakings and
certain speculative ventures. In his 1890 report,
therefore, the Secretary indicated that he felt that
the protests raised a fundamental question as to the
Government's policy so he requested Congress to pass
supplementary legislation"to meet the difficulties apt
to arise from any national system of irrigation intended."[14] In the following year Congress responded by
appropriating an additional $325,000 and amending the
1888 law so that the Secretary could no longer reserve
lands that would be irrigated by the reservoirs built

---

13. Ibid., 1890, p. xiii; and L.O.R., 1891, p. 51. By 1891 181
    sites had been selected. In 1883 Donaldson estimated that only
    30,000,000 acres could be irrigated but by 1891 estimates
    reached 120,000,000 acres. Final Desert Land entries affected
    only about 1,717,120 acres. L.O.R., 1891, pp. 48-9.
14. Sec. of Int. Report, 1889, pp. xxv-xxvi.

on the withdrawn sites.[15] Instead, therefore, of endeavoring to establish a national system of irrigation
Congress responded to western sentiment and partly reversed the beginnings of a far-sighted policy.

The necessity for settling the private land
claims of the Southwest, to which the President had referred, was also urged upon Congress by his Secretary.
The latter found that, "The commotions in New Mexico
have been somewhat serious already and the subject needs
careful treatment to avoid graver difficulties."[16] He
demanded legislative action and again, as in the case of
the railroad grants, Congress put aside its policy of neglect and in March, 1891, established the above mentioned
Court of Private Land Claims. The Court was authorized
to adjust all claims in Nevada, Colorado, Wyoming, New
Mexico, Arizona and Utah. It was well constituted and
although its task was extremely difficult it affected a
careful adjustment of all claims with a very great saving of land for the Government. Congress deserves additional credit for affording the Court continuous support by repeatedly extending the time within which its
work must be completed.[17]

Secretary Noble also recommended that Congress
provide for adjusting all questions connected with
swamp land grants. He was amazed at the fact that although nearly two-thirds of Florida had been claimed as
swamp land these claims did not embrace the southern
part of the State where the lands were, in fact,
swampy.[18] But he was disappointed in Congress' failure
to act both in response to that suggestion and to the
request to allow Registers and Receivers the power to
summon witnesses for cases in which they suspected
fraud.[19] Moreover Secretary Noble was balked in his

---

15. This probably reduced the amount of land reserved to 385,000
    acres. Cf. L.O.R., 1891, p. 51.
16. Sec. of Int. Report, 1890, p. v.
17. 26 Stat. 854. See ante, Chapter XI and Reports of the Attorney
    General, 1895-1904.
18. Sec. of Int. Report, 1889, p. xxxi.
19. Ibid., p. xxxv.

attempt to thwart speculation in mineral lands.[20] There
were thousands of old mining applications lying dormant
because their promulgators were waiting for a purchaser
Secretary Noble urged that these delinquent applicants
be forced to complete their claims to patent or subject
them to cancellation. Congress made no response to
this request.

The Secretary also discovered a great deal of
speculation in coal lands. Consequently in his first
report he suggested that the Geological Survey be authorized to determine the character and location of
such lands and then that they be reserved, except
through leasing, for use in the localities where they
existed.[21] He felt that the Government should compel
the sale of coal at a moderate price in those localities
but Congress apparently did not agree with him. One of
the most important subjects which the Secretary considered dealt with timber lands. In his first report
he asked Congress to establish a Commission which would
ascertain the best methods for the "treatment, management, preservation and disposal" of timber.[22] He noted
the great losses which occurred through forest fires.
Later the Secretary backed his Commissioner's recommendation for what amounted to an extension of the Timber
Cutting Act to regions where it did not then apply. He
also endorsed the views of the American Forestry Association and thus gave his support to a program that
achieved fruition in the Omnibus reform bill of 1891.[23]
Reserving further discussion on this conservation movement until later it is evident, from the foregoing cita-
tions, that Secretary Noble presented a comprehensive
set of proposals for legislative action, many of which
found an appropriate response.

On the other hand the Secretary's record is open
to serious criticism on three counts: first, his handling of the Oklahoma Indian Reservation opening;

---

20. Ibid., p. xxxv.
21. Ibid., pp. xxxvi-xxxvii.
22. Ibid., 1890, p. xvi. He also backed a demand for improvements
    in the General Land Office. Ibid., p. xxxvii.
23. Ibid., p. xxxv.

second, his liberal policy in issuing patents; and
third, his dismissal of Special Land Office Agent Conrad.   In Congress Representative T. C. McRae of Arkansas took the Secretary to task on several additional
points, though of the above three he included only the
Oklahoma opening.   With some justice the Congressman
felt that the Secretary should have taken greater pre-
caution, prior to the opening rush, to prevent fraud.[24]

It is scarcely necessary to recall the great
event which occurred in what was to be Oklahoma, on
April 22, 1889.   For the better part of a decade "boom-
ers" had been attempting to settle illegally in the
Indian Reservation and just before President Cleveland
left office he signed a bill which arranged for turning
over a part of the land to the public.[25]   Under this
law President Harrison proclaimed April 22 the date for
the opening.[26]   The contest for land which took place
immediately after noon on that day has been frequently
portrayed in history, novel and movie and is worth re-
calling here chiefly because it illustrates the avidity
with which westerners sought fresh lands.   The Land Office claimed that by nightfall of the Twenty-second,
there were two claimants for every available tract.[27]
Unfortunately there was also fraud and favoritism on the
part of Government officials.   Eastern newspapers reported that United States Marshalls Jones and Tom Nee-
dles of Illinois had appointed about 450 "land sharks
and particular friends" as deputies and that these men
took advantage of their commissions, which gave them the
right to be within the Reservation before the opening,
by locating on choice lots in both Guthrie and Oklahoma

---

24. Other criticisms were: issuing patents to the defaulting North-
    ern Pacific Railroad; delivering a list of uncalled for patents
    to lawyers who used it in an attempt to defraud the patentees;
    and refusal to answer a Congressional resolution of inquiry. 51
    Cong. 1 Sess. Cong. Rec., p. 3802. Anent the attempted patent
    frauds, see N.Y. Times, July 3, 1890.
25. 25 Stat. 1005-6.
26. Cf. Schlesinger, op. cit., pp. 47-50; L.O.R., 1889, pp. 338-9;
    and W. A. Burnap, One Man's Lifetime.
27. L.O.R., 1891, p. 49.

City.[28] Many individuals in Oklahoma charged that the
favoritism was the result of a conspiracy hatched in
Washington and carried out with the aid of high officials. Secretary Noble ordered an investigation of the
charges but little seems to have come of it.[28] If he
could not have checked the "conspiracy" or the favoritism which preceded the opening he might have moved
vigorously to rectify the results of such actions.

The second charge against Secretary Noble concerns his liberality in issuing patents. He not only
permitted the Land Office to adopt very generous interpretations of the settlement laws but he himself is
credited with great partiality toward timber land violations. R. S. Yard declared that the Secretary found
an accumulation in the Land Office of 105,000 untried
cases against depredators but that he disposed of them
by "liberalizing" the regulations for the laws.[29] It
was in this manner that laws were practically nullified
by what might be termed executive legislation.

On the third charge Secretary Noble is not alone
to blame. The Harrison administration was equally at
fault in dismissing Special Agent Conrad just prior to
the time set for prosecuting the Benson ring survey
frauds. It will be recalled that the Democrats had
thoroughly exposed the ring's machinations, largely
through Mr. Conrad's able investigation. In the course
of his work Mr. Conrad had also uncovered the special
interest which certain railroads and banks held in Mr.
Benson's work. These groups were allied with Senators
Stewart and Stanford of California and Jones of Nevada.
Mr. Conrad had gained additional enmity by aiding in
the preparation of twenty-three civil suits to recover
$500,000 from bondsmen for deputies who had done fraudu-
lent work.

Less than a month after the Republican Party
came into office Mr. Conrad and a few other Special

---

28. N.Y. Times, April 26, 1889; Washington Post, April 25, 1889;
     both quoted in Copp, op. cit., May 1, 1889. Congress received
     but did not adopt a resolution for an inquiry regarding the
     fraud. 51 Cong. 1 Sess. Cong. Rec., p. 1110.
29. Yard, op. cit., p. 101.

Agents were dismissed, reputedly for reasons of economy.
Mr. Conrad, however, was shortly reinstated but soon released a second time when Senators Stewart, Stanford and
Jones, along with three western Congressmen, sent a tele-
gram from the Pacific Coast requesting his dismissal.[30]
They claimed that Mr. Conrad was "thoroughly unfit for
his position." This was scarcely a very definite
charge and it contradicted the opinion of Mr. Conrad's
superiors. In fact Acting Land Office Commissioner
Stone considered him indispensable for the successful
prosecution of the Benson cases. After another reinstatement Mr. Conrad was dismissed for the third and
last time. He was assured by the Secretary that there
was no reflection upon his personal character or official integrity. In fact he was given to understand
that political pressure had become too strong to be resisted.[31]

Secretary Noble was placed in an unenviable position when he tried to explain the dismissal to a New
York World reporter.[32] The former defended his actions
by saying that Mr. Conrad was too suspicious, particularly of Republicans. It seemed that the Special Agent
became suspicious of one of the Secretary's friends
while investigating a case of alleged fraud to which
the Secretary himself had assigned him. Mr. Conrad had
also expressed a "suspicion" in a private report to the
Land Office that Secretary Teller might not have been
unaware of a certain fraud that had transpired while
the latter was in office. But the most absurd reason
which Secretary Noble gave was connected with the false
charge printed in a practically unknown paper that Mr.
Conrad had claimed that all the women in the office of
the Surveyor General of California were prostitutes.
The Secretary declared that he did not believe the
charge but he maintained: "I can't have such things
even reported about special agents of this office. It
materially impairs their usefullness!"[33]

---

30. N.Y. Times, Oct. 26, 1889.
31. N.Y. World, Oct. 25, 1889.
32. Ibid., Oct. 26, 1889.
33. Ibid.

If these were the reasons used to explain the
dismissal to a reporter it is evident from other statements that the Secretary was also moved by a desire to
assist the defendants in the Benson trials. At first
he had carefully avoided discussing Conrad's value for
the trials, though he did admit that Mr. Conrad might
serve as a witness. Then later the Secretary attempted
to nullify the value of any evidence which the former
might produce by publicly stating that, "if they knew
his record his testimony would not amount to a feather
before any jury that could be got together."[34] This
astounding declaration was followed by what a newspaper
called a "parting black eye" for Mr. Conrad, for the
Secretary told him: "You must go back as a witness if
anybody will believe you."[34]

The New York Times claimed that lawyers who read
the Secretary's statements were amazed and wondered if
his sentiments were sustained by the President.[34] Two
New York World editorials were headed, "Protecting
Criminals" and "The Administration's Disgrace."[35] One
of the latter declared that the Secretary's actions
would be more clearly understood if the Government entered "no prosecution" in the Benson cases, even though
the Secretary had promised that they would be vigorously pushed. The paper also demanded that President Harrison secure Secretary Noble's resignation. It concluded one discussion of the Conrad dismissal by stating:
"It affords a suggestion of what and how much the
Tribune meant when it exultantly exclaimed, upon Harrison's accession to power, that the Republican party has
come into its own again." The Secretary was not dismissed, however, and ultimately his actions seem to have
been forgotten.

During his four-year term Secretary Noble was
served in rapid succession by two partisan and one unscrupulous Land Office Commissioners. While he, himself, refrained from partisan statements, every one of
his Commissioners began his own report by following the

34. N.Y. Times, Oct. 27, 1889.
35. Ibid., Oct. 25, 28, 1889.

President's lead in denouncing the Democratic administration.[36] For several months in 1889 the Land Office
was managed by Acting Commissioner William M. Stone of
Iowa.[37] Mr. Stone had been appointed Assistant Commissioner on May 15, 1889, with the backing of Iowa Congressmen and the railroad Senator, William B. Allison.[38]

    Mr. Stone prepared the Land Office Report for
1889 and in it he unjustly charged that Commissioner
Sparks' reforms were "attempted nullifications of the
land laws."[39] He also declared that the Board of Review
established a "superficial process" which delayed public
business and served "what would appear to have been a
specific and defined purpose, namely, that of greatly
hindering the determination of cases, causing their indefinite pendency." In addition he claimed that Democratic policies made for a great arrears of Land Office
business and greatly "discouraged settlement on the
public domain."[40] This latter point is untrue, judged
by the number of entries made under Commissioner McFarland, and the charge that the Democrats produced a great
arrears of business is true for only a short period. According to Mr. Stone's own figures there were only about

---

36. For a very partisan criticism of Democratic policies see the
    Minneapolis Tribune's praise of a partisan speech by Senator
    Plumb. Public Opinion, Vol. V, p. 558.
37. A native of New York State, Mr. Stone had been an editor, law-
    yer, judge and soldier in various localities. He was also a
    State legislator and Governor in Iowa, the latter from 1864-68.
    In 1880 he became interested in mining ventures and for a time
    practiced law in Pueblo, Colo. Nat. Cyclop. Am. Biog., Vol. XL,
    p. 431.
38. Mr. Stone's strong rival was ex-Senator G. M. Chilcott of Colo-
    rado, one of the manipulators of the Maxwell grant. The latter
    was backed by Senators Teller and Stewart. N.Y. Times, Apr. 26,
    1889.
39. L.O.R., 1889, p. 4.
40. Secretary Lamar claimed that because of the great amount of
    fraud, his predecessor had suspended hearings on disputed cases
    until Congress provided him with greater assistance. This
    policy accounts for some of the arrears which the Democrats in-
    herited. Sec. of Int. Report, 1886, pp. 4-7.

20,000 agricultural land patents in 1886 but thereafter
the number had risen until for the eleven months preceding his administration, there was about the normal
53,000. Of course this latter figure did not compare
with that established under Mr. Stone. As soon as he
took office he obtained the Secretary's consent to
abolish the Board of Review, formulated more liberal
rules for entry requirements and, for a time, ground out
patents at the rate of 500 a day. Within three months
he had issued 33,400 patents and his successors followed the same open-handed policy.[41]

        Mr. Stone was also quite misleading in his state-
ments about Democratic exposure of fraud. He declared
that cases of fraud were "exceedingly rare and notably
exceptional" on the part of the settlers.[42] This was
true, but the Democratic reforms had been aimed at the
speculator and the man who was not a settler in good
faith. Mr. Stone admitted, however, that corporate interests had been known to perpetrate frauds and he declared that for the future the special agents would see
that such "embryo frauds, it is to be believed, are
watched, detected, and successfully thwarted."[43] But
for some reason the Acting Commissioner overlooked the
fact that his efforts to minimize fraud were nullified
by the fact that he was forced to devote a considerable
portion of his Report to the usual subjects of abuses in
connection with timber, coal, swamp and agricultural
lands. On the other hand Mr. Stone must be credited
with a realistic attitude toward the problem of controlling timber lands for he keenly analysed the weakness of
the Government's policies and urged a thorough revision.[44]

---

41. L.O.R., 1889, p. 8.
42. Ibid., p. 9.
43. Ibid., p. 10.
44. He listed the faults as: loose construction of railroad rights
    to timber under the right-of-way law; the indefinite character
    of the 1878 Timber Cutting law with its clauses of an "and-so-
    forth" type; no active cooperation from the officers of the
    Department of Justice; and, finally, diverse and conflicting
    judicial decisions on identical questions.

On the day that the Acting Commissioner signed
his Report Judge Lewis A. Groff of Nebraska was appointed Commissioner. Perhaps the President's choice
was partly dictated by a desire to placate the dissat-
isfied landed interests of that State. In any case
Judge Groff's background and his Land Office record differ little from Mr. Stone's.[45] His first decision as
Commissioner is said to have caused the reinstatement
of an entryman who, because of ill health, had been unable to establish his claim within the time required by
law.[45] This apparent bid for popularity was successful
and was followed by similar "liberal" interpretations
so that in 1890 and 1891 the number of agricultural patents issued totalled 117,247 and 114,360, respectively.[46]
Such a policy undoubtedly helped to clear up the arrears
of work and, as Commissioner Groff's successor declared,
enabled the Office to patent "cases long suspended on
suspicion of fraud or under harsh technical rules!"[47]

Mr. Groff's term was cut short by ill health and
on March 31, 1891 he was succeeded by perhaps the most
unfortunate of the Republican appointees. The President
selected Thomas H. Carter, later known as "Slippery Tom"
Carter,[48] of Montana, for his Commissioner. The latter
was a native of Ohio but he had successively moved to
Illinois, Iowa and, in 1882, to Helena, Montana.[49] He
entered politics and was elected a Representative to
Congress in 1889 when Montana was admitted as a State.
Then in the Democratic landslide of 1890, he failed to
secure reëlection, though according to one outspoken
newspaper his defeat was attributed not to popular dislike, but to opposition from the Northern Pacific Railroad.[50] The road's attitude was traced to the fact that
while in Congress Mr. Carter had strongly advocated a
bill "relating to mineral lands, their survey and appraisement, which was objectionable" to the company.

---

45. Nat. Ency. Am. Biog., Vol. XIII, p. 106.
46. L.O.R., 1891, p. 5.
47. Quoted from the life of T. H. Carter in Dict. Am. Biog., Vol.
   III.
48. J. Ise, "The United States Oil Policy," p. 317.
49. Dict. Am. Biog., op. cit., p. 554. He was later Senator from
   Montana.
50. Philadelphia Press, March 31, 1891.

Nevertheless this opposition did not last long.
Mr. Carter apparently changed his tactics for when he
was appointed Commissioner, the Philadelphia Press
claimed that the Northern Pacific was convinced that he
would be "just and fair to it because his appointment
was urged on the President by Senator Sanders, whose
friendly relations with the Northern Pacific are well
known." Whatever the term "just and fair" may mean it
is evident that the railroad which had abused its grant
and privileges most flagrantly had secured a "friend in
court." The Commissioner's attitude toward the road is
illustrated by his amazing suggestion that instead of
proceeding against the railroad for its timber depredations along its line, the Government and the road should
jointly proceed against other violators.[51]

If he thus showed a friendliness to one western
corporation the Commissioner also satisfied other western interests. A recent sketch of his life has claimed
that his appointment was received with pleasure throughout the West.[52] At least one westerner, Charles A.
Guernsey, according to his own testimony, received something more than pleasure when Commissioner Carter illegally issued twenty-three agricultural land patents,
along with seventy-two mineral land patents, to him personally after Senator F. E. Warren had introduced the
two men to each other.[53] Not many recipients of administrative largess would be quite so frank as Mr. Guernsey.

Commissioner Carter's term is also outstanding
because of the great amount of fraud which occurred,
despite his broad interpretation of the laws,[54] and because of the liberal appropriations which he received
for protecting and surveying the public domain.[55] This

---

51. Cummings and McFarland, op. cit., p. 267.
52. Dict. Am. Biog., loc. cit., p. 544.
53. Senator Warren told Commissioner Carter, "He's one of our kind,
    Tom, see what you can do for him." Mr. Guernsey seems to have
    confused his dates. C. A. Guernsey, "Wyoming Cowboy Days,"
    pp. 155-6.
54. L.O.R., 1891, pp. 53-4.
55. Ibid., pp. 56-7; and H. Ex. Doc. #352. 51 Cong. 1 Sess.

generosity of funds was particularly noticeable when
compared with the appropriations for the Democratic administrations, both that which preceded and that which
followed the Republican term.[56] Whether the difference
in amounts arose from partisanship in Congress or from
a willingness to place more adequate funds in "safe"
hands, is impossible to say. Nevertheless Congress did
not display any indulgence toward the Land Office itself. Commissioner Carter earnestly requested a new
building, one that would house the entire staff.[57] He
showed that one of the most important divisions of the
Office, in which forty clerks were employed, occupied
quarters separate from the main Office building. While
Congress had appropriated an extra $16,000 for the Of-
fice in March, 1891, the money could not be used because
there was no nearby building that would serve and the
only alternative lay in further "scattering divisions
around the city." Yet neither Commissioner Carter nor
his immediate successors were able to secure a proper
remedy from Congress.

Another factor which required Congressional attention lay in the increasing demand for the extension
of the 1887 Alien Land Law. The rising Populist movement especially, supported this demand as labor organi-
zations had previously done. As already pointed out the
effectiveness of the Democratic measure had become materially reduced when, because its provisions restricted
investments, it helped to bring about the admission of
six new States.[58] Meanwhile foreigners continued to
make acquisitions in States. For instance during the
summer of 1890, the Memphis Avalanche reported that an
English syndicate had recently purchased 750,000 acres
of timber land in Alabama.[59]

---

56. Sec. of Int. Report, 1894, pp. 15 and 17.
57. L.O.R., 1891, pp. 61-2 and 66. He asserted that he needed a
    fifty percent increase in floor space. Land Office files were
    piled nine and one-half feet high and they were still greatly
    exposed to the dangers of fire.
58. Cf. Philadelphia Press, March 21, 1889. Columbia University
    Clipping Bureau.
59. Quoted in Public Opinion, Vol. 8, p. 345.

Congress received numerous bills which were intended either to exempt mineral land from the restrictions on foreign investments or to broaden the prohibition on alien holdings.[60] The latter question was debated in the press throughout the country and there was
widespread publicity for outstanding or notorious examples of foreign absentee ownership.[61] In 1890 the New
York World devoted three columns to exposing William
Scully's system of rack-rents in Illinois. The paper
estimated that Mr. Scully drew $200,000 annually. Simi-
lar prominence was accorded an account of the Schenley
estate near Pittsburgh.[62] The latter holding was valued
at $35,000,000 and it reputedly paid its owner not less
than $100,000 annually. Congress, however, did not
adopt any measure to further restrict holdings but the
States began to enact measures of their own. By 1901
the London Times recorded that only fifteen out of the
forty-five States made no distinction between alien and
other owners.[63]

II

Despite many failures the Republican legislative
accomplishments were rather impressive. In addition to
laws for aiding the adjustment of railroad grants, for
creating a private land claims court and for continuing
water site selections, there was a law to limit the

---

60. The Committee on Mines and Mining favored exempting mineral
    lands, according to a report of March 29, 1890. 51 Cong. 1
    Sess. H. Rep. #1140. The Committee on Judiciary favored ex-
    cluding alien holdings, December 19, 1890. 51 Cong. 2 Sess.
    H. Rep. #3323.
61. For example the New Orleans Picayune, Atlanta Constitution,
    San Francisco Bulletin, Indianapolis Journal and St. Paul
    Globe favored restrictions. The Omaha Bee, St. Paul Pioneer
    Press and Springfield Republican opposed them. Cf. Public
    Opinion, Vols. 8 and 9, passim; Columbia University Clipping
    Bureau.
62. N.Y. World, July 4, 1890 and June 23, 1890.
63. Clipping in Columbia University Clipping Bureau.

amount of land which one person could enter.[64]   Commissioner Sparks had endeavored to establish a 160 acre
maximum but Secretary Lamar had doubled that amount for
those using the settlement laws.   On August 30, 1890,
his regulations were written into the Statute books.[65]
But the most far-reaching of the Republican enactments
is found in the Omnibus reform bill of 1891.   The adoption of so inclusive a measure, with its important sections like that which provided for forest reserves, is
attributed not only to the factors noted at the beginning of the present chapter, but also to the efforts of
a conference committee and, perhaps, the fatigue which
over-burdened legislators felt from an end-of-the-ses-
sion rush of bills.

The Omnibus bill originated somewhat inauspi-
ciously when, in February, 1890, Representative Payson
reported to the House one of the frequent bills to repeal the Timber Culture Act.[66]   After some desultory
debate the bill passed[67] but the Senate took no action
on it until the following May when Senator Plumb reported as a substitute an entirely new bill of thirteen sections.[68]   This comprehensive measure was not debated for
several months but it is interesting to observe that
with perhaps one exception, its provisions promised honest and realistic reform.[69]   It not only repealed the
Timber Culture Act but it required thirty months between the time of entry and the time of commuting under
the Homestead law.

Moreover there was considerable promise in several amendments for the Desert Land Act for both the
myth of rugged individualism and the hypocritical care
for the poor settler were abandoned.   The bill permitted

---

64. 26 Stat. 371 ff. The act is curiously worded.
65. There had been earlier efforts in Congress. Cf. 49 Cong. 1
    Sess. Cong. Rec., p. 6000.
66. 51 Cong. 1 Sess. Cong. Rec., p. 1523.
67. Ibid., p. 2349.
68. Ibid., p. 2537. During the debate a petition from the American
    Forestry Association, calling for timber reservations was read.
69. Ibid., p. 5272.

a group of settlers to file joint maps of the plans
which they proposed to follow for irrigating their sections and it required each entryman to spend $1.00 per
acre for each of three successive years or forfeit his
claim. In order to thwart speculation one section authorized officials, if they considered it necessary, to
call for proof of construction and reclamation at any
time during the three years. The questionable part of
the Senate measure lay in the proposal to push to patent
settlement entries where no fraud had been reported
prior to final entry and in place of land department action, to require the Attorney General to sue for the
cancellation of all entries where fraud was found if
they had been encumbered or had passed to other parties.[70] This latter provision revived the feature over
which the Senate and the House had split in 1887.

During the course of the debate in September
Senator Plumb offered an amendment which duplicated the
law for withdrawing reservoir sites.[71] Senator Teller
presented several amendments which, in addition to establishing certain requirements, guaranteed rights-of-
way to ditch companies and protected their reservoirs
and canals to the extent of fifty feet on each side.
Both Senator Plumb's single proposal and Senator Teller's
four were accepted without opposition. There was considerable discussion, however, over a timber amendment
offered by Senator Sanders of Montana.[72] He felt that
since it was so difficult to obtain timber in many localities where it was needed and since many regions had
no law for acquiring timber land, the Government should
permit the free cutting of timber in all but the Pacific
Coast States and Nevada. Senator Edmunds strongly opposed this liberality though some of his objections were
met by arguments from westerners like Senators Sanders,
Stewart and Teller. They declared that more timber was

---

70. There was also a provision establishing a time limit of five
    years within which all suits to annul patents must be brought.
    Several sections dealing with the public lands in Alaska have
    been excluded arbitrarily from this discussion.
71. Ibid., p. 10,086.
72. Ibid., pp. 10,087-94.

destroyed by fire than cut for constructive purposes
and they felt it obviously more preferable to supply
human needs than to allow the timber to perish. Senator Sanders' amendment was finally accepted after its
phrasing had undergone considerable change. Instead of
granting permission to cut timber it declared that if
any individual was subject to civil or criminal action
by the Government for acquiring public timber, he could
be excused if he showed that the timber had been cut for
use in the State or Territory in which it grew. This
privilege was confined to Colorado, Montana, Idaho,
North and South Dakota and the gold and silver regions
of Nevada and Utah. Incidentally the debate showed that
Senator Plumb as Chairman of the Public Lands Committee
was aware of the fact that there was no timber law for
other States such as Wisconsin and Alabama but he seems
to have made no effort to supply one.

    The bill passed the Senate with only three dis-
senting votes but the House refused to accept it.[73] Consequently it went to conference and was then held over
until the Second Session. Meanwhile the conference committee, consisting of Senators Plumb, Pettigrew and
Walthal and Representatives Payson, Pickler and Holman,
made several important changes.[74] In the first place
Desert Land entries were restricted to 320 instead of
640 acres and the commutation provision of the Homestead law was reduced from thirty to fourteen months.
A new section providing for the repeal of the Preëmption
Act was added to that which repealed the Timber Culture
law but the most important change of all was provided
for by the addition of a section which permitted the
President to establish forest reserves. The full story
of how Secretary Noble, at the instigation of B. E.
Fernow and E. A. Bowers of the Forestry Association,
persuaded the conference committee to write in this section twenty-four, is ably related in John Ise's The
American Forest Policy and it need not be repeated here.
Mr. Ise believed that no measure for forest reserves
could have passed alone at that time and he considered

---

73. Ibid., p. 10,760.
74. Ibid., 2 Sess., p. 3611.

the provision "by far the most important piece of timber legislation ever enacted in this country."[75] The
Senate conferees were apparently won over to the House
position on one point for the Committee dropped the section which required the Attorney General to bring suit
for voiding completed entries. And by some curious
means Senator Sander's timber amendment and the provision establishing a time limit for instigating suits to
void patents were omitted.

The conference report came before the Senate on
Saturday, February 28, a few days before the close of
the Fifty-first Congress.[76] On that day the Senate met
from before noon until midnight and its preoccupation
with an abundance of work may account for the fact that
when Senator Plumb announced that there was nothing in
the bill that had not already been considered, the Senate passed it after only one short stump speech in behalf of the poor settler. In the evening of the same
day the House also took up the committee report.[77] Representative Payson read a summary of the bill and then
asked for its passage. He was forced to answer several
questions on the Senate changes and to report that the
provision for timber land reservation was the only feature that the House had not passed upon at some previous
time. Representative McRae of Arkansas objected to such
a provision because he felt that "the power granted to
the President....is an extraordinary and dangerous power
to grant over the public domain."[78] He did not expand
this thesis but he was reminded that the executive already had the power to reserve irrigation sites.

When there was a request that the bill wait over
until the following Monday Representative Payson made a
strong personal plea in its behalf but because of objections, including that based on the fact that the bill
had not been printed, he consented to delay the vote.[79]
On Monday, however, it passed the House without further

75. Ise, op. cit., p. 109.
76. 51 Cong. 2 Sess., op. cit., p. 3545.
77. Ibid., p. 3611.
78. Ibid., p. 3614.
79. Ibid., p. 3615.

discussion[80] and President Harrison signed it the following day.[81] At the same time someone discovered that
the timber cutting section was missing and consequently
under suspended rules, Senator Sander's amendment was
rushed through both Houses and quickly became a law.[82]
This measure not only protected depredators who cut timber for local State and Territorial consumption but it
also contined the unfortunate provision which set a time
limit of five years for bringing suits to annul patents
that had already issued and six years for those which
issued in the future.

In several important respects the reform bill
contained provisions which the Public Land Commission
had recommended in 1880. Moreover the general policies
of permitting only small individual entries, establishing more adequate provisions for desert land development
and reserving timber lands mark the end of an era because they at last demonstrated the realistic recognition of some outstanding western needs. It is true that
surveying, administrative, mining and other improvements
were not included and also that there was no possibility
of correcting abuses that had developed since the needs
first became recognized. In fact abuses were protected
by the provision requiring the Land Office to issue patents in certain classes of cases.[83] The section establishing a relatively short time within which to bring
suit for annulling patents based on fraud falls in the
same category. Furthermore it was unfortunate that one
admirable feature for handling forests should have been
accompanied by a provision that allowed more extensive
free cutting of timber. Incidentally since there was no
provision for protecting the reservations which President Harrison soon established they were subject to extensive depredation.[84] But despite its drawbacks the

---

80. Ibid., p. 3685.
81. 26 Stat. 1095.
82. 26 Stat. 1093.
83. In part this section resulted from Commissioner Sparks' poli-
    cies. He had tied up business in the Northwest as well as
    elsewhere. S. V. Proudfit interview.
84. Sec. of Int. Report, 1894, p. 18.

reform bill was a decided gain for proper administration.

Some elements in the West were not pleased by the reforms. For example, the Cheyenne Daily Leader[85] suggested that had the bill been drawn by the cattle kings especially in their own interest it could not have been done better. There is little doubt that the ditch companies, which were assisted by several sections of the act, were apt to include cattle companies in their number. And furthermore, the restrictions on the former privilege of entering under several laws, which had aided in the acquisition of large holdings, seemed to indicate that since the cattlemen had secured what they desired, they were ready to cut off the same opportunity for others. But the forces which produced the bill cannot be attributed entirely to cattlemen, for it sprang from the desires of many groups. In any case Liefur Magnusson has aptly suggested that a change in laws had little effect on policies of rapid disposal for most administrators favored liberality when dealing with the public lands.[86]

As already noted the adoption of the Omnibus bill marks a dividing line in public land history. In conclusion, therefore, it is pertinent to recall that the questions originally posed dealt with the Government's policies for meeting problems raised by the last frontier. Because, as examination has shown, these policies were so frequently shameful, it is evident that the problems were not faced honestly and intelligently by those who should have solved them. The short-sighted actions of interested parties, the heavy hand of heritage, the indifference or uninformed character of public opinion, the betrayal of official responsibilities, the lack of a desire to face realities and the decrepid condition of administrative agencies, are interrelated factors which help to account for the failure of efforts to administer properly the public domain.

---

85. Quoted in Osgood, op. cit., p. 245.
86. L. Magnusson, "The Disposition of the Public Lands of the United States," pp. 19-20.

Many of the results of the Government's policies
have already been pointed out. For instance the failure to survey the public lands scientifically and to
classify them provided an incentive to fraud and illegal exploitation by railroad, mining, timber and other
groups. The indifference toward making the railroads
live up to a strict interpretations of the acts establishing their grants resulted in, and was caused by, unwarranted influences on the various branches of the
Government. And although the disposition of railroad
grant land is foreign to a consideration of Government
policies it is relevant to note that this disposition
fostered timber land monopolies, mineral land monopolies
and large scale farming and ranching possessions. The
effect of the Government's timber policies was to promote fraud, corruption, thievery, waste, occasional
violence, defiance of authority and monopolization.
Mineral land laws encouraged law suits and extensive
speculation. The lack of proper administrative safeguards for handling swamp and school lands made them a
prize for unscrupulous politicians and designing exploiters. Private land claims, long unadjusted, permitted fraud, illegal exploitation and occasional violent clashes. And the lack of a pastoral land law also
resulted in widespread fraud and extensive violence.[87]

But one of the most significant of these unfortunate results is to be found by examining the extent
to which the Government accomplished its avowed aim of
encouraging settlers. Foregoing accounts have emphasized the too frequent speculation in farming land
through abuse of relinquishment rights or other techni-
calities. And, to repeat, large holdings developed from
the use of scrip and purchase of lands granted for encouraging various enterprises. But by and large, was
the West fulfilling Thomas Jefferson's expectations by
creating a nation of small scale farmers? In particular

---

87. Admittedly these evils represent the darker side of the pic-
    ture. And the question readily arises, could these evils have
    been avoided. While the historian should be chary of "if's"
    a reply might be hazarded that they could not have been en-
    tirely avoided but they might have been mitigated.

how successful was the Homestead law?

In 1889 Acting Commissioner Stone boasted that the Homestead law had brought 297,208 "actual settlers on the public domain."[88] But the total number of final Homestead entries added to an estimate of the number of commuted Homestead entries indicates that there should have been about one-third, or 90,000, more settlers than the Commissioner claimed were there.[89] This fact would indicate a considerable abuse of the law. Other statistics reveal still greater discrepancies. Prior to 1890 a total of 120,000,000 acres were entered under the Homestead law, as compared with the 47,500,000 acres patented to the above mentioned "actual settlers." The former figure would have provided quarter sections of land for 750,000 settlers. Apparently homesteaders found that the "game" was not worth the candle or there was extensive abuse of the law.

It is also interesting to compare the number of farms created during the decade of the 1880's with the amount of land claimed from the Government and with the increase in the number of farm workers. In all the public land States and Territories west of the Mississippi River, excluding Arkansas, Oklahoma and Louisiana, there were about 800,000 farms in 1880.[90] During the following decade there was an increase of over 260,000 farms absorbing about 70,000,000 acres.[91] Yet during the same period nearly 190,000,000 acres of the public domain were claimed from the Government.[92] Most all of this absorption was west of the Mississippi River in the States and Territories selected for consideration. Only a portion of the public domain had as yet gone to railroads; the total amount selected by all roads, including those east of the Mississippi, amounted to but 50,000,000 acres, since the beginning of railroad grants.[a]

88. L.O.R., 1889, p. 82.
89. Ibid., 1931, p. 41; Hibbard, op. cit., p. 386 ff.
90. Abstract of the Census, 1910, p. 282.
91. Ibid.
92. Calculated from the Land Office Reports for the 1880's. Over the period of a decade there were undoubtedly duplications of entries.
93. L.O.R., 1890, p. 22.

It would seem, therefore, that during the 1880's only
about 37% of the public domain was providing farms of
whatever size or kind.[94]

In comparing the number of farms with the number of farm workers it is necessary to use statistics
for the entire United States and not just for the region west of the Mississippi River. During the 1880's
there was an increase of 555,734 farms under a Census
classification which included tenant farms.[95] At the
same time there was an increase of 270,000 tenants, accounting for nearly half the number of new farms.[95] Incidentally, this meant that there were 1,296,000 tenants
in the United States by 1890, or, tenant farms accounted
for 28.4% of all farms.[96] The increase in tenancy during the 1880's was more pronounced in mid-Western regions like Iowa, Minnesota, the Dakotas, Nebraska and
Kansas than it was in the Southern States of Louisiana,
Mississippi, Alabama, Georgia and South Carolina.[97] In
the Rocky Mountain and Pacific Coast States tenancy was
on the decline. In view, therefore, of the increase in
tenantry and of the comparatively small amount of
claimed land that was devoted to farming, it is evident
that the Government's land policies conspicuously failed
to establish a nation of independent, small farm owners.[98]

Any discussion of the results of the period under review would naturally include a comment on the
Census Report reference to the end of the frontier.

---

94. The Homestead law alone claimed 70,000,000 acres, enough to
    have provided 445,000 farms of the quarter section size.
95. Abstract of the Census, 1910, pp. 265, 282 and 286.
96. Ibid., p. 286.
97. Certain Aspects of Land Problems and Government Land Policies.
    Part VII of the Supplementary Report of the Land Planning Com-
    mittee of the National Resources Board, 1935, p. 22.
98. The subject of mortgages has been omitted as not relevant here.
    For an eloquent comment on "settlers" seeking land there are
    the statistics for tenantry in Oklahoma. In 1890, one year
    after the opening, there were practically no tenants but within
    ten years 42% of the farmers were tenants. National Resources
    Board, Supplementary Report, Part VII, op. cit., p. 22.

Every analysis of this statement should begin with the
words of the Report. It declared, "Up to and including
1880 the country had a frontier of settlement, but at
present, (1890), the unsettled area has been so broken
into isolated bodies of settlement that there can hardly be said to be a frontier line."[99] The rapid exhaus-
tion of free arable land in humid regions has been referred to frequently in the foregoing pages.[100] Of
course the movement of population toward a common center from both East and West, the construction of several
transcontinental railroads, and the establishment of
mining, cattle and agricultural communities beyond any
frontier line, all tended to eliminate any line of settlement. But was the frontier gone? Not in the sense
that there was no more free public land. Statistics
are surprisingly conflicting but in 1894, the Secretary
of Interior estimated that there were still over
606,000,000 acres unabsorbed.[101] The fact that land
could be taken up in such large quantities as 26,391,000
and 19,000,000 acres yearly, in 1910 and 1916 respectively, indicates the continuance of free land.[102] And
despite a widespread belief to the contrary, especially
during the 1930 depression era, there was still land
for homesteading in the industrial age, for in 1932
there were 4,000,000 acres entered under original Homestead entries.[102] Beginning with 1934 the public lands
were progressively withdrawn from private entry but in
that very year there were over 2,800,000 acres of original Homestead entries.[102] Nevertheless after 1890, the
economic and social development of the country tended to
diminish the importance of the type of free land which

---

99. Quoted in D. E. Clark, "The West in American History," p. 623.
100. In 1887, A. B. Hart had called attention to the fact that because fine arable land was nearly gone American conditions
must become more like those of old and crowded countries.
Hart, op. cit.
101. Sec. of Int. Report, 1894, p. 13. In 1891 the Land Office estimated that there were 580,000,000 acres unabsorbed. L.O.R.,
1891, p. 45. L. Magnusson quotes the Dept. of Agric. Yearbook
for 1898 as recording 573,994,854 acres, about 39% of the U.S.
10% more was reserved. Magnusson, op. cit., p. 26.
102. Sec. of Int. Report, 1934, p. 61.

remained and the entire question must be reserved for further investigation.

The existence of large quantities of free land in the country in 1890, calls attention to other opportunities as well as accomplishments of that time. The Government had secured on paper a comprehensive program that would serve to guide future land reform efforts. It had begun, with far-sighted and disinterested backing from non-political sources, a scientific inventory of its resources, even though the process did not assist the work of land disposal. It had deprived the railroads of some of their extra benefits. Again with excellent outside assistance it had begun to follow a policy of timber and soil conservation, which had reached a climax in the Forest Reserve section of the 1891 law. And finally, it had been able to secure either a moderate defense of Government rights, as in the services of Secretaries Schurz and Lamar and President Cleveland, or a militant defense, as in the services of Commissioner Sparks, Colonel Le Barnes, Representative Payson and Senator Van Wyck.

BIBLIOGRAPHY

PRIMARY SOURCES AND GOVERNMENT PUBLICATIONS

General Land Office Report, 1875-1893. These also contain the Reports of the Surveyors General.

Secretary of Interior Reports, 1875-1893. The full reports after 1878 contain the Reports of the Governors of the Territories.

Statutes of the United States, Vols. 13-26.

United States Supreme Court Reports, 1874-1892.

Abstract of the Census, 1910.

Copp, H. N., "Public Land Laws, 1875-1882."

Congressional Record, 1877-1891.

House and Senate Documents and Reports of Committees.

Donaldson, Thomas, "The Public Domain," 1884.

46 Congress 2 Session--House Executive Document #46. Preliminary Report of the Public Land Committee, 1880. Serial #1923.

45 Congress 2 Session--House Executive Document #80. Major J. W. Powell's Report on the Rocky Mountain Regions of the United States, April 1, 1878. Serial #1805.

Powell, J. W., Report to the Secretary of Interior on the Methods of Surveying the Public Domain, November 1, 1878. Printed separately by the Government Printing Office.

Land Planning and Land Use. Supplementary Report #7 of the Land Planning Commission of the National Resources Board, 1935.

NEWSPAPERS AND PERIODICALS

The Clipping Bureau in the School of Journalism at Columbia University has a helpful collection of newspaper material.

New York Times, 1877-1891. Index on file in the Public Library of New York, 42nd Street and Fifth Avenue, New York, N.Y.

New York Tribune, 1875-1891.
Various New York and Washington papers for special
    topics. New York World, New York Herald, New York
    Sun, New York Evening Post, Washington Post, Wash-
    ington Critic.
The Nation, 1885-1889, passim.
Public Opinion, 1886-1891.
Copp's Land Owner, 1874-1891.

                          BOOKS

Burnap, W. A., "One Man's Lifetime," 1923.
Burkley, F. J., "The Faded Frontier," 1935.
Guernsey, C. A., "Wyoming Cowboy Days," 1936.
Ellis, G. D., "Platforms of the Two Great Political
    Parties," 1920.
Peck, H. T., "Twenty Years of the Republic," 1906.
Pettigrew, R. F., "Triumphant Plutocracy," 1922.
Puter, S. A. D., "Looters of the Public Domain," 1908.
Richardson, A. D., "A Compilation of the Messages and
    Papers of the Presidents." 1900. Vols. VII-IX.
Schurz, Carl, "Speeches, Correspondence and Political
    Papers," ed. by G. Bancroft, Vols. III-IV. "Remi-
    niscences of Carl Schurz," Vol. III, 1908.
Author's interview with S. V. Proudfit and Mauchlin
    Nivens, employees of the Interior Department from
    the time of Secretary H. M. Teller and L. Q. Lamar,
    respectively.

                    SECONDARY SOURCES

                    MAGAZINE ARTICLES

"Stealing Uncle Sam's Farms"--Independent. December 18,
    1902, Vol. 54, 3037-81.
Adams, H. B., "The Land Question." Article XXXVI on
    National Land Problems, August 30, 1886. Galley
    proofs in Columbia University Clipping Bureau files.
Atkinson, ed., "Farm Ownership and Tenancy in the
    United States," American Statistical Association,
    December, 1897.

Dunham, H. H., "Some Crucial Years of the Land Office,"
    Agricultural History, April, 1937.
Ganoe, F. T., "The Desert Land Act in Operation, 1877-
    1891," Agricultural History, April, 1937.
Gates, P. W., "The Homestead Law in an Incongruous Land
    System," American Historical Review, July, 1936.
Gill, Thomas P., "Landlordism in the United States,"
    North American Review, January, 1886.
Hart, A. B., "The Disposition of Our Public Lands,"
    Quarterly Journal of Economics, Vol. I, 169 (1887).
Johnson, J. W., "Railway Land Grants," North American
    Review, March, 1885, Vol. 140, 280.
Julian, G. W., "Our Land Policy," Atlantic Monthly,
    March, 1879, Vol. 43, 325.
        -"Our Land Grant Railways in Congress,"
    International Review, February-March, 1883, Vol. 14,
    198.
        -"Railway Influence in the Land Office,"
    North American Review, March, 1883, Vol. 136, 237.
Martin, H. M., "Time to Repeal Bad Land Laws," National
    Magazine, January, 1904, Vol. XIX, #4.
Millard, B., "The West Coast Land Grafters," Every-
    body's Magazine, May, 1905
Paine, V. B., "Our Public Land Policy," Harper's Monthly,
    October, 1885.
Peters, E. T., "Evils of Our Public Land Policy,"
    Century, February 3, 1883.
Rae, J. R., "Commissioner Sparks and the Railroad Land
    Grants," Mississippi Valley Historical Review, Sep-
    tember, 1938.
Robbins, Roy M., "The Public Domain in the Era of Ex-
    ploitation, 1862-1901," Agricultural History, April,
    1939.
Smith, H. A., "The Early Forestry Movement in the United
    States," Agricultural History, October, 1938.
Stevenson, F. B., "The Land Grabbers," Harper's Weekly,
    Vol. XLIX, June 24, 1905

REFERENCE WORKS

Appleton's Annual Encyclopedia
Appleton's Encyclopedia of American Biography

Biographical Directory of the American Congress, 1789-
    1927.
Cyclopedia of American Government, especially article
    on "Public Lands" by P. J. Treat.
Dictionary of American Biography.
National Cyclopedia of American Biography.
Lamb's Biographical Directory.

BOOKS

Brockett, L. P., "Our Western Empire," 1881.
Cate, W. A., "Lucius Q. C. Lamar," 1935.
Clark, D. E., "S. J. Kirkwood," 1917.
                -"The West in American History," 1937.
Conover, Milton, "The General Land Office," 1923.
Cummings, H. C. and McFarland, C., "Federal Justice,"
    1937.
Democratic Campaign Handbook, 1884.
Detroit Post and Tribune, "Zachariah Chandler," 1880.
Dewey, D. R., "National Problems," 1907.
Dick, Everett, "Sod House Frontier," 1937.
Fine, N., "Labor and Farm Parties in the U. S.," 1928.
Ford, H. J., "The Cleveland Era," 1921.
Fuess, C. M., "Carl Schurz, Reformer," 1932.
George, Henry, "Our Land and Land Policies," Works, Vol.
    8, 1900.
Haney, L. H., "A Congressional History of Railways,
    1850-1887," 1910.
Haynes, F. E., "James Baird Weaver," 1919.
                -"Third Party Movements Since the Civil
    War," 1916.
Hicks, J. D., "The Populist Revolt," 1931.
Howe, G. F., "Chester A. Arthur," 1934.
Ise, John, "The United States Forest Policy," 1920.
            -"The United States Oil Policy," 1928.
Magnusson, Liefur, "The Disposition of the Public Lands
    of the United States," 1919.
Mayes, Edward, "Lucius Q. C. Lamar," 1896.
Moody, W. G., "Land, Labor and Capital," 1883.
Myers, Gustavus, "The History of Great American Fortunes,"
    1936 ed.
Muzzey, D. S., "James G. Blaine," 1934.
National Conservation Commission Report, 1909.

Nevins, Allan, "Grover Cleveland," 1932.
- "Hamilton Fish," 1936.
- "Abram Hewitt," 1935.
Oberholtzer, E. P., "A History of the United States,"
Vols. IV-V, 1931, 1937.
Orfield, M. H., "Federal Land Grants to the States,"
1915.
Osgood, E. S., "The Days of the Cattlemen," 1929.
Palmer, Ben, "Swamp Land Drainage," 1915.
Paxson, F. L., "History of the American Frontier, 1763-
1893," 1924.
- "The Last American Frontier," 1910.
Pomerantz, Sidney, "Samuel J. Randall: Protectionist
Democrat, 1863-1890," M. A. Thesis, Columbia Uni-
versity, 1932.
Proudfit, S. V., "Public Land System of the United
States," 1923.
Rhodes, J. F., "History of the United States," Vol. 8,
1920.
Richardson, R. N. and Rister, C. C., "The Greater South-
west," 1934.
Sanborn, J. B., "Congressional Grants of Land in Aid of
Railways," 1899.
Sandoz, Mari, "Old Jules," 1936.
Sato, Shosuke, "History of the Land Question in the
United States," 1886.
Schlesinger, A. M., "The Rise of the City, 1878-1898,"
1933.
Sheldon, A. E., "Land Systems and Land Politics in
Nebraska," 1938.
Shinn, C. H., "Land Laws of the Mining Districts," 1903.
- "The Story of the Mine," 1901.
Stephenson, G. W., "The Political History of the Public
Lands, 1840-1862," 1917.
Stewart, L. O., "Public Land Surveys, History, Instruc-
tions and Methods," 1935.
Tarbell, I. M., "The Nationalizing of Business, 1878-
1898," 1936.
Treat, P. J., "The National Land System, 1785-1820,"
1910.
Webb, W. P., "The Great Plains," 1931.
Woodward, C. S., "The Public Domain - Its Surveys and
Surveyors," 1897.
Yard, R. S., "Our Federal Lands," 1928.

MAXWELL GRANT BIBLIOGRAPHY

Land Office Reports, 1885 and 1887. (Also contain re-
    ports of Surveyor General of New Mexico.)
36 Cong. 1 Sess. H. Rep. #321. Sen. Report. #228
                    Cong. Globe., pp. 816-3291, <u>passim</u>.
52 Cong. 1 Sess. H. Rep. #1253, #1824.
                    Cong. Rec., Vol. 23, pt. 2.
Laws of the Territories of New Mexico and Colorado,
    1876-80.
History of New Mexico, Its Resources and People, 2 vols.,
    1907. Pacific States Publishing Co.
Bancroft, H. H.,"History of Nevada, Colorado and Wyom-
    ing." Works, Vol, XXV, 1890.
                -"History of Arizona and New Mexico."
    Works, Vol. XVII, 1889.
Bloom, L. B. and Donnelly, T. C.,"New Mexico - History
    and Civics," 1933.
Bradley, G. D.,"Winning the Southwest," 1912.
Coan, C. F., "History of New Mexico," Vol. I, 1925.
Conrad, H. L.,"'Uncle Dick' Wooton," 1890.
Garrard, L. H., "Wah-To-Yah and the Taos Trail," 1927.
Grant, B. C. (ed.), "Kit Carson's Own Story of His Life,"
    1926.
Hayes, A. A., "New Colorado and the Santa Fe Trail,"
    1880.
Inman, Henry, "The Old Santa Fe Trail," 1899.
Otero, M. A., "My Life on the Frontier," Vol. II. 1939.
Peters, DeW. C., "Life and Adventures of Kit Carson,"
    1857.
Rives, G. L., "The United States and Mexico, 1821-48,"
    1913.
Twitchell, R. E., "Leading Facts of New Mexican History,"
    2 vols., 1912.
                -"Military Occupation of the Territory
    of New Mexico," 1909.
                -"Old Santa Fe," 1925.
                -(ed.)"Archives of New Mexico," 1914.

<u>New York Times</u>, Sept. 10, 1870; Mar. 24, 1880; Jan. 26,
    1885; June 13, 1885; June 30, 1885; July 1, 1885;
    Jan. 4, 1886; Oct. 16, 1886; Dec. 6, 1886; Oct. 12,
    1887; and June 22, 1890.

New York Tribune, Sept. 22, 1879; June 30, 1885; Oct. 17,
    1885; Dec. 11, 1885; Apr. 18, 1886; June 9, 1886;
    Oct. 14, 1886; Apr. 19, 1887; Apr. 22, 1887.
New York Sun, Sept. 1, 1884.
New York Herald, May 23, 1887.
Philadelphia Press, June 7, 1887 (?); May 14, 1892; and
    Sept. 29, 1893.
New Orleans Times, Oct. 9, 1881.
Washington Critic, Jan. 25, 1888.
Copp's Land Owner, Jan., 1880
Proposal of John Collinson to the Stock and Bondholders
    of the Maxwell Land Grant and Railway Company for
    Reorganization. Dated 20th Nov. 1874.
Noel, Leon, "The Largest Estate in the World," Overland
    Monthly, Vol. XII, n.s. Nov. 1888.
Morrow, Wm. W.,"Spanish and Mexican Private Land Claims."
    Pamphlet.
Keleher, W. A., "Law of the New Mexican Land Grant," New
    Mexican Historical Review, Vol. 4, #4, Oct. 1929.

                    COURT RECORDS

U. S. vs. Maxwell Land Grant Co., 5 N. M. 297
DeMares vs. Gilpin, 15 Col. 76 (Involves part of the
    Sangre de Christo grant).
Colorado Fuel Co. vs. Maxwell Land Grant Co., 22 Col. 71.
Tameling vs. United States Freehold and Emigration Co.,
    93 U. S. 644.
U. S. vs. Maxwell Land Grant and Railway Co., 21 Fed.
    Rep. 19; 26 Fed. Rep. 118; 121 U. S. 235, (including
    the Transcript of the Record and supplementary ma-
    terial from the Land Office Files not contained in
    the Transcript); 122 U. S. 365.
U. S. vs. San Pedro and Canon del Agua Grant, 4 N. M.
    405 and 146 U. S. 120.
Maxwell Land Grant Co. vs. Dawson, 7 N. M. 133 and 151
    U. S. 586.
Russell vs. Maxwell Land Grant Co., 158 U. S. 253.
Bent vs. Miranda, 8 N. M. 78 and 168 U. S. 471
Thompson vs. Maxwell Land Grant and Railway Co., 3 N. M.
    269 and 168 U. S. 451.
Interstate Land Co. vs. Maxwell Land Grant Co., 139 U. S.
    569.

71
72
74

75
76

77
79
81
83
85

88